STUDIES IN
BIBLIOGRAPHY

STUDIES IN
BIBLIOGRAPHY

EDITED BY

DAVID L. VANDER MEULEN

Volume Forty-Eight

Published for

THE BIBLIOGRAPHICAL SOCIETY OF THE UNIVERSITY OF VIRGINIA

BY THE UNIVERSITY PRESS OF VIRGINIA, CHARLOTTESVILLE

1995

107089

Founding Editor
Fredson Bowers (1905–1991)

Assistant to the Editor
Elizabeth Lynch

Virginia. University. Bibliographical Society.

Studies in bibliography; papers v.1—
1948/49—
Charlottesville.
    v. illus. 26cm. annual.
Title varies: 1948/49—

  1.   Bibliography—Societies.   I.   Title.
Z1008.V55   010.6275549–3353 Rev.*

ISBN 0–8139–1617–8

The editors invite articles and notes on analytical bibliography, textual criticism, manuscript study, the history of printing and publishing, as well as related matters of method and evidence. Send manuscripts to David L. Vander Meulen, English Department, Bryan Hall, University of Virginia, Charlottesville, VA 22903.

All other correspondence, concerning membership, subscriptions, and other business, should go to Penelope F. Weiss, Executive Secretary, Bibliographical Society, University of Virginia Library, Charlottesville, Va. 22903.

This journal is a member of the Council of Editors of Learned Journals.

Contents

CONTENTS

Preface

Most of this volume consists of essays designed to honor J. D. Fleeman on the completion of his life's principal endeavour, a comprehensive bibliography of Samuel Johnson. Galvanized by two of David's ardent admirers, Professor Daisuke Nagashima and Professor Howard D. Weinbrot, we as co-editors found ourselves casting a net from—if not China to Peru—then Oxford to Otago. That the field of potential contributors proved so diverse and so distinguished is one measure of David's achievement. Throughout his career, he devoted himself selflessly to the work of others; indeed, several of the articles included in this volume bear his direct imprint. All exemplify one of his most cherished ideals—that of scholarly community. For David, no pains were excessive when it came to teaching, learning, and collaborating. As a consequence, the epigraph to this collection might well be taken (with the change of a single pronoun) from King Alfred's preface to his version of Gregory's *Cura Pastoralis*: "Her mon maeg giet gesion hiora swaeth."

From its inception David knew of this undertaking and took a discerning, albeit somewhat rueful, interest: his deep humility did not impede an accurate assessment of his own worth, but he had to grow accustomed in stages to seeing himself pushed firmly into the limelight. During the final months of his life, moreover, he was able to read several of the essays collected here. He guided the choice of the photograph that appears as frontispiece, a picture (taken on 10 June 1994) that also serves as the official portrait for Pembroke College, Oxford (from which David officially retired in that month). Within weeks before his death on 20 July 1994, we were able to send him the completed table of contents.

It remains a great grief to us that David did not live to see, in its final form, this testimony to the affection and admiration he inspired in so many. His *magnum opus*, however, he knew to be in the most capable hands: Dr. James McLaverty had agreed to take primary responsibility for the final editing and proof-reading of the Johnson bibliography, which is to be published by the Oxford University Press.

On 17 February 1994 (at what proved to be his last public appearance) David addressed the Oxford Bibliographical Society on the subject of "A Bibliography of Dr. Johnson." During the course of his talk, he made eloquent reference to the high standards that every bibliographer must aspire to uphold: "James Maxwell used to assert that the only appropriate epitaph on the grave of a scholar should be 'He got it right.'" David went on to say, "I wish I could hope for that." Our conviction is that his hope was realized, time and time again.

DAVID L. VANDER MEULEN
BRUCE REDFORD

J. D. Fleeman
1932–1994

J. D. Fleeman: A Memoir

by

DAVID FAIRER

VERY RECENTLY DAVID FLEEMAN CAME UPON A WORK BY SAMUEL Johnson that had eluded all previous scholars and is recorded in no bibliographies. It is a forty-line fragment 'On the Character and Duty of an Academick' published for the first and only time as an appendix to John Moir's *Hospitality. A Discourse* (London, 1793), and its words are appropriate for the man whose work this volume celebrates: "An academick," says Johnson, "is a man supported at the public cost, and dignified with public honours, that he may attain and impart wisdom. He is maintained by the public, that he may study at leisure; he is dignified with honours, that he may teach with weight. The great duty therefore of an academick is diligence of inquiry, and liberality of communication." If, as Johnson avers, public honours impose a duty, then David Fleeman's long-laboured duties, his "diligence of inquiry, and liberality of communication" to eighteenth-century scholars worldwide, demand to be publicly honoured. It is Johnson's implicit blessing on this volume, and perhaps a personal acknowledgement of someone who has worked with absolute devotion in his cause.

As tutor and fellow of Johnson's own college since 1965, and its librarian from 1969 to 1984, David Fleeman has been in every way at the heart of Johnsonian studies. In 1984 he brought scholars from around the world to Pembroke for the bicentenary conference, and for so many students of the eighteenth century he is a mine of expertise on Johnson and his circle. In private communication, whether by letter, telephone, or bubbling talk, he delights in the circulation of knowledge, offering new leads to anyone with a scholarly problem, putting one individual in touch with another, or supplying just the obscure fact or detail that will open up someone's work in exciting ways. He is generous to a fault with his time, and has always been conscious of the duty that scholars owe to each other and to the field of endeavour they share. It is a Johnsonian conviction. To quote the fragment again: "The great effect of society is, that by uniting multitudes in one general co-operation, it distributes to different orders of the community the several labours and occupations of life." Knowledge is held in common, and truth can best advance through the pooling of expertise. In his 1984 "Valediction," delivered to the departing conference-goers, he spoke in similar tones on behalf of the Johnsonian community, skilfully surveying the various projects in hand and setting out some of the tasks that lay ahead. Typically he looked forward as well as back, to new techniques as well as to familiar problems, and he urged those present to have a mind to the tercentenary in 2009 when the work of the intervening years would once again be held to account: "Much remains to be done," he exhorted; "Johnsonians cannot stand idle if we are to make a respectable showing at our next meeting."

Fleeman's contribution over more than thirty years to this enterprise deserves celebration: he is someone for whom being brought to book is no throwaway metaphor, but a due responsibility. In his published editions and studies of Johnson's writings, soon to be crowned by his massive bibliography, Fleeman has considerably increased our understanding of the great man, but not by any commanding theory or dramatic reinterpretation (these are for him a dubious combination of metaphysics and egotism). Instead, what we are offered is a scrupulous attention to the workings of Johnson's mind and the particular struggles by which his conceptions made their way into print and out to their readership. The picture is always a dynamic one: Fleeman's Johnson is not a man of monumental certainties, but a mind at work, facing practical difficulties and encountering challenges at every stage, whether in the progress of a subscription or a set of proofs. Bibliography for Fleeman never loses touch with biography. In a paper on Johnsonian Bibliography delivered to the Oxford Bibliographical Society on 17 February 1994 (as yet unpublished) he acknowledged the "biographical bias" that close attention to an author's text will inevitably give, and commented about his own project that "it was this which led me to think that an account of the emergence of Johnson's thoughts into the form in which we now meet them, might serve instead of yet another 'critical biography.'" In his work on bibliography and textual criticism Fleeman has never lost sight of Johnson's thoughts, or his principles either, and it is interesting to discover that he thinks of his body of Johnsonian scholarship in terms of an alternative intellectual biography.

I

John David Fleeman is a Yorkshireman and a "Johnson" on his mother's side. He was born at Holme-on-Spalding-Moor in the old East Riding on 19 July 1932, the son of Mary (née Johnson) and Joseph Fleeman. "Fleeman," derived from Flamanc/Flamand, or Fleming, is a scarce name, but several graveyards in the Isle of Axeholme, the district beyond the southern tip of the riding around the villages of Snaith and Rawcliffe, house generations of Fleemans who farmed the lands in the area. It was his grandfather, John William (1866–1936), who broke away from the agricultural life and by dint of self-education eventually became an Inspector in the West Riding Constabulary, and his son Joseph (1906–1983) took up schoolteaching as a career. When David Fleeman was very young the family moved to Laxton, an isolated hamlet on the flood plain of the River Ouse near the point where it becomes the tidal Humber, and here his father was the village schoolmaster and a lay preacher at the small church of St. Peter. The young Fleeman's most formative childhood experiences were as a choirboy in this church, chanting the Psalms and hearing intoned the words of Cranmer's prayerbook and the King James Bible. Later, when he read Johnson for the first time, he felt an immediate kinship with his solemn tones and measured phrases, as though he were hearing a familiar congenial voice.

In 1943 he entered Pocklington School (founded 1514), a public (i.e., "private") boarding school fifteen miles north of Laxton, where he was taught English by a man who during the First World War had taught his father before him. His methods were those that had implanted English Literature into many generations of Pocklingtonians: the pupils memorised poems, and they were made to stand up and recite them. In history, dates were learned by rote; in divinity, psalms and parables. But in this ritual of recollection and recital Fleeman excelled. He enjoyed the stirring rhythms of Bridges and Hopkins, or Tennyson's Light Brigade, and he won a prize for declaiming a passage from Shakespeare's *Richard the Second*. It is no surprise that a boy who relished an author's memorability, and who had an instinctive feel for pattern and cadence, would find Dr. Johnson a powerful writer.

In fact, Fleeman was hooked on Johnson before he read Boswell. What first stirred him was a copy of the selected essays, and especially the solemnity of the last *Idler*, number 103: "Though the Idler and his readers have contracted no close friendship they are perhaps both unwilling to part. There are few things not purely evil, of which we can say, without some emotion of uneasiness, 'this is the last.'" Dark and sober words, and not perhaps those that an adolescent might appreciate—at least not those Rasselas meets—but they struck home "like a sledgehammer." Johnson's horror of the last was one Johnsonian's beginning.

In 1951 Fleeman went up to St. Andrews University, that venerable seat of learning on the Fife coast in Scotland, and in his freshman year studied French and German, Modern History, Philosophy, and English.

At first it seemed that modern languages were to be his speciality (the previous year he had applied to read French and German at St. John's College Oxford, which did not then admit for English). He attended lectures in French on Corneille and Voltaire, and in German on Goethe and Lessing. The yearning Romanticism of Lamartine and others disgusted him (in the eighteenth-century sense), and it was Balzac, Maupassant and Zola who hit his taste. In English he came under the influence of Richard Logan, a lecturer who combined a contempt for romanticism with a conviction that Horace was in fact an Englishman. Logan's view of vernacular English Literature as an intellectually unsatisfactory offshoot of the classical tradition was never unequivocally shared by Fleeman, but it is no surprise that the Age of Pope and Johnson became his great love. In general he relished wit, intellect, social realism, and responded to doubt, difficulty, struggle ("we are not to repine, but we may lawfully struggle"). He developed a conviction that would stay with him for life: that nothing easy is worth doing. Slick methods and glib answers were anathema. Already Johnson was providing the scenario for a life that embraced effort and sought firm evidence and sure results.

Having graduated in 1956 with a First in English Language and Literature (he won the class medal), Fleeman confronted what for many of his generation was certainly a struggle—National Service. He joined the Twentieth Foot of the Lancashire Fusiliers at Bury, and after basic training entered the Royal Army Education Corps as a Sergeant. It was a life built on order and hierarchy. He felt happily at home with army discipline, teaching everything from the writing of reports to the reading of ordnance survey maps (something he had learned at school), and he developed a relish for Pythagorean geometry. With the confidence of youth he committed himself to attainable knowledge and satisfying conclusions. Having instructed the officers on how to write clearly, he was attached to the Lifeguards at Windsor, teaching recruits to the elite Household Cavalry. During this time, in 1957, he married Isabella Macaskill from the Isle of Harris in the Outer Hebrides, whom he had known since his undergraduate days in St. Regulus' Hall, and together they moved into married quarters in Windsor.

Leaving the army the following year, he returned to Yorkshire and taught as a schoolmaster for a year at Selby, from where he applied to do graduate work at Oxford. Somewhat unconventionally he was met by Graham Midgeley, English tutor of St. Edmund Hall (a notoriously "sporty" college), at the South Door of York Minster, and the interview was conducted in Betty's tearooms. (To a fellow Yorkshireman this does not seem incongruous: Betty's to this day has more formality than many an Oxford common room.) "Do you row?" he was asked. "I'm afraid not," was the reply. "Good!" said a relieved Midgeley. And so he gained his place at Oxford. It was All Fools Day 1959.

There was little doubt that he would settle on some Johnsonian research topic, but the choice was not easy. The immediate possibility was, predictably, a study of how Johnson's style was coloured by the Prayerbook and the Authorized Version of the Bible (the first Yale volume containing the prayers and meditations had appeared the previous year), and before coming up to Oxford Fleeman began compiling an index of phrases. But his supervisor for the first two terms, Mary Lascelles, persuaded him that the research would lead to no surprising conclusion, and so for a time his thoughts turned to a wider stylistic essay on Johnson. Things seemed to come into focus again when he found in Blackwell's second hand department a first edition copy of *The Adventurer* and decided that he would like to edit it. This discovery coincided with his introduction to the delights of bibliography through attending Herbert Davis's printing class, part of the course work for any probationer B. Litt. student. The fascinating detective work of investigating printing practices, type, paper etc., offered a combination of difficulty, fact, and physical detail to which he was by nature responsive, and it made a powerful impression.

It was at this moment that the discipline of bibliography came into conjunction with the powerful moral presence of Johnson, and it was a decisive combination. He was sent to talk to L. F. Powell, who was then preparing the Yale second volume, and Fleeman proudly marched in with his *Adventurer* under his arm. "An interesting project," remarked the great man, "but what will you do when you've finished it? Why work for three years on Hawkesworth, when Johnson can offer you a life sentence? You'd better work on *him*." Intriguingly Powell led him to the 1825 "Oxford" edition of Johnson's works (published by Pickering, Talboys and Wheeler): "This is still the standard edition; but nobody knows how it came to be as it is. Go and have a look at the text and make some comparisons." Fleeman found that in chapter one of *Rasselas* alone fifty commas had been added, and it was clear that this edition, which dominated traditional stylistic analyses of the "ponderous" Johnson, offered a thoroughly corrupt text in which some three quarters of the punctuation is unwarranted. So he began work comparing it with earlier editions, charting variant readings and listing errors in the text, until a family tree of Johnson's complete works began to take shape. It also revealed to him how significantly punctuation can affect the way we hear the words of an author, and the revelation of lifting away those thick overlays from Johnson's sentences forever sharpened his eagerness to recover exactly what Johnson wrote.

Settled onto a Johnsonian topic, and now with L. F. Powell as his supervisor, Fleeman became a protégé of a scholar of almost mythic status in Oxford. Never having sat an academic examination in his life, or completed any thesis, Powell had retired over a decade earlier from his post as Librarian of the Taylor Institution and was finding a useful role at the age of seventy-nine supervising a few postgraduates while pursuing his own research. He was a model of capacious knowledge harnessed to diligent and disciplined inquiry, but it is clear that his influence came as much from the man as from the work. When Fleeman wrote the entry on Powell for the *DNB* "Missing Persons" volume, he took the opportunity of expressing his deep admiration in phrases of a Johnsonian weight and intensity:

Powell's career displayed native tenacity. An orphan boy with few material advantages, he was largely self-taught, undeterred by difficulties, ever alert for information, and he kept his memory in full activity. A formidable indexer, he rightly considered his memory superior to card indexes, and drew together disparate source material, references, and recondite information, with effortless skill. For his pupils he resembled Johnson without the danger: cheerfulness was always evident. He was eminently 'clubbable', loved a *bon mot* or anecdote, and despised gossip. He defied the doctors of 1914 with energetic pedestrianism, and in his eighties would sometimes trick unwary visitors by suggesting a stroll. A shrewd and learned editor, a patient mentor, and a courteous friend, his *Boswell* is a lasting memorial.

Powell spent his final years in a nursing home in Banbury, not far from Oxford but beyond the buzz of scholarly conversation. In order to remedy this deficiency Fleeman suggested to Roger Lonsdale that each should pay him a visit on alternate Sunday afternoons for some eighteenth-century chat, and they both maintained this with only rare interruptions for several years until LFP's death in 1975.

In Oxford the Fleemans lived at 32 New Inn Hall Street, a historic house notable as a place where John Wesley preached in the 1780s (the Wesley Memorial Church was later built across the road)—but for the Anglican Fleeman a more stirring association was that Charles the First had kept the royalist silver in their cellar during the Civil War. The genuine treasure-house, however, was the Bodleian Library, and here Fleeman had a wealth of manuscript and printed material at his disposal. As he set about examining hundreds of individual Johnson items the emphasis of his work shifted from the primarily textual to the bibliographical, and he began to identify many reprints and editions not known to Courtney or other bibliographers, besides finding that so-called "new editions" were occsasionally merely reissued sheets. Fleeman's research had led him progressively from the redolence of Johnson's language, to the development of his texts, and on to the underlying bibliographical problems.

In the Autumn of 1961 Donald and Mary Hyde visited Oxford. They had asked Powell to suggest someone who might take on the task of cataloging their superb eighteenth-century collection, and a party was thrown at the Mitre attended by all L. F.'s pupils, including Roger Lonsdale, John Hardy, and Christian Deelman (Powell was proud of his eighteenth-century "chaps"). In the event Fleeman accepted an invitation for a period of two years to catalogue the library at Four Oaks Farm, and this went along with an appointment as bibliography consultant at Harvard. It was a bold move, considering that his Oxford thesis remained unfinished, but the opportunity to work on such a wonderful hoard of material was too tempting. His brief was to complete the catalogue in two years, and indeed two years later, to the day, the task was done. Twenty-eight thousand filing cards were processed, and Isabel Fleeman proved a meticulous and helpful collaborator in the later stages, herself responsible for indexing the miscellaneous manuscript correspondence.

A further year followed with Fleeman's appointment as "Hyde Fellow in Bibliography" at Harvard, and the project was extended to develop the catalogue into a bibliography. In 1964 the catalogue of printed books was privately produced in three volumes as *Catalogus Bibliothecae Hydeianae*. During this time he also took the opportunity to travel around the States accumulating information: the Library of Congress, the Huntington Library, Chicago, Texas, Philadelphia, all were visited and many original documents examined. His Oxford D. Phil. thesis made good use of these primary sources and was finally submitted from the U.S. and successfully defended in January 1965. "A Critical Study of the Transmission of the Texts of the Works of Dr. Samuel Johnson" (Bodleian MS D. Phil. c. 444) shows that at that early date Fleeman already had an impressive command of an extremely wide range of material. The thesis describes in detail the transmission of Johnson's texts from their first publication to their inclusion in the collected editions of 1787–89, and supplies a general view of their subsequent development through the various collected editions to the 1825 "Oxford" volumes. Every text is analysed, the stemma indicated, and the textual features of each edition recorded. This thesis, which still repays consultation by the Johnsonian scholar, provided not only the basis for an editorial assessment of any given version or reprint of a Johnsonian text, but the textual foundation for a new bibliography of Johnson's works. The massive project was already under way.

In terms of a career Fleeman's first wish was to be a librarian, but there were no openings available. However, the sudden death of Robert Browning, the English tutor at Pembroke College, created an unexpected vacancy there. The possibility of a fellowship at Johnson's *alma mater* was tempting, and he was well acquainted with its Johnsonian holdings (a few years earlier Browning had allowed him to see the manuscripts and catalogue them). In spite of a feeling that teaching was not his main love, and acutely aware of the narrowness of his literary interests during the previous six years, he rose to the occasion at interview. In response to the question, "What would you expect your students to take away from your teaching?" the former army instructor gave the reply, "I hope they would learn how to write a decent English sentence." He was elected.

Along with the security of a college fellowship came the responsibility for tutoring on literature from the Renaissance to the end of the Romantic period. With an intake in English of up to ten students, Pembroke has at any one time about thirty undergraduates reading English (a tenth of the student body), and the teaching duties are shared with an English Language/Medieval tutor, and some bought-in assistance. As a teacher Fleeman is tough, tactical, interrogatory, oppositional, but fair, and it is never easy to forget the bibliographer behind the tutor. Sweeping conjectures, ingenious theories, unsupported generalizations, second-hand commonplaces—all are given short shrift. But underneath is a deep love of books and a respect for the individual writer's struggle to find the right word.

Fleeman does take pleasure in literary criticism and can enjoy tutoring undergraduates, but its relish for him lies in playing a game by the rules, with rallies of words and argument. His students need to be able to return his serve. Perhaps it is precisely because he does not see "truth" as being at issue in mere literary criticism that he is able to appreciate it as a rhetorical exercise or battle of wits. (He remains conscious of the fact that where Harvard's motto is *Veritas*, and Oxford's *Dominus illuminatio mea*, that of St Andrews is *Ever to be best*.) Teaching for him is an enjoyable encounter that exploits the energy of debate, but it cannot be a search for truth because it exercises itself in the play of ideas. Sometimes a student would be reminded of the rigorous argumentative powers of Ursa Major, but where Johnson's unpredictable swings from game to earnest could injure the unwary, Fleeman, like his mentor, resembles "Johnson without the danger." As a teacher he has always been conscious of working within formal rules—"then *each side* knows what

it's doing," he once remarked, alluding directly to the adversarial encounter of the tutorial. Until women entered the college in 1979, he
would insist on academic gowns being worn, and surnames were used
("Mr Smith" in the first year, the more intimate "Smith" in the second,
and "John" in the third). Placed either side of the fire, the players would
begin the match.

College work kept him busy: a schedule during term of twelve hour-
length tutorials a week was the norm, and administrative duties increasingly impinged on the remaining hours of the day. Like many a recently
recruited fellow he found himself handed the job of Secretary to the
Governing Body (1966–71), but a pleasanter task came his way in 1968
when he succeeded Douglas Gray as Pembroke's Librarian (like other
college posts this brought no remission in teaching). The college's books
were at that time widely scattered, having overflowed their original de-
pository; and so his chief task was to oversee the building of a new library, opened by the Chancellor, Harold Macmillan, in 1974. One event
that gave him particular personal pleasure was Pembroke's award in 1966
of an honorary fellowship to L. F. Powell, then at the ripe age of eighty-
five. A devoted college man, Fleeman became its acting head during
1991–93 at a difficult time, and as Vicegerent he superintended the pro-
tracted appointment in 1992–93 of a successor to the Mastership. This
was an exhaustive and exhausting process, but according to one colleague
he saw the business through with an impressive combination of fairness
and efficiency, integrity and good humour.

Beyond the confines of the college, the English Faculty also imposed
duties. As a Lecturer he has regularly taught the M. Litt. probationer
class in Bibliography and Textual Criticism, passing on to a new generation of students the intriguing delights of inner formes and cancels, and
the darker tales of corruption, contamination and foul papers. Especially
memorable were the classes he taught jointly with David Foxon, when
they made a superb doubles pair: Fleeman striking the ball hard down
the baseline, while the flamboyant genius Foxon vollied spectacularly at
the net. When Foxon unexpectedly retired as the University's Reader in
Bibliography, the post was frozen and Fleeman had to shoulder a considerable extra burden for several years until a replacement was appointed.

He also proved a valuable Faculty member as a postgraduate supervisor, and from his first probationer in 1966 to the present day he has
seen fourteen students successfully through to their Oxford B. Litt. or
D. Phil., supervising theses on a surprisingly wide range of topics—and
only one of them specifically on Johnson. Subjects have included Edward Cave, Elizabeth Carter, Percy's *Reliques*, William Tytler, Roger

North, Sheridan's *The Rivals*, and McKenzie's *Man of Feeling*, and have extended to the sporting novels of R. S. Surtees and no less than four theses on Thomas Hardy. The experience of my own first supervision in October 1969 is probably not unique. His opening move was pre-emptive and a little startling: "Of course, you know there's only one writer you should be doing a thesis on. . . ." My reply, delivered with as much uncertain confidence as possible, that I was interested in working on Thomas Warton, seemed to hover invitingly in the air for ever. "That's all right. At least he was a friend of Johnson's." Immediately the practicalities were entered into: there was no discussion of Warton's milieu, his ideas, his influence, his poetic development, his theory of history. I was asked to return in two weeks' time with a card index of every item of Warton's correspondence I could trace. In the first hour I had received my own life sentence.

To have access, through Fleeman, to a store of useful information on works of reference, manuscript collections, editorial procedures, bibliographical questions, whom to write to and where to look, was a boon to any fledgling research student, and supervisions gave the impetus for many weeks of work. The talk was always buoyant and fascinating, the interest genuine, the help practical. He knew when to leave a student to get on with the job, and when immediate help was needed. I answered the telephone early one morning to hear a single word being forcefully enunciated—"*Propagate!*"—a startling injunction, especially at 8.30 a.m. It was, however, the solution to a hiatus in a torn letter, mentioned to him the day before, which had come to him while shaving.

Beyond the college and the Faculty, Fleeman's workload increased dramatically during 1976–77 when he was appointed one of the two University Proctors (a post dating back to the Middle Ages). Marked out by white tie and clerical bands, the two Proctors, who traditionally represent the colleges and are independent of the Vice-Chancellor, are jointly responsible for student discipline—although they and the "bull-dogs" (their thick-set, bowler-hatted deputies) do not command quite the same awe among the student body as they did in Johnson's day. As a Proctor Fleeman held overall responsibility for the conduct of university examinations and was *ex officio* a member of every administrative committee of the university, participating in the work of over sixty bodies. Not surprisingly, the job is taken on for only a year.

In 1977 this responsibility was handed on, only for another to take its place: when J. C. Maxwell was knocked down and killed by a motorcycle while walking home to his Oxford flat, Fleeman generously took on the joint editorship of *Notes & Queries* (the language/medieval editor was his Pembroke colleague, Professor Eric Stanley). No single human being could replace the indefatigable Maxwell, with his carrier-bag filing system and panoptic learning, but for the next seven years he had a worthy successor. Contributors, especially inexperienced ones, could rely on Fleeman's encouragement and practical help: a submitted note might call forth a four-page letter full of ideas for fresh lines of inquiry and a host of questions for further deliberation. It is impossible to say how many young scholars found new impetus for their researches through such editorial support. Also during this period he was General Editor of the publications of the Oxford Bibliographical Society, and as such was responsible between 1974 and 1984 for the planning and overseeing of at least one volume a year. Between them the two editorships imposed a heavy burden.

They also came at a time when Fleeman's health was giving serious cause for concern, and the physical strain was considerable. Acute kidney failure followed, which was fortunately remedied in September 1979 by a successful transplant. Although his energy returned and he was soon able to resume work, this unsettled period was especially disruptive of research and left his major project suspended for a time. But happily he was about to enter his most productive decade to date, during which a series of publications confirmed him as the leading British Johnson scholar.

As early as 1971 Fleeman's devotion to Johnson was given public recognition when he was elected President of the Johnson Society of Lichfield, following in the footsteps of such luminaries as David Nichol Smith, L. F. Powell, Mary Lascelles, Mary Hyde, James Clifford, and Helen Gardner. The Annual Supper that year was more than ever a splendid occasion: "Liveried footmen served the traditional fare in the panelled Guildhall; the City plate—candelabra, punch bowls etc.,—was much in evidence, while the churchwarden pipes, smoke curling upwards in the candlelight, created a passable reproduction of an 18th century atmosphere" (so the report in the society's *Transactions* reads). In his Presidential address Fleeman (who had read *Handley Cross* by the age of six) likened himself to R. S. Surtees's Jorrocks: "O, John Jorrocks! John Jorrocks! you are indeed a most fortunate man! a most lucky dog! O dear! —O dear! was ever anything so truly delightful!" But instead of continuing in this vein with an after-dinner talk of Johnsonian anecdote and reminiscence, the Presidential Address soon became an informative lecture on Johnsonian bibliography. Fleeman has always been uneasy about what he referred to in a 1988 review as the "hoary old business" of "The Great Cham" whose main claim to greatness is his talk. For him Johnson is primarily a writer, a maker of books, not the anecdotal Johnson of dinner-table delight; his Johnson is more the man of the essays, prefaces and poems, speaking directly in his own words and not dependent on the note-taking of others. It is as though Fleeman wants to discover Johnson from within, not as caught in performance by his friends. This uneasiness with the Johnson of many Johnsonians has worked to sharpen the rigour of his scholarship and the image of Johnson that it conveys.

As past President of both the Lichfield Society and the Johnson Club (1972–73), and a governor of Johnson's House since 1980, he was invited by the Johnson Society of London to lay the commemorative wreath in Poets' Corner, Westminster Abbey, on 19 December 1981. On this occasion he chose to speak Johnson's haunting words on Iona: "To abstract the mind from all local emotion would be impossible, if it were endeavoured, and would be foolish if it were possible. Whatever withdraws us from the power of our senses; whatever makes the past, the distant, or the future predominate over the present, advances us in the dignity of thinking beings." In this powerful passage, memory and imagination, recollection and hope, relieve momentarily the struggle of the present, and Johnson in that spot senses a kind of eternity. But the next day he is busy again with practicalities: "In the morning we rose and surveyed the place. . . . I brought away rude measures of the buildings, such as I cannot much trust myself, inaccurately taken, and obscurely noted." The diurnal, self-deprecating human endeavour in a way brings us closer to Fleeman's Johnson; and it is this man, the brilliant master of words who recognised (to quote Fleeman's 1984 "Valediction") that "language is a mysterious and ultimately devious medium," who has been the focus of his scholarly research for over thirty years.

II

For some people books themselves are invisible, and the power of literature resides in the ideas and images which transcend the material that contains them. For Fleeman the bibliographer, however, books embody physically the effort to get things right, to see ideas through to the point at which they communicate, and from the chain lines and the press marks, to the imprint or the cancels, they tell a human story. Fleeman's uneasiness with "pure" literary criticism is partly a distaste for things that float free (like the yearnings of Lamartine), and a conviction that, as Pope said, "when we are confined to truth, we soon find the shortness of our tether." This Johnsonian belief that what is right and true is not mysterious, ideal, or distant, but is embedded in the present and tangible, means that its recovery is both a practical and ethical challenge.

Difficulty is the moral warrant of truth, and it is difficult because self-deception, human frailty and circumstance will always offer an easier path into conjecture. Bibliography, with its actualizing of literary endeavour, engages with fact, not opinion. For Fleeman one is either a Platonist or an Aristotelian, an idealist or an analyst. He distrusts the secret and the subjective. Certainly the truth can be lured from its hiding place, but once recovered it must be demonstrable and submit itself to general acceptance. Private truth is a contradiction in terms; a truth that only one person can see is madness. So at the heart of the matter is a very Johnsonian combination—a preparedness to play and "argue for victory" alongside a passionate conviction about the actuality of truth. Fleeman's strength of feeling on this matter comes through in an early essay on "Johnson and the Truth" (1962), where he approvingly opens with a quotation from the life of Cowley: "the basis of *all* excellence is truth." His footnote significantly adds: "My italics."

Before gaining his Oxford fellowship Fleeman had already published four papers on Johnson, and the earliest of these exemplifies his concern for the processes of Johnson's thought. "Some Proofs of Johnson's *Prefaces to the Poets*" (*The Library*, 1962) demonstrates the great man's solicitude and attention to minutiae at the proof stage, and also his consideration for his printer. Fleeman reveals how "the restrictions of time and space . . . stimulated his critical faculties to acute and incisive activity" as Johnson reworked ideas sometimes through the smallest stylistic emendations. In an appendix, along with a checklist of the surviving proofs of the *Prefaces*, Fleeman offers a full tabular analysis of the many kinds of proof-changes under various headings, a fascinating record of Johnson's sustained commitment to stylistic accuracy, to getting things right. This detailed work on Johnson's proofs convinced him that beneath the public image of the confident critical dictator was the scrupulous craftsman and conscientious refiner of language, and the article set him off on a lifelong exploration of the dynamics of the Johnsonian text, its creation, revisal, printing, and distribution.

The most enjoyable of the early papers on Johnson is "The Making of Johnson's *Life of Savage, 1744*" (*The Library*, 1967), a highly satisfying blend of detection and reasoned conjecture which exemplifies bibliography's forensic role in tackling a literary mystery. After demonstrating bibliographically that the *Life* was printed in two parts, he relates the final part (of forty-eight pages) to those "forty-eight printed pages" that Johnson told Boswell had been written "at a sitting." An examination of Johnson's marginalia in the Glasgow University Library copy suggests that the hurried rewriting may have been the result of new material from a Popean source, but "whether he obliged Johnson to remove explicit references to himself, or whether he supplied new information cannot yet be known." The article ends with the intriguing possibility that there may somewhere survive a copy containing the first version of those forty-eight pages, Johnson's earliest account of Savage's latter days.

In his *R.E.S.* note (1968) on Johnson's Prayers and Meditations he gives the results of a close re-examination of the Pembroke College manuscripts. From beneath George Strahan's heavy obliterations he is able to recover a considerable number of new readings, and although the censored details are unremarkable, the very anti-climax of the conclusion has a vindicatory ring to it: "References to doubts, scruples, uncertainties, and perplexities of mind and to melancholy ($\mu\chi$) are the targets of Strahan's Indian Ink; those who seek sensational disclosures need not look for them in Johnson's papers." Reminiscent of Johnson striding into the cave to dispel Boswell's delicious mystery, Fleeman relishes making conjecture face up to the empirical evidence, wittily substituting for the abstract word "disapproval" the all-too-tangible "Indian Ink."

In fact, a subtext of much of Fleeman's scholarship is his distinction between the practical bibliographer and the over-sensitive "litterateur." This term appeared in his 1969 review of *Papers Read at a Clark Library Seminar*, in which he responded to Edmund Wilson's slight on Fredson Bowers as a "monomaniac bibliographer." In making that comment, says Fleeman, Wilson reveals himself as someone "for whom 'literature' is a self-evident phenomenon, whose sensibilities are sufficient to define it." Bibliographers are needed, he continues, to remind such people that "the translation from inspiration to publication is a far from simple matter. ... A text is not a stable entity but rather needs interpretation through an understanding of the ways in which it came into existence and that those ways are less than finely metaphysical and too often grossly physical." A critic who disowns bibliography is placing literature on a Platonic plane, cutting it free of its incarnation as a series of human processes. For Fleeman "literature" is inseparable from the act of giving physical form to an idea: "It is too easy" he concludes, "for the litterateur to dismiss the bibliographer because he occasionally wants to spell 'literature' as 'books.' "

It was an exciting moment for Fleeman the booklover when, in the Spring of 1963, he discovered William Bowyer's ledgers in the Grolier Club of New York. While searching with Gabriel Austin for general information on eighteenth-century printing practices, he came across the seven volumes which had lain forgotten since their purchase in 1929 and immediately saw their significance. Having reported his findings in the *Times Literary Supplement,* he demonstrated in a 1964 article on Somervile's *The Chace* how the progress of a particular edition could be traced through Bowyer's printing accounts.

Fleeman's tireless efforts to track down every surviving item of Johnsoniana have led to a number of very useful reference volumes that should be on any self-respecting Johnsonian's shelf. The earliest of these was partly the result of his travels around American libraries and especially of his work on the Hyde Collection; modestly entitled *A Preliminary Handlist of Documents & Manuscripts of Samuel Johnson* (1967), it consists of 265 items and includes documents bearing Johnson's autograph annotations or endorsements. A companion volume listing 285 copies of "books associated with Dr. Samuel Johnson" appeared in 1984. His substantial *C.B.E.L.* entry for "Samuel Johnson" (1971) is a significant contribution to Johnsonian bibliography and offers some further helpful lists, including works dedicated to Johnson, his contributions to others' books, his periodical writings, and his many "proposals." In 1975 Fleeman published a facsimile edition of the sale catalogue of Johnson's library (reproduced from the annotated Harvard copy), adding an introduction, and providing an index of authors, titles and purchasers, along with a census of all known copies, some not identified in the catalogue. In the same year his article "The Revenue of a Writer" brought together all the available information on Johnson's literary earnings during his career, and made good use of William Strahan's bank account to present a striking picture of the financial realities behind the man of letters. In 1985 he published a detailed list of thirty-one prospectuses and proposals in which Johnson was concerned, and in the 1993 volume of *Studies in Bibliography* he and Donald Eddy offered a further "preliminary handlist" of the many books to which Johnson subscribed. Taken together, these bibliographic publications provide a wealth of Johnsonian knowledge that eighteenth-century scholars can be grateful for.

For Fleeman all bibliographies are in a sense "preliminary," all knowledge finally tentative. In his 1984 "Valediction" he offered the sobering remark that, thanks to the increasing refinement of analytical techniques, "every modern critical edition is obsolescent on the day of publication:"

The more we examine the business, the more we find that this emphasis upon the singularity of the origin of a text, with its consequential concern to eliminate all other contaminations, not least those of the printer, lies open to question.

Johnson himself had second, third, and even further thoughts, and he frequently acquiesced in the intrusions of others (as with John Nichols's interventions in the *Lives of the Poets*): "By what means are such intrusions to be identified? Are they to be eliminated? or should we not leave them as our author did?" These are the questions of a committed pragmatist.

One of Fleeman's strengths as an editor is his keen awareness that a literary text is a flux upon which any printed edition is bound to impose an artificial fixity. In a review of Cornford's edition of Young's *Night Thoughts* (*Notes & Queries*, 1991), he echoes the 1969 review quoted earlier, but develops his point in terms of the compromised role of the editor: "Language is undoubtedly a slippery and elusive agency," he writes, "and despite the apparent certainty of the written or printed form, it cannot be wholly settled in an unequivocal state. Editors nevertheless undertake to do exactly that." This healthy awareness of textual pragmatics causes him to be suspicious of tidy impositions of consistency upon a text that may reflect its author's uncertainties or oversights. Although editors have to make choices, these should not be decided through a desire to impose a comforting predictability that will not trouble a reader. It is as though Fleeman even wants that reader to notice inconsistencies or quirks in a text, as reflecting more truly its conception in the fallible human brain. A regularized text is therefore anathema to him. In his reviews he criticizes editions that invoke a publisher's "house style" as an excuse for regularizing, or, under the cloak of a comment that "such matters as punctuation and capitalization were left to the compositors," tidy up a text so that the idiosyncrasies are wiped out.

As an editor Fleeman is prepared to be equivocal, even inconsistent, when he deems it appropriate, and he will weigh the balance of probabilities at those points where certainty is impossible. He feels that an editor must show his hand and reveal exactly why a particular reading is being emended or retained. In fact a stubborn retention of readings is a marked feature of his work, which is only conservative in the most literal sense. His "conservatism" can be bold and daring when a safer course might have been to emend something awkward, inconsistent or strange. He insists, however, that editions should preserve a degree of unfamiliarity, so that the reader is reminded that the text is not a modern one, just as the mind that produced it was not a modern mind. In welcoming Fleeman's 1985 edition of the *Journey to the Western Islands of Scotland* ("a model of its kind"), Mervyn Jannetta commented: "it is heartening to encounter such straightforward statements of editorial policy, which are the more reassuring for the openness with which they acknowledge the pressures of practical necessity on editorial ambition. Time and again in the textual notes we are made acutely aware of how expediency is anything but a soft option" (*The Library*, 6th ser., 8 [1986], 284–285).

A characteristic of Fleeman the editor is his capacity to keep an open mind and think each specific problem through. Rather than apply a textual theory and work to produce a neat, consistent answer, he is an intelligent realist who works with the grain of the material, however knotty, and develops a method appropriate to each instance; furthermore, his knowledge of Johnson is profound enough to appreciate the writer's own inconsistencies.

There is a note of comprehending sympathy in this, and it is no surprise that the introduction to his edition of *A Journey to the Western Islands of Scotland* tells a story worthy of his author. Setting out on an idealistic mission to reconstruct the lost manuscript from which the text had been set, he had hoped to identify individual compositors and work back to the holograph they had in front of them (this early optimism is evident in his 1981 lecture to the Johnson Society of London, summarized in *The New Rambler*). But in the end the fact had to be faced that typesetting conventions and variations in spelling and punctuation did not form a consistent pattern, and so his task changed to a humbler but far more Johnsonian one:

That has led to caution and conservatism, when I had at first hoped for an opportunity to indulge greater freedom with the text . . . no great changes could have been expected anyway, but I have to confess some disappointment in the collapse of some cherished theories. They were the dreams of a textual critic doomed to wake at last an editor.

This Johnsonian awakening from a "dream of hope" highlights Fleeman's editorial decorum.

In his introduction to the *Journey* he remarks that "a text, and certainly not this one, is not a single entity but is rather a process. Its witnesses are merely markers on the continuum of that process," and it is this awareness of process which justifies some of his decisions. Inconsistency is embraced as an authentic mark of human fallibility which it is not the editor's job to override, and the reader of this edition is brought intriguingly close to Johnson's thought processes and seems to be leaning over Johnson's shoulders as he writes. Some of Fleeman's more daring decisions are to resist emendation. Perhaps the most outrageous is his retention of the printed "Frith of Forth" in the third paragraph, even though later in the text the word appears as "Firth" (as in "Firth of

Tay" on p. 7) to which it is normally emended. In this case he even accepts that "Frith" must have been a compositor's misreading of MS "Firth," but he proceeds to argue that in reviewing it in proof Johnson may have allowed the word to remain, assuming as he did so a possible derivation from Latin 'fretum': "Such a train of thought would be highly characteristic of Johnson who retained a misreading 'fecundine' for 'secundine' (placenta) in his *Preface* to 'Cowley', 1779 (116, line 7; *Lives,* ed. Hill, i. 42, para. 136; cf. *The Library,* 5th ser. xvii (1962), 216), and so no emendation is here proposed." The editor puts us in touch with Johnson's mental processes so that we see how he might retain a misreading of his manuscript at one moment but allow a different spelling to stand a few pages later. Mere consistency carries no weight in the argument.

Perhaps Fleeman's most triumphant emendation (all the more convincing because of the many carefully argued refusals to emend) concerns Johnson's description of the Armadale otter. The published texts read: "I expected the otter to have a foot particularly formed for the art of swimming; but upon examination, I did not find it differing much from that of a spaniel." Fleeman's brilliant emendation of "art" to "act" is the result not merely of close acquaintance with Johnson's handwriting, but of a sure sense of Johnson's mind: "Though swimming may be an 'art' for men," he comments, "it is not so for otters. Johnson defined *art* as 'the power of doing something not taught by nature and instinct'." Johnson's sureness and clarity of mind have been absorbed by his editor. The majority of its readers will value the edition for the almost two hundred pages of commentary and appendices, which reveal a range of erudition and eye for detail worthy of his mentor Powell (in his *Notes & Queries* review, A. F. T. Lurcock commented that "it could be reviewed properly only by a committee"); but it will not surprise some to know that he himself is proudest of the thirteen pages of textual notes. Indeed, as the above examples show, it is there that we come closest to Johnson's mind and art.

The text of Johnson's poems may have offered less scope for annotation and emendation, but here too Fleeman took a firm stand. His Penguin edition of 1971 (subsequently revised) remains for many the standard edition (in a 1975 review O M Brack concluded that it contained the best texts of the poems). The policy of the Penguin series required a modernized text, but after a sustained struggle Fleeman persuaded the publishers that in Johnson's case the updating of his spelling and reduction of his capitalizations would prevent the full meaning from coming through. His two-page discussion of this point in the introduction makes a watertight case and should be read by any editor of eighteenth-century poetry who may be tempted to impose modern conventions. He convincingly argues for a link between spelling and stress, in Johnson's tendency for example to give added weight to the final syllable, so that we even begin to *hear* Johnson as we read (*dreadfull, controul, compleat* and many more). Though they are not idiosyncratic spellings, the point holds, and if we turn to the poems themselves the verse in places begins to sound with more gravity. Ever conscious of Johnson's own views on editorial matters, Fleeman quotes the poet's disapproval of Lord Hailes's modernized edition of John Hales of Eton: "An author's language, Sir, is a characteristical part of his composition, and it is also characteristical of the age in which he writes. Besides, Sir, when the language is changed we are not sure that the sense is the same. No, Sir, I am sorry Lord Hailes has done this." Once again, the weight of Johnson himself is placed behind the argument. Rather than accommodate Johnson to the language of the present, Fleeman is adamant that Johnson is emphatically "not a modern author . . . his is not a modern mind."

Consistent with his interest in the workings of Johnson's mind, he chose in this edition to supply a critical text: "one advantage of the construction of a critical text is that the recorded variants will illustrate the progress of a composition by which a rough draft develops into a finished work." This dynamic principle extends to the contents of Fleeman's edition: two texts of the same translation of Horace *Odes* I.22 are placed side by side. As he says in the introduction, "the changes are slight, but the two together illustrate the kind of polishing to which Johnson often subjected his compositions." In his selections from *Irene* he gives extracts from Johnson's draft notes so as to "give some idea of the development of his thoughts and expression." It is clear throughout Fleeman's scholarly work that it is the *movement* of Johnson's mind that fascinates him: his Johnson is never the self-confident dictator occupying a firm position on every subject, but a writer who is always thinking things through, reworking ideas and developing his responses in a context of human uncertainty and fallibility. The crucial poem for Fleeman is, not surprisingly, *The Vanity of Human Wishes,* and he ends the Penguin volume with the text of the original manuscript in the Hyde Collection "so that the curious reader may see for himself the progress of Johnson's mind and art." This point was developed in his 1985 *R.E.S.* review of *The Unknown Samuel Johnson*: "It is clear from the manuscript of the *Vanity of Human Wishes* that the act of composition was a dynamic process in which Johnson was both maker and audience interacting to generate words and ideas sometimes in conflict, sometimes harmonious." Fleeman's contributions to Johnsonian bibliography never ignore this sense of dynamic process, and they are everywhere strengthed by it.

Fleeman's well known dissatisfaction with the editorial principles of the Yale Edition of Johnson's works is best seen in terms of this concern for the dynamics of the Johnsonian text. His objections are clearly presented in his 1971 *R.E.S.* review of the three-volume *Rambler*. In reprinting a modernized version of a "best" text, the "straitjacket of editorial policy" allows no consideration of Johnson's "processes of thought;" the reduction of initial capitals and elimination of italics sacrifices subtleties of meaning; and the editor's defensive appeal to the house style of the original publisher gets short shrift: " 'House style'," says Fleeman, "is assumed to exist in the eighteenth century even though there are no surviving manuals of it, no analyses of it, and no definitions of it: it has become a kind of magic handkerchief into which editorial problems may be persuaded to disappear." Furthermore, in rejecting the layout of the original folio *Ramblers*, the edition ignores Johnson's care for the appearance of his texts (witness the displayed compliments in his letters), and so the "spaciousness, dignity, and public statement" of the Folio is replaced by the crowded page "of a mere commercial venture." Another Yale principle of which Fleeman disapproves is the separation of the textual editing from the writing of the critical introduction. The assumption behind this division of labour contradicts his belief that the textual editor has the true critical warrant: "One of the best ways to approximate to an understanding of an author's work is to try to edit him. However carefully Mr. Bate may have read the *Rambler* there will remain tracts of Johnson's mind which only Mr. Strauss has traversed, and it is regrettable that we have not been given the results of that journey." (In that single word "tracts" we gain a sense of Fleeman's conviction that bibliography is the reverse of a narrow pursuit.)

Fleeman was given the chance to enter the arena of criticism when he was invited to deliver the British Academy's prestigious Warton Lecture on 3 November 1983. Rather than map out "Johnson's ideas" or "Johnson's style" (those static concepts beloved of so many undergraduate essays) Fleeman took the dynamic principle as his key, finding the clue to Johnson's art in his revisions, and the *Vanity of Human Wishes* manuscript played its role in this. For Fleeman, Johnson's mind and art were always in progress together—his words were not idea-led. To demonstrate this he follows the poem's third line, "Remark each anxious Toil, each eager Strife," through its earlier stages (from "Explore each restless . . ."):

Yet it is not evident that the revision or development of the line is the effect of an anterior *idea*. It is rather (subject to the constraints of 'metrical composition') a simple verbal adjustment, in that the language is not so much subordinate to the idea, as that the language itself provides the dynamic of the composition of the line and engenders whatever ideas the line can express.

This is a simple but remarkable statement, with significant implications for our view of Johnson as a writer. The word is anterior—no reach exceeding grasp here. The passage also shows how Johnson for him is forever in close-up, recutting his pen, weighing words and working from them to the ideas, not glimpsing an idea and attempting to capture it in words. For Fleeman, the word is the "thing" from which Johnson the poet starts (all those years of dictionary making), and although Fleeman does not, and probably would not, say this, line three in its successive reworkings exemplifies in miniature Johnson's own properly laboured art, eventually discarding the merely "restless" and pushing through to a thoughtful pairing of the "eager" with the "anxious." A writer on Johnson needs to understand the nuance that such a disentangling allows.

What drives Fleeman's lecture, as well as his scrupulous editing, is a conviction of the immanence of meaning, contained and expressed in the words themselves. There is no fashionable interplay of multiple meanings, it is not imported by the reader's own independent experience or transformed by a modern perspective. All is contained in the "now" of Johnson's words to which our minds should be addressed. But that "now" is itself in process and leads outwards. Fleeman concludes: "It is this feature of Johnson's poetry which projects its interest beyond the words which make it. It is projected into a dimension which is not backward from or anterior to those words, but which looks forward to something which is yet to arise from the words. The interest of his words is not so much in where they start but in where they lead."

The "life sentence" that L. F. Powell promised him in 1960 is still being served. For over thirty years Fleeman has been working towards a complete account of every published piece by Johnson, and of every known fragment of manuscript material which can be traced. Not resting content with describing the editions published in Johnson's lifetime, he has set himself the task of listing all later printings including translations, abridgments, chap-books and school text books, a detailed examination of which can give valuable information on the dissemination of Johnson's writings during the nineteeenth century when it has often been supposed that his reputation was in eclipse. The fact that

Rasselas alone has run through more than five hundred editions in English, in addition to over 130 editions of translations (one of which, into Italian, Fleeman welcomed in a 1984 review), indicates the scale of the enterprise. Looking back, Fleeman attributes his comprehensive scheme to the idealistic ambitions of "Rash Youth" (Johnsonian capitals), which "Crabbed Age" has come to view in a more sober light. But the commitment is being heroically carried through.

Some shifts in approach have been necessary as the work entered areas of study not envisaged at the outset, and the bibliographer has even had to become reconciled to the sociologist. For example, nineteenth-century school editions of *Rasselas* or the *Dictionary* (see his 1993 essay, "Johnson in the Schoolroom") needed to be placed in the context of the educational curriculum on both sides of the Atlantic. In his 1994 Oxford Bibliographical Society paper Fleeman recognised that the project has widened his view of the nature and possibilities of bibliography:

This somewhat sociological element in the development of my notions of a bibliography was new to me, and indeed at first, repugnant. The initial determination of Rash Youth to eschew, even to counter psychological biography by emphasizing intellectual evolution, was not easily persuaded that the record of the reception of an author's work need spill over into any sort of endorsement of "la sociologie de texte." Yet imperceptibly something of that view has crept into the compilation almost as an inevitable consequence of the range of material surveyed.

For Fleeman, certainty is at every moment vulnerable to new facts. The predominant tone of his writing is therefore elegiac, and sometimes rueful. The incremental advance of knowledge is won in the face of doubt rather than on a surge of confidence, and it is more a matter of recognising misconceptions than of constructing theories. Above all, scholarship is a moral activity conducted at the meeting point of honesty of purpose and clarity of method. Any scholar of Johnson's *Dictionary* or the *Shakespeare* will be familiar with the way in which (to quote Fleeman again) "a clear plan of action turns fuzzy and unclear once we leave the early stage of projecting, and begin to wrestle with uncomplaisant data."

Throughout his scholarly life Fleeman has struggled to come as close as possible to Johnson's mind and art. The energy of his researches, the integrity of his principles, and the generosity of his commanding knowledge deserve our gratitude. But for all his unrivalled expertise he has never forgotten that the work of the scholar must never supersede or blur the direct message of the great man himself. As he reminds himself and us in a 1985 *R.E.S.* review: "[Johnson] did not write to set arcane puzzles for professors in academies, but in order to say something, despite his recognition of the devious nature of language, to his readers, and happily, some of those 'common readers' still exist." Certainly, something of Johnson's own powers as a writer and man can be glimpsed in everything Fleeman has written. In all senses of the verb, he represents Johnson to us.

———

It would be appropriate to conclude this memoir with the full text of *"A FRAGMENT of the late Dr. JOHNSON,* ON THE CHARACTER AND DUTY OF AN ACADEMICK," printed as an appendix (pp. 42–43) to *Hospitality. A Discourse Occasioned by Reading His Majesty's Letter in Behalf of the Emigrant French Clergy, in St. Dionis Back Church, May 26, 1793 ... By John Moir, A. M.* It is introduced by Moir as follows: "The affinity of the subject has induced me to present the reader with the following STRICTURES, by one of the most illustrious moralists in modern times, presented to me, in the Author's own handwriting, by a friend whose confidence is one of my best comforts, and whose communications are all valuable, and merit the highest gratitude. The utility of the order is implicated in the functions thus forcibly described and inculcated."

David Fleeman agreed that the word originally printed as "national" in the second paragraph was probably a misreading of Johnson's handwritten "rational" ("his initial ragged 'r' is very like an 'n' to those unfamiliar with his hand"), and he also cited in favour of the emendation Johnson's sense of the internationalism of learning and knowledge.

In the month before his death David Fleeman had managed to do some preliminary research into Moir's background. He apparently was born in Scotland of English parents, and brought up a "Seceder," i.e. a schismatic of the Kirk (1733), but he was bright enough to do well in various Scottish schools, and studied divinity at Edinburgh (though did not graduate), before coming to England and joining the Church of England. He published a number of books and sermons, and a collection called *Gleanings* (2 vols., 1785), which includes a whiggish essay on Johnson, and an even more whiggish one on "Majesty," but which is published by the Author, from his house "8 Bolt Court, Fleet Street," viz. the house in which Johnson died in December of the year before. Nowhere in *Gleanings* does Moir indicate that he had this "Fragment," nor does he at that time show much respect for his predecessor in the house, so it may be assumed he acquired the paper some time later. In 1788 he was living in Southwark, and held a curacy and a lectureship in London. His most successful work was called *Female Tuition,* which ran into several editions.

ON THE CHARACTER AND DUTY OF AN ACADEMICK

The great effect of society is, that by uniting multitudes in one general co-operation, it distributes to different orders of the community the several labours and occupations of life. The general end is general happiness, which must result from the diversified industry of many hands, and the various direction of many minds. From this distribution every man being confined to his own employment, derives opportunities of attaining readiness and skill by improving daily on himself, and to this improvement must be ascribed the accommodations which are enjoyed in popular cities, and countries highly civilised, compared with those which are to be found in places thinly inhabited, where necessity compels every man to exercise more arts than he can learn.

From this complex system arise different obligations. Every man has his task assigned, of which, if he accepts it, he must consider himself as accountable for the performance. The individuals of this illustrious community are set apart, and distinguished from the rest of the people, for the confirmation and promotion of rational knowledge. An academick is a man supported at the public cost, and dignified with public honours, that he may attain and impart wisdom. He is maintained by the public, that he may study at leisure; he is dignified with honours, that he may teach with weight. The great duty therefore of an academick is diligence of inquiry, and liberality of communication. Of him that is appointed to teach, the first business is to learn, an unintermitted attendance to reading must qualify him to be heard with profit. When men whose active employments allow them little time for cultivating the mind, and whose narrow education leaves them unable to judge of abstruse questions, may content themselves with popular tenets, and current opinions, they may repose upon their instructors, and believe many important truths upon the bare authority of those from whom they received them; but the academick is the depositary of the public faith, it is required of him to be always able to prove what he asserts, to give an account of his hope, and to display his opinion with such evidence as every species of argument admits. Our colleges may be considered as the citadel of truth, where he is to stand on his guard as a sentinel, to watch and discover the approach of falsehood, and from which he is to march out into the field of controversy, and bid defiance to the teachers of corruption. For such service he can be fitted only by laborious study, and study therefore is the business of his life; the business which he cannot neglect without breaking a virtual contract with the community. Ignorance in other men may be censured as idleness, in an academick it must be abhorred as treachery.

THE PUBLICATIONS OF J. D. FLEEMAN

by

DAVID FAIRER

1961

"Dr. Johnson in the Highlands," *Times Literary Supplement*, 29 September 1961, 645. [Letter.]

"A Dr. Johnson Mystery," *The Scots Magazine*, n.s., 76.2 (November 1961), 120–125.

1962

"Johnson and the Truth," in *Johnsonian Studies*, ed. Magdi Wahba (Cairo, U.A.R.: Société Orientale de Publicité, 1962 [distributed outside the U.A.R. by Oxford University Press]), 109–113.

"A Letter of Dr. Johnson," *Times Literary Supplement*, 22 June 1962, 461. [Letter.]

"Some Proofs of Johnson's *Prefaces to the Poets*," *The Library*, 5th ser., 17 (September 1962), 213–230.

1963

"The Reprint of *Rambler* No. 1," *The Library*, 5th ser., 18 (December 1963), 288–294.

"Eighteenth-Century Printing Ledgers," *Times Literary Supplement*, 19 December 1963, 1056.

1964

"William Somervile's *The Chace*, 1735," *Papers of the Bibliographical Society of America*, 58 (First Quarter 1964), 1–7.

"Johnson's *Journey* (1775), and its Cancels," *Papers of the Bibliographical Society of America*, 58 (Third Quarter 1964), 232–238.

"The Johnsonian Collection of Mr. and Mrs. Donald F. Hyde," *Manuscripts*, 16.4 (Fall 1964), 39–40.

[Compiler of] *Catalogus Bibliothecae Hydeianae*, 3 vols., 1964. [Privately printed.]

"Some of Dr. Johnson's Preparatory Notes for his *Dictionary*, 1755," *Bodleian Library Record*, 7 (December 1964), 205–210.

1965

[Joint editor, with Mary Lascelles, James L. Clifford, and J. P. Hardy, of] *Johnson, Boswell and their Circle: Essays Presented to Lawrence Fitzroy Powell in Honour of his Eighty-Fourth Birthday*. Oxford: Clarendon

Press, 1965. xii, 338 pp. [Includes "Dr. Johnson and Henry Thrale, M.P.," pp. 170–189.]

"Johnson as a Subscriber," *Johnsonian News Letter*, 25.1 (March 1965), 2.

[Review of *Dr. Johnson's Printer: The Life of William Strahan*, by J. A. Cochrane, 1964], *Review of English Studies*, n.s., 16 (November 1965), 432–434.

1966

[List of books dedicated to Johnson], *Johnsonian News Letter*, 26.1 (March 1966), 7.

[Unsigned review of *A Bibliography of Edmund Burke*, by William B. Todd, 1964], *Times Literary Supplement*, 7 July 1966, 604.

[Review of *English Prose Fiction 1700–1800 in the University of Illinois Library*, comp. William H. McBurney and Charlene M. Taylor, 1965], *The Library*, 5th ser., 21 (December 1966), 347–348.

1967

A Preliminary Handlist of Documents & Manuscripts of Samuel Johnson. Oxford Bibliographical Society Occasional Publication no. 2. Oxford: Oxford Bibliographical Society, 1967. 51 pp.

[Review of *Freshest Advices: Early Provincial Newspapers in England*, by R. M. Wiles, 1965], *The Library*, 5th ser., 22 (March 1967), 79–81.

[Review of *The Collected Works of Oliver Goldsmith*, ed. Arthur Friedman, 5 vols., 1966], *Review of English Studies*, n.s., 18 (May 1967), 212–214.

"Hill's Johnson," *Times Literary Supplement*, 24 August 1967, 768. [Letter.]

"The Making of Johnson's *Life of Savage*, 1744," *The Library*, 5th ser., 22 (December 1967), 346–352.

1968

[Review of *The Cambridge University Press 1696–1712: A Bibliographical Study*, by D. F. McKenzie, 2 vols., 1966], *The Library*, 5th ser., 23 (March 1968), 75–79.

"Some Notes on Johnson's Prayers and Meditations," *Review of English Studies*, n.s., 19 (May 1968), 172–179.

[Review of Henry Fielding, *Joseph Andrews*, ed. Martin C. Battestin, 1967], *Review of English Studies*, n.s., 19 (May 1968), 208–209.

1969

[Review of *Bibliography: Papers Read at a Clark Library Seminar, May 7, 1966*, by Fredson Bowers and Lyle H. Wright, 1966], *Notes & Queries*, 214 (July 1969), 280.

[Review of Laurence Sterne, *A Sentimental Journey through France and Italy by Mr. Yorick*, ed. Gardner D. Stout, Jr., 1968], *Review of English Studies*, n.s., 20 (August 1969), 347–351.

[Review of *An Introduction To The Study of Bibliography, To Which is Affixed a Memoir on the Public Libraries of the Antients*, by Thomas Hartwell Horne, 1814, reprinted 1967], *The Private Library*, 2nd ser., 2 (Autumn 1969), 127–128.

1970

[Revisal and correction of] Boswell, *Life of Johnson*, ed. R. W. Chapman. 3rd ed. Oxford: Oxford University Press, 1970. xxiv, 1492 pp. [Reprinted and reissued as a World's Classics edition, Oxford, 1980.]

Introductory note to facsimile edition of Johnson's *London, 1738 and 1748* and *The Vanity of Human Wishes, 1749 and 1755*. Menston: Scolar Press, 1970. Reprinted 1973.

Introductory note to facsimile edition of Johnson's *Plan of a Dictionary, 1747*. Menston: Scolar Press, 1970. [*English Linguistics 1500–1800 (A Collection of Facsimile Reprints)*, selected and edited by R. C. Alston, no. 223.]

[Notice of *The Bibliothek*, 5.4 (1968)], *Notes & Queries*, 215 (January 1970), 3–4.

[Review of *Prince of Publishers*, by Harry M. Geduld, 1969], *Notes & Queries*, 215 (March 1970), 105–106.

"Dr. Johnson and the Laird of Lochbuie," *Times Literary Supplement*, 16 October 1970, 1195. [Letter.]

[Review of *Johnson on Shakespeare*, ed. Arthur Sherbo, 1968. The Yale Edition of the Works of Samuel Johnson, Vols. VII–VIII], *Notes & Queries*, 215 (November 1970), 435–439.

1971

Introductory note to facsimile edition of Johnson's *Life of Richard Savage, 1748*. Menston: Scolar Press, 1971.

[Editor of] *Samuel Johnson: The Complete English Poems*. Penguin English Poets. Harmondsworth: Penguin Books, 1971. 260 pp. [2nd ed. revised, Allen Lane, 1974; 3rd ed. New Haven and London: Yale University Press, 1982.]

"Samuel Johnson" in *The New Cambridge Bibliography of English Literature*, ed. George Watson, vol. 2, 1660–1800 (Cambridge: Cambridge University Press, 1971), columns 1122–1174 (main entry).

"Johnson's 'Rambler,' " *Times Literary Supplement*, 21 May 1971, 594. [Letter.]

[Review of *The Rambler*, ed. W. J. Bate and A. B. Strauss, 1970. The Yale Edition of the Works of Samuel Johnson, Vols. III–V], *Review of English Studies*, n.s., 22 (August 1971), 348–352.

[Review of *The Letters of Tobias Smollett*, ed. Lewis M. Knapp, 1970], *Notes & Queries*, 216 (September 1971), 357–358.

1972

[Review of *A Catalogue of Horace Walpole's Library*, by Allen T. Hazen. With *Horace Walpole's Library*, by W. S. Lewis, 3 vols., 1969], *The Book Collector*, 21 (Summer 1972), 275–279.

"Johnsonian Bibliography," *Transactions of the Johnson Society of Lichfield*, December 1972, 34–45. [Presidential Address.]

1973
[Editor of] *Early Biographical Writings of Dr. Johnson*. Westmead, Hampshire: Gregg International, 1973. xi, 522 pp. [Includes "Introduction," pp. 7–11. Facsimile edition.]

Introductory note to facsimile edition of Johnson's *Irene, 1749*. Menston: Scolar Press, 1973.

[Review of *Samuel Johnson: A Survey and Bibliography of Critical Studies*, ed. James L. Clifford and Donald J. Greene, 1970], *Notes & Queries*, 218 (June 1973), 230–233.

1974
[Revisal of] *The Poems of Samuel Johnson*, ed. David Nichol Smith and Edward L. McAdam. 2nd ed. Oxford: Clarendon Press, 1974.

"Johnson on Shakespeare," *Times Literary Supplement*, 17 May 1974, 528. [Letter on John Wain's *Johnson as Critic*.]

"An Emendation to Johnson's *Life of Pope*," *The Library*, 5th ser., 29 (June 1974), 227. [Letter.]

[Compiler of] *Johnson's Prayers and Meditations. Facsimiles of the MSS at Pembroke College*. Oxford: Pembroke College, 1974. [Fourteen booklets in a slipcase. Includes unsigned four-page "A Note on the Facsimiles." Printed for the 350th anniversary of the founding of the college.]

1975
The Sale Catalogue of Samuel Johnson's Library. A Facsimile Edition. ELS Monograph Series no. 2. Victoria, B.C.: English Literary Studies, Department of English, University of Victoria, 1975. 118 pp.

"The Revenue of a Writer: Samuel Johnson's Literary Earnings," in *Studies in the Book Trade. In Honour of Graham Pollard* (Oxford Bibliographical Society Publications, n.s. 18; Oxford: Oxford Bibliographical Society, 1975), 211–230.

[Review of William Shaw, *Memoirs of the Life and Writings of the Late Dr. Samuel Johnson*, and Hester Lynch Piozzi, *Anecdotes of the Late Samuel Johnson, LL.D. During the Last Twenty Years of His Life*, ed. Arthur Sherbo, 1974], *Review of English Studies*, n.s., 26 (August 1975), 335–337.

1976
[Review of *The Early Biographies of Samuel Johnson*, ed. O M Brack, Jr., and Robert E. Kelley, 1974], *Modern Language Review*, 71 (1976), 136–138.

"A Productive Career," in *Our Friend L. F.: Recollections of Lawrence Fitzroy Powell*. 1976. [Privately printed for the thirty-first annual dinner of the Johnsonians, Friday, 17 September 1976, at the Metropolitan Club, New York.]

1977
[Review of *A Bibliography of George Berkeley*, by Geoffrey Keynes, 1976],
  Notes & Queries, 222 (June 1977), 286–287.
[Review of *Samuel Johnson in the British Press, 1749–1784: A Chronological
  Checklist*, by Helen Louise McGuffie, 1976], *Analytical & Enumerative
  Bibliography*, 1.3 (July 1977), 209–214.
[Notice of *Research in Progress in English and History, in Britain, Ireland,
  Canada, Australia, and New Zealand* (2nd ed.), ed. S. T. Bindoff and J. T.
  Boulton, 1975], *Notes & Queries*, 222 (December 1977), 482–483.
[Review of *Titles of English Books (and of Foreign Books Printed in England)*,
  vol. 1 (1475–1640), by A. F. Allison and V. F. Goldsmith, 1977], *Notes &
  Queries*, 222 (December 1977), 566–567.
[Review of *Abraham Cowley: A Bibliography*, by M. R. Perkin, 1977],
  Notes & Queries, 222 (December 1977), 573.

1978
[Notice of *The Thrales of Streatham Park*, by Mary Hyde, 1977], *Notes &
  Queries*, 223 (August 1978), 290.

1979
"Concealed Proofs and the Editor," in *Studies in the Eighteenth Century. IV.
  Papers presented at the Fourth David Nichol Smith Seminar, Canberra
  1976*, ed. R. F. Brissenden and J. C. Eade (Canberra: Australian National
  University Press, 1979), 207–221.
[Review of *Samuel Johnson and the Age of Travel*, by Thomas M. Curley,
  1976], *Modern Language Review*, 74 (1979), 418–419.
[Review of *Dryden: A Selection*, ed. John Conaghan, 1978], *Notes & Queries*,
  224 (December 1979), 577.
[Review of *Samuel Johnson, Biographer*, by R. Folkenflik, 1978], *Notes &
  Queries*, 224 (December 1979), 578.
[Review of Samuel Johnson, *Sermons*, ed. Jean Hagstrum and James Gray,
  1978. The Yale Edition of the Works of Samuel Johnson, Vol. XIV], *Notes
  & Queries*, 224 (December 1979), 578–579.

1980
"A Johnsonian Crux," *Notes & Queries*, 225 (February 1980), 48–49.
"Samuel Beilby *alias* Herbert *alias* A Yorkshire Freeholder," *Notes & Queries*,
  225 (February 1980), 56–57. [Identifies the author of an anonymous attack
  on Johnson's *Lives*.]
[Review of *Augustan Worlds: Essays in Honour of A. R. Humphreys*, ed. J. C.
  Hilson, M. M. B. Jones, and J. R. Watson, 1978], *Review of English
  Studies*, n.s., 31 (February 1980), 81–83.
[Review of *Index to British Literary Bibliography*, vols. 4 and 5, by T. H.
  Howard-Hill, 1979], *Notes & Queries*, 225 (October 1980), 424.
[Review of *Charles Dickens and his Publishers*, by Robert L. Patten, 1978],
  Notes & Queries, 225 (October 1980), 462–463.

1981

[Notice of facsimile reprint of Johnson's *Dictionary*, Times Books, 1979], *Notes & Queries*, 226 (October 1981), 385–386.

[Brief commemorative address on laying the wreath to Samuel Johnson on behalf of the Johnson Society of London, Westminster Abbey, Saturday, 19 December 1981], *The New Rambler*, 1981 issue, 18.

"Editing Johnson's Journey," *The New Rambler*, 1981 issue, 19–20. [Summary of paper read 19 December 1981.]

1982

1983

[Review of *A Chesterfield Bibliography to 1800*, by Sidney L. Gulick, 1979], *Review of English Studies*, n.s., 34 (February 1983), 119.

[Notice of *Hebridean Decade, Mull, Coll and Tiree, 1761–1771*, by Major N. M. Bristol (1982)], *Notes & Queries*, 228 (April 1983), 100–101.

"Johnson's Poetry," *Proceedings of the British Academy*, 69 (1983), 355–369. [British Academy Warton Lecture on English Poetry, read 3 November 1983.]

1984

A Preliminary Handlist of Copies of Books Associated with Dr. Samuel Johnson. Oxford Bibliographical Society Occasional Publication no. 17. Oxford: Oxford Bibliographical Society, 1984. 101 pp.

"Dr. Johnson's *Dictionary*, 1755," in *Samuel Johnson 1709–84* [Arts Council Commemorative Exhibition Catalogue], ed. Kai Kin Yung (London: The Herbert Press, 1984), 37–45.

"Bibliographer," *Notes & Queries*, 229 (March 1984), 30–31. [A note on Johnson's manuscript revision to the *Dictionary*'s definition of "bibliographer."]

[Review of *The Guardian*, ed. John Calhoun Stephens, 1982], *Notes & Queries*, 229 (March 1984), 93–94.

[Review of *Development of the English Book Trade, 1700–1899*, ed. Robin Myers and Michael Harris, 1981], *Notes & Queries*, 229 (March 1984), 128–129.

[Review of *Sale and Distribution of Books from 1700*, ed. Robin Myers and Michael Harris, 1982], *Notes & Queries*, 229 (March 1984), 129.

[Review of Samuel Johnson, *Rasselas Principe d'Abissinia*, trans. Goffredo Miglietta, 1982], *Notes & Queries*, 229 (March 1984), 135–136.

[Review of *A Critical Edition of Mary Wollstonecraft's A Vindication of the Rights of Woman*, ed. Ulrich H. Hardt, 1982], *Notes & Queries*, 229 (March 1984), 137–138.

[Review of *A Bibliography of Jane Austen*, by David Gilson, 1982], *Notes & Queries*, 229 (March 1984), 138–140.

[Catalogue of] *An Exhibition for the Johnson Conference at Pembroke College, Oxford, 8–13 July 1985*. [Privately printed.]

"A Valediction." Beirut: Librairie du Liban; The Egyptian Publishing Co.-

Longman, 1984. [Lecture delivered in Pembroke College Hall on Friday, 13 July, 1984 at 9.30 a.m.]

1985

[Editor of] Samuel Johnson, *A Journey to the Western Islands of Scotland.* Oxford: Clarendon Press, 1985. lx, 371 pp.

"Johnsonian Prospectuses and Proposals," in *Augustan Studies: Essays in Honor of Irvin Ehrenpreis,* ed. Douglas Lane Patey and Timothy Keegan (Newark: University of Delaware Press; London and Toronto: Associated University Presses, 1985), 215–238.

[Review of *The Nichols File of* The Gentleman's Magazine*: Attributions of Authorship and Other Documentation in Editorial Papers at the Folger Library,* by James M. Kuist, 1982], *Review of English Studies,* n.s., 36 (February 1985), 99–101.

[Review of *The Unknown Samuel Johnson,* ed. John J. Burke, Jr., and Donald Kay, 1983], *Review of English Studies,* n.s., 36 (November 1985), 573–575.

1986

[Review of *Dr. Johnson's Household,* by Lyle Larsen, 1985], *The New Rambler,* 1985/86 issue, 39–40.

[Review of *Blue Guide. Literary Britain and Ireland,* comp. Ian Ousby, 1985], *The New Rambler,* 1985/86 issue, 40–42.

"Dr. Johnson and 'Miss Fordice,' " *Notes & Queries,* 231 (March 1986), 59–60.

1987

[Review of *The Correspondence of Thomas Percy and John Pinkerton,* ed. H. Harvey Wood, 1985], *Notes & Queries,* 232 (March 1987), 91–94.

"Dr. Johnson's Desk," *The Times,* 18 April 1987, 17. [Letter.]

"Johnson's Dictionary (1755)," *Trivium,* 22 (Summer 1987), 83–88.

[Review of *Irish Booksellers and English Writers, 1740–1800,* by R. C. Cole, 1986], *Review of English Studies,* n.s., 38 (November 1987), 568–569.

[Review of *Index of English Literary Manuscripts, vol. 3, 1700–1800, Part 1, Addison-Fielding,* comp. M. M. Smith, with P. Boumelha, 1986], *Notes & Queries,* 232 (December 1987), 545–546.

1988

[Review of *Dr. Johnson: Interviews and Recollections,* ed. N. Page, 1987], *The New Rambler,* 1987/88 issue, 48–50.

[Review of *Selections from Johnson on Shakespeare,* ed. B. H. Bronson and J. M. O'Meara, 1987], *Notes & Queries,* 233 (March 1988), 98–99.

[Review of *The Birth of Shakespeare Studies,* by Arthur Sherbo, 1986], *Modern Philology,* 86 (August 1988), 90–92.

1989

"Memorabilia," *Notes & Queries,* 234 (March 1989), 1–5. [*Addenda* and *corrigenda* to *Samuel Johnson: A Survey and Bibliography of Critical Studies,* by J. L. Clifford and Donald J. Greene, 1970, and *A Bibliography of Johnsonian Studies, 1970–1985*, by John A. Vance, 1987.]

1990

"Johnson and Boswell in Scotland," *Transactions of the Johnson Society of Lichfield*, 1989–1990, 51–72. [An address delivered at a study day in the Guildhall, Lichfield, 21 April 1990.]

"Commemorative Address (Uttoxeter September 24th 1990)," *Transactions of the Johnson Society of Lichfield*, 1989–1990, 77–80. [A commemoration of Johnson's penance in Uttoxeter Market Place.]

[Review of *Fresh Reflections on Samuel Johnson: Essays in Criticism*, ed. Prem Nath, 1987], *The New Rambler*, 1989/90 issue, 38–41.

[Review of *William Heberden. Physician of the Age of Reason*, by Ernest Heberden, 1989], *The New Rambler*, 1989/90 issue, 41–43.

[Review of *The Sublime Savage: A Study of James Macpherson and the Poems of Ossian*, by F. J. Stafford, 1988], *Notes & Queries*, 235 (June 1990), 224–225.

1991

[Review of *Collected Poems of Thomas Parnell*, ed. C. Rawson and F. P. Lock, 1989], *Notes & Queries*, 236 (September 1991), 388–389.

[Review of Edward Young, *Night Thoughts*, ed. S. Cornford, 1989], *Notes & Queries*, 236 (September 1991), 389–390.

[Review of *Index of English Literary Manuscripts, vol. 3, 1700–1800, Part 2, John Gay-Ambrose Philips, with a First-line Index to Parts 1 and 2*, comp. M. M. Smith, 1989], *Notes & Queries*, 236 (September 1991), 390–392.

1992

[Review of *Samuel Johnson and Biographical Thinking*, by Catherine N. Parke, 1991], *The New Rambler*, 1991/92 issue, 39–40.

[Review of *The Eighteenth Century: A Current Bibliography. New Series 11, for 1985*, ed. Jim Springer Borck, 1990], *Review of English Studies*, n.s., 43 (November 1992), 604.

1993

"Johnson in the Schoolroom: George Fulton's Miniature Dictionary (1821)," in *An Index of Civilisation: Studies of Printing and Publishing History in Honour of Keith Maslen*, ed. R. Harvey, W. Kirsop, and B. J. McMullin (Clayton, Victoria: Centre for Bibliographical and Textual Studies, Monash University, 1993), 163–171.

"Dr. Johnson and Revd. William Dodd," *Edinburgh Bibliographical Society Transactions*, 6.2 (1993), 55–56.

[With Donald Eddy] "A Preliminary Handlist of Books to which Dr. Samuel Johnson Subscribed," *Studies in Bibliography*, 46 (1993), 187–220. [Reprinted, with corrections, as Occasional Publication no. 2 of the Bibliographical Society of the University of Virginia, 1993.]

"Lawrenceson Fitzroy Powell," in *Dictionary of National Biography: Missing*

Persons, ed. C. S. Nicholls (Oxford: Oxford University Press, 1993), 531–532.

1994–

"Johnson's *Shakespeare* (1765): The Progress of a Subscription," in *Writers, Books, and Trade: An Eighteenth-Century Miscellany for William B. Todd,* ed. O M Brack, Jr. (New York: AMS Press, 1994), 355–365.

[Review of *Johnson and Boswell in Scotland: A Journey to the Hebrides,* ed. Pat Rogers, 1993], *Notes & Queries,* 239 (March 1994), 106–109.

[Review of *Samuel Johnson,* by Pat Rogers, 1993], *Notes & Queries,* 239 (June 1994), 249–250.

[Review of *Samuel Johnson's Translation of Sallust: A Facsimile and Transcription of the Hyde Manuscript,* ed. David L. Vander Meulen and G. Thomas Tanselle, 1993], *The Library,* 6th ser., 16 (June 1994), 155–156.

[Review of *A Preface to Samuel Johnson,* by Thomas Woodman, 1993], *Notes & Queries,* 239 (September 1994), 395–396.

[Review of *Robert Surtees and Early Victorian Society,* by Norman Gash, 1993], *Notes & Queries,* 239 (September 1994), 401–404.

"Johnson's Secret," in *The Age of Johnson,* 6 (1994), 147–149.

POPE IN THE PRIVATE AND PUBLIC SPHERES:
ANNOTATIONS IN THE SECOND EARL OF OXFORD'S
VOLUME OF FOLIO POEMS, 1731-1736

by

JAMES McLAVERTY

A VOLUME of separately published folio poems now in the Bodleian Library, shelfmark M 3.19 Art, provides an unusual perspective on Pope's publishing activities between 1731 and 1736 and evidence of the response of his friend Edward Harley, second Earl of Oxford. Of the twenty-five pieces in the collection, fourteen are written by Pope himself, three are attacks on him by opponents, and eight are the work of supporters or friends. Central are the four epistles to several persons (or moral essays), *An Essay on Man,* and *The First Satire of the Second Book of Horace* and its consequent attacks and counter-attacks. Twenty of the poems are annotated by Harley, fourteen are dated, and five have detailed commentary. Harley's notes show that he sided with Pope, even when members of his circle became entangled in the satire, that he was fascinated by questions of reference, and that he attended to textual variation. His annotation has special interest because it coincides with Pope's own first systematic attempts to mediate between his poems and their public by providing a commentary. Following Maynard Mack, I shall also argue that in one of the poems in the collection, *An Epistle to Dr. Arbuthnot*, Pope has made three changes in his own hand.[1]

The early history of the volume leads to the Harleian library, and then, through the sale of the library (which peripherally draws in one of its cataloguers, Samuel Johnson), to one of the Bodleian's greatest benefactors, Richard Rawlinson. The Harleian library, built up by Edward and his father, the statesman Robert Harley, was one of the greatest of all British libraries, and its manuscripts became one of the founding collections of the British Museum.[2] Edward Harley (1689–1741) was an inveterate collector from his undergraduate days, when he was already running up large bills for books. To his father's extensive collection of genealogy, heraldry, history, politics, bibles, and prayer books, he added incunabula, printing on vellum, illuminated manuscripts, Greek and oriental manuscripts, coins and medals, and much more. When the library was sold it amounted to around 50,000 printed books (which had been kept at the country house, Wimpole) and 7,639 volumes of manuscripts, with 14,236 deeds, rolls, and charters (which had been stored at the town house in Dover Street). Harley took a detailed interest in the library, directing its organization and furnishing, and dating his purchases; he was generous to scholars, helping Maittaire, Palmer, and Hearne among others. His generosity extended to Pope, who treated the Dover Street house as something of a London base and found his own uses for the library.[3]

Pope saw that Harley's interest in books and his great library had potential value to him, and in the period immediately preceding the 1730s folios he involved him in two of his most complicated publishing operations. When the arrangements for *The Dunciad Variorum* in 1729 seemed likely to prove dangerous, with the printer and bookseller liable to prosecution, he asked Harley for help, suggesting that if a group of peers were prepared to publish the work, no action could be taken against them for libel. Harley agreed to act and consequently Pope sent him instructions about the distribution of

1. Pope's role was first noted by Mack in 'Some Annotations in the Second Earl of Oxford's Copies of Pope's *Epistle to Dr. Arbuthnot* and *Sober Advice from Horace*', *Review of English Studies*, n.s. 8 (1957), 416–420. I am deeply indebted to Professor Mack's work, not least to his transcription of Pope's note on Atticus; I shall dispute one of his three ascriptions to Pope while adding another. Harley's notes are referred to in the *Twickenham Edition of the Poems of Alexander Pope*, 11 vols (1939–69), III, ii, 48, 103; IV, 84–85; VI, 370; and in Margaret Smith and Alexander Lindsay, *Index of Literary Manuscripts*, III (1700–1800), Part 3 (1992), pp. 9–10, PoA 11, PoA 83, PoA 306.

2. The best account of the library, on which I have drawn freely, is the introduction to *The Diary of Humfrey Wanley 1715–1726*, ed. C. E. Wright and Ruth C. Wright, 2 vols (London, 1966), which supersedes the brief accounts in Edward Edwards, *Lives of the Founders of the British Museum* (1870) and William Younger Fletcher, *English Book Collectors* (1902). The manuscripts were acquired for the nation for £10,000.

3. See Maynard Mack, *Alexander Pope: A Life* (1985), p. 881. Mack suggests *The First Satire of the Second Book of Horace* may have been written there. Pope gave a Persian manuscript to the library (*Diary of Humfrey Wanley*, II, 247 [13]).

the books, down to the most explicit details: 'I beg your Lordship to send about 20 books to Cambridge, but by no means to be given to any Bookseller, but disposd of as by your own Order at 6s. by any honest Gentleman or Head of a House.'[4] Subsequently Harley was one of those (the others were Burlington and Bathurst) who assigned the copyright of *The Dunciad* to Lawton Gilliver. The second operation involved Harley's library directly. As early as September 1729 Pope wrote to Harley with the request 'That you would suffer some Original papers & Letters, both of my own and some of my Friends, to lye in your Library at London' (*Correspondence*, III, 54). Later, with publication in mind, he asked for permission to say that the originals were in Harley's library and was told, 'what ever mention you make of that Library I shall be pleased with' (*Correspondence*, III, 56). In consequence, Harley's library became the home for Pope's letters, the place of transcription (Harley even became involved in checking the transcriptions himself), and the vital stage on the route to 'involuntary' publication. Other works were transcribed there, and for some of Pope's shorter poems Harleian transcriptions provide the most authoritative witness. There can be little doubt that during the period Harley was collecting and annotating the Bodleian folios, he was, through his library, becoming intimately acquainted with many aspects of Pope's career.[5]

When Harley died, the state of his financial affairs necessitated the sale of the library. The books were bought by the bookseller Thomas Osborne for £13,000, and it was probably at the Osborne sale of the Harleian library that Richard Rawlinson bought the volume now in the Bodleian.[6] It appears from his correspondence that Rawlinson had not liked Harley, finding him 'incommunicative' and believing that he helped scholars in order 'to beg the applause of the world',[7] and he liked Osborne's sale, or so he claimed, even less, fearing that the bookseller would blend in his own stock with Harley's books. He resolved not to buy, but when he saw the books, 'a beautiful sight it was', he soon gave way and started making purchases.[8] His dislike of Os-

---

4. *The Correspondence of Alexander Pope*, ed. George Sherburn, 5 vols (1956), III, 26–27, 27 March [1729]. See also the account of this episode in David Foxon, *Pope and the Early Eighteenth-Century Book Trade* (1991), 108–114.

5. See Sherburn's account of the publication of Pope's letters (*Correspondence*, I, xi–xviii), and the suggestion that *An Essay on Man* may have been transcribed in the library (*Correspondence*, III, 193). Papers from the Harleian library have been important in establishing Pope's text; see *Twickenham* IV, xlii, and VI *passim*, and *Index of Literary Manuscripts*, III, iii, 9.

6. A good short account of Rawlinson is provided by Ian Philip, *The Bodleian Library in the Seventeenth and Eighteenth Centuries* (1983), 82–84, 93–98. A splendidly detailed account, on which Philip draws, is provided by B. J. Enright, 'Richard Rawlinson: Collector, Antiquary, and Topographer', unpublished D.Phil. thesis, University of Oxford, 1956. *Richard Rawlinson: A Tercentenary Memorial*, by Georgian R. Tashjian, David R. Tashjian, and Brian Enright (Kalamazoo, Michigan, 1990) gives information on other aspects of his career.

7. Bodley MS Ballard 2, f. 113, 24 June 1742. I suspect Enright is wrong in saying Rawlinson thought Harley 'dog in the manger'; that applies to Mr. West.

8. He complains in Bodley MS Ballard 2, f. 119 ([23 October] 1742), MS Ballard 2,

borne was something he shared with Pope and Johnson. Osborne's advertisement of subscription copies of the *Iliad* at half price had led to Pope's installing him as Curll's rival in the urinating contest in *The Dunciad* in 1743,[9] but Johnson's attack on the bookseller may have been more effective. Employed with William Oldys, who had been Harley's literary secretary, to supervise the cataloguing of the library, he took offence at Osborne's treatment of him, as Boswell explains: 'It has been confidently related, with many embellishments, that Johnson one day knocked Osborne down in his shop, with a folio, and put his foot upon his neck. The simple truth I had from Johnson himself. "Sir, he was impertinent to me, and I beat him. But it was not in his shop: it was in my own chamber." ' But, with characteristic fairness, Johnson noted that though the sum paid for the Harleian books would not have covered the cost of the original binding, 'the slowness of the sale was such, that there was not much gained by it.'[10]

Rawlinson died on 6 April 1755, leaving 5,205 volumes of manuscripts and between 1,800 and 1,900 printed books to the Bodleian Library. In his Will be specifically bequeathed to the Bodleian books such 'as shall appear to have therein any manuscript additions, or explanatory enlightning or controversial notes, either by myself or any other person or persons whatsoever'.[11] The volume which is now M 3.19 Art clearly falls into that category, but it did not come to the Library with the other volumes in the bequest that started to arrive from 1756 onwards. It seems to have arrived there between 1874 and 1880, the period during which a book by Devèze de Chabriol that had previously been at M 3.19 Art was moved to Physics b. 13. The history of the volume in the intervening period remains at present unknown.[12]

The folio poems collected by Harley cover the period following the publication of the *Dunciad Variorum* in March 1729 and culminating in the issue of the second volume of *Works* in April 1735. The collection was probably given to the binder over a year after the appearance of *Works* II; the last poem in the collection, *Bounce to Fop*, was published in May 1736, and the first Pope poem to be published after that, presumably too late to be bound

---

f. 123 (24 March 1743), and MS Ballard 2, f. 161 (16 October 1744); sees the books in MS Ballard 2, 129 (18 May 1743), and buys some 'not incurious' in MS Ballard 2, f. 146 (25 October 1743). I have not found the volume that is now M 3.19 Art listed in *Catalogus Bibliothecae Harleianae*, 5 vols (1743), though that may be because of the complex ordering of the catalogue. The Bodleian has Rawlinson's copy with some items marked (8° Rawl. 66–70), and I have noted these Pope items, without claiming to have made an adequate check: I, 4864, 4893, 4916; III, 3618, 6158, 6164; V, 1128.

9. See *Twickenham*, V, ed. James Sutherland, pp. 303–304, and David Foxon, *Pope and the Early Eighteenth-Century Book Trade*, pp. 248–249.

10. See *Boswell's Life of Johnson*, ed. George Birkbeck Hill, rev. and enlarged L. F. Powell, 6 vols (1934–50), I, 154.

11. Enright, p. 299, cites the relevant part of the Will. The printed books were a relatively minor part of the bequest, and the major problem for the Library was the cataloguing of the manuscripts; see R. W. H[unt], 'The Cataloguing of the Rawlinson Manuscripts, 1771–1844', *Bodleian Library Record*, 2, no. 26 (December 1947), 190–195.

12. I am most grateful to Mr. Clive Hurst of the Bodleian Library for his generous advice and his skilled detection of the period of the volume's arrival in the Library.

with these, was *Horace his Ode to Venus* on 9 March 1737.[13] Some of Harley's notes, those on *An Epistle from a Nobleman* (title-page) and *To Arbuthnot* (15.9), which are transcribed with the others at the end of this essay, show knowledge of the quarto or folio *Works* of 1735, but that does not mean all the notes (even in those poems) were made after that date, and the most likely pattern is of annotation shortly after receipt followed by some further notes around the time of binding. The book is bound quite plainly, which befits its status as a collection of folio pamphlets rather than a subscription edition of Homer or a fine-paper copy of the *Works*. The front and back covers are bound in marbled brown calf, with a gilt double-rule border; the spine is in smooth calf with a red gilt-bordered label, gilt-stamped 'EPISTLES BY M^r· POPE & OTHERS'. On the top left-hand side of the front cover a strip, measuring c. 3 x 10 (all measurements are in cms.), has been torn away. The volume measures 37.2 (high) x 23 (wide) x 3.6 (deep). The endpapers are marbled and the inside of the front cover bears the Rawlinson bookplate based on his diploma as Doctor of Laws.[14] On the first page after the end-papers, someone has written in pencil in an open sprawling eighteenth-century hand, 'MSS. Notes of the hand writing of Lord Oxford'. This identification is confirmed in an ink annotation by a librarian. The volume has been bulked out with blank sheets: eight leaves before item 1, two in item 2 before p. 5, six before item 15, and eight more at the end. Item 1 has been repaired by the Library; item 2 has two readily perceptible stab-holes. One item in the collection, 12*, I do not understand. It consists of two leaves of *An Essay on Man* with a line already present written out at the foot. I do not think the writing is Harley's or Pope's.

The poems in the collection fall into three groups, though there are various interlinkings and Harley's own arrangement is loosely chronological. First, and as the heart of the collection, come the poems Pope planned as part of the *opus magnum* which was to be founded on the basis of the *Essay on Man*: the *Essay* itself, represented by the first edition and revision of the first epistle and first editions of the other three (1733–34); and first editions of the supplementary poems, *To Burlington* (1731), *To Bathurst* (1732), *To Cobham* (1733), and *To a Lady*.[15] Second comes the group associated with Horatian imitations. Perhaps to help ensure the anonymity of the *Essay on Man*, Pope published his imitation of *The First Satire of the Second Book of Horace* in 1733 and followed it with an imitation of *The Second Satire* of the same book. *The First Satire* rapidly whipped up a controversy of its own: responses included an attack from Lady Mary Wortley Montagu, Lord Hervey, and William Wyndham, *Verses Address'd to the Imitator . . . of Horace* (1733), with an anonymous riposte, *Advice to Sappho* (1733), and an

13. The dates are taken from D. F. Foxon, *English Verse 1701–1750*, 2 vols (1975), hereafter abbreviated to Foxon.

14. The bookplate is discussed and illustrated in Enright's thesis, pp. 105–106.

15. I have used short titles for Pope's poems throughout this essay. The choice of abbreviation for Pope's epistles is influenced by F. W. Bateson's presentation in *Twickenham*, III, ii, of the four that Warburton called 'Moral Essays'.

attack from Hervey alone, *An Epistle from a Nobleman to a Dr. of Divinity* (1733), with its anonymous riposte, *Tit for Tat* (1734). To this group also belong Pope's *Sober Advice from Horace* (1734) and his reply to his critics, *An Epistle to Dr. Arbuthnot* (1735). The final group consists of poems by friends and protégés. Three young friends developed themes that were important to Pope. David Mallet attacked Bentley and Theobald in *Verbal Criticism: An Epistle to Mr Pope* (1733); Gilbert West praised Lord Cobham's gardens in *Stowe . . . Address'd to Mr. Pope* (1732); and Walter Harte contributed *An Essay on Reason* (1735), whose title echoes that of the prospective first epistle of the second stage of the *opus magnum*. Mallet was at pains to emphasize his independence of Pope: 'this poem was undertaken and written entirely without the knowledge of the Gentleman to whom it is addressed', but we know from a letter of 7 November [1732] that Pope had seen it before publication, 'The Epistle I have read over & over, with great & just Delight; I think it correct throughout, except one or two small things that savor of Repetition toward the latter End' (*Correspondence* III, 330). Of the four Swift poems included at the end of the collection, *On Poetry* (1733), *An Epistle to a Lady* (1734), *The Life and Genuine Character of Doctor Swift* (1733), and *Bounce to Fop* (1736), the two last have been attributed to Pope, and it is quite possible he had a hand in their revision or publication.[16]

Harley's collection represents both the new direction Pope was giving to his career and the publishing arrangements that went with it. The *opus magnum* was to be combined with *The Dunciad* to make a new volume of *Works*. The plans for the *opus magnum* are known to us mainly through the account Pope gave to Spence in 1730 and through a cancelled leaf in the fine-paper quarto edition of the complete *Essay on Man*. This leaf, containing the 'Index to the Ethic Epistles', is preserved in a copy in the Cambridge University Library and shows a division into two books.[17] The first book contains the four epistles of *An Essay on Man*; the second book contains nine projected epistles, arranged to correspond to the four epistles of *An Essay on Man*. The plan may be summarized in modernized typography by giving Pope's account of the first book and following each epistle with the parallel material of the second book in brackets: Of the nature and state of man [Of the use of things]; Epistle I, With respect to the universe [Of the limits of human reason; Of the use of learning; Of the use of wit]; Epistle II, As an individual [Of the knowledge and characters of men; Of the particular characters of women];

---

16. See *The Poems of Jonathan Swift*, ed. Harold Williams, 3 vols (1958), II, 541–543, III, 1135–36; *Jonathan Swift: The Complete Poems*, ed. Pat Rogers (1983), 844–845, 895–897; and Pat Rogers, 'The Authorship of "Bounce to Fop": A Re-examination', *Bulletin of Research in the Humanities*, 85 (1982), 241–268.

17. Joseph Spence, *Observations, Anecdotes, and Characters of Books and Men*, ed. James Osborn, 2 vols (1966), I, 131, Anecdote 299. The edition is Foxon P853. The Index is reproduced in Foxon, *Pope and the Early Eighteenth-Century Book Trade*, p. 125, and in Foxon's facsimile of *An Essay on Man* (Menston, 1969), which was reprinted, with *To Arbuthnot* and others, in *Alexander Pope: Poems in Facsimile*, intro. *Geoffrey Day* (Aldershot, 1988). The original facsimile of *To Arbuthnot*, with Foxon's introduction, was published at Menston, 1970.

Epistle III, With respect to society [Of the principles and use of civil and ecclesiastical polity; Of the use of education]; Epistle IV, With respect to happiness [A view of the equality of happiness in the several conditions of men; Of the use of riches, etc.]. As Miriam Leranbaum has explained, the project was never completed, though it continued to haunt Pope's thinking for the rest of his career.[18] The four poems Bateson decided to call 'Epistles to Several Persons' represent, more or less explicitly, contributions to the grand design: *To Cobham* and *To a Lady* correspond to the two epistles planned for the second section, while *To Bathurst* and *To Burlington* correspond to aspects of the final section. Other material seems to have been used in the fourth book of *The Dunciad*, published in 1742. Pope clearly anticipated that Harte's *Essay on Reason* would be taken as part of the design, and a letter to Mallet in the summer of 1734 suggests that he welcomed the prospect:

I fancy the Title of an *Essay on Reason* is the best, & am half of opinion, if no Name be set to it, the public will think it mine especially since in the Index, (annext to the large paper Edition of the Essay on Man) the Subject of the next Epistle is mentioned to be of *Human Reason* &c. But whether this may be an Inducement, or the Contrary, to Mr Harte, I know not: I like his poem so well (especially since his last alterations) that it would no way displease me. (*Correspondence*, III, 408–409)

The extent of Pope's contribution to *An Essay on Reason* is in doubt, but it appeared anonymously, and was indeed mistaken for Pope's work.[19]

It is not clear when Pope decided that he would not himself be able to complete the *opus magnum* in time for the 1735 *Works* or when he decided to abandon the scheme altogether. David Foxon has shrewdly suggested that the publication of *The Impertinent* as a scruffy quarto on 5 November 1733 may be the first sign of self-doubt, while the *Works* in quarto and folio suggest a certain amount of dithering.[20] Gilliver's advertisement leaf in *To a Lady*, which appeared a couple of months before the *Works*, simply gives a twofold division, *Essay on Man* and 'Epistles to Several Persons'; the *Works* themselves hedge their bet with a division into *An Essay on Man* and 'Ethic Epistles, The Second Book: Epistles to Several Persons', under which heading *To Cobham*, *To a Lady*, *To Bathurst*, and *To Burlington* fall indifferently with *To Addison*, *To Oxford*, and *To Arbuthnot*. But it is clear from the organization of the epistles in the series of octavo *Works* that followed the publication of the quarto and folio *Works* II in 1735 that Pope still clung to some of his original vision. The half-titles of the subsequent octavo volumes (Griffith 388, 389, and 430) revived the *opus magnum* plan by implementing a four-part division: 'An Essay on Man, Being the First Book of Ethic Epistles'; 'Ethic Epistles, The Second Book'; 'Epistles, The Third Book. To Sev-

18. Miriam Leranbaum, *Alexander Pope's 'Opus Magnum' 1729–1744* (1977) gives an intricate account of which I have given only the baldest summary here.

19. See Leranbaum, pp. 25–27. Harte's views on these matters were not strictly orthodox, but I have found no attack on Pope on that basis.

20. See Foxon, *Pope and the Early Eighteenth-Century Book Trade*, p. 123, and Reginald Harvey Griffith, *Alexander Pope: A Bibliography*, 2 vols (1922, 1927), books 370–372.

eral Persons'; 'Satires of Horace Imitated, With the Satires of Dr. Donne, Versified by the same hand'. This was accompanied by careful paralleling of the first two books: both had a 'Contents' section which presented a schematic account of the epistles, and that account then shadowed the text in footnotes. This was the pattern in the first three editions of octavo *Works* II in 1735 and 1736, but in 1739 the pattern changed: the influence of the original quarto and folio reasserted itself and the new *Works* II (Griffith 505) divided the epistles into two sections only, *An Essay on Man* and 'Epistles to Several Persons'; the 'Contents' relating to the four epistles was dropped; commentary linking the first and second books (for example, on pp. 19, 24) was omitted; and commentary suggesting an abandoned plan was added ('The Deduction and Application of the forgoing Principles, with the *Use* or *Abuse* of *Civil* and *Ecclesiastical Policy*, was intended for the subject of the third Book', p. 46). This collection, planned in 1738, probably marks the point when Pope finally abandoned the *opus magnum*, but during the time of Harley's collecting, the project was still very much alive, and the evidence of the early *Works* II octavos is that Pope regarded his inability to complete it by 1735 as setback rather than a defeat.

To Burlington, which is the first item in the collection, was probably something of a trial run for the *opus magnum* epistles, and it is representative of Pope's new publishing arrangements. It was printed by John Wright for Lawton Gilliver and so continued the pairing that Pope had established to publish the *Dunciad Variorum*. After quarrelling with Lintot over the subscription for the *Odyssey*, Pope decided to control the publication of his works himself. He employed John Wright, who had formerly been manager of John Barber's printing shop but had now set up on his own account—or Pope's—on St. Peter's Hill, and Lawton Gilliver, a bookseller almost out of his apprenticeship, who had just set up in Fleet Street at the appropriately named Homer's Head.[21] This combination of experienced printer and novice bookseller was perfectly suited to Pope's needs. Heavy demands were to be made on the printer's skill and patience by complex books (*The Dunciad Variorum*) and extensive revision (everywhere), while copyrights were to be guarded and profit margins squeezed. After the publication of *To Burlington*, which, because of the furore over the 'Timon's Villa' episode, must have been a critical nightmare for Pope but a commercial success for Gilliver, the poet and bookseller signed an agreement which was clearly designed to take care of the completion of the *opus magnum*. The basis for the agreement of 1 December 1732 was that Pope intended to 'publish certain Poems or Epistles', that he might choose to offer some of them to Gilliver, and that Gilliver would pay £50 for the privilege of printing and publishing each one for a year. A subsidiary interest was entry in the Stationers' Register to protect the copyright; Gilliver promised to enter each poem correctly in the Register, to enjoy the benefit of the entry for one year, and after that to hold

21. I summarize the account in Foxon, *Pope and the Early Eighteenth-Century Book Trade*, pp. 102–108.

it in trust for Pope. It was probably at this same time that Pope made the declaration that is kept with the agreement in the British Library. The declaration is undated and it refers quite formally to the agreement without giving its date, which suggests it was written on the same day. The Declaration deals with the possibility of Pope's death before he has finished the *opus magnum*, ensuring that Gilliver would be free to publish the existing epistles in a volume of *Works*. Gilliver, as the declaration points out, owned the *Dunciad* copyright, so there was a joint interest in the *Works*, which was finally entered to Pope and Gilliver in half shares in the Register.

The agreement and declaration had their impact on the twenty-five items (fourteen by Pope) in Harley's collection. Nine are printed by Wright and published by Gilliver (four have both names in the imprint), and in addition each was involved in one publication without the other, Wright printing the fourth epistle of *An Essay on Man* and Gilliver publishing *Of Verbal Criticism*. I suspect that only the need for anonymity deprived them of a full hand of all fourteen Pope items. Maynard Mack has stressed Pope's determination to obtain an unprejudiced critical reception for *An Essay on Man*, and this extended to avoiding the by then well established association with Gilliver and Wright (*Twickenham*, III, i, xv). For the publication of the *Essay* Pope turned to the printer and publisher of *The Grub Street Journal*, which he seems to have been involved with, through Gilliver, in the early stages. Official publication of *An Essay on Man* was by John Wilford, a shareholder in the *Journal* from 7 September 1732 and subsequently its publisher, and printing was by Samuel Aris (Epistle III) and John Huggonson (Epistle I), successively printers of the *Journal*, with Edward Say (Epistle II), who, as far as I know, has no other Pope connection, making up the number.[22] *Sober Advice* was also kept anonymous, but for reasons of decency. The bookseller was Thomas Boreman and the printer John Hughs. That completes the account of the Pope poems, except for *Bounce to Fop*. The names of the same printers appear surprisingly often in an account of the other eleven. On the evidence of imprints and ornaments, Wright and Gilliver produced West's *Stowe* and Harte's *Essay on Reason* ('Printed by J. Wright for Lawton Gilliver' in the latter suggesting an official Pope publication); Gilliver and Say produced Mallet's *Of Verbal Criticism*, and Say printed Swift's *The Life and Genuine Character of Doctor Swift* and possibly (from the style of the ornaments only) *Tit for Tat*; Huggonson printed *Verses Address'd to the Imitator . . . of Horace*, in its first and fifth editions, and Swift's *On Poetry*; and Aris printed Swift's *An Epistle to a Lady*. The printers of *Advice to Sappho*, Hervey's *Epistle to a Nobleman*, and *Bounce to Fop* remain unidentified. This concentration on a relatively small circle of book

22. Huggonson was a shareholder in the *Journal* from the time of the first records (28 August 1730) and held two shares (Gilliver held 6 and four others had 1 each); he replaced Aris as printer in October 1733. See Michael Turner's transcription of 'The Minute Book of the Partners in the *Grub Street Journal*', *Publishing History*, 4 (1978), 49–94. I have identified printers freely on the basis of association of ornaments; such identifications are necessarily tentative.

trade figures suggests the influence of Gilliver as Pope's bookseller. He was doubtless sought out by Pope's admirers, and those given Pope's or Swift's anonymous works to print tended to be otherwise associated with him in his business.

One of the major interests of Harley's volume is the annotation of dates of publication and receipt. The established relationship between Pope and Gilliver may explain the regularity with which Harley not only received these poems but was sent pre-publication copies. However, the single reference to the topic in Pope's correspondence suggests otherwise. On 30 December 1734 Pope wrote to Harley, 'I hoped to have had Interest enough with my negligent Bookseller [Gilliver] to have procur'd a Copy of the Epistle to Dr A. to accompany my Letter. I doubt whether I shall do it yet?' (*Correspondence*, III, 446). In this case Harley notes the date of publication, 'Publisht Janu. 2. 1734/5', which coincides with the date of entry in the Stationer's Register and of advertisement in the *London Evening Post*, but does not make it clear when he received his copy. Pope's correspondence shows that he was well aware of the value of providing pre-publication copies to interested parties and influential friends. Off-prints of *The Rape of the Locke*, for example, were sent to Arabella Fermor, Robert Petre, and John Caryll in May 1712 (*Correspondence*, I, 145), and, towards the end of his life, in a letter to Warburton of 21 February 1744 Pope advised him, 'I would also defer . . . the publication of the Two Essays [*On Criticism* and *On Man*] with your Notes in Quarto, that (if you thought it would be taken well) you might make the Compliment to any of your Friends (& particularly of the Great ones, or of those whom I find most so) of sending them as Presents from yourself' (*Correspondence*, IV, 500). Such pre-publication copies would be especially valued by a collector like Harley. He frequently annotated his volumes with dates of receipt, and he would have been encouraged in the practice by an unusual letter from Pope of 16 May 1729, seeking his help in compiling a case against Burnet, Duckett, and Dennis, the authors of *Pope Alexander's Supremacy*, 'I therfore beg your Lordship to send a Careful hand to buy the Book of Lintot, (who must not be known to come from you) & to enter down the day of the month. . . . Let the same Man, after he has the book, go to Roberts the Publisher in Warwick lane and threaten him, unless he declares the author' (*Correspondence*, III, 33–34).

Harley's annotation of the date of receipt or publication is not systematic, only fourteen out of the twenty-five poems are dated, and it is not easy to discern a pattern. Inadvertance may have played its part, but the most likely explanation is that poems were dated if they were complimentary copies. The attacks on Pope by Lady Mary Wortley Montagu and Lord Hervey, *Tit for Tat*, and three of the Swift poems, for example, were unlikely to be sent by their authors. And Gilbert West, the nephew of Lord Cobham, may not have felt himself in need of powerful friends to the same extent as 'Mr Mallet. a Scots Gentleman' whose poem was 'Sent by the Author'. On the other hand, it would be very surprising if Harley had not been sent the revised version of *To Burlington*, *To Bathurst*, and *To Cobham* by Pope himself, especially since *To Bathurst* contained the lines,

> Who copies Yours or OXFORD's better part,
> To ease th'oppress'd, and raise the sinking heart?

It may be that in this and some other cases, Harley was sent a fine-paper copy that was bound elsewhere; only the joint satires of the *Satires of the Second Book of Horace* are in fine-paper copy here. It is not clear either why some poems are annotated with the date of publication rather than of receipt. The distinction between the two is clear in the copy of *To a Lady*, where the half-title is annotated with the date of receipt, 6 February 1735, and the title with the date of publication, 7 February 1735. In another case, that of the two *Satires of the Second Book of Horace*, the publication date recorded, quite accurately, as 15 February 1733, is the date of publication of the first satire, not of both satires, which did not appear together until 9 July 1734. It seems possible that these dates were given to Harley by Pope, otherwise he must have given scrupulous attention to the newspapers and journals.[23] The dates of receipt may usefully be compared with the dates of publication as given by David Foxon in his catalogue, which makes good use of Harley's datings. The general pattern is of receipt one or two days before publication: *Advice to Sappho*, 12 April 1733 (13 April); *Essay on Man* III, 4 May 1733 (8 May); *Essay on Man* IV, 22 January 1734 (24 January); *Verbal Criticism* 14 April 1733 (16 April); *Sober Advice*, 20 December 1734 (21 December); *To a Lady*, 6 February 1735 (7 or 8 February); *Essay on Reason*, 6 February 1735 (7 February); *The Life and Genuine Character of Doctor Swift*, 12 April 1733 (?20 April). The very early receipt of the last item is another small grain in the balance towards establishment of Pope's authorship, while the presence of Harte's *Essay on Reason* in this list confirms the impression that Pope was contriving to have this work mistaken for his own.

Harley's other annotations have special importance because they coincide with Pope's own growing interest in the editing and annotation of his work. When Pope wrote to Jacob Tonson, senior, about the publication of Bentley's Milton and Theobald's Shakespeare, I suspect his reference to his own work was only half in jest: 'I think I should congratulate your Cosen on the new Trade he is commencing, of publishing English classicks with huge Commentaries. Tibbalds will be the Follower of Bentley, & Bentley of Scriblerus. What a Glory will it be to the Dunciad, that it was the First Modern Work publish'd in this manner?' (*Correspondence*, III, 243–244.) *The Dunciad Variorum* itself seems to have been modelled on Claude Bossette's edition of Bolieau, published in Geneva in 1716.[24] The typography, especially the

---

23. The following items have publication dates: 1, 5, 8, 9, 10, 17, 19. The dates on all items except 8 and 10 are endorsed by Foxon; the date of 8 is indefinite and 10 seems to have been sent with 9 and caught its date.

24. See McLaverty, 'The Mode of Existence of Literary Works of Art: The Case of the *Dunciad Variorum*', *Studies in Bibliography*, 37 (1984), 82–105. Pope's copy of the Geneva

division of the notes into 'Remarks' and 'Imitations' (though the *Variorum* lacks the 'Changemens' found in the Boileau) seems to derive from that edition, and Pope's *Variorum* could claim like Boileau's *Oeuvres* to be 'Avec Eclaircissemens Historiques, Donnez par lui-meme'. Although much of the *Dunciad* apparatus is comic and parodic, much of it also is highly informative and justificatory (most 'Imitations', for example, simply identify allusions), and the influence of Boileau did not die with publication of the *Variorum* but lived through the preparation of the *Works*. Jonathan Richardson has explained that he was given the manuscripts of the *Essay on Man* 'for the pains I took in collating the whole with the printed editions . . . on my having proposed to him the making an edition of his works in the manner of Boileau's'.[25] The original plan must have been for *Works* II to appear with annotations to both the *Dunciad* and the *opus magnum* epistles, as the 'Postscript' to the quarto and folio *Works* makes clear:

It was intended in this Edition, to have added *Notes* to the *Ethic Epistles* as well as to the *Dunciad*, but the book swelling to too great a bulk, we are oblig'd to defer them till another Volume may come out, of such as the Author may hereafter write, with several Pieces in Prose relating to the same subjects.

In the mean time, that nothing contained in the former Editions may be wanting in this, we have here collected all the *Variations* of the separate Impressions, and the *Notes* which have been annexed to them, with the addition of a few more which have been judg'd the most necessary.

Some notes, therefore, remain at the foot of the page as they were in the individual editions; others are placed at the end. The 'Changemens' lacking in the *Dunciad* are here provided as endnotes, though only for *An Essay on Man* and *To Arbuthnot*, and there are 'Remarques', now 'Notes', on *To Bathurst* and *To Arbuthnot*. The two octavo editions of *Works* II of 1735 and their successors elaborated the notes, which were placed at the foot of the page, but they did not include the 'Variations'.[26] By comparing Harley's notes with those in the quarto, folio, and octavo *Works*, we can contrast Pope's implied reader with an actual one, though it is important to recognise that Pope was constrained by the laws of libel, as Harley working in his library was not.

Harley shows no interest in 'Imitations', which is suprising for a man of keen scholarly interests. Pope provides literary notes on Oppian at *Essay on Man*, III, 178, on Virgil at *To Bathurst*, 75, 184 (octavo only), on *Don Quixote* at *To Burlington*, 160 (octavo only), and on Pitholeon (49, octavo only), Chaucer (72), Horace (88, octavo only), and Milton (319, octavo only) in *To Arbuthnot*. It is possible that Pope included these notes in the octavo editions

Boileau, given to him by James Craggs, is at Mapledurham House; see no. 26 in Maynard Mack's listing of surviving books from Pope's library, *Collected in Himself* (1982), p. 399.

25. *Richardsoniana* (1776), p. 264.

26. In conception, if not execution, it is Warburton's 1751 edition which comes closest to achieving an edition of Pope in the 'manner of Boileau's': the notes are of three sorts (under the headings, 'Imitations', 'Variations', and 'Notes') and, as Warburton is anxious to remind us, they were communicated to the editor by the author himself.

because they were for a general, and less educated, public, whereas the quartos and folios were aimed at the wealthy, including scholars and collectors like Harley, who, it might be thought, needed no help in identifying references and allusions. Certainly the development of a running explanatory commentary and system of cross-references in the octavos suggests their readers are in need of a helping authorial hand. But in the case of the 'Imitations', it seems more likely that Pope really was short of time in preparing the quarto and folio and had to leave some things out; many purchasers of the quartos and folios were probably, like Harley, more interested in personalities than intertextuality.

Where the *Works* II octavos do seem to be responsive to Pope's sense of his readership is in the omission of 'Variations'. The *Works* I octavos published at the same time do include them, but those editions provided Pope's first serious opportunity to elaborate his early texts. It is clear from the 'Postscript' in the large-format *Works* that Pope attached the need for 'Variations' to the purchase of expensive editions; purchasers spending a guinea would want a truly complete *Works*, one that included the readings of individual editions that their friends told them about. The 'Variations' would also appeal to another category of reader, the persistent purchasers of Pope's poems in folio (and sometimes quarto), who would be interested in having their attention drawn to novelties in the new book. In the octavos space was at a premium, and the difference in format and price removed the sense of obligation to provide variant readings.

In his attention to textual variation Harley shows a scholarly enthusiasm lacking in the treatment of 'Imitations'. This is particularly evident in his comparison of the two versions of the first epistle of *An Essay on Man*. In some ways his annotation is superior to that supplied in the quarto and folio *Works*, presumably by Jonathan Richardson working under Pope's supervision. Harley compared his copy of the first edition of the first epistle with the revised edition Pope published two months later, and marked the changes in the first edition. On the first page he notes the change made famous by Johnson, from 'A mighty Maze! of walks without a Plan' to 'A mighty Maze! but not without a Plan' (*Lives of the Poets*, III, 162). Although Mack in his Twickenham volume points out that both lines are susceptible of orthodox interpretation, Pope's failure to include the original line in the *Works* 'Variations' suggests that he was not anxious to keep it before his public. Harley notes further detailed verbal changes in the early stages of the poem, without providing a comprehensive collation. Some of the changes may be recorded because they particularly appealed to his sensibility. For example, the revision of the word 'spreads' to 'swells' in the line 'Suckles each herb, and spreads out ev'ry flow'r' (134) is ignored by the *Works* 'Variations' but recorded by Harley, whereas the complicated revision of the lines about bliss (93-94) are recorded in the 'Variations' but ignored by Harley. What is particularly impressive about Harley's collation is the neat recording of major deletions and shifts by the use of marginal 'x's. On page 6 at lines 14-15, for example, he notes that six lines from later in the poem are inserted at this point, and he duly marks the lines with an 'x' (7.1). On page 10 he marks lines 7–12, two of which were transferred and four omitted. It must be conceded that Harley lacked stamina as a collator, and that towards the end of the poem the 'x's are used in a general way to note a complex revision of a whole passage (13.1–2 and 14.18–19), but his notes suggest an admirably careful and attentive reader, with an awareness of the sort of distinctions that became so important in later controversies about this poem.

Other poems provided few opportunities for collation, but Harley's notes on *To Arbuthnot* show an attentiveness to minor changes in the representation of Lord Hervey in the *Works* text, even though he ignores some of the omissions and developments picked up by the *Works* 'Variations'. The change from 'Damon' to 'Fanny' is noted at page 8 line 13, and in the margin of the reference to 'Paris' on page 15 line 9 he writes, 'In a late edition the name is changed to Sporus a more proper nick name' (see Figure 1). In this instance a difference in the use of the pen suggests that Harley has come back to the poem some time after making the original annotation, which presumably preceded the 1735 *Works*. His note draws attention to the increased harshness of treatment of Hervey in the *Works* text, and, of course, he had no need to record the other variants when the *Works* did it for him. *Verses to the Imitator of . . . Horace* is a parallel case, and the two stages of annotation suggest, if rather weakly, that the first was probably not long after receipt.

Harley's main interest in annotating the poems is in the personalities represented. This form of interest goes back at least as far as *The Dunciad*, when he wrote to Pope in a letter of 27 May 1728, 'I see curl has advertised a Key to the Dunciad, I have been asked for one by several [Sherburn signifies a gap here] I wish the True one was come out' (*Correspondence*, II, 496). It was an interest Pope encouraged and shared. The question of naming preoccupied him at this time: it is discussed in the 'Cleland' preface to *The Dunciad Variorum*; in Boileau's discourse annexed to Walter Harte's *Essay on Satire, Particularly on the Dunciad*; and in *The First Satire of the Second Book of Horace, To Arbuthnot*, and *To a Lady*. Harley shows no scruples about naming; he merely wants to know who's who. Most of the annotations are simple identifications. The best example is *The First Satire of the Second Book of Horace*, where there are five straightforward identifications, four of which are accepted as correct by modern editors. A fifth, that of Dr. Hollings as 'Celsus', is ignored by John Butt in the *Twickenham* edition, perhaps because Hollings has proved impossible to identify. The five identifications are accompanied by what I take to be seven queries, represented by underlinings in red pencil. In a letter which is unfortunately undated but which Sherburn allots to 1733, Pope writes to Harley from Dover Street, 'I find here Two red Lead pencils, one of which I presume is for me, & therfore I have taken it away (for it writes well)' (*Correspondence*, III, 359). I assume that Harley is using another of these pencils for his underlinings here and elsewhere, though the colour is now a reddish-brown. The underlinings probably precede publication of *To Arbuthnot*, which would have identified Budgell, and they show that Harley had some difficulty in spotting allusions

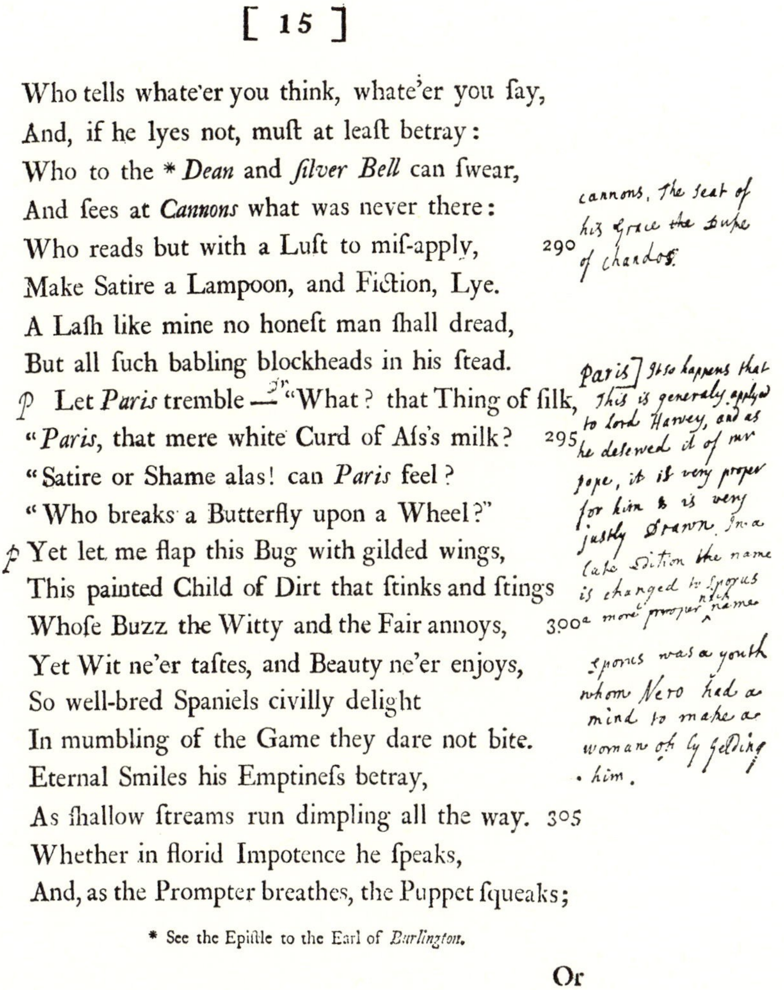

[15]

Who tells whate'er you think, whate'er you fay,
And, if he lyes not, muſt at leaſt betray:
Who to the * *Dean* and *ſilver Bell* can ſwear,
And ſees at *Cannons* what was never there:
Who reads but with a Luſt to miſ-apply,
Make Satire a Lampoon, and Fiction, Lye.
A Laſh like mine no honeſt man ſhall dread,
But all ſuch babling blockheads in his ſtead.
P Let *Paris* tremble —"What? that Thing of ſilk,
"*Paris*, that mere white Curd of Aſs's milk?
"Satire or Shame alas! can *Paris* feel?
"Who breaks a Butterfly upon a Wheel?"
p Yet let me flap this Bug with gilded wings,
This painted Child of Dirt that ſtinks and ſtings
Whoſe Buzz the Witty and the Fair annoys,
Yet Wit ne'er taſtes, and Beauty ne'er enjoys,
So well-bred Spaniels civilly delight
In mumbling of the Game they dare not bite.
Eternal Smiles his Emptineſs betray,
As ſhallow ſtreams run dimpling all the way.
Whether in florid Impotence he ſpeaks,
And, as the Prompter breathes, the Puppet ſqueaks;

* See the Epiſtle to the Earl of *Burlington*.

Or

Figure 1. Annotations of *An Epistle to Dr. Arbuthnot*, p. 15. Bodley M 3.19 Art (published by kind permission of the Bodleian Library).

to members of his own circle. 'Shylock and his Wife', although unidentified
by Butt, are surely Edward and Mary Wortley Montagu, who appeared under
the same name (and as 'Worldly') in *To Bathurst*, though Harley does not
identify them there either.[27]

Sometimes Harley's identifications are confirmed by Pope in subsequent
editions, as when Gage (*To Bathurst*, 8.2) is given his full name in the first
Works II octavo, or when a full note is supplied on Sir John Blount (*To
Bathurst* 8.7) in the large-format *Works* II. Sometimes confirmation is de-
layed until Warburton's edition, as in the case of Arthur Moore (*To Arbuthnot* 2.13). None of the identifications has been discredited by modern scholarship, though Butt suggests that 'Lady M———' in *Sober Advice* (7.20) may
be Lady Mary Wortley Montagu rather than Lady Mohun, and he omits
the identification of Theobald as the butt of 'Three things another's modest
wishes bound, / My Friendship, and a Prologue, and ten Pound' (*To Arbuthnot* 3.16), of the Duke of Argyll as the man Welsted wishes to be commended
to (*To Arbuthnot* 3.17), and of 'one Hamilton' as the man offering to 'go
snacks' (*To Arbuthnot* 4.12–13). Sometimes Harley himself expresses an intelligent caution. His note on 'Bufo' in *To Arbuthnot* (12.8) seems to have
been written in three stages. First he wrote a cautious 'this character made
fit many I think it is cheifly the right of mr Bubb Doddington'. Then, possibly
on immediately reading what he had written, he added 'but' before the 'I' to
admit his daring. Finally he added in red pencil, possibly after talking to
Pope, 'it would also fit the late earl of Halifax'. This is a shrewd recognition
of Pope's practice of double reference that might serve as guide to modern
editors.[28] Similarly, next to 'Fannia' in *To a Lady*, he notes 'It is said this
hints at the Countess of Pembroke, who used to be drawn in these several
attitudes', showing respect for Pope's concern in his preface that ladies should
not be identified. He has no hesitation, however, in identifying the addressee
of the poem as Martha Blount; in doing so he shows that contemporaries
were willing to accept the poem as a tribute in a way that Warburton, possibly out of personal dislike for Martha Blount, would not, insisting that the
addressee is 'imaginary'.[29]

In three cases, Harley provides longer notes. On page 8 of *To Bathurst*
he gives a very specific anecdote illustrating Lady Mary Herbert's meanness,
which contrasts with the more general one provided by Pope in the *Works*.
Pope's note deals with Lady Mary and Gage together:

The two Persons here mentioned were of Quality, each of whom in the time of the
Missisipi despis'd to realize above *three hundred thousand pounds:* The Gentleman
with a view to the purchase of the Crown of Poland, the Lady on a Vision of the like
Royal nature. They since retired into Spain, where they are still in search of Gold
in the Mines of the Asturies.

27. The identification is made by Bateson in *Twickenham*, III, ii, and the coupling of
the miser and his wife makes it plausible. Oxford may at this time have been unaware of
the extent of Pope's animosity towards Lady Mary.

28. It would lead to a recasting of Bateson's appendix on Atossa, for example. It may
be that the couplet in *Sober Advice* (7.20 [124–125]) is another example of the same technique.

29. *The Works of Alexander Pope*, ed. William Warburton, 9 vols (1751), III, 193, 195.

Pope's note lacks some of the tang of specific social transgression supplied by Harley's, but it gives a more general picture. Harley's gift for vivid anecdote also shows in the *Miller's Tale*-style story told of Lady Mohun as a note to *Sober Advice* (7.20). This story suits the bawdy tone of *Sober Advice*, and chimes in perfectly with the annotated couplet,

> A Lady's Face is all you see undress'd;
> (For none but Lady M——— shows the Rest),

The anecdote is entirely apposite, though the point of the story (does Lord Mohun recognize his wife's buttocks or not?) is not entirely clear. The third longer note is on 'Paris' in *To Arbuthnot* (15.9; see Figure 1). This is composed of three parts: a variant reading; a scholarly account of Sporus's 'Gelding' (an interesting feature of this and the previous anecdote is Harley's use of capital letters to highlight impropriety); and a judgement, 'It so happens that this is generaly applyed to Lord Harvey, and as he deserved it of Mr Pope, it is very proper for him & is very justly Drawn'. It is significant that Harley is here endorsing Pope's treatment of an important court figure at a point in Pope's career when the question of birth and status had been made important to him. The issues raised by *Verses Address'd to the Imitator . . . of Horace* and Pope's reply in *To Arbuthnot* make the response of an aristocrat like Harley especially interesting.

Harley is our most important source for the authorship of the *Verses*. To the usual co-authors, Lady Mary Wortley Montagu and Lord Hervey, he adds a third, William Wyndham, 'under Tutor to the Duke of Cumberland and married to my Lady Deloraine'. Maynard Mack ingeniously, and surely correctly, suggests that this explains an allusion in *To Arbuthnot*, one of those marked in red pencil:

> To please a *Mistress*, One aspers'd his life;
> He lash'd him not, but let her be his *Wife*.[30]

Isobel Grundy, in her fine article on the *Verses Address'd to the Imitator . . . of Horace*, points out that the marriage did not take place until April 1734, over a year after the publication of the poem, and takes this as the date after which Harley's annotation must have been made.[31] But the 'and' of 'and married to my Lady Deloraine' starts more than an ordinary space away from 'Cumberland' and a little lower than the line established by the earlier writing. It is at least possible that Harley identified the authors at an early stage (his wife, as Grundy points out, was a friend of Lady Deloraine) and added the information about the marriage when he was looking through later, either on the publication of *To Arbuthnot* or at the time of binding the folios together. After all, if Harley himself did not give the information on the authorship of the *Verses* to Pope, somebody like him must have done so. Harley shows no hostility to Lady Deloraine or Lady Mary Wortley Mon-

---

30. Mack, 'A Couplet in the *Epistle to Dr. Arbuthnot*', *TLS*, 2 September 1939, p. 515.
31. Grundy, '*Verses Address'd to the Imitator of Horace*: A Skirmish between Pope and Some Persons of Rank and Fortune', *Studies in Bibliography*, 30 (1977), 96–119 (110).

tagu (another of Lady Oxford's friends), but he clearly sided with Pope against Lord Hervey as he gleefully annotated *An Epistle from a Nobleman,* 'that is my Lord Harvey alias Lord Fanny, alias Paris, alias Sporus alias &c &c &c.' and wrote of the addressee, 'The Dean of Chichester Dr. Shewin a very great scoundrel'. The relationship between the *Verses Address'd to the Imitator . . . of Horace* and *To Arbuthnot* interested Harley, as at this stage it interested Pope and his implied readers. He notes that the 'Fifth Edition Corrected' of the *Verses* is no such thing and that it was a reprint in response to *To Arbuthnot.* On page 19 he improves on Pope's footnote reference to the *Verses* by giving page and line numbers; in the 'Fifth Edition' of the *Verses* he would have found a reference to page 19 of *To Arbuthnot.* Harley makes no comment on Pope's account of his parentage. In the light of Johnson's debunking information that his father was 'a linen draper in the Strand',[32] it is easy to forget that many of the country's leading figures, Harley, Burlington, Bathurst, Cobham, must have read this account and believed it; it is not improbable Pope believed it himself.

In Harley, therefore, Pope found a careful and attentive reader, a collector sharing his own interest in first editions and textual variation, and an interpreter with an eye for personal satire but a willingness to rest in doubts and uncertainties when they were necessary. What we cannot know is how far Harley's reading was guided by Pope himself, and unfortunately Pope's own annotations of *To Arbuthnot* are far from having the self-explanatory quality that might help us. There is even some doubt about where Pope's contribution starts and Harley's ends, for although there are two interventions convincingly attributed to Pope, and I shall go on to propose another, three more single-letter annotations, cautiously proposed as Pope's by Maynard Mack, are not, I believe, by him. The doubtful annotations are not without importance. On page 15 (Figure 1) someone has designated speakers of the dialogue: 'P' (Pope) speaks first; 'Dr' (Arbuthnot) replies; and the 'P' begins the Sporus portrait. When Warburton produced his edition of Pope in 1751, he gave all the speeches in *To Arbuthnot* to either 'P' or 'A', and *To Bathurst* was similarly divided. If Pope made the changes to Harley's copy, the probability that Warburton was following Pope's instructions is increased. Although the difficulties of distinguishing handwriting on so narrow a base are self-evident, I think these capitals can be identified as Harley's. The 'P' has a distinctive foot, which is also to be found in the margin in 'Paris'. The 'D' is also distinctive, looking a little like a treble-clef; the vertical line rises above the bowl of the letter, which curls away behind it to form a complete circle; a similar 'D' is found in the margin in 'Drawn'.[33]

32. *Lives of the English Poets,* ed. G. Birkbeck Hill, 3 vols (1905), III, 83.

33. Confirmation that this is Harley's writing can be found in his letters to Thomas Hearne in the Bodleian. That dated 12 December 1723 (MS Rawl. Lett. 8 f. 336; letter 184) has a good example of the 'P' in the title *A Memorial of suche Princes,* while that dated 25 December 1731 (MS Rawl. Lett. 8 f. 377; letter 206) has good examples of the 'D' in '*Durandus*'. These extracts also give other valuable information about his writing: that capital 'M' is almost indistinguishable and has to be interpreted generously, that some capital 'T's are

The two undisputed Pope interventions are both substantial. The couplet added on page 12, between lines 12 and 13, appeared in Pope's manuscript, and was included in the notes to Warburton's edition as a 'Variation':

> To Bards Reciting he vouchsafd a Nod
> And snuff'd their Incence like a gracious God.[34]

Harley would not have been able to include this couplet without Pope's help, and the handwriting is of a quite different quality from Harley's. Even more significant is the note on 'Atticus' on page 11. Mack correctly identifies this as being in Pope's handwriting, and in any case the degree of revision suggests composition not transcription. Mack thinks the explanation of the presence of this note is that Harley was sent Pope's own working copy in which he was preparing the note for the quarto and folio *Works*. That note certainly presents interesting parallels:

ATTICUS] It was a great Falshood which some of the Libels reported, that this Character was written after the Gentleman's death, which see refuted in the Testimonies prefix'd to the Dunciad. But the occasion of writing it was such, as he would not make publick in regard to his memory; and all that could further be done was to omit the Name in the Edition of his Works.

The notes follow a similar structure: they state the accusation, point to the previously established defence, deny the reader further information on the grounds of tenderness to the memory of 'Atticus', and say that all that can be done is to omit the name. The handwritten annotation picks up a further problem, why the character was ever printed, but denies any knowledge of it. Mack is certainly correct in seeing a relation between the two, but there are some difficulties in seeing the folio sent to Harley as a working copy. For one thing the implication of Pope's letter of 30 December is that he had no copies of *To Arbuthnot* but was planning to send one to Harley as soon as he received it; if the Harley copy was received on 2 January, which seems likely, that leaves no time for Pope to establish a working copy. Of course, Pope may in exasperation have sent Harley a copy he had had for some time, but that chimes in ill with the letter. Another problem is that Pope was unlikely to draft the notes to the *Works* on copies of the individual epistles. The texts sometimes differed quite substantially, and it would have been reckless to annotate the wrong text, especially when the large-format *Works* version represented an earlier text and had probably been printed off in advance. There is also the question of the interpolated couplet. There is little sign that Pope seriously intended to incorporate it into the poem, nor is the insertion made in Pope's characteristically professional way. The alternative to the suggestion that Harley's copy was Pope's working copy must be that

little more than a straight line with a lead-in stroke, and that capital 'B's and 'R's have a flourish quite foreign to the rest of the hand.

34. *Works*, IV, 30. Pages of manuscript are reproduced in John Butt's 'Pope's Poetical Manuscripts', *Proceedings of the British Academy*, 40 (1954), 23–39, and Maynard Mack, *The Last and Greatest Art* (Newark, 1984), 419–454. The couplet appears on p. 438 of the latter; it has been interlined by Pope in a transcript by another hand.

Pope was annotating the poem for him, perhaps on the occasion that Harley entered the second identification of 'Bufo' in the margin. Some signs support that idea: the footnote is keyed to the text with a dagger, which would be inappropriate for a draft endnote; Pope begins by attempting to work within the measure, avoiding straying into the margin by breaking the words 'provocation' and 'perpetuate', and only his revisions make the page untidy. If Pope was annotating the text some time after Harley received it but before the appearance of *Works*, he would have been trying to remember a note he had penned only a short while before.

The further annotation I wish to propose as Pope's is that of the note on page 16. The note, linked by an asterisk to 'Or at the Ear of *Eve*, familiar Toad' is itself unusual:

In the fourth book of *Milton*, the Devil is represented in this Posture. It is but justice to own, that the Hint of *Eve* and the *Serpent* was taken from the *Verses on the Imitator of* Horace.

Pope rarely reveals so much of his technique as he does here. Isobel Grundy has written of the power with which Pope appropriated and transformed the insults offered him in the *Verses to the Imitator of . . . Horace* (pp. 117–118), and in this note he is directing our attention to that achievement, just as he directs attention to the insult to his birth on pages 18 to 19. Someone has added to this note 'shape &' before 'Posture'; the change successfully clarifies the relation between Pope's line and *Paradise Lost*. I do not believe Harley would have made this emendation himself (he is a conservative annotator) and I do not think he could have found it printed elsewhere. In these circumstances I am readily persuaded that the writing is Pope's: the 'h' closes to resemble a 'k' as his sometimes does; the 'p' has a gap between vertical and bowl; the ampersand is not Harley's usual one. More important, the movement of the pen seems to have been Pope's rather than Harley's, with the ink spreading more widely. Pope was improving a footnote a few pages after composing or recollecting the 'Atticus' one.

The creation of a separate note on 'Atticus' had repercussions on the annotation of this poem in general. The individually published folio of *To Arbuthnot* had included a long note on 'Lyes so oft o'erthrown':

Such as those in relation to Mr. *A*———, that Mr. *P.* writ his Character after his death, &c. that he set his Name to Mr. *Broom*'s Verses, that he receiv'd Subscriptions for *Shakespear*, &c. which tho' publickly disprov'd by the *Testimonies* prefix'd to the *Dunciad,* were nevertheless shamelessly repeated in the Libels, and even in the Paper call'd, *The Nobleman's Epistle.*

The provision of a separate note on Addison for the large-format *Works* led to a revision of this note, with Addison omitted and the Shakespeare charge being placed before the Broom one. But then, after all this trouble, in the octavo *Works* the 'Atticus' note was omitted altogether and so was the note on 'Lyes so oft o'erthrown'. It was not reintroduced until Warburton's edition of 1751. The note on *Paradise Lost* had a rather different fate. It was omitted from the large-format *Works* but resurfaced in the second octavo of 1735 in

the truncated form 'See Milton. Book 4'. The attention this note originally
gave to *Verses Address'd to the Imitator of . . . Horace*, and its revision, omission, and final abbreviation suggest Pope's special interest in the relation
between the two poems. If the *Verses* were not only published by Dodd but,
as it appears, printed by Huggonson, it might be worth investigating the
possibility that Pope had a hand in their publication.[35]

Differences in annotation between Pope's folios and quartos on the one
hand and his octavos on the other are difficult to interpret, but they suggest
authorial attention to the needs of different readerships. As we have seen,
the large-format editions gave 'Variations', provided a cross-reference to the
aristocrats' *Verses Address'd to the Imitator of . . . Horace* (in the individual
folio), and defended Pope's conduct with respect to Addison; the octavos had
none of this but they did have more 'Imitations' and a running commentary,
as well as a few more ordinary notes. Purely material questions of space must
have played their part, but Pope probably knew that readers, like Harley,
who moved in society and collected books would be interested in variant
readings and in contemporary personalities belonging to their circle; it is
Lord Hervey and Lady Mohun that really interest Harley, not Budgell and
Welsted. Pope cared for the opinion of these readers and took account of
rumours and accusations that would damage his reputation. For the wider
readership purchasing the octavos, variants were not necessary, though some
guidance in reading was; if these readers were unaware of the aristocrats'
contempt or the charges about Addison, the Shakespeare, and Broome, there
was little point in informing them; the task of self-justification before the
jury of peers had already been essayed in the quartos and folios. Harley's
annotations suggest that at least one member of that jury was convinced.

A Transcription of Annotations in Bodley M 3.19 Art
(published by kind permission of the Bodleian Library)

The poems are by Pope unless the contrary is indicated. Titles and imprints are simplified and abbreviated, and title-page dates are in arabic.
Reference numbers are given to D. F. Foxon, *English Verse 1701–1750*. I
have based my transcription on the system advocated by Fredson Bowers in
'Transcription of Manuscripts: The Record of Variants', *Studies in Bibliography* 29 (1976): 212–264, and adapted by David Vander Meulen in *Pope's
Dunciad of 1728: a History and Facsimile* (Charlottesville and London, 1991),
166–169. Each entry gives the page number (or 'title-page'), the line number
on that page, the line in the Twickenham Edition ('ʌ' indicates that the
relevant line does not appear there), a lemma or location on the page ('head'
or 'foot'), and a transcription of the annotation. Italic comments in brackets

---

35. There are other interesting differences between the notes in the large-format *Works*
and the octavos. The note on 'Welsted's Lye' originally ended with 'He took no notice of
so frantick an Abuse; and expected that any man who knew himself Author of what he was
slander'd for, would have justify'd him on that Article', an attack on the editors of the
Grub Street Journal that was dropped in the octavos. Notes on Blount and Ward in *To
Bathurst* are corrected.

apply to the whole annotation, or all following the last bracket, or all following the last asterisk (single asterisks and their brackets enclose double asterisks and their brackets). The following abbreviations are used: del[eted],
interl[ined], marg[in], underl[ined]. Because there is no accompanying text,
I have given some small preference to intelligibility over brevity in lemmata
and comment. I have not followed the original lineation. Superscripts are
retained except in dates, which are levelled. Marks in grey pencil, which I
take to be the work of librarians, are not transcribed.

1. An Epistle to the Right Honourable Richard Earl of Burlington. Printed
for L. Gilliver. 1731. (Foxon P908)

title-page	head 'Called TASTE'; 'The True Title is False Taste'; 'first edition was publisht Dec. 13. 1731 [fi-nal '1' over '2']'

2. Of False Taste. An Epistle to the Right Honourable Richard Earl of Burlington. The Third Edition. Printed for L. Gilliver. 1731. (Foxon P912, with
intervening sheet before p. 5.)

3. Of the Use of Riches, An Epistle to the Right Honorable Allen Lord Bathurst. Printed by J. Wright, for Lawton Gilliver. 1732. (Foxon P923, with corrected reading on p. 13)

8.2 (130)	———] r. marg. 'Gage'; l. marg. 'Gage esq₃ Brother to my Lord Gage'
8.3 (131)	Maria's] preceded by 'x' ; l. marg. 'Lady Mary Her-bert'; foot 'Lady Mary Herbert in the Mississipi time borrowed of Her servant 10 Luidores for neces-sary expences because she said she would not Break a million never paid the servant.'
8.7 (135)	Bl———t] l. marg. 'Sʳ John Blount'

4. An Epistle to the Right Honourable Richard Lord Visctᵗ· Cobham. Printed
for Lawton Gilliver. 1733. (Foxon P920)

5. The First Satire of the Second Book of Horace, Imitated in Dialogue Between Alexander Pope of Twickenham, in Com' Mid' Esq; and his Learned
Council. To Which is Added, The Second Satire of the Same Book. Printed
for L. G. 1734. (Foxon P895, with engraving on p. 36)

title-page	head 'Publist Feb. 15. 1732/3'
3.3 (3)	Peter] underl.; r. marg. 'Peter] Walter'
3.6 (6)	Fanny] underl.; r. marg. 'Lord *Harvey [overwrites illegible]'
5.9 (19)	Celsus] both occurrences underl.; r. marg. 'Dʳ Hol-lings'
5.13 (23)	Richard] underl.; r. marg. 'Blackmore'
5.17 (27)	Budgell's] underl. in red pencil
7.12 (44)	Bond] r. marg. 'Bond] Dennis Bond'

13.4 (100)	Lee] *underl. in red pencil*
	B**ll] *underl. in red pencil*
13.7 (103)	Plums] *underl. in red pencil*
	Directors] *underl. in red pencil*
	Shylock] *underl. in red pencil*
	Wife] *underl. in red pencil*

6. [See attribution below], Verses Address'd to the Imitator of the First Satire of the Second Book of Horace. By a Lady. Printed for A. Dodd. (Foxon V39)

| title-page | *By* a LADY.] *above* 'The Authors of this poem are Lady Mary Wortley Lord Harvey & Mr Windham under Tutor to the Duke of Cumberland *and married to my Lady Deloraine [*spacing suggests a later addition*]' |

7. [Unknown], Advice to Sappho. Occasioned by Her Verses on the Imitator of the First Satire of the Second Book of Horace. By a Gentlewoman. Printed for the Authoress; and sold by J. Roberts. 1733. (Foxon A86)

| title-page | *head* 'R. April. 12. 1733' |
| 6.12 | hope] 'p' *del.; l. marg.* 'm/' [*prepublication correction*] |

8. An Essay on Man. . . . Part I. Printed for J. Wilford. (Foxon P822)

title-page	*head* 'February' [*over* 'March'] 1732/3'
5.6 (6)	of walks] *underl.; r. marg.* 'But Not'
6.14–15 (22/29)	*l. margin.* 'six lines *from [*over illegible*] x'
6.15 (29)	Of] *del.*
	vast] *del.*
	l. marg. 'But'
6.17 (31)	And Centres] *del.; l. marg.* 'Gradations'
7.1 (23)	*l. marg.* 'x'
7.6 (∧)	has] *del.*
	us as we are] *del.*
	r. marg. 'all things as they are'
10.6–7 (98/73)	*l. marg.* 'x' *underl.*
10.13 (99)	*l. marg.* 'x'
11.2–3 (108/∧)	*r. marg.* 'x'
11.6–7 (∧/110)	*l. marg.* 'x'
	r. marg. '———'
12.10 (134)	spreads] *del.; l. marg.* 'swells'
13.1–2 (∧)	*l. marg.* 'x'
14.18–19 (184/∧)	*l. marg.* 'x'

9. An Essay on Man. . . . Epistle I. Corrected by the Author. Printed for J. Wilford. (Foxon P827)

| title-page | *head* 'Publisht April. 23. 1733.' |

10. An Essay on Man. . . . Epistle II. Printed for J. Wilford. (Foxon P833)
    title-page   *head* 'Publisht April. 23. 1733.'

11. An Essay on Man. . . . Epistle III. Printed for J. Wilford. (Foxon P840)
    title-page   *head* 'R. May 4. 1733'

12. An Essay on Man. . . . Epistle IV. Printed for J. Wilford. (Foxon P845)
    title-page   *head* 'R. Janu. 22. 1733/4'

12*. Two leaves of An Essay on Man. . . . Epistle IV, pp. 17–18 and advert leaf.
    17.   *foot* 'Come then, my friend! my Genius come along'

13. [Mallet, David], Of Verbal Criticism: An Epistle to Mr Pope. Printed for
Lawton Gilliver. 1733. (Foxon M51)
    title-page   *head* 'Sent by the Author April. 14. 1733.'
                       Mr. Pope.] *r. marg.* 'By Mr Mallet. a Scots Gentle-
man'

14. Sober Advice from Horace, to the Young Gentlemen about Town. (Foxon
P968)
    title-page   *head* 'R. .Dec. 20: 1734'
    6.4 (92)   Lady or Lord *Fanny*] *r. marg.* 'Lord and Lady Har-
vey'
    7.16 (121)   *Ty——y*] *r. marg.* 'Lady Tyrawley very near
sighted'
    7.20 (125)   Lady M——] *r. marg. and foot* 'Lady Mohun
there is a famous story of her she was in a Hackney
coach with some fellows and my Lord came up &
would know who was there, she did not care to be
found out at last she said that she would show her
Bare Arse to him if that would satisfy him, he
agreed & she put her Arse out at the Window to
him, and he went away'
    8.8 (133)   *N——dh——m's*] 'Mother Needham a famous
Bawd'
    9.4 (150)   *Bedford-head*] *underl. in red pencil*
    9.12 (158)   *B——t*] *r. marg.* 'Lord Bathurst'
    9.14 (160)   nor pay too dear] *underl. in red pencil*
    9.20 (166)   *M——ue*] *r. marg.* 'Mountague'
    10.10 (176)   *B——ck*] *r. marg.* 'Buck'
    10.12 (178)   *L——l, J——ys, O——w*] *foot* 'L——l Mr
Richard Lyddel *J——ys* Mr Jefferies *O——w*
Ld Onslow'

15. [Hervey, John], An Epistle from a Nobleman to a Doctor of Divinity.
Printed for J. Roberts. 1733 (Foxon H157)
    title-page   Nobleman] *above interlined* 'that is my Lord Har-
vey ['v' *over* 'l'], alias Lord Fanny, alias Paris, alias

Sporus alias &c &c &c.'
Doctor of Divinity] *r. margin.* 'The Dean of Chichester Dr. Sherwin a very great scoundrel.'
H————n C————t] *below interlined* 'ampto' 'our'

16. [Unknown], Tit for Tat. Or an Answer to the Epistle to a Nobleman. Printed for T. Cooper. 1734. (Foxon T322)

17. An Epistle from Mr. Pope, to Dr. Arbuthnot. Printed by J. Wright for Lawton Gilliver. 1734. (Foxon P802)

title-page	*head* 'Publisht Janu. 2. 1734/5.'
2.10 (20)	Charcoal] *underl. in red pencil*
2.13 (23)	Arthur] *l. marg.* 'Arthur Moore'
	whose giddy son] *underl. in red pencil*
2.19 (29)	Drop] *preceded by* 'x'; *l. marg.* 'Wards famous Drop'
	Nostrum] *underl. in red pencil*
3.16 (48)	My] *preceded by* 'x'
	Friendship] *underl. in red pencil*
	Prologue] *underl. in red pencil*
	ten Pound.] *underl. in red pencil*
	r. marg. 'xTibbald'
3.17 (49)	Pitholeon] *underl. in red pencil; preceded by* 'x'; *r. marg.* 'x Welstead'
	Grace]; *preceded by* 'x'; *r. marg.* 'x the Duke of Argile'
3.22 (54)	Journal] *underl. in red pencil*
4.12–13 (66–67)	*l. marg.* 'one Hamilton'
6.4 (100)	Bishop] *underl. in red pencil*
6.5 (101)	nay see you] *underl.; l. marg.* 'the Drs common phrase'
6.17 (113)	Letters] *underl. in red pencil*
8.4 (140)	nod the head,] *underl. in red pencil*
8.13 (149)	Damon] *del.; l. marg.* 'Fanny'
11.14 (214)	Atticus] *preceded by* '†'; *foot* 'The assertion of some anonymous authors that Mr P. writ this Character after the Gentlemans death, was utterly untrue; it having been sent him several years before; [*followed by del.* 'on a Provocation of that nature, wch *he had too much regard to his memory to' [*above del.* '(unless obliged to it) we wd not perpetuate':]] and then shown to Mr Secretary Crags, & ye present Earl of Burlington; who approvd our author's Conduct on an Occasion, wch *he has to much regard to that Gentlemans memory willingly to make publick [*interl. with caret above del.* 'out of Regard to his Memory to perpetuate']. By what accident it

	came into print, he never could learn, but [*interl.*] All he can now do is to omit the Name.'
12.8 (230)	*Bufo*] *l. marg.* 'Bufo] this *character [*over illegible*] made fit many *but [*later insertion?*] I think it is cheifly the right of Mr Bubb Doddington*, it would also fit the late earl of Halifax [*in red pencil*]'
12.12–13 (234–235)	*interlined with caret* 'To Bards reciting he vouch-safd a Nod And snuff'd their Incence like a gracious God.'
13.13 (260)	QUEENSB'RY] *r. marg.* 'Gay] he was neglected by the court & had no place though often promised, He lived with the Duke of Queensberry & died at his House Dec. 4. 1732. He was buried at the Duks expence and will set up a monument for him'
14.8 (280)	Sir *Will.*] *l. marg.* 'Sr Will, Sr William Young, a great scribler of Libels & Lampoons.'
14.8 (280)	*Bubo*] *l. marg.* 'Bubo, Bubb Dorington of the same stamp.'
15.4 (300)	*Cannons*] 'Cannons, the seat of his Grace the duke of Chandos [*final 's' over ? 'e'*]'
15.9 (305)	Let *Paris*] *preceded by* 'P'; *r. marg.* 'Paris] It so happens that this is generaly applyed to Lord Harvey, and as he deserved it of Mr Pope, it is very proper for him & is very justly Drawn *In a late edition the name is changed to Sporus a more proper **nick [*interlined with caret*] name Sporus was a youth whom Nero had a mind to make a woman of by Gelding him. [*ink suggests later addition*]'
15.9 (305)	'What] *preceded above by* 'D^r'
15.13 (309)	Yet] *preceded by* 'P'
16.n (319n)	Posture] *preceded by* 'shape &' *above with caret*
18.9 (376)	To please a Mistress] *underl. in red pencil*
18.10 (377)	but let her be his *Wife:*] *underl. in red pencil*
18.12 (379)	except his *Will*;] *underl. in red pencil*
19.4 (385)	M*] 'oore' *over the asterisk*
19.10 (391)	*Bestia*] *underl. in red pencil*
19.12 (393)	Noble Wife,] *underl. in red pencil*
19.n (381n)	*Verses to the Imitator of Horace*] *r. marg.* 'p. 4 Line 10'

18. [See attribution of item 6], Verses Address'd to the Imitator of the First Satire of the Second Book of Horace. By a Lady. . . . The Fifth Edition Corrected. Printed for A. Dodd. (Foxon V44)

title-page	Fifth Edition] *r. marg.* 'This wch is called the fifth edition is not true but a sham of the Booksellers upon Mr Popes printing his Epistle ['pis' *over il-*

legible] to Dr. Arbuthnot where these verses are mentiond they supposed that some copies would be called for.'

19. Of the Characters of Women: An Epistle to a Lady. Printed by J. Wright, for Lawton Gilliver. 1735. (Foxon P917)

half-title	*head* 'R Feb. 6. 1734/5.'
title-page	*head* 'Publisht. ['P' *over* 'B'] Feb. 7. 1734/5.
5.5	*To a LADY*] *r. marg.* 'Mrs Martha Blount'
6.3 (9)	*Fannia*] *underl.; l. marg.* 'It is said this hints at the Countess of Pembroke, who used to be drawn in these *several ['a' *interlined with caret*] attitudes'
9.5 (63)	Now] *preceded by* 'x'
9.6 (64)	Grace] 'e' *below* 'x'; *r. marg.* 'The Duke of Wharton'
	Ch**] *r. marg.* 'Coll Charters'; 'see miscellanies vol. 3. p. 137.'

20. [West, Gilbert], Stowe, the Gardens of the Right Honourable Richard Lord Viscount Cobham. Address'd to Mr. Pope. Printed for L. Gilliver. 1732. (Foxon W360)

title-page	Address'd to Mr. *POPE.*] *r. marg.* 'By Mr West Nephew to My Lord Cobham'
7.20	Dy'd for the Laws he] *underl. in red pencil*

21. [Swift, Jonathan], On Poetry: A Rapsody. Printed at Dublin, and reprinted at London: And sold by J. Huggonson. 1733. (Foxon S888)

22. [Swift, Jonathan], An Epistle to a Lady, Who Desired the Author to Make Verses on Her, in the Heroick Stile. Also a Poem, Occasion'd by Reading Dr. Young's Satires, Called, The Universal Passion. Dublin printed: and reprinted at London for J. Wilford. 1734. (Foxon S841)

23. [Harte, Walter], An Essay on Reason. Printed by J. Wright for Lawton Gilliver. 1735. (Foxon H93)

title-page	*head* 'R. Feb: 6. 1734/35'

24. Swift, Jonathan, The Life and Genuine Character of Doctor Swift. Written by Himself. Printed for J. Roberts. (Foxon S884)

title-page	*head* 'R. April. 12 1733'

25. [Pope, Alexander, and Swift, Jonathan], Bounce to Fop. An Heroick Epistle from a Dog at Twickenham to a Dog at Court. By Dr. S———T. Dublin printed, London reprinted for T. Cooper. 1736. (Foxon B326)

title-page	By Dr. S———T.] *followed by* 'much altered by Mr Pope.'

SAMUEL JOHNSON AND THE TRANSLATIONS
OF JEAN PIERRE DE CROUSAZ'S
EXAMEN AND *COMMENTAIRE*

by

O M BRACK, JR.*

THANKS in part to Alexander Pope's shrewdness in publishing his ambitious *Essay on Man* anonymously, so that his enemies were beguiled into praising the poem on its merits, there was a "chorus of approbation" for some years after its appearance in 1733–34.[1] On the Continent, however, after the publication in 1736 of a French prose translation by Etienne de Silhouette,[2] it aroused the suspicion of Jean Pierre de Crousaz (1663–1750), professor at Lausanne, mathematician, logician, and Protestant theologian. That Pope was a Roman Catholic may have had something to do with Crousaz's hostility, but his first attack, *Examen de l'essai de monsieur Pope sur l'homme* (1737), is chiefly directed at what Crousaz believed to be its Leibnitzian content. Being told that Silhouette misrepresented Pope, Crousaz, who knew no English, then turned to a new translation—more accurately, a translation-imitation—by the Abbé Jean-François du Bellay du Resnel (1737). For his poem Du Resnel rearranged the *Essay on Man*, omitting some sections but adding others to extend Pope's 1,300 lines to 2,000 in French Alexandrines.[3] Crousaz

* I am grateful to Bruce Redford and David L. Vander Meulen for inviting me to contribute an essay to this volume and to the Huntington Library for an Andrew W. Mellon Fund Fellowship to allow me time to write it. David has read several drafts of this essay and it is better for his wise counsel. David Fleeman also graciously commented on a draft. Special thanks to Huidi Tang for assistance in tracking down several obscure matters. Heartfelt gratitude must also be expressed to friends and librarians who make this kind of bibliographical scholarship possible. Friends have generously shared their bibliographical expertise: Michael J. Crump, John Dussinger, Donald D. Eddy, Frank Felsenstein, C. Y. Ferdinand, Gwin Kolb, Vincent Giroud, Stephen Parks, Alvaro Ribeiro, and William B. Todd. Several librarians kindly supplied information: John Ahouse, Kathryn L. Beam, John Bertram, Michele Fagan, Diane Gatscher, James Green, Alan Michelson, Margaret M. Sherry.

1. The history of the reception of the *Essay on Man* is concisely told by Maynard Mack in his Twickenham Edition of the poem (1950; xv–xxvi). The quoted phrase appears on p. xvi. The four epistles were published successively on 20 February, 29 March, 8 May 1733, and 24 January 1734 (p. 3).

2. *Essai sur l'homme. Par M. Pope. Traduit de l'Anglois en François, par M. D. S.*****. N.p. M.DCC.XXXVI. The first edition is no. 14 in E. Audra, *Les traductions Françaises de Pope (1717–1825)* (1931).

3. *Les principes de la morale et du goût, en deux poëmes, traduits de l'Anglois de M. Pope, par M. Du Resnel, Abbé de Sept-Fontaines, de l'Académie des Inscriptions et Belles Lettres.* A Paris, chez Briasson Libraire, rue Saint-Jacques, à la Science. M.DCC.XXXVII. The first edition is no. 22 in Audra. Du Resnel explains how and why he changed Pope's

reprinted the entire poem with remarks interspersed in his *Commentaire sur la traduction en vers de Mr. l'abbé Du Resnel, de l'essai de M. Pope sur l'homme* (1738).

Considerable confusion has surrounded Samuel Johnson's role in the translations into English of Crousaz's two attacks on Pope's *Essay on Man*. *An Examination of Mr Pope's Essay on Man* and *A Commentary on Mr Pope's Principles of Morality, or Essay on Man* were easily confused: both are projects of Edward Cave, publisher of the *Gentleman's Magazine*, and both are dated "M.DCC.XXXIX." and "Printed for A. DODD" (Anne Dodd was a mercury used by Cave as a trade publisher).[4] Once it was known that it was Elizabeth Carter who translated the *Examen* and Johnson who translated the *Commentaire*, Johnsonians ignored the *Examination*. J. D. Fleeman, however, in his forthcoming bibliography of the writings of Samuel Johnson, observes, "Several of the notes in the *Examination* have the tone and manner of SJ's comments in his own translation of the *Commentary*."[5] Taking as a starting point this observation, the following essay will trace the history of the confusion about Johnson's role in the *Examination* and *Commentary*, clear up problems surrounding their publication, show that both works are indebted to Charles Forman's translation of the first epistle of the *Commentary*, and demonstrate that Johnson had a larger role in preparing the *Examination* for publication than has hitherto been recognized, not only providing editorial assistance but writing two substantial footnotes.

I

Identifying Johnson's contribution to the translations and publications of Crousaz's two attacks on Pope's *Essay on Man* has been difficult. James Boswell reports in *The Journal of a Tour to the Hebrides* (1786) that on 19 August 1773 when visiting St. Andrews, Johnson, in speaking of how quickly he could compose, mentioned that he had "written six sheets in a day of translation from the French."[6] Later, on 3 June 1781, Boswell records in his

<hr>

Essay on Man in his Preface, included by Johnson in his translation of the *Commentaire*. In the same preface Du Resnel identifies the faults of Silhouette's French prose translation: "those who are in the same Degree Masters of the *English* and *French* say, in plain Terms, that there is nothing of Mr. *Pope* to be found in them [*Essai sur l'homme* and *Essai sur la critique*], and that if they sometimes discover the Philosopher, the Poet is always lost" (324). Crousaz responded in the *Commentary*: "I do not understand *English*, and how loudly soever I might declare my Approbation of the judicious Comparison of the Poetry of the two Nations made by Mr DU RESNEL, my Suffrage ought to be made no account of, being given upon a Subject I do not understand" (3).

4. See Michael Treadwell, "London Trade Publishers 1675–1750," *Library* 6th ser., 4 (1982): 123–124. More precisely, the title page of the 1739 issue of the *Commentary* has "M.DCC.XXiX."

5. See the "Notes" to no. 39.10CP/1, the first edition, first issue of Johnson's *Commentary*.

6. *Boswell's Life of Samuel Johnson*, ed. G. B. Hill, rev. and enl. by L. F. Powell (1934–

journal that Johnson "Told us at night he had once written six sheets in one day: forty-eight quarto pages of translation of Crousaz on Pope, published by itself in 1740 or 1741."[7] If this is exactly what Johnson said, the confusion about the role Johnson may have had in a translation of Crousaz was introduced for Boswell by his source. One problem is the publication date for the translation: all copies of the *Commentary* are dated either 1739 or 1742, although the latter was issued in late 1741. A second problem is the format: the *Commentary* is not a quarto but a duodecimo. A third problem, although less obvious, is the amount of translation Johnson performed in one day. The text of the volume fills fourteen and a half sheets. Translating six sheets, 144 duodecimo pages of prose and verse, or about forty-two percent of the total work, would seem to be beyond the reach of even Johnson. Perhaps two sheets or forty-eight duodecimo pages is closer to the truth.[8]

By the time Boswell came to write the *Life of Samuel Johnson, LL.D.* (1791) he was convinced that the *Examination* had been translated by Elizabeth Carter but apparently was unaware of the *Commentary*. In spite of the confused account Boswell received from Johnson, he gathers three pieces of evidence in the *Life* to prove that Johnson did not translate Crousaz and leaves the impression that the issue has been settled. After reprinting Johnson's letter to Cave of 21 or 22 November 1738 suggesting that "the Examen

---

50, 1964), 5:67. L. F. Powell suggests that since this sentence does not appear in the manuscript of the *Tour* Boswell may have taken it from his journal of 3 June 1781. In perusing this journal Boswell may have been reminded that Johnson had first mentioned the six sheets of French translation while in St. Andrews.

7. James Boswell, *Laird of Auchinleck 1778–1782*, ed. Joseph W. Reed and Frederick A. Pottle (1977), 375.

8. A. D. Barker suggests that translating two sheets or forty-eight duodecimo pages, about fourteen percent of the work, in one day would be "quite a feat" and "is probably right" ("Edward Cave, Samuel Johnson, and the *Gentleman's Magazine*" [D.Phil. thesis, Oxford University, 1981], 316). Perhaps Johnson thought he remembered translating forty-eight pages. If he also remembered that the book was in quarto, a little arithmetic, of which he was very fond, would have given him six sheets to make forty-eight pages, instead of two to make the same number in duodecimo. I am assuming that "sheets" refer to *printed* sheets. Johnson, as a commercial writer, who was also "bred a Bookseller," certainly knew that translators were paid by the printed sheet (*The Letters of Samuel Johnson*, ed. Bruce Redford [1992–94], 3:159). Johnson, of course, may have been talking loosely or he may have been misunderstood by his auditors. David L. Vander Meulen has suggested that Johnson may be remembering the amount of paper on which he wrote the translation. The Sallust translation, for example, is written on sheets folded into a quarto format. Each Sallust manuscript page contains about 140 words and each Crousaz printed page about 300 words, if completely in prose (although many pages have varying amounts of poetry). At this ratio forty-eight manuscript pages would fill a little over twenty-two printed pages, or slightly less than one sheet. Poetry would make Johnson's task easier as a manuscript page would fill faster. If, in fact, Johnson is referring to *printed* sheets, which seems most likely, perhaps the number of sheets grew with the years. One of Johnson's harmless vanities was his pride in the speed with which he could compose and reports of his Herculean labors should be viewed with skepticism. See, for example, William Cooke, *The Life of Samuel Johnson, LL.D.* (1785) in *The Early Biographies of Samuel Johnson*, ed. O M Brack, Jr., and Robert E. Kelley (1974), 131–132, and Sir John Hawkins, *Life of Samuel Johnson, LL.D.*, 2d ed. (1787), 381–382 n.

should be pushed forward with the utmost expedition," Boswell comments, "But although he corresponded with Mr. Cave concerning a translation of Crousaz's Examen of Pope's Essay on Man, and gave advice for its success, I was long ago convinced by a perusal of the Preface, that this translation was erroneously ascribed to him."[9] As early as 12 March 1786 Boswell had written to Edmond Malone that Dr. Richard Palmer "shewed me the translation of Crousaz which has been ascribed to Dr. Johnson; But which is certainly not his. I agree with you that the translation itself is not a test. But the Preface is."[10] Boswell's statement in the Life, it should be noted, is a hit at Sir John Hawkins who, in his Life of Samuel Johnson, LL.D. (1787), attributes the Examination to Johnson, citing the letter of 21 or 22 November as evidence (Hawkins, Life, 66–67). As will be seen below, Boswell's attempt to keep as much distance as possible between his biography and that of Hawkins prevented him from using valuable information that Hawkins offered. In any case, Boswell's first piece of evidence, based on a recognition of Johnson's style, is also faulty, for the Preface is only a translation from Crousaz; Johnson's translation of the Commentaire would undoubtedly be rejected on the same stylistic grounds.

With his second and third pieces of evidence, Boswell is on safe ground. He first cites a manuscript in the British Museum: "ELISÆ CARTERÆ. S.P.D. THOMAS BIRCH. Versionem tuam Examinis Crousaziani jam perlegi. Summam styli et elegantiam, et in re difficillimâ proprietatem, admiratus, Dabam Novemb. 27° 1738."[11] Then he says, "Indeed Mrs. Carter has lately acknowledged to Mr. Seward, that she was the translator of the 'Examen.' "[12] Boswell, apparently unaware of the Commentary, but aware that the Examination had been translated by Elizabeth Carter, was at a stand. When he arrived at 3 June 1781 in the Life he revised his journal account to read: "He told us, that he had in one day written six sheets of a translation from the French," bringing it into accord with his earlier published account in the Tour, in which he also omits any reference to Crousaz (Life, 4:127).

Boswell, Hawkins, and other early biographers had received no help from Johnson on his role as translator of Crousaz. In the Life of Pope there is no indication that Johnson has any connection with a work by Crousaz: "It was

9. Life, 1:137–138. Letters, 1:20–21. James L. Clifford suggests that this letter might be dated 21 or 22 November 1738 (Young Sam Johnson [1955], 346 n.19). Since the letter is in response to Edmund Curll's announcement in the Daily Advertiser for 21 November of the publication of a translation of the Commentaire and the advertisement for the Examen suggested by Johnson appears in the Daily Advertiser for 23 November, Clifford is surely right in his dating of the letter. See below.

10. The Correspondence of James Boswell with David Garrick, Edmund Burke, and Edmond Malone, ed. George M. Kahrl, Rachel McClellan, Thomas W. Copeland, James M. Osborn, and Peter S. Baker (1987), 299.

11. Life, 1:138. "I have now perused your translation of Crousaz's Examination; and admire the great propriety and elegance of the style in a subject attended with so much difficulty." (Translation from Montagu Pennington, Memoirs of the Life of Mrs. Elizabeth Carter, 2d ed. [1808], 1:45.)

12. Life, 1:138. William Seward (1747–99), man of letters, and friend of Johnson, the Thrales, and other members of the circle.

first turned into French prose, and afterwards by Resnel into verse. Both translations fell into the hands of Crousaz, who first, when he had the version in prose, wrote a general censure, and afterwards reprinted Resnel's version with particular remarks upon every paragraph."[13] Nevertheless the *Commentary* was attributed to Johnson shortly after his death, in plenty of time to allow Hawkins and Boswell to avoid omitting the attribution.[14]

The earliest attribution in print of a translation of Crousaz to Johnson seems to be that in "An Account of the Writings of Dr. Samuel Johnson, Including Some Incidents of His Life" in the *European Magazine* for January 1785: "In November [1738], he is believed to have published a translation of An Examination of Mr. Pope's Essay on Man, by M. Crousaz, Professor of Philosophy and Mathematics at Lausanne, 12mo. whose Commentary on Pope's Principles of Morality, or Essay on Man, we can ascribe to him with confidence" (*Early Biographies*, 46). For some reason Boswell appears not to have consulted this work, or at least not this portion of it, even though it may have been written by Isaac Reed or George Steevens, or both.[15] In his haste to condemn Hawkins for attributing the *Examination* to Johnson, Boswell fails to note that Hawkins follows Johnson's account by mentioning a second work by Crousaz:

Cave engaged him to undertake a translation of an Examen of Pope's Essay on Man, written by Mr. Crousaz. . . . The reputation of the Essay on Man soon after its publication invited a translation of it into French, which was undertaken and completed by the Abbé Resnel, and falling into the hands of Crousaz, drew from him first a general censure of the principles maintained in the poem, and afterwards, a commentary thereon containing particular remarks on every paragraph. The former of these [*Examination*] it was that Johnson translated, as appears in the following letter of his to Cave, which is rendered somewhat remarkable by his stiling himself *Impransus*. (Hawkins, *Life*, 65–66)

Further clues in Johnson's own writings suggested the existence of not one but two attacks by Crousaz on Pope's *Essay on Man*. The most important

13. *Lives of the English Poets*, ed. George Birkbeck Hill (1905), 3:164, par. 181. See Hawkins's indebtedness to this passage in the quotation from his *Life* given below. Whitwell Elwin, who splices together Johnson's discussions of the *Essay on Man* from the *Life of Pope* in his introduction to the poem, adds a footnote to this passage: "The first treatise of Crousaz was translated by Miss Carter, and published in 1738 [1739], under the title of An Examination of Mr. Pope's Essay on Man. The second treatise was translated by Johnson himself, and published in 1742, with the title, A Commentary on Mr. Pope's Principles of Morality." See *The Works of Alexander Pope*, vol. 2, ed. Whitwell Elwin (1871), 264 n.2.

14. Arthur Murphy, having had the opportunity of consulting Boswell's *Life* when writing his *An Essay on the Life and Genius of Samuel Johnson, LL.D.* (1792), knew that Elizabeth Carter had translated the *Examination* but observes that "This translation has been generally thought a production of Johnson's pen." He mentions the *Commentary*, perhaps using Hawkins as his source, but makes no suggestion that Johnson may have translated it. See *Johnsonian Miscellanies*, ed. George Birkbeck Hill (1897), 1:374, 480.

15. *Early Biographies*, 301–302. Dr. Richard Brocklesby in a letter to Boswell, 13 December 1784, reports hearing that Steevens had taken away the Catalogue of Johnson's works, which seems to have served as the basis of this "Account." See *The Correspondence and other Papers of James Boswell Relating to the Making of the* Life of Johnson, ed. Marshall Waingrow (1969), 26 and n.6, 146 n.1.

hint is Johnson's letter of 21 or 22 November to Cave. The letter begins: "I am pretty much of your Opinion, that the Commentary cannot be prosecuted with any appearance of success," and after suggesting to Cave an advertisement for the *Examen* to forestall a rival, Johnson adds: "It will above all be necessary to take notice that it is a thing distinct from the Commentary." Hawkins, even though he misses the full significance of the sentence, recognizes that there are two works, whereas Boswell apparently does not. Had Boswell, for example, looked carefully at the *Examination* when he read the Preface, he would have noticed on the verso of the last leaf a full-page advertisement for the forthcoming *Commentary*. Had he actually read carefully the two-part essay in the 1743 *Gentleman's Magazine* that he attributed to Johnson on the basis of internal evidence, " 'Considerations on the Dispute between Crousaz and Warburton, on Pope's Essay on Man,' in which, while he defends Crousaz, he shews an admirable metaphysical acuteness and temperance in controversy," Boswell would have discovered that the English translation of the *Commentaire* is mentioned explicitly and nearly half of the essay consists of quotations from it. In fact, the second installment has as its title: *"Specimens of M. Crousaz's Sentiments from the English Translation of his Commentary on Mr Pope's Essay on Man, continued from p. 152."* The running head reads *"Sentiments from M. Crousaz's Commentary, &c."* [16] Hawkins, who first attributed the essay to Johnson, had he been taken more seriously by Boswell, would have alerted Boswell to the real nature of the essay, although not to Johnson's role in the *Commentary*. Johnson, Hawkins suggests, decided to become a moderator between Crousaz's attacks on the *Essay on Man* in his *Examination* and *Commentary* on one side and William Warburton's defence in his *Vindication*, as it has come to be known,[17] on the other, "but proceeded no farther than to state the sentiments of Mr. Crousaz respecting the poem, from a seeming conviction that he was discussing an uninteresting question."[18] Another clue, admittedly difficult to locate, is a quotation from Johnson's *Commentary* in his *Dictionary* under "Consoler."

16. The first installment of the essay has no title; it appears as a letter to the editor, "Mr. Urban," in the *Gentleman's Magazine* for March and November 1743 (13:152, 587–588). The entry in the index reads *"Crousaz* M. Specimens of his Sentiments 587." G. B. Hill in the 1887 *Life* observes, "It is not easy to believe that Boswell read this essay, for there is nothing metaphysical in what Johnson wrote. Two-thirds of the paper is a translation from Crousaz. Boswell does not seem to have distinguished between Crousaz's writings and Johnson's" (1:157 n.4). Some unintended irony is here as Hill, like Boswell, did not know that the translation was taken from a work by Johnson. The best discussion of the essay is in Thomas Kaminski, *The Early Career of Samuel Johnson* (1987), 157–158.

17. Warburton began his defence in December 1738 in the *History of the Works of the Learned.* Four more letters appeared in January, February, March, and April 1739. These five letters, with the addition of a sixth, were published as *A Vindication of Mr. Pope's Essay on Man, from the Misrepresentations of Mr. Crousaz* 15 November 1739. Then a seventh letter was published separately 13 June 1740, with a final revision incorporating all of the letters, entitled *A Critical and Philosophical Commentary on Mr. Pope's Essay on Man,* published 10 August 1742. See Mack, Twickenham Pope, xxi n.3.

18. Hawkins, *Life,* 70, 351. Boswell could also have found the essay in the 1787 *Works* (9:364–368).

John Wilson Croker and other editors of Boswell's *Life* made ingenious attempts to explain the 21 or 22 November 1738 letter, but it was not until L. F. Powell undertook his massive revision of G. B. Hill's edition of the *Life* that the attribution to Johnson of the *Commentary* was finally resolved. True, Whitwell Elwin in his 1871 introduction to the *Essay on Man* in *The Works of Alexander Pope* quoted a sentence from Johnson's long footnote on the ruling passion: " 'Every Observer,' says Johnson, 'has remarked, that in many men the love of pleasure is the ruling passion of their youth, and the love of money that of their advanced years.' " Elwin's footnote reads: "Crousaz's Commentary on Pope's Essay, translated by Johnson, p. 109."[19] But this reference, and an earlier footnote identifying Johnson as the translator, were overlooked by Johnsonians. Also ignored was a reference in William John Courthope's 1889 *The Life of Alexander Pope*, included as part of the same edition of *The Works of Alexander Pope*, that "Johnson was himself engaged with Crousaz' Commentary on the Abbé du Resnel's translation of the 'Essay on Man,' but he temporarily abandoned it in deference to the opinion of his publisher, Cave."[20] Powell, then, unaware of the earlier attributions of the *Commentary* to Johnson by Pope scholars, made an independent attribution in 1934.[21] Powell had seen only the 1742 issue of the *Commentary* and gave a quasi-facsimile description of the title page. Allen T. Hazen, while preparing an exhibition of Johnson books and manuscripts, which opened at Yale University on 8 November 1935, identified what to date is the unique copy of the 1739 issue. The discovery was reported initially by Hazen in the *Times Literary Supplement* for 2 November 1935 with a fuller account and a reproduction of the title page the following January in an essay co-authored with E. L. McAdam, Jr., in the *Yale University Library Gazette*.[22]

II

Identifying the various components of the controversy surrounding Johnson's role in the translation of the *Commentary* has been the first step; sorting out the chronological and textual relationships of the various translations of Crousaz is the next. Confusion surrounds the dates of publication of both the *Examination* and the *Commentary*. As Johnson points out in his letter

19. *Works of Pope*, 2:307. See n.13 above. Elwin cites Johnson's *Commentary* (page references in parentheses) in the following footnotes to the *Essay on Man*: 2:358 n.4 (47), 360 n.1 (55), 361 n.6 (57), 381 n.6 (99), and 433 n.3 (223).

20. *The Works of Alexander Pope* (1889), 5:327. Courthope draws on Johnson's letter of 21 or 22 November, although he misdates it September 1738, citing Croker's edition of the *Life* as his source. The index to the *Works* appears in vol. 5; under "Johnson, Dr.," under the subheading "*An Essay on Man*," is an entry: "translated a treatise of Crousaz on."

21. *Life*, 4:494–496. The *Commentary* has now been attributed to Johnson once in each century (1785, 1871, 1934). To prevent the work from having to be attributed to Johnson anew in the twenty-first century the author of this essay is completing an edition to be published as the next volume in the Yale Edition of the Works of Samuel Johnson.

22. *TLS*, p. 704; "First Editions of Samuel Johnson, An Important Exhibition and a Discovery," *YULG* 10 (1936): 45–51.

of 21 or 22 November 1738, in a controversy such as that surrounding Pope's *Essay on Man* "the names of the Authours concerned are of more weight in the performance than its own intrinsick merit," thus "the Publick will be soon satisfied with it." To make a profit from the controversy it was necessary for Cave to publish the two works in a timely fashion and forestall any rivals, neither of which he managed to do.

It is not known when Cave and Johnson decided to publish translations of Crousaz's two attacks on the *Essay on Man*, but Carter apparently began work on the translation of the *Examen* by late summer 1738, as it is difficult to imagine Cave making a preliminary announcement of its publication without some copy in hand. The translation of the *Examen* was announced in the *Daily Advertiser* for 9 September 1738 and in the *London Evening Post* for 7–9 September as in the press; a similar advertisement appeared at the end of the "Register of Books" in the *Gentleman's Magazine* for September 1738 (8:496):

In the Press, and speedily will be publish'd by *A. Dodd*, An Examination of Mr. *Pope*'s Essay on Man. Translated from the *French* of Monsi. *de Crousaz*, Member of the Royal Academies of Sciences at *Paris* and *Bourdeaux*. With Remarks by the Translator.[23]

Perhaps a preliminary announcement was deemed necessary because a rumor of a rival publication had reached St. John's Gate but, if so, a search of the newspapers and magazines has not uncovered an advertisement for any publication Cave might have felt the need to preempt. In any case, what occurred during the next ten weeks is something of a mystery. In a letter of 26 September 1738 to his daughter, Nicholas Carter suggests one explanation. He expresses satisfaction with Johnson's praise of the translation but frustration with Cave's lack of progress in printing the work: "That will, I suppose, please Cave; but is not sufficient it seems, to make him hasten the Press. . . . Dilatoriness is an inseparable Part of his Constitution."[24] This letter suggests that Elizabeth Carter had completed her share of the work on the translation before 26 September and was only awaiting its appearance in print.

23. The announcement in the *Daily Advertiser* for 9 September reads: "*In the Press, and speedily will be publish'd, Printed for* A. Dodd, AN Examination. . . . Translated from the French of Monsieur De Crusar. . . . With Remarks by the Translator." Except for the *Daily Advertiser* in the Beinecke Library, Yale University, kindly searched for me by John Bertram, I have used the Burney Collection of Eighteenth-Century Newspapers available on microfilm.

24. Quoted in Barker, p. 274, citing the introduction to Gwen Hampshire, "Elizabeth Carter's Unpublished Correspondence" (B.Litt. thesis, Oxford University, 1971), xii. There would be a similar delay in publishing Carter's translation of Francesco Algarotti's *Il Newtonianisimo per le Dame*. On 13 December 1738 in the *Daily Advertiser* Cave announced it as "In the Press," and announced its publication as 10 May 1739, although Thomas Birch's copy with his signature has an inscription dated 31 May 1739, probably a more accurate date of publication as Birch, patron of the translation from the beginning and one of its reviewers, must have received an early copy. See Edward Ruhe, "Birch, Johnson, and Elizabeth Carter: An Episode of 1738–39," *PMLA* 73 (1958): 496. As Kaminski observes, Cave frequently had difficulty publishing a work in a timely fashion. See, for example, his discussion of Cave's edition of Jean Baptiste Du Halde's *Description of China* (pp. 66–67).

But before Cave could publish Carter's translation of the *Examen*, Edmund Curll advertised on 21 November a translation by Charles Forman of Crousaz's *Commentaire*:

This Day is publish'd, (Price 1 s. 6 d.)
Translated by CHARLES FORMAN, *Esq;*
A Commentary upon Mr. POPE's Four Ethic Epistles, entitled *An Essay on Man*. Wherein his System is fully examin'd. By Monsieur DE CROUSAZ, Counsellor of the Embassies of Sweden, &c. formerly Governor to the Prince of Hesse, and Member of the Royal Academies of Sciences of Paris and Bourdeaux.
This Commentary is a critical Satire upon the Essay on Man. "We have endeavour'd to be impartially just in our Translation of it; and had we not been persuaded that Mr. Pope will think his Honour engaged to make some Reply to the heavy Charge brought against him by Monsieur Crousaz, we would have enlarged the Remarks we have made on Abbe Du Resnel, the Translator of The Essay on Man into French Verse."
Printed only for E. Curll, at Pope's Head in Rose-Street, Covent-Garden. And sold by Mess. Jackson, Jolliffe, and Dodsley, at St. James's; Brindley and Shropshire, in Bond-Street; Winbush and Amy, at Charing-Cross; Gilliver, in Fleet-Street; Dodd, without Temple-Bar; and Cooke and Nutt, at the Royal Exchange.[25]

The news of Curll's publication caused a flurry at St. John's Gate. Cave apparently wrote to Johnson seeking his advice and the letter of 21 or 22 November is his response:

I am pretty much of your Opinion, that the Commentary cannot be proscecuted with any appearance of success. . . . And I think the Examen should be push'd forward with the utmost expedition. Thus, This day, etc. An Examen of Mr. Pope's Essay etc. containing a succinct account of the Philosophy of Mr. Leibnitz on the System of the Fatalists, with a confutation of their Opinions, and an Illustration of the doctrine of Freewil; [with what else you think proper.]
It will be above all necessary to take notice that it is a thing distinct from the Commentary.

Cave followed Johnson's advice and on 23 November in the *Daily Advertiser* appeared the following advertisement, perhaps written by Johnson:

This Day is publish'd,
An Examination of Mr. POPE's Essay on Man: Containing a succinct View of the System of the Fatalists, and a Confutation of their Opinions; with an Illustration of the Doctrine of Free Will; and an Enquiry what View Mr. Pope might have touching upon the Leibnitzian Philosophy.
By Mons. CROUSAZ,
Professor of Philosophy and Mathematics at Lausanne &c. Printed for A. Dodd, without Temple-Bar; and sold by the Booksellers.
Where may speedily be had, having been some Weeks in the Press, translated likewise from the French of Mr. Crousaz, A COMMENTARY on MR. POPE's *Principles of Morality*: or, *Essay on Man*; being a more minute Enquiry into the Tendency

25. This announcement in the *Daily Advertiser* was repeated on 22 and 23 November. Forman's name does not appear on the title page or elsewhere in the work. The "Monthly Catalogue" in the November 1738 issue of the *London Magazine* has the following entry: "21. A Commentary upon Mr. *Pope*'s Essay on Man. Part I. By M. *de Crousaz*. Translated by *Ch. Forman*, Esq; Printed for *E. Curll*, price 1s. 6d." The item immediately above reads: "20. An Examination of Mr. *Pope*'s Essay on Man. By M. *Crousaz*. Printed for *A. Dodd*, price 1s. 6d." (7:582).

of the said Principles, occasion'd by a Letter written to Mr. Crousaz concerning his *Examination*, &c. To which are added, The Abbe *Du Resnel*'s Preliminary Discourse on English and French Poetry, and some cursory Observations by the Translator.

N.B. As the Commentary is built upon the Abbe *Du Resnel*'s Translation of the Essay into French Verse, the entire Translation is inserted, with an interlineary English Version, exactly correspondent to the French, for the Use of those who do not understand that Language, or are newly engaged in the Study of it.[26]

Before proceeding it is necessary to know something of the makeup of the book, which may be described as follows:

AN | EXAMINATION | OF | Mr *POPE*'s Essay ON MAN. | Translated from the *French* of | M. *CROUSAZ*, | Member of the Royal Academies of | Sciences at *Paris* and *Bourdeaux*; and Pro-|fessor of Philosophy and Mathematics at | *Lausanne*. | [single rule] | [printers' ornament] | [single rule] | LONDON: | Printed for A. Dodd, at the *Peacock*, without | *Temple-Bar*. M.DCC.XXXIX.

Collation: 12° in 6s (160 x 95 mm.): A⁶ (–A2; A3 as 'A2') B⁶ (±B5) C⁶ (±C1) D⁶ (±D3) E–F⁶ G⁶ (±G4, G6) H–U⁶. Title page, *i–viii* Preface, *1–227* text, *228 In the Press, Translated likewise from the* French of *Mr* Crousaz. A COMMENTARY. . . .

Typography: Catchwords ii *them*ₐ] ~. 24 the] as 59 Sounds ₐ] ~, 61 short ₐ] ~, 63 duction] tion 78 ₐIT] "~ 98 [catchword *NERO* below footnote rather than above] 114 HE] He 148 lead] ead 180 does ₐ] ~: 211 pos–] their 212 be] lose 214 for ₐ] or,

Press figures: None.

Paper: Crown with "WB" and fleur-de-lys with "IV." Like Heawood nos. 1073 and 1706.[27]

27. Edward Heawood, *Watermarks Mainly of the 17th and 18th Centuries* (1950).

Notes: The chain line patterns reveal that, in the five-leaf gathering A, leaf 2 has been deleted and leaf 3 signed 'A2'. That the signing is right for the gathering as it finally appears seems to indicate that the cancellation was planned. One replacement for a leaf cancelled elsewhere in the volume, therefore, may originally have been printed as leaf A2, with the remaining four cancel leaves printed as a unit.[28] The copy at Yale is Elizabeth Carter's own, with the inscription in

28. On page 66 (cancel leaf G3) the "y" in "*They*", the first word of the first line of verse in the footnote, is corrected in some copies, by what appears to be the same hand, to "n".

her hand "E Libris Eliza Carter." It descended to her nephew, executor, and biographer, the Reverend Montagu Pennington, who has written his name on the flyleaf and added an ascription to E. Carter on the title page.

Copies: CSmH, CSt, CtY, ICU, IU, MeB, MiU, NbU, NjP, NIC, PPL, TxU, ViU, David L. Vander Meulen; L (2), LeU, O

26. Publication of the *Examination* was also announced in the *General Evening Post* for 21–23 November, *London Evening Post* for 23–25 and 25–28 November, and the *Daily Gazetteer* for 28 November, where we are told it is "Translated from the French of M. CROUSNER." It appears prominently displayed as the first item in the "Register of Books for November, 1738" in the *Gentleman's Magazine* with a large numeral "1" and an initial "A" five lines high: "AN EXAMINATION of Mr *POPE*'s Essay on Man. By Mons. *Crousaz*, Professor of Philosophy and Mathematicks at *Lausanne*. Printed for *A. Dodd*. Price 2 *s*." (8:608). At the bottom of the right-hand column at the end of the "Register of Books for December, 1738" appears an additional advertisement. Beginning "*This Month* was publish'd," it repeats the announcement as it appears in the *Daily Advertiser* for 23 November but only for the *Examination* (8:664).

Because Johnson's letter of 21 or 22 November suggests that Cave's *Commentary* had little chance of appearing soon, the announcement of 23 November in the *Daily Advertiser* seems an attempt to ward off the competition by arguing a prior claim, at least for the *Commentary*: "*Where may speedily be had, having been some Weeks in the Press.*" Johnson himself used a similar ploy a month earlier for the *History of the Council of Trent* when he wrote on 20 October 1738 to the *Daily Advertiser,* "It is generally agreed, that when any person has inform'd the world by advertisements, that he is engag'd in a design of this kind, to snatch the hint and supplant the first undertaker, is mean and disingenuous."[29] When Cave reprinted the advertisement of 23 November for the *Examination* and the *Commentary* in the 24 November *Daily Advertiser,* he inserted as the second line the description "*Beautifully printed, Price Two Shillings sew'd*", and he tried to ward off the threat from Curll by noting: "N.B. The Commentary of Mr. Pope's four Epistles publish'd by Mr. Curll, Price 1 s. 6 d. goes no further than the first Epistle."[30] Curll countered in the *Daily Advertiser* of 25 November by revising the opening of his advertisement and adding a note of his own: "*This Day is publish'd, (With* The Essay on Man *inserted) Price but* 1 s. 6 d. MR. FORMAN's Translation of A COMMENTARY. . . . N.B. We shall pursue M. Crousaz in his Attacks upon Mr. Pope regularly, but not precipitately, without regarding whatever comes from Mrs. Dodd, who is only a Screen for anonymous Persons and Performances. E. Curll." Mrs. Dodd, it is curious to note, is among the booksellers and publishers listed in Curll's advertisement of 21 November.[31] In the *Daily Advertiser* for 27 November, Cave's advertisement appears as the second item and Curll's as the third item from the top of a left-hand column, allowing the reader to compare conveniently the two offerings.

As will be argued below, it is unlikely that Cave was able to ready the *Examination* for publication on 23 November, two days after Curll announced his publication of the *Commentary* on 21 November. Thomas Birch, because of his close relationship with Carter at the time, must have received one of the first complete copies of the *Examination,* and likely wrote his note of praise to her immediately. Therefore, Monday, 27 November, the date of Birch's note, would very probably be the first day the book was available.[32]

29. The letter appeared in the 21 October 1738 issue of the *Daily Advertiser* above Cave's signature but it is certainly by Johnson.

30. The announcement in the *London Evening Post* of 23–25 November has the note in a slightly different form: "N.B. The Commentary advertis'd by Mr. Curll, price Six-pence, takes in no more than the first Epistle of the Essay on Man." It is repeated 25–28 November.

31. In this 25 November version of the advertisement, Curll has omitted all of the booksellers and publishers except himself.

32. To keep the *Examination* before the public Cave advertised it on 23, 24, 27 November and after in the *Daily Advertiser* so the announcements are not a reliable record of the actual publication date. Announcements also appeared in the *London Evening Post* for 23–25 and 25–28 November. See n.26 above. Cave's letter to Birch of 28 November 1738, reporting Johnson's advice that Carter translate Boethius, suggests that the *Examination* had just been published and it was time to look for a new project. An advertisement for the *Examination* appears on the verso of the final leaf of the first volume of *Sir Isaac Newton's Philosophy Explain'd For the Use of the Ladies* published by Cave in late May

The *Examination* was now published, but what was the status of Johnson's *Commentary*? There is no evidence that Cave thought of abandoning the *Commentary*; instead he continued to spar with Curll. The advertisement for the *Commentary* on the verso of the last leaf of the *Examination*, taken from the announcement in the *Daily Advertiser* of 23 November—"*In the Press, Translated likewise from the* French *of Mr* Crousaz. A COMMENTARY. . . . French*, for the Use of those who do not understand that Language, or are newly engaged in it"—argues for the superiority of Cave's publication. Cave needed to establish both that he was the first to have the idea of publishing Crousaz's two attacks on the *Essay on Man* and that he alone was making available not only the *Examination* but also the complete *Commentary*. Curll's initial announcement in the *Daily Advertiser* and his general threat to continue to pursue Crousaz was serious enough, but on acquiring a copy of Curll's publication Cave and Johnson discovered from the end of his Preface that Curll was proceeding with his translation: "The COMMENTARY of Monsieur DE CROUSAZ upon Mr POPE's *Second* EPISTLE is in the Press; and in the *Conclusion* of this *Work* will be subjoined the *various Readings* of its *several Editions*, with REMARKS thereon" (x). This volume never appeared and Forman died 28 April 1739.[33] In fact, unknown apparently to Cave and Johnson, Forman's translation of the first epistle was not selling well; it was reissued by Curll, without the title page and Preface, in *Miscellanies In Prose and Verse, By the Honourable Lady Margaret Pennyman* in December 1740.[34]

Johnson, then, in spite of threats from Curll, continued to press on with his translation of Crousaz's *Commentaire*, even though for all Cave and Johnson knew Curll and Forman were hard at work preparing the second epistle of their *Commentary* for publication. It must have been in late November or early December 1738 that Johnson made his heroic effort to complete the *Commentary* and translated "six sheets," or at least a substantial amount, in one day. Exactly when he completed his translation is unknown. He presumably finished it in the winter of 1738–39, but certainly in time to have it printed with 1739 on the title page. No announcement of its publication has been discovered, suggesting that it was never published. It appears to have been withdrawn in order to privilege Elizabeth Carter's *Examination*, and the only known copy of the *Commentary* with "Printed for A. DODD" and

---

1739. The *Examination* is also advertised, along with the Algarotti, in "*BOOKS lately printed and sold by* EDWARD CAVE, *at St* JOHN's GATE, LONDON", which appears on the verso of the final leaf of January 1740 issue of the *Gentleman's Magazine* (10:40). The *Examination, Commentary*, and Algarotti appear in a four-leaf advertisement with a similar heading tipped into some copies of the 1742 *Commentary*. Of the twenty-four items on the list, none seems to have been published after the *Parliamentary Register* in May 1741. Carter is mentioned as translator of Algarotti, but not of Crousaz.

33. *Gentleman's Magazine* 9 (May 1739): 272. For an account of Forman's career, see Georges A. Bonnard, "Note on the English Translations of Crousaz' Two Books on Pope's 'Essay on Man,'" in *Recueil de Travaux à l'occasion du quatrième centenaire de la fondation de l'Université* (Lausanne, 1937), 178–181.

34. J. V. Guerinot, *Pamphlet Attacks on Alexander Pope, 1711–1744* (1969), 274–275.

"M.DCC.xxxix" in the imprint once belonged to Carter.[35] Cave, for reasons now obscure, stored the work for three years. Then in November 1741, the 1739 title page was cancelled and replaced by a bifolium containing the 1742 title page with Cave's name in the imprint and an Errata listing three errors discovered by Johnson.[36] The work was advertised in the November 1741 issue of the *Gentleman's Magazine* (11:614) and in the *Scots Magazine* of the same month. Johnson's prediction that "the Publick will be soon satisfied" proved correct. In an attempt to clear Cave's warehouse, Johnson puffed the work in a two-part essay in the *Gentleman's Magazine* for March and November 1743. The book did not sell well, and Cave was still advertising it as late as 1753.[37]

III

Besides prodding Cave to move more quickly with his own Crousaz books, the publication of Curll's *Commentary* also affected the text of both of Cave's works. Curll's *Commentary* is, in fact, a translation and abridgement by Forman of the first epistle of Crousaz, with Pope's lines substituted for the Du Resnel text, essentially vitiating Forman's attack on the verse translation since the reader has few examples of it. The "Remarks" on his translation of the *Commentary* are in footnotes to the text. These notes, largely favorable to Pope, attack both Du Resnel's translation and Crousaz's commentary based on it.

The influence on Johnson's activities by Curll's publication of a translation of the *Commentaire's* first epistle can best be shown by looking at Johnson's *Commentary* first. Although Johnson may have read over the *Commentaire* in anticipation of translating it, he could not have begun serious work on the first epistle of his *Commentary* before the publication of Forman's translation on 21 November 1738 since he clearly used it to make his own. Johnson's translation is superior to Forman's and includes the whole text; nevertheless there are a number of verbal parallels, several too close to be dismissed as coincidence. Johnson, for example, translated "à la gayeté" (60) as "Mirth and Gaiety" (27) and Forman as "Gaiety and Mirth" (24). The

35. John Nichols says that the *Commentary* "was kept back until November 1741." See *Literary Anecdotes of the Eighteenth Century* (1812), 5:550. J. D. Fleeman in his bibliography of the writings of Johnson concurs. See no. 39.10CP/1a. The CtY copy of the 1739 *Commentary* has an inscription in Elizabeth Carter's hand: "E Libris Elizæ Carter."

36. Fleeman, bibliography, no. 39.10CP/1b.

37. The work appears as item XXII, immediately below the listing of the *Examination*, in an undated advertisement, "Books Printed for E. Cave at St. John's Gate," bound at the end of *A General Index to the First Twenty Volumes of the Gentleman's Magazine* (1753) in the Bodleian Library, Oxford. Although the advertisement is a separately printed gathering, it could not have been printed earlier than 1753, as it advertises the third edition of *The Entire Works of Dr. Thomas Sydenham*, to which Johnson's life was prefixed, published that year. The advertisement reproduces all of the information on the title page except Crousaz's credentials and, of course, the imprint. Underneath Cave adds a comment: "The two foregoing proper to be bound with Mr. Warburton's defence of the Essay on Man."

French "on en prend ce qu'il faut pour se conserver en vigueur; & on n'a garde de se laisser séduire par des plaisirs qui émoussent l'attention & la vivacité de l'intelligence" (103) is translated by Forman as "We take what is necessary for preserving us in *Health and Vigour*; but we also take Care not to suffer ourselves to be seduced by Pleasures that take off the Attention, and blunt the Vivacity of the *Understanding*" (56–57) and by Johnson as "We take what is necessary to preserve *Health and Vigour*, but are not to give ourselves up to Pleasures that weaken the Attention, and dull the *Understanding* (61; italics added). Johnson is misled by taking a cue from Forman's translation of "alloit plus loin que la bêtise de cet animal" (55). Forman, confusing "bêtise" with "bête," writes "was more a Beast than that Animal" (20) and Johnson "was much more despicable than the Brutality of that Animal" (23).

Curll's edition of the *Commentary* served Johnson not only while he translated the first epistle; it also suggested the tone and form his footnotes should take. Curll's remarks in the Preface—"Impartiality and Justice obliges us to ask Mr *De Crousaz*, as he had two *French* Translations of Mr *Pope*'s *Essay on Man* in his Hands, why he did not take the Prose to comment upon rather than the Verse, since he did not understand *English*?"—provide the point of attack for both Forman and Johnson.[38] Both translators make numerous complaints about how Du Resnel's French verse translation has distorted Pope's meaning and hence Crousaz's commentary, and in six instances Johnson has a footnote at or near the same point in the text, even though he does not always agree with Forman. On *"just Balance"* Forman's footnote suggests, "This is the Translator's Way of rendering *equal Eye*, which he likewise has too in the next Line; or *sa juste* Balance is a Flight of his own" (31). Johnson says, "These two Lines that give Occasion to these Questions, are entirely inserted by the Translator" (34). Forman's "These six lines are not in the Translation; how they came to be passed over, the Translator knows best" (33) is condensed by Johnson to "In this Place six whole Lines are omitted" (36).[39] To a quotation of lines 99–108 of Pope, which Forman has substituted for those of Du Resnel, Forman adds a footnote: "To these ten Lines, the Translator, tho' counted one of the French First Rates, has hobbled out their Meaning within the Compass of twenty four of his own; but he has left their Spirit behind him" (33). Johnson, of course, includes Du Resnel's verses with a translation, so he takes a slightly different approach, in part answering Forman:

---

38. I follow E. Audra in attributing the Preface to Curll. See *L'Influence Française dans l'oeuvre de Pope* (1931), 93. The Preface, unlike the notes, is hostile to Pope, calling the *Commentary* "a Critical Satire on the *Essay on Man*" and challenging Pope for "his Honour" to reply "to the heavy Charge brought against him by a *Frenchman*" (viii–ix). Curll has adapted a portion of his Preface for the advertisement in the *Daily Advertiser* for 21 November and later.

39. Johnson makes a similar, but more expansive, observation later: "In this Place the Translator has, with great Fidelity and Judgment, entirely omitted a Paragraph of Twenty-two Verses, from the Fifty-third to the Seventy-fourth" (166).

Mr *Pope*, in the Original, has not made use of the Word *Nature* in the passage here refer'd to; his Expression being only

Lo! *the poor* Indian, *whose untutor'd Mind.*

But he has, indeed, us'd the Word a few Lines after,

Yet simple Nature to his Hope has given, &c.

to which, perhaps, all that Mr Crousaz has written may be apply'd with Propriety. (37–38)

In another footnote Forman writes, "Mr *Pope* has nothing to do with these Words, they are one of the Translator's Flights, which the Critick is only exposing at the same time that he thinks he is demolishing Mr *Pope*" (36). Johnson says, "Mr *Crousaz* is so watchful against Impiety, that he lets Nonsense pass without Censure. . . . I take this Opportunity of observing, once for all, that he is not sufficiently candid in charging all the Errors of this miserable Version upon the original Author. . . . He had a Prose Translation in his Hand, which he might have compared with *Du Resnel's* . . ." (49). Then Forman writes, "Here we omit some of the Criticism, because it is upon a few Lines of the Translation that neither shew Mr *Pope*'s Words not his Meaning" (48). Johnson, who reprints the lines in his text with a translation, also adds a footnote: "This Couplet is an Addition by the Translator" (53). Again, Forman writes, "The Translator's Vein is, no doubt, fertile enough sometimes; for it makes Mr *Pope* say many Things which he never thought of, tho' not in this Place, which is the first of Mr *Pope*'s that has met with the Commentator's entire Approbation; notwithstanding the Beauty of the Original is quite lost in 23 Lines of *French*" (62). Johnson comments, "On this Passage where sixteen Lines are translated into thirty three, it is not necessary to make any other Remark than may be made in general on the whole Work, that it is extremely below the Original in Spirit, Propriety, and notwithstanding the Diffuseness of his Expression, in Perspicuity" (67).[40] Even such a Johnsonian-sounding note as "The address of one is the Exclamation of a Freeman, that of the other the Murmur of a Slave" (3) echoes Forman's "Notwithstanding all Mr *Crousaz*'s Logick, this Argument smells more of the Slave than Mr *Pope*'s Philosophy does of the Poet" (66). Forman even anticipates Johnson in discussing the significance of individual words: "The Translator takes *vile* to signify *poor* and *wretched* as to worldly Circumstances, and therefore places the Man in a *Chaumiere* (a *Cottage*); after which he gravely shews that a *poor* Man may *sometimes* have good Qualities; but, it seems, never such good ones as are enjoyed by the *Rich*" (69). A parallel case is Johnson's discussion of *"End"* or *"Destinee."*[41]

---

40. In this instance Johnson is taking issue with Forman as well as Du Resnel. Two notes later, Johnson, like Forman, praises Du Resnel's translation (78). Johnson is referring to ll. 207–222 of Pope but the passage in French is only twenty-three lines, as Forman says.

41. "Mr *Crousaz* seems to impose upon his Readers, or at least upon himself, by the equivocal and variable Import of the Word *End*, [or *Destinee*] which signifies either the Period of our Being, or intentional End for which we are sent into the World. So that his Argument against Mr *Pope* seems to stand thus: *Heaven,* says the Author, conceals from all earthly Beings their End, or Time of their Dissolution. *Heaven,* says the Commentator, discovers clearly to Man his End, or the Intention for which he was created" (32).

Forman substitutes Pope's verses for those of Du Resnel throughout his translation of the first epistle of the *Commentary*. Johnson, however, follows Crousaz in reproducing Du Resnel's poem in its entirety, although adding his own line-for-line translation. But when Crousaz repeats a line or lines of Du Resnel's poem in his text for analysis, Johnson substitutes the lines of Pope. He also cites Pope's verse in the footnotes. This helps Johnson reinforce his point about the difference in quality between Pope's and Du Resnel's verses.

IV

Twenty-one-year-old Elizabeth Carter was essentially responsible for the translation of Crousaz's prose in the *Examination*. That she was the translator we have the testimony of Carter herself, her father, Nicholas Carter, Thomas Birch, Samuel Johnson, William Seward, and her nephew, Montagu Pennington. But Johnson probably had an important stake from the beginning in her translation of the *Examen*, as well as his own of the *Commentaire*, for the combined project may well have been his own idea. Thomas Kaminski is certainly correct in observing, "That Johnson was instrumental in Cave's decision to publish the Crousaz translations may be inferred from their unique place in all of Cave's publishing ventures. Never before or after did he stray into the area of literary or moral controversy, yet these topics would have had considerable appeal for Johnson" (223 n.49). The appeal of the topic, coupled with the appeal of Elizabeth Carter, was irresistible. Johnson had met Carter through Cave in April 1738. In that month he wrote to Cave, "I have compos'd a Greek Epigram to Eliza, and think She ought to be celebrated in as many different Languages as Lewis le Grand" (*Letters*, 1:17). The epigram, with a Latin translation, was published in the April issue of the *Gentleman's Magazine*, and in the July issue Johnson published a second epigram in Latin praising her, with his English translation of it in the August issue.[42] It may have been Johnson's admiration for Carter and a desire to find a literary project for her which would allow them to work together that had suggested the translation to him in the first place. There can be no doubt that there was competition, friendly at least on the surface, for Carter's attention between Johnson and Thomas Birch, both of whom believed that the way to her heart was through her mind.[43] Both men, having chosen to play the role of Mentor, found it necessary to have a literary project for a medium. Johnson had Crousaz, and when it was completed he suggested that Carter "undertake a Translation of *Boethius de. Cons.* because there is

42. *The Poems of Samuel Johnson*, ed. David Nichol Smith and Edward L. McAdam, 2d ed., rev. J. D. Fleeman (1974), 57, 82–83.

43. I am not suggesting that the two men had the same motive. Johnson was married and "seems to have had just the kind of warm, friendly, gallant, but limited interest in Eliza that he later showed to . . . other pretty and talented younger women." Birch appears to have been courting Carter with a view to marriage. See Ruhe, 495.

prose & verse & to put her name to it when published," Cave reported to Birch in a letter of 28 November 1738.[44] Instead Carter took Birch's suggestion that she translate from Italian a work by Francesco Algarotti, *Il Newtonianisimo per le Dame* (1737), published in May 1739 as *Sir Isaac Newton's Philosophy Explain'd For the Use of the Ladies. In Six Dialogues on Light and Colours. From the Italian of Sig. Algarotti* (London: Printed For E. Cave, at St. John's Gate, MDCCXXXIX).

The competition between Johnson and Birch to decide who would be the director of Elizabeth Carter's next translation project is revealing. Although Carter had an excellent knowledge of languages, she welcomed outside assistance. On all three of her translations, including *All the Works of Epictetus* (1758), she received generous help, relying first, it appears, on Johnson, then on Birch, and finally on Thomas Secker, always with her father as advisor in the background. An overview of her major projects and the evidence for the assistance she received will make this clear.[45]

To begin with *Epictetus*, the last translation, because its history is the best documented, it is clear that she relied heavily on the advice of Bishop Thomas Secker and her friend, Catherine Talbot. Both gave advice on the introduction and notes and Secker not only read several drafts of the translation, but even read proofs. Secker's corrections and revisions must have been extensive, for Talbot tells Carter in a letter of 9 July 1755 that "the Bishop of Oxford shut himself up with him [Epictetus] for near a month, never leaving his study but for his morning ride and afternoon walk." James Harris, an excellent Greek scholar who had assisted John Upton with his important edition of Arrian's Epictetus (1739–41), answered queries on the translation. Carter used Upton's edition for her translation and he is frequently cited in the footnotes.[46]

44. Quoted in Ruhe, 495; *Life*, 1:139.
45. This is only an overview. Elizabeth Carter's literary career—poet, prose writer, translator—deserves an in-depth study.
46. See *A Series of Letters between Mrs. Elizabeth Carter and Miss Catherine Talbot*, ed. Montagu Pennington, 3rd ed. (1819), 2:82. For the history of the composition of the translation of Epictetus, which began in 1749 and was published in April 1758, see *A Series of Letters*, 2:24, 71, 75–76, 82–83, 96 and Pennington, *Memoirs*, 1:159–212. Thomas Secker (1693–1768) was at this time bishop of Oxford and in 1758 became archbishop of Canterbury; Catherine Talbot (1721–1770), the bulk of whose literary works were published posthumously by Carter, resided with her mother in Secker's house until his death in 1768; and James Harris (1709–80) was the author of *Hermes*. The footnotes draw numerous parallels between Epictetus and the New Testament. In addition to correcting Carter's Greek and reading proofs, Secker may have given some assistance on these notes. For Harris's assistance on Upton's edition of Arrian's Epictetus, see Clive T. Probyn, *The Sociable Humanist, The Life and Works of James Harris 1709–1780* (1991), 70–71. Harris's role in assisting Carter is made clear from a manuscript of 26 January 1754 quoted by Probyn (343–344). Carter, in a footnote to *All the Works of Epictetus* (1758), says "The Translator is obliged for this Note, as well as many other valuable Hints, to Mr. HARRIS; so well known for many Works of Literature and Genius" (112). See also pp. xxxiii, 183. At the end of her Introduction Carter says, "I have been much indebted to Mr. *Upton's* Edition: by which, many Passages, unintelligible before, are cleared up. His Emendations have often assisted me in the Text; and his References furnished me with Materials for the historical Notes" (xxxiv).

Her second translation, Algarotti's *Il Newtonianisimo per le Dame*, received extensive assistance from Thomas Birch, who read drafts of it and provided editorial assistance. Anyone who reads through the footnotes to the translation and is familiar with Birch's work will recognize at various points his heavy hand. Numerous notes appear, diminishing in number after the early portion of the work, some lengthy, most unnecessary, reminding the reader of Johnson's description of Birch given to Sir John Hawkins: "a pen is to Tom a torpedo, the touch of it benumbs his hand and his brain; Tom can talk; but he is no writer." [47] Carter's translation of Algarotti, unlike her deservedly praised Epictetus, can best be described as serviceable, lacking the elegance of the original. [48]

Carter's first translating project, the *Examen* of Crousaz, also received editorial assistance, in this case from Samuel Johnson. [49] As previously men-

47. Hawkins, *Life*, 209. Birch contributed 618 lives to *A General Dictionary, Historical and Critical*, 10 vols. (1734–41). Two footnotes on Aristotle, one on p. 24 and the other on p. 25 of volume one of Algarotti, which fill three-quarters of each page, are particularly reminiscent of the *General Dictionary*. In fact, the reader is told at the end of the first footnote to "See Bayle's *Life of* Aristotle *in the* General Dictionary, Vol. II. [265–275]." Birch contributed the life of Galileo to the *General Dictionary* (5:372–374), and two footnotes for the Algarotti are taken directly from it (1:x, 28). Another footnote is taken from his life of Roger Cotes (4:441–445), where Robert Green's *Principles of Natural Philosophy* is also mentioned (Algarotti, 1:141–142). Birch's life of Epimenides (5:61–64) supplies another footnote (Algarotti, 1:157–158). John Donne's anecdote on Francesco Guiccardini (Algarotti, 1:2), although not included in Birch's life of Donne (4:631–637), may have been discovered in the course of his reading for it. Neither Birch or Carter needed to be familiar with the *Os Lusiadas* as all the comments on it in a footnote (1:183–184) are taken directly from Pierre Bayle's Life of Luíz de Camoes ("Camoens (Luis de)"; 4:81, n.[X], col. b.). Undoubtedly information for other footnotes is to be found in the *General Dictionary*, but there is no index. Some footnotes may also have been supplied from Birch's extensive reading for the project. See James Marshall Osborn, "Thomas Birch and the *General Dictionary*," *Modern Philology* 36 (1938): 25–46, and Ruhe, 495–496.

48. Birch corrected the translation from the Italian but exactly what it owes to him is difficult to tell. Algarotti introduces numerous literary allusions, including a number of passages of poetry in Italian, even if originally written in another language, such as English or Latin. The poetry is usually omitted or turned into prose unless an English text is available. Milton and Pope's verse, no surprise, are substituted for the Italian but Edward Fairfax's translation of Tasso and Thomas Creech's translation of Lucretius are used, suggesting, perhaps, a sense of discomfort with Italian verse translation. At one point eight lines of Italian poetry are not translated but have appended a curious footnote: "As Seignor *Algarotti* does not mention where he had these Verses, I would not venture to translate them from the *Italian*, since I am not certain, whether they were not originally in *English*" (1:72). English "Ladies" who do not read Italian still need to know what the verses say. Is the "I" Carter, or is this, as perhaps was the introduction of Fairfax and Creech, more Birch pedantry? In fairness to Birch it must be said that Carter is often timorous. A similar although not identical situation occurs in *Epictetus* in chapter 26: "The Text is so very corrupt in some Parts of this Chapter, that the Translation must have been wholly conjectural; and therefore is omitted" (87). Also, when Carter has passages from Homer in *Epictetus*, she uses Pope's translation. See pp. 301, 303, 312, and 417, for example.

49. Birch too may have assisted Carter in some way on the *Examination*. It is likely that he had known Carter for several years through their association with Cave. In letters to Cave of 24 June and 31 July 1738 Carter sends "compliments to . . . Mr Birch & Mr Johnson," but it is only on 8 August 1738 that she is deemed of sufficient importance to be first entered in his diary. At this time Carter must have been translating the *Examen*. If

tioned, Carter was responsible for the translation itself, including turning Silhouette's French prose rendition of Pope's verse into English prose. Although the preliminary announcements for the *Examination* in September 1738 indicate that it would be published "With Remarks by the Translator," this phrase is omitted from all later advertisements. Carter presumably completed the translation before 26 September 1738, but without remarks.[50] The translation has remarks, however, and evidence suggests that it was Johnson who added them, in the same manner he added "Annotations" to his own *Commentary*.[51]

The *Examination*, like Forman's *Commentary*, substitutes Pope's verses for Crousaz's quotations from the French prose translation of Silhouette. In some instances Pope's verses are inserted in the text and in others placed in footnotes. Johnson at this period was one of the "miners in literature" for Cave, translating, writing occasional pieces in prose and verse, and handling a variety of editorial chores, including revising the parliamentary debates. As Kaminski has shown, much of Johnson's work for Cave had little to do with the *Gentleman's Magazine*.[52] Johnson would have been the logical person to have gone through Carter's prose translation, inserting Pope's verse into the text and footnotes, especially since he was doing the same thing for his own *Commentary* about that time.

V

Crousaz's examination of the first epistle of the *Essay on Man* fills pages 1–112 (or B1 through L2) of Carter's translation of the *Examination*. All five of the cancel leaves are in this portion of the text. It is surely no coincidence that Forman's *Commentary* also happens to cover only the first epistle. Of

---

Birch gave her any assistance, other than encouragement, it could only have been with the French translation, as the footnotes are in Johnson's style. Judging by Birch's assistance on the Algarotti, had he annotated Crousaz we might have expected footnotes on Homer and the wrath of Achilles (5), Leibnitz (16), the minister in Scotland who assassinated his son (27), Mr. Collins's *Essay on Liberty* (38), etc. See Barker, 264, 275; Ruhe, 499. The two letters are included in Hampshire, "Carter's Unpublished Letters."

50. As in the case of *Examination, Sir Isaac Newton's Philosophy Explain'd for the Use of the Ladies* does not have Elizabeth Carter's name, or a mention of remarks or notes by the translator, on the title page. The title page of *All the Works of Epictetus* reads: "Translated from the Original GREEK. By *ELIZABETH CARTER*. WITH An INTRODUCTION, and NOTES, by the TRANSLATOR."

51. The title page to the *Commentary* reads, "Some Annotations by the Translator." The announcement for the *Commentary* in the *Daily Advertiser* for 23 November and on the verso of the last leaf of the *Examination* say, "some cursory Observations by the Translator."

52. "Of these men it may be said that they were miners in literature, they worked, though not in darkness, under ground; their motive was gain; their labor silent and incessant" (Hawkins, *Life*, 219). See Kaminksi, Chapter 3 ("A Miner in Literature"), for an excellent account of Johnson's activities during this period. Johnson mentions his involvement in a variety of editorial activities in a letter to Cave of late August (*Letters*, 1:18–20).

the eleven footnotes occurring in the rest of the books, covering the other three epistles (pp. 113–227), nine are verses from Pope without commentary.[53] Of the two remaining, one in the final gathering informs the reader "The *Illinois* are a People of *North America*" and the second is a quotation from Du Resnel's verse translation with which Johnson was familiar, even though it is unlikely he had reached this far in his translation of the *Commentaire*. The text says, "Prepared by the Effect of Poetic Prose, when he begins his third Epistle with calling me *bounded man!**" to which a note has been added: "**Apprens, Homme borné, que le maitre du monde. Resnel*'s French Translation."[54] Of the thirteen footnotes to the first epistle, eleven are verses from Pope—seven with commentary, and four without.[55] Some of the comments are simple: "*Mr* Pope'*s Words are*," "*Mr Crousaz has this Distich in view*," "See the subsequent verses," "See Mr *Pope*'s *Universal Prayer*, the third Stanza," and "The whole Passage stands thus."[56] One footnote simply defines "*Conscientia sui*" as "*Consciousness*."[57]

Two of the footnotes that introduce passages of Pope's verse are more critical, much in the style Johnson uses in the *Commentary*: "I suppose the following Lines are alluded to; perhaps the Remarker strains them a little too much" (28, D2^v), and "Had the ingenious Author of the Examination regarded the Whole of this Passage, which he so much objects to, and not only a Part of it, he would perhaps have given a more favourable Interpretation" (67–68, G4^{r-v}).

The final two footnotes provide an even more detailed critical commentary on the text. On the passage from the first epistle of the *Essay on Man* beginning "Presumptuous Man! the reason wouldst thou find, / Why form'd so weak, so little, and so blind!" (ll. 35–36), which Crousaz, of course, read in Silhouette's French prose translation,[58] Crousaz observes (here in Carter's translation):

We are very far from being nothing but Weakness; for, with regard to the Body, Man has invented Machines, by the Means of which he can lift and transport Burdens too heavy for the strongest Animal; and as to the Mind, to what a Length have Discoveries already been carried, and how large a Way is opened for those who are willing to use their Endeavours to extend them farther!

The Terms, *little* and *great*, are relative Terms; this is so true, that we are at the same time both very great and very little: Nor is this peculiar to us; there are no

53. The footnotes occur on p. 115 (L4^r), p. 121 (M1^r), p. 143 (N6^r), p. 153 (O5^r), p. 165 (P5^r), p. *168* (P6^v), p. 192 (R6^v), p. 206 (T1^v), and p. 211 (T4^r).

54. The first of these footnotes is on p. 218 (U1^v) and the second is on p. 138 (N3^v).

55. The footnotes without commentary are on p. 66 (G3^v), p. 72 (G6^v), p. 98 (K1^v), and p. 99 (K2^r).

56. The first two footnotes occur on p. 7 (B4^r) and the others on p. 10 (B5^v), p. 29 (D3^r), and p. 71 (G6^r).

57. The footnote is on p. 41 (E3^r).

58. "Homme présomptueux, prétens-tu découvrir la raison d'où vient que tu as été formé si foible, si petit, si aveugle?" See *Essais sur la critique et sur l'homme* (A Londres, 1737), 104. This is no. 19 in Audra. According to Audra this is the second London edition and the first to have Pope's verse facing the French prose translation. For convenience of the reader, quotations from the *Essay on Man* are taken from the Twickenham Edition.

Objects but what are at the same Time infinitely great and infinitely little. As to that Blindness which Mr *Pope* imputes to us, the Expression is strong, but metaphorical. We are not born blind, nay, have the immediate Use of our Eyes. With regard to our Understanding, 'tis true, we are born likewise with an Ability of extricating ourselves from it. It is in our Power to produce in ourselves a Knowledge capable of enlightening us; we are born very imperfect, but with the rich and invaluable Present of being able ourselves to work out our own Perfection.

I will add too (but by the way) that the Question why we are form'd so weak, so little, and so blind, may be interpreted in all ill Sense; for 'tis to ourselves that we ought to impute our *(a)* Errors.

To this passage is appended the following footnote:

(a) Mr *Pope* in this Place considers Man only in his *natural* State, and does not speak of his *moral* Defects. Nor does he at all dissent from *Solomon*, in describing Man as weak, and little, and blind; for so he certainly is, when compared with Beings of a superior Rank, and yet may be very perfect in his own. For (as Mr *Crousaz* observ'd of *great* and *little*) Perfection is a relative Term, and varies its Signification according as it is differently apply'd. (14, cancel C1^v)

Later Crousaz takes objection to this passage by Pope:

> In Pride, in reas'ning Pride, our error lies;
> All quit their sphere, and rush into the skies.
> Pride still is aiming at the blest abodes,
> Men would be Angels, Angels would be Gods.
> Aspiring to be Gods, if Angels fell,
> Aspiring to be Angels, Men rebel;
> And who but wishes to invert the laws
> Of ORDER, sins against th'Eternal Cause. (123–130)[59]

After devoting a paragraph to *pride* and a discussion of the need for man to be thankful "that he is the Work of the eternal and perfect Being," Crousaz observes that man

ought to neglect no Means of being assured of the Will of his Creator, in order to conform his own to it. His Desires ought continually to be bent on improving himself more and more *(a)*, and rend'ring himself every Day more virtuous. He receiv'd these Talents from the Author of his Life. Wou'd this infinitely wise Author, and who never acts casually, and without an End, have given him Leave to make no use of them? At seeing such a Resolution, shall we cry out, ———— *What Pride! This Man is never content.*

To this passage is appended the following footnote:

(a) Mr *Crousaz* certainly argues very justly, upon the Necessity of Men's improving the Talents which they have received from their Creator; but there does not seem to be any thing in the Passage he cited from Mr *Pope*, that at all contradicts this. For does his exclaiming against the Pride and Folly of *Mortals*, in aspiring to the Perfection of *Angels*, at all imply that they are not to look upon themselves

59. "Nos erreurs ont leur source dans les raisonnemens de l'orgueil. On sort de sa sphere & l'on s'élance vers les Cieux. L'orgueil a toûjours en vue les demeures célestes: les hommes voudroient être des Anges, & les Anges des Dieux. Si les Anges qui ont aspiré à être Dieux sont tombés, les hommes qui aspirent à être Anges, se rendent coupables de rebellion. Qui ose seulement souhaiter de renverser les loix de l'ordre, peche contre la cause éternelle" (*Essais*, 111).

as *Men?* and act agreeably to that Rank in the Creation wherein they are placed? (78, H3ᵛ)

Not only is the technique for footnoting similar to that used by Johnson in his *Commentary*, but there are occasional verbal echoes as well. The *Examination* introduces a quotation from Pope with *"Mr Pope's Words are"* (7), repeated exactly in the *Commentary* (62), and with slight variations such as "Mr *Pope* only says" (28, 141) and "Mr *Pope* has only these Words" (89). The *Examination* introduces another quotation from Pope with "The whole Passage stands thus" (71). "Stands thus" appears in a footnote in Johnson's translation of Du Resnel's Preface, included at the end of the *Commentary* (308); it is repeated in another footnote as "his Argument against Mr *Pope* seems to stand thus" (32), with a variation on the use of "thus" later in the *Commentary*, "Mr. POPE *thus concludes his first* EPISTLE" (83). One of the footnotes on a cancel leaf in the *Examination* concludes, "Perfection is a relative Term, and varies its Signification according as it is differently apply'd" (14); "signification" appears in a similar sense in a footnote to the *Commentary* (63), as does "signifies" (32). The two longer footnotes, which provide critical commentary on the text, share a common phrase, "at all." The first footnote says, "Nor does he at all dissent from *Solomon*" and the second "For does . . . aspiring to the Perfection of *Angels*, at all imply." This phrase does not appear elsewhere in the *Examination*. Johnson sometimes uses it when translating "ne . . . point," as "not at all unhappy" for "n'est point malheureux" (137). Crousaz's "Il ne faut donc pas s'étonner" (5) is translated as "It is therefore not at all surprising" (iv) and Du Resnel's "S'il est permis de flater les Hommes" is translated as "If it be at all allowable to flatter Men" (315). Altogether "at all" appears fourteen times in the *Commentary*.[60]

The instance in which *"Conscientia sui"* is defined in a footnote would seem to be another manifestation of Johnson's hand. Although the Latin phrase *"Conscientia sui"* appears in Crousaz's *Examen*, the footnote with a definition as *"Consciousness"* does not. When Johnson turned to editing the texts of Browne, Ascham, and Shakespeare, he frequently annotated them by defining a word or words which he thought the reader would not understand.[61]

A more important sign of Johnson's hand in editing the *Examination* is the quotation in a footnote from Du Resnel's French verse translation, *"Ap-*

60. See the *Commentary*, pp. iv, 25, 82, 124, 137, 157, 169, 192, 223, 244, 272, 310, 315, 317; *Commentaire* (Geneve, 1738), pp. 5, 29, 130, 181, 196, 217, 229, 251, 285, 309, 340; Du Resnel, *Les Principes de la morale et du goût*, "Discours preliminaire du traducteur" (Paris, 1737), pp. xxi, xxxiii, xxxviii. Footnotes do not follow these forms in Algarotti's *Il Newtonianisimo per le Dame*, translated and edited about the same time. The annotations to *Epictetus* were written much later and present special problems as they incorporate material from several contributors.

61. O M Brack, Jr., "Samuel Johnson Edits for the Booksellers: Sir Thomas Browne's 'Christian Morals' (1756) and 'The English Works of Roger Ascham' (1761)," *University of Texas Library Chronicle* 21 (1991): 13–39.

prens, Homme borné, que le maitre du monde" (3.2) to explain *"bounded Man"* (138). Du Resnel's translation is quoted in its entirety in Johnson's *Commentary*, with a literal line-for-line English translation. *"Homme borné"* appears in Crousaz's *Examen*, indicating that he also consulted Du Resnel's verse translation, which he was later to use in his *Commentaire*, for nothing resembling it appears in Silhouette's prose version.[62] The footnote, however, does not appear in Crousaz's *Examen*, but was added to the *Examination* by Johnson. In the *Commentary* Johnson translates Du Resnel's second line of epistle three as "Learn, bounded man, that the master of the world" (158). Perhaps Carter in the text of the *Examen* chose to translate "borné" as "bounded" instead of "limited," "confined," "restrained," or "restricted," but a more likely explanation would be that Johnson was at work here.

There are three footnotes in the *Examination* that are extensive enough to argue they are in Johnson's style and more nearly resemble those he was writing for the *Commentary*. One of the three occurs on a cancel leaf and all are marked with an *"(a)"* instead of the usual asterisks and obelisks used not only in the text elsewhere to mark footnotes, but also, by Cave, in the *Gentleman's Magazine* and in Johnson's *Commentary*. Of all the footnotes on cancel leaves, only two passages from Pope appear with asterisks, but these markers may be holdovers from the text on the original leaves, since the remainder have *"(a)"*. A. D. Barker has demonstrated that Cave shared his printing during this period with Thomas Gardner.[63] The *Examination*, which went through Cave's press, uses asterisks and obelisks, with the exceptions noted, and *Sir Isaac Newton's Philosophy Explain'd for the Use of the Ladies*, which went through Gardner's press, uses superscript lowercase roman letters for notes, although not enclosed in parentheses. In Cave's haste to complete the printing of the *Examination*, perhaps some of the work was put out to Gardner. Gardner's compositor, familiar with a different system for footnoting, might then have introduced the letter designations himself, although it is possible that he was copying what he saw in the manuscript.[64]

62. Pope's first paragraph of epistle three says,
> Here then we rest: "The Universal Cause
> "Acts to one end, but acts by various laws."
> In all the madness of superfluous health,
> The trim of pride, the impudence of wealth,
> Let this great truth be present night and day;
> But most be present, if we preach or pray.

Silhouette says, "C'est donc à ce principe que nous nous arrêtons; 'la CAUSE UNIVERSELLE n'agit que pour UNE FIN, mais elle agit par différentes loix.' Dans toute la folie que peut inspirer la santé la plus vigoureuse, dans toute la pompe de l'orgueil & l'impudence des richesses, que cette grand vérité nous soit présente jour & nuit; qu'elle nous le soit sur tout dans le tems consacré à instruire ou à prier" (143).

63. Barker, Appendix K; A. D. Barker, "The Printing and Publishing of Johnson's *Marmor Norfolciense* (1739) and *London* (1738 and 1739)," *Library* 6th ser., 3 (1981): 287–304.

64. A look at some of the works printed by Samuel Richardson points out the difficulty of trying to establish printing-house practice. *Epictetus*, printed by Richardson, uses lowercase italic letters for footnotes which he also uses, for example, in the third edition of *Clarissa* (1751). But the second volume of John Leland's *A View of the Principal Deistical*

Leaf G4, which has a footnote with a relatively lengthy introduction to a quotation from Pope, and leaf H3, which has a substantial footnote by Johnson, are both marked "*(a)*" and are not on cancel leaves. Johnson may have added the passage from Pope just before printing of gathering G began. After G was printed, Johnson had second thoughts and had leaves G3 and G6 cancelled to add three passages from Pope, passages included by Forman in his *Commentary*. The two passages on leaf G6 are also singled out for comment by Johnson in his *Commentary*.[65] If the book was being printed seriatim, perhaps printing was complete only through gathering F when Curll announced his edition of the *Commentary* on 21 November, with printing on gathering G about to proceed. Type may have been set for gathering H and, perhaps, the remainder of the volume, at least through gathering T.

Unfortunately, the watermarks are of no assistance in ordering the printing of the sheets as all the gatherings but one contain the crown and a "WB," including at least one of the cancel leaves.[66] Only gathering U has a different watermark, a fleur-de-lys and a "IV." Gathering U was probably printed near the end of the press run and has the full-page announcement for Johnson's *Commentary* as "*In the Press*" on the verso of leaf U6.

It may well have been with gathering H that Cave and Johnson decided to push "forward with the utmost expedition," for the relatively large number of errors indicates that it was printed in haste and not proofread carefully.[67] There are also signs that gathering T was rushed through the press. On the verso of leaf T1 the footnote has no obelisk in the text. Then on the recto of leaf T4 a one-line footnote, indicated with an obelisk, was added, apparently at the last minute, to the bottom of the page: "His greatest *Virtue*—his greatest *Bliss*, V.340,". To make room for the footnote the last line on the recto was moved to the top of the verso, with the penultimate line, now the last line, containing an error: "inthose." The compositor, however, failed to

---

Writers (1755) has footnotes designated by asterisks, obelisks, etc. It might be argued that since Richardson "put out" to another printer the first volume, published in 1754 with these figures for footnotes, he wished to be consistent. But the second edition of Leland's *Reflections on the Late Lord Bolingbrokes's Letters on the Study and Use of History* (1753), printed by Richardson, also uses these figures, and he had himself printed the first edition. The first volume of *The Modern Part of an Universal History* (1759), also printed by Richardson, has marginal notes with no sigla and footnotes designated in the following ways: sources used in the text have superscript lowercase roman letters, commentary by the compiler has roman capitals enclosed in parentheses, and sources used in the commentary have small arabic numerals enclosed in parentheses. See William M. Sale, Jr., *Samuel Richardson: Master Printer* (1950), 103, 184, 247–248.

65. The following passages from epistle one are added: on G3v, ll. 69–72; on G6r, ll. 91–98; on G6v, ll. 99–102. See Forman, 21, 33–34. For a discussion of the passages from Pope on G6 of the *Examination* and their appearance in Forman and in Johnson's *Commentary*, see above.

66. For example, cancel leaf G3 in the Vander Meulen copy has the crown.

67. Page 73 (H1r), l. 7: "absur'd" [absurd]; 75 (H2r), l. 11: "enter'd" [apostrophe wrong font]; 82 (H5v), l. 15: "*whon*" [*when*]; 83 (H6r), ll. 5–6: pre$_\wedge$|sided [no line-end hyphen]; 83 (H6r), l. 26: "Perfection,Knowledge" [no space after comma]; 84 (H6v), l. 20: "ver$_\wedge$ 123.that" [no period after "ver" and no space after period].

change the catchword so that it now catches the second line on the verso. The extra line added to the top of the verso of leaf T4 forced the compositor to move the last line to the top of leaf T5 recto, again forgetting to change the catchword which now catches the second line, and again failing to catch an error in the penultimate line, now the last line: "so ar" [so far].[68]

In summary, Elizabeth Carter finished her prose translation of Crousaz's *Examen* at least by 26 September 1738 and, perhaps, by 9 September when Cave made the preliminary announcement of its publication, as it was about this time she traveled to Deal with her father, returning later in the month. Johnson had seen all or part of the manuscript before 26 September, when Nicholas Carter refers to Johnson's commendation of the translation.[69] Sometime, probably early November, Johnson, who served as Cave's editor on a number of projects, revised Carter's manuscript, inserted Pope's verses into the text and footnotes, and rewrote the text to accommodate the verses; printing then began. Production may have moved slowly because Cave was printing the November issue of the *Gentleman's Magazine* and a portion of volume two of the *Description of China* at the same time.[70] When Curll announced the publication of Forman's translation of the first epistle of the *Commentaire* on 21 November, the printing of the *Examination* probably had not proceeded past gathering F. Realizing that the rival publication of the *Commentary* did, in fact, have "Remarks," Cave and Johnson made hurried adjustments to make the *Examination* more competitive. Footnotes were added to gatherings H, T, and perhaps others, and on the five cancel leaves. Printing proceeded on gathering G and the remainder of the volume, finally reaching gathering U with the announcement of Johnson's *Commentary* on the verso of the last leaf, the preliminary gathering A, which included the title page and perhaps one of the cancel leaves printed as A2, and the partial sheet containing the four cancel leaves. Cave and Johnson, after showing early signs of "Dilatoriness," completed the *Examination* between Curll's announcement on Tuesday, 21 November and its publication on Monday, 27 November 1738.

68. The compositor continued to have difficulties. The catchword on T5 verso is "for" but the first word on T6 recto is given incorrectly as "or" and on the third line a "to" has been omitted: "to come [to] pass."

69. "*Johnson* (as her father expressed it) 'gave it his suffrage free from bias' before it was printed." See Pennington, *Memoirs*, 45; Barker, 274.

70. Barker, Appendix K. In September Cave printed Mark Akenside's *Voice of Liberty; or A British Philippic, Dr Waterland Imitated*, Proposals for Moses Browne's *Poems on Various Subjects*, the September *Gentleman's Magazine*; in October Andrew Burrell's *Hebrew Tongue*, Proposals for Johnson's edition of the *History of the Council of Trent*, and the October *Gentleman's Magazine*.

DR. HOADLY'S 'POEMS SET TO MUSIC BY DR. GREENE'

by

KEITH MASLEN

A BROKEN and partly dismembered volume in the de Beer Collection of the University of Otago Library offers the means of expanding our understanding of the collaboration between John Hoadly, eighteenth-century poet and dramatist, and Maurice Greene, whose reputation as a musician and composer has, somewhat unfairly, been eclipsed by that of Handel. From close scrutiny of this unspectacular survival, this paper is able to identify unrecorded verse libretti and shorter poems by Hoadly. The latter are presented in full. It also offers rare details of performances and performers, of a kind not usually to be found in standard reference sources. Further, it points to new items from the press of Samuel Richardson.

The volume in question, minus covers and lacking an indeterminate quantity of leaves, fortunately retains its finely tooled leather spine and red label reading 'POEMS SET TO MUSIC BY DR. GREENE'. The fifty-eight leaves remaining, still loosely sewn in place, contain seven sets of words for musical performance, four printed and three in manuscript, plus four allied shorter poems.[1] The four separately printed works, occupying thirty-seven leaves, are *Love's revenge* (1737?), *Jephtha* (1737), *The force of truth* (1744), and *Phoebe* (1748). These are bound with twenty-one intercalated leaves on which have been written three other works of similar character, 'The Choice of Hercules . . . 1740', 'Love's Artifice', no date, and 'The Song of Moses . . . 1743', as well as four short poems in manuscript, relating to three of the printed works. The handwriting throughout the volume, on the intercalated leaves and here and there in the printed works, is Hoadly's own.[2] A summary of the contents of the whole volume as it stands is given in the notes.[3]

1. Its full library classification is ZDU: Eb 1737 H—ZDU for New Zealand, Dunedin, and University of Otago respectively. The remains are enclosed in a wrapper bearing the bookplate of the de Beer Collection, the words 'The Gift of E. S. de Beer Esq.', and in pencil 'I. A. Williams' Collection', also the accession number [19]73–18724. The front and back covers are missing; the leather spine, elaborately gold-tooled, retains its red label with the words 'POEMS SET TO MUSIC BY DR. GREENE'. The largely intact head-band projecting some 5 mm to one side of the remaining leaves shows that a quantity of leaves, perhaps as many as 16 to 24, are missing at the front. Leaf size (trimmed) is a uniform 195 by 125 mm, save for *The force of truth*, which is 195 by 121 mm.

2. The handwriting has been checked against Hoadly's autograph letter of 'Sepr. 6th. 1763'—see footnote 14—and by Miss Pamela J. Willetts, Department of Manuscripts, British Library, who compared a photograph of the 'Sonnet in Imitation of Milton' with BL. Add. MS. 35612. (Miss Willett's letter of 6 March 1961 is held with ZDU: Eb 1737 H.

3. It will be helpful to summarise the several contents of ZDU: Eb 1737 H in due order.

The four printed works and 'The Choice of Hercules' name Dr. Greene as composer of the music. Maurice Greene, born 1696, died 1755, held a number of the plum musical posts in London, and from 1735 was Master of the King's Music. Unfortunately, none of his music is included, and indeed none is known to exist for *The force of truth* or for the three libretti in manuscript.

Who wrote the words? The anonymous author of the printed works and 'The Choice of Hercules' is well known to have been Dr. John Hoadly. Three of the four shorter poems are signed J. Hoadly. Hoadly, born 1711, died 1776, was youngest son of Benjamin, the controversial bishop of Bangor, and brother to Benjamin, author of the hugely successful comedy *The suspicious husband*, whose title role was one of Garrick's favourite parts. In 1735 John took holy orders and, thanks to his father's considerable powers of patronage, at once became chaplain to the Prince of Wales. Thereafter, his life was that of fashionable clergyman, able through his passion for the theatre tastefully to administer sound moral doctrine mixed with a great deal of sweetness. John's collaboration with Maurice Greene during the 1730s and 1740s in private theatrical entertainments is vividly recorded in the Francis Hayman portrait of 1747, now in the National Portrait Gallery, London.[4] Here Greene is depicted sitting, with his hand on a copy of their latest joint production, *Phoebe*, while Hoadly stands modestly behind.

What do the several bibliographical facts imply? Surely that this was Hoadly's own book, that all the shorter poems and all seven libretti were his own compositions. It may further be inferred that all seven were set to music by Greene and that the title on the spine means what it says. Presumably Hoadly, perhaps after his fruitful collaboration had come to an end—possibly in 1749, when Greene retired because of worsening health—decided to gather

---

A. χ1r,v 'Dedication of ye. Pastoral of Love's Revenge to Diana Duchess of Bedford' (2 pp.); χ2r,v 'To James Harris Esqre. of Salisbury' (2 pp.)

B. *A*2 B–D2 E1, *Love's Revenge*, [1737]

C. A–B4, *Jephtha*, 1737

D. χ1r–χ6r, 'The Choice of Hercules . . . 1740' (11 pp.); χ6v, 'To Mrs. Bowes with ye. *Force of truth*' (1 p.)

E. A8, *The force of truth*, 1744

F. χ1r–χ2r (χ2v blank), 'To the most Honourable the Marchioness Grey' (3 pp. of text, 1 blank)

G. A–C4 D2, *Phoebe*, 1748

H. χ1r (χ1v blank) χ2r,v 2χ4 3χ1r,v (3χ2r,v blank), 'Love's Artifice' (13 pp. of text, 3 blank); 3χ3r-4v 4χ1r,v, 'The Song of Moses . . . 1743' (6 pp.)

The twenty-one unprinted leaves, described in sections A, D, F, and H, presumably added at the time of binding (with others now missing), all have horizontal chain lines, and they represent two stocks of Britannia paper. The first two leaves are distinguished by showing, in appropriate places, a Britannia watermark with motto. The remaining nineteen leaves, distributed in three sets of six and two and eleven, are distinguished by a Britannia watermark without motto and the prominent countermark 'C. TAYLOR'.

4. The painting is reproduced in the article on Greene in *The New Grove dictionary of music and musicians*, ed. Stanley Sadie (1980), vol. 7.

into one volume all his poems to music by Greene, both printed and unprinted. That Hoadly transcribed the manuscript pieces *after* the volume had been bound may be seen from his insertion of final punctuation below extra full lines of verse, when room ran out in the outer margin. A question arises from the obvious fact that the University of Otago volume has been partly and clumsily dismembered, leaving occasional stubs. Did it once hold other sets of words by Hoadly for music by Greene?

To analyze in greater detail the works in this volume, it is perhaps easier to begin with the printed ones. Even these offer some points of new information: details of performances and performers (scarce for this period) written in by Hoadly, and discovery of the identity of the printer of two of the printed items. The present whereabouts of all four University of Otago copies has recently been recorded in the Eighteenth Century Short Title Catalogue, two with the cryptic rider that they contain manuscript notes by the author. (As of January 1994, ESTC records the existence of other copies of the four works in these editions as follows: *Love's revenge* ([1737])—two copies; *Jephtha* (1737)—three copies; *The force of truth* (1744)—four copies; *Phoebe* (1748)—seven copies.)

These four copies are briefly described below, in order of their position in the volume.

1. *Love's revenge; a dramatic pastoral, in two interludes. Written in the Year, 1736* [*sic*]. *Set to music by Dr. Greene. 1737.* Winchester: Printed and Sold by W. Greenville [1737?]. The four characters are Cupid, a satyr, Myrtillo, and Florimel, plus choruses of shepherds and shepherdesses. Hoadly has inserted the cast lists for two performances. One was sung 'at Dr. Greene's House, by Miss Ayliffe. Dr. Greene. Mrs. Hastings. Miss Gilbert afterwards Mrs. Bowes'. Note that on this occasion the composer himself sang the part of satyr. The other performance was 'at The Academy in ye. Apollo. [with] Mr. Lloyd. Mr. [William] Savage. Mr. Mence ['Abbott' scored through]. Mr. Bailley'.[5] The shepherds and shepherdesses were represented by 'Gentlemen of ye. King's Chapel, and St. Paul's Choir'. Greene had been organist at St. Paul's since 1718, and at the Chapel Royal since 1727. Roger Fiske has already noted the 'extraordinary' use of an all-male cast on some occasion or other, reporting a copy in the Royal College of Music, but he could only suppose that 'for some strange reason either the Society of Apollo or the Three Choirs Festival sometimes favoured concert performances with all-male soloists' (p. 178). Hoadly's annotations in the Otago copy indicate that the men sang in the Apollo Room of the Devil Tavern, Temple Bar. This was the meeting-place of the Apollo Society, founded in 1731 by Maurice Greene and Michael Festing as a place where music other than Handel's and

---

5. Identification of some of the singers has been made from *The London stage 1660–1800: a calendar of plays, entertainments & afterpieces together with casts, box-receipts and contemporary comment, compiled from the playbills, newspapers and theatrical diaries of the period, Part 3: 1729–1747*, vol. 2, ed. Arthur H. Scouten (1961), and from Roger Fiske, *English theatre music in the eighteenth century*, 2nd edn (1986), p. 178.

the Italian opera could be performed—hence the remark attributed to Handel, 'De toctor Creen is gone to the tefel'.[6]

2. *Jephtha, an oratorio. In two parts. Compos'd by Dr. Greene.* London; Printed in the Year MDCCXXXVII. Again, Hoadly has noted a performance 'at ye. Academy in the Apollo' and filled in the cast list: Jephtha, by 'Mr. Abbott', Jephtha's daughter by 'Mrs. Lampe', First and Second Elder of Gilead, 'Mr. Whaley. Mr. Cheriton', Chorus, 'Gentlemen and Boys of ye. K's Chapel'. Mrs. Lampe is no doubt Isabella, née Young, newly married wife of John Frederick Lampe (Fiske, p. 631).

3. *The force of truth. An oratorio. Set to Music by Dr. Greene.* ['1743' inserted in MS.] London; Printed in the year MDCCXLIV. Hoadly has inserted only the names of the singers: Darius 'Savage', First Persian Youth 'Lloyd', choruses sung by 'Gentn. & Boys of ye. Kings Chapel, & St. Pauls Choir'.

The printer's ornaments are those used by Samuel Richardson. They include ornaments number 3 (insert only), used on the title page, and numbers 8, 57, and 103, as reproduced in William Sale, *Samuel Richardson: master printer* (1950); also two other ornaments among the four hundred or so Richardson ornaments identified by Maslen (to be reproduced in his forthcoming revision of Sale). *Jephtha* is not listed by Sale.

4. *Phoebe. A pastoral opera. Set to music by Dr. Greene.* London: Printed in the Year M.DCC.XLVIII. Hoadly has added 'Perform'd at ye. Academy' and identified the singers: Amyntas 'Mr. Savage' (with 'Mence' scored through), Linco 'Mr Wasse' ('Savage' scored through), Sylvio 'Mr. Beard' ('Bailley' scored through), Phoebe and Celia 'Mr. Jones', choruses 'Gentlemen & Boys of the K's. Chapel, & St. Paul's Choir'. Mr. Beard must be John Beard, the celebrated tenor.

Again, the printer's ornaments are those used by Samuel Richardson. They include numbers 16 and 51—the latter on the title-page—as reproduced by William Sale, as well as five other Richardson ornaments as identified by Maslen. *Phoebe* is not listed by Sale.

Hoadly's annotations in the printed copies are the least of his manuscript contributions to the volume. Next to be considered are the four short poems written on added leaves and prefixed to three of the printed pieces. All are apparently unpublished, except for ten lines of a version of the second poem, referred to below. The first is a 'Dedication of ye. Pastoral of Love's Revenge to Diana, Duchess of Bedford' in twenty-four lines of octosyllabics.[7] The

---

6. Quoted in *Händel-Handbuch* (1985), 4.263.

7. In all the transcriptions long s has been modernised, superscript letters brought down, hyphens regularised, and line numbers added. The text is as follows:

> Madam,
> The Sigher of Arcadia's Plain
> (As Stories tell, or Poets feign)
> When Chloe's gone, to kill the Hours,
> Stroles round the Fields & gathers Flow'rs,
> 5   And of his Myrtles, Pinks, & Roses
> A Crown for Chloe's Head composes.

second, containing twenty-two lines of octosyllabics, is addressed 'To James Harris Esqre. of Salisbury, with the following Pastoral, and the Music in Score. 1743'.[8] The 'following Pastoral' is the copy of the Winchester edition of *Love's revenge*, presumably printed in 1737. Clive T. Probyn, in *The sociable humanist: the life and works of James Harris 1709–1780* (1991), quotes ten lines of a variant copy of this poem from British Library Add. MSS 37683, with line 2 reading 'No sweeter Harris than of your Mind' instead of 'No sweeter notes, than of the Mind'.[9] Probyn supposes that the 'Pastoral'

But vain is all his Art & Care,
Vain the Beauty that They wear,
Vain their Hue, their fragrant Breath,
10   Unless his Fair accept the Wreath:
Unless his Chloe deign to take 'em
Their fragrant Breath & Hue forsake 'em.
    O Bedford, shou'd You thus refuse
This humble Garland of the Muse,
15   Or view it with neglectfull Eye,
The little Bloom it boasts would die;
Each Flow'r would mourn ye. absent Ray,
And ev'ry Beauty fade away.
    But if in the fantastic Twine
20   Some Blossom should superior shine,
Some fav'rite Sprig your Eye shd. meet
Pure, innocent, and simply-sweet,
Accept the All the Muse can give,
—Add new Grace, and bid it live.
                  J. Hoadly.

8. The text is as follows:

Friendship is Musick—and we find
No sweeter Notes, than of The Mind.
The Thracian Youth ye. Woods among,
Made Hearts of Oak attend his Song;
5   Quarries obey'd Amphion's Call,
And danc'd into the Theban Wall.
These shew'd the Virtue of their Strings
On Stocks, & Stones, & senseless Things;
But You, great Master of the Lyre,
10   To nobler Harmony aspire:
You, by Analogy divine,
Can Sounds to moral Truths refine,
This universal Fabrick scan,
And read The Harmony of Man:
15   Can see the Parts in Concert roll,
And join to form One beauteous Whole;
And in angelic Strains can raise
The great *Composing Spirit's* Praise.
    Thence, (if such mean Relief need be)
20   Look down on *Greene*, & think on *Me*,
And own a Friend like Musick finds
In skillfull Notes and equal Minds.
                  J. Hoadly.

9. Oxford (1991), p. 77. I am grateful to Professor Probyn for sending me a transcript of the full text of the British Library version, and for other advice and encouragement.

was 'almost certainly *Phoebe: A Pastoral set to music by Dr. Greene* (1748)', and that 'the poem was also by Hoadly'. Certainly, in this Otago copy, Hoadly claims the lines as his, but it now appears that the pastoral was *Love's revenge*, perhaps in a copy of this very Winchester edition, and that the gift was made in '1743', which was presumably also the date of composition of these lines.

The third little poem, an Italian sonnet written on the verso of a leaf immediately preceding *The force of truth*, is addressed 'To Mrs. Bowes with ye. *Force of Truth, an Oratorio. Sonnet in Imitation of Milton*'. The first line is 'O *Florimel*, whose tunefull Skill once gave'—the full text is given in the notes.[10] 'Florimel' flatteringly recalls Mrs. Bowes' performance of this role in the production of *Love's revenge* held at Dr. Greene's house—see above.

The fourth poem, fifty lines of octosyllabic couplets occupying most of the two leaves immediately preceding *Phoebe*, is addressed 'To the most Honourable the Marchioness Grey, with my Pastoral Opera of Phoebe, set to Musick by Dr. Greene'.[11] Its text begins 'From polish'd Circles of ye. Fair, / From gilded Domes, and tainted Air . . .'. The full text is given in the notes.[12]

10. The text is as follows:

> O *Florimel*, whose tunefull Skill once gave
> To Verse of mine such Harmony & Grace,
> 　　With Innocence of Mind & Voice & Face,
> 　　Mixing thy Rill with my Castalian Wave;
> 5　Now that your virgin Hand you given have
> 　　To thy *Myrtillo* in that Holy Place,
> 　　Let artfull Fuges renew ye. harmonious Chase,
> 　　And Musick's ev'ry Charm his Heart enslave.
> 　　Of Verse & Harmony the Muses join'd
> 10　Shall teach him (Knowledge seen but of the Few,)
> 　　Great in his Works ye. *God of Truth* to find,
> 　　　And praise that Greatness greatly shewn in you:
> 　　There see ye. nobler *Temple* of the Mind,
> 　　　And own ye. *Force of Truth & Beauty* too.
> 　　Octr. 30, 1743.　　　　　J. Hoadly.

This poem was printed, perhaps for the first time, 'in the Year M.CM.LXI. at the Press Room, Department of English [University of Otago].'

11. Jemima, marchioness Grey and baroness Lucas of Crudwell, first daughter of John Campbell, third earl of Breadalbane, was born 9 October 1722, and married 22 May 1740 to Philip Yorke, second earl of Hardwicke (*Complete Peerage*, 1926, 6.118–119).

12. The text is as follows:

> 　　From polish'd Circles of ye. Fair,
> 　　From gilded Domes, and tainted Air,
> 　　From Pleasures toilsome, Time a Load
> 　　Retirement but from Croud to Croud;
> 5　Where Love but drives a Trade at best,
> 　　(An Alley-Broker He profess'd)
> 　　Not giving corresponding Hearts,
> 　　But chaff'ring with his golden Darts;
> 　　Where Innocence the World amazes,
> 10　(A Face scarce known in publick Places,)
> 　　But rather loves—at Home—to share

There is much more. The dedicatory poems already described take up a mere eight pages. On the remaining thirty (discounting blanks) Hoadly has transcribed fair copies of three libretti: two masques and a Biblical verse paraphrase. The first of these, placed in chronological order immediately after *Jephtha*, is 'The Choice of Hercules, A Mask, set to Musick by Dr. Greene, 1740'. The second, placed after *Phoebe*—and therefore arguably later —is the undated, and apparently unreported, 'Love's Artifice, A Mask. Set to Musick by [space left blank]'. At the very end of the volume comes 'The Song of Moses paraphrased for Musick from Exod: Chr. 15, 1743', also seemingly unreported.

'The Choice of Hercules' between pleasure and virtue obviously required much deliberation. Hercules was sung by 'Mr. Abbot', Virtue by 'Mrs. Lampe',

One Corner of St. James's Square—
  Far hence permit the simple Swain
To lead Thee to the guiltless Plain,
15 Where Phoebe innocent and gay,
Dares with the dangerous Passion play;
And Celia, uninstructed Maid,
Stoops her pure Cause Herself to plead.
Nor scornfully wilt Thou disdain
20 The Shepherd's Pastimes pure tho' plain.
Thou, (whose well-cultivated Mind
Nor for Enjoyment too refin'd,
Nor Other's Woes to feel too wise,
Knows all but Nature to despise,)
25 Serene shalt teach the madding Train,
False Pleasure is but real Pain.
Superior to her Syren-Song
Prudent Thou glid'st the Stream along,
Not heedless of the Baits of Youth,
30 But steddy to the Pilot, Truth.
With Her upon the Helm advanc'd
In purer Joys Thou sit'st intranc'd,
And seest with Pity and Amaze
The voluntary Herds, that graze
35 Th'inchanted Shore of Circe's Isle,
Transform'd so foully by her Smile.
  Lady from all their painted Pride,
Come, let the Shepherd be thy Guide—
He'll lead Thee to the Fountain's Brink,
40 Where the Sylvan Muses drink;
Whose spotless & translucent Face
Heaven reflects with Heav'n's own Grace,
And pure by Nature's Arts refin'd
Presents a Mirror to thy Mind.
45   He'll lead Thee, (go with Him along)
Where Greene's sweet Muse attunes her Song,
And plays her not unusual Part,
Mixing Simplicity with Art:
Thy Genius shall according move,
50 And self-approving Her approve.

Pleasure by 'Miss Young', and followers of these two were represented by
'Gentn. & Boys of ye. Kg's. Chapel'. The piece begins and ends this way:

> Scene, a wild Wood. / Hercules enters alone. / Recitative.
> Whither hath roving Thought my Steps misled?
> How wild this Gloom! How awefull is this Shade!
>
> . . . .
>
> His Memory lives in godlike Minds,
> Himself enroll'd amongst ye. Gods a God.

Following the verse, Hoadley has written, 'Taken from Prodicus in Xeno-
phon, and from Silius Italicus'.

This is evidently the work in four scenes generally known as 'The Judgment of Hercules'. Roger Fiske, in discussing the 'popularity in the 1740s of
this triangular theme', tentatively gives priority to this version by Greene,
with its libretto 'probably' by John Hoadly.[13] According to Fiske, the title
'The Choice of Hercules' belongs to an undated, unpublished, and perhaps
unperformed cantata by John Stanley, as well as to Handel's 'interlude' of
1751. However, here Hoadly himself, perhaps in the late 1740s, has also
chosen to call his work by that name.

'Love's Artifice' is a pastoral drama in four scenes. The 'Persons represented' are Camacho the Rich, Basilius the Poor, Quiteria, and Friends of
Camacho, and Friends of Basilius, forming the two choruses. The first scene
is 'a Bower artfully decorated for the Nuptials of Quiteria and Camacho'—
there can be no doubt how the plot will shape. 'The Subject is taken from
Don Quixote, Book 2. of ye. 2 Part, Chap. 2, 3, and 4th'. Friends of Camacho
begin:

> Yon fleecy Wealth more white than Snow,
> Those countless Herds, that feed below,
> Quiteria scorns no more.

The text concludes with a 'Grand Chorus' of Basilius's Friends.

> Live, happy Pair, ye. Force to prove
> Of plighted Vows, and mutual love!
>
> Content shall on your Cottage smile,
> And honest Labour Want beguile;
> While Avarice, in Excess unbless'd,
> Shall sad Camacho's Roofs infess'd [sic]
> Live, happy Pair, ye. Force to prove
> Of plighted Vows, & mutual Love.

Hoadly's failure to assign a date or to state who set the words to music is
unsettling. Does this perhaps mean that it was not in fact set to music, but
only intended to be, and never performed? The absence of information in
The London stage proves nothing, for works by Greene and Hoadly privately
performed at the Apollo Society were unlikely to be publicly advertised.

13. Fiske, pp. 199–200. The standard literary account of this theme is Maren-Sofie
Røstvig, 'Tom Jones and the Choice of Hercules', in *Fair forms: Essays in English literature
from Spenser to Jane Austen*, ed. Maren-Sofie Røstvig (1975), pp. 147–177.

'The Song of Moses . . . 1743' would seem to be a more fitting creation for the ecclesiastical Chancellor of Winchester. The 'Persons represented are Moses. Miriam. Chorus of Israelites. Chorus of Virgins'. The first chorus, of Moses and Israelites, begins:

> Praise be to God, and God alone,
> Who hath his Pow'r wth Glory shewn!

The finale, by the Grand Chorus, ends:

> To Ages shalt Thou stretch thy Sway,
> Thy Reign be one eternal Day!
> Who mad'st the Sea all Ægypt's Tomb,
> While, safe within its watry Womb,
> Thou bad'st all Israel take his dryshod Way.
>   Da Capo.
>   The end.

What of the missing leaves, whose original existence is revealed by the length of the head-band and a few remaining fragments in the spine, showing the excision to have been rather brutal? Had Hoadly written on these perhaps other of his words for music by Dr. Greene? The note on Hoadly in John Nichols's *Literary anecdotes* (3.141–143) lists five dramas written by Hoadly: '1. "The Contrast," a comedy, acted at Lincoln's-inn Fields, 1731, but not printed. 2. "Love's Revenge," a pastoral, 1737. 3. "Phoebe," another pastoral, 1748. 4. "Jephtha," an oratorio, 1737. 5. And another, intituled, "The Force of Truth," 1764.'—a slip for 1744. 'The Contrast' seems not to have been printed, nor would it have contained words 'set to music'. (Nichols seems not to have known the 1734 edition of *Love's revenge*.) Nichols continues: 'He left several dramatic Works in MS. behind him; and among the rest, "The House-keeper, a Farce," . . . together with a tragedy on a religious subject'. Nichols further remarks that the 'tragedy was on the story of Lord Cromwell, and he once intended to give it to the stage'. A subjoined letter of Hoadly to William Bowyer the younger, dated August 1st 1765, explains that it was Garrick's retirement which finally put an end to any idea that Hoadly might with propriety 'break through the prudery of my profession, and (in my station in the Church) produce a play upon the Stage'. Another, presumably unpublished, letter from Hoadly to Bowyer (the recipient may now be clearly identified) dated 'Sepr. 6th. 1763' shows further that Hoadly had been hoping not only to have this 'historical Tragedy on the Fate of ye. great & good Lord Cromwell, the great Promoter of the Reformation in England', produced on the stage by Garrick, but to have it printed by Bowyer and to give him the copyright, thus 'acknowledging not merely by Words, the Sense I have of the Obligations due to Mr. Bowyer as mine and my Father's Friend'.[14] Clearly this too was no poem for setting to music.

14. The original is in the Harvard Theatre Collection, Harvard College Library. I thank the Curator of the Harvard Theatre Collection, Dr. Jeanne T. Newlin, for permission to quote from this letter. The recipient is not identified in the catalogue entry. The Bowyers, father and son, printed much for Hoadly's father, the bishop, but the only printing done

One is left wondering what other 'dramatic Works in MS.', if any, Hoadly wrote that might once have been present in this volume. Nevertheless, his own collection, depleted as it seems to be, is a valuable reminder of a poet prominent in his day, and of his composer friend.

by Bowyer junior for John Hoadly was the edition of his father's *Works . . . Published by his son John Hoadly, LL. D.*, 1773 (*The Bowyer ledgers*, ed. Keith Maslen and John Lancaster [1991], item 4986).

VIRTUAL READERS: THE SUBSCRIBERS TO FIELDING'S *MISCELLANIES* (1743)

by

Hugh Amory*

In a magisterial prolegomenon (1961) to his edition of Volume I of Fielding's *Miscellanies* (1972), Henry Knight Miller carefully discussed and illustrated the list of subscribers, which then, curiously enough, he never printed in his edition.[1] He never explained this decision—nor the omission of some other features of his copy-text, such as divisional title pages—and probably saw no need to do so, for such edition-specific features, like illustrations, imprints, dust-jackets or advertisements, were not then regarded as part of the work for which the editor was responsible. In that bygone age, when self-referentiality was the peculiar (but excellent) privilege of literary language, documents like subscription lists seemed extra-literary and even extra-textual—part of the "background" of the work, no doubt, but operating by different rules and subject to different disciplines. Whatever else subscription lists may have been, they were not verbal icons or well-wrought urns, and certainly no reviewer questioned Miller's decision, if one pondered the matter at all.

Now, thirty-three years later, Bertrand Goldgar and I are continuing Miller's edition in a very different scholarly climate. The Project for Historical Bio-Bibliography at Newcastle has greatly stimulated interest in subscription publishing,[2] and Bibliography itself has slouched toward a History

---

* An earlier version of this paper was delivered at a seminar on "Booksellers, readers and reviewing," chaired by Michael J. Suarez, at the 24th annual meeting of ASECS, 25 April 1993. I am grateful for criticism and comments from Bertrand Goldgar, Michael Treadwell, Robert D. Hume, and Martin Battestin.

1. Henry Knight Miller, *Essays on Fielding's* Miscellanies (1961); *Miscellanies by Henry Fielding, Esq;: Volume One*, ed. H. K. Miller (1972) (hereafter cited as *Misc.* I).

2. P. J. Wallis, "Book Subscription Lists," *The Library*, 5th ser., 29 (1974), 255–286.

of the Book, in which all the physical features of the editor's sources take on heightened significance. Our sense of textuality, moreover, has broadened—some would say, blurred, but to particularize the rocks, human bodies, street signs, and other objects that are now acceptable literary texts would be invidious. Suffice it to say, that the inclusion of Fielding's list in our edition should be theoretically unobjectionable, though in practice I can no longer print it where it belongs, at the head of Volume I.

This deferment of the list in no way affects its value as a document, but transforms and disguises its textuality. Fielding, unusually, set his list at the traditional site of dedications, invocations, and proems. Here, at a green oak by the edge of the sea, on a golden chain, says Pushkin, a learned cat walks to and fro. Half in, half out of the work, simultaneously authors, characters and readers, the muses, noblemen and cats that inhabit this place ambiguously recommend both its truth and its fiction. Matthew Hodgart compares the "haughty territorial magnates" among Pope's subscribers to the Homeric heroes in the Catalogue of Ships.[3] Though many of these heroes never reappear in the *Iliad*, they continued to haunt the imagination of the audience, providing a grip for their *paesani*, or *semblables*, to appropriate the text. I call them "virtual readers" in the rather esoteric sense that the electronic simulation of experience through VCRs and electromechanical gloves is known as "virtual reality." Depending on the reality, of course, the difference may be small or great: virtual sex, for example, may be indistinguishable from the real thing, whereas virtual representation is a poor substitute for direct elections. When we have assessed the adequacy of the list as an account of Fielding's actual readers, we can better appreciate its virtues.

I

THE SUBSCRIBERS AND THEIR COPIES

Our earliest notice of the *Miscellanies* is a squib by Horace Walpole satirizing Fielding's poverty, written in March or April 1742; here it appears that Fielding was already soliciting subscriptions, a year before the book was finally published.[4] No copy of the proposals survives, but their substance is recorded in an advertisement of 5 June 1742, which also implies, as Miller notes, that subscription "must have been underway for some time." How long is anyone's guess, but Miller and Martin Battestin plausibly propose that it began in late 1741.[5] The form of subscribers' names, however, usually dates from after that time, when it can be dated: not only the Earl of Orford, but the Earls of Bath, Harrington and Lichfield acquired their titles in 1742 or 1743; the Countess of Dalkeith, *née* Lady Caroline Campbell, and Mrs.

3. Matthew Hodgart, "The Subscription List for Pope's *Iliad*, 1715," in Robert B. White (ed.), *The Dress of Words: Essays . . . in Honor of Richmond P. Bond* (1978), p. 34.

4. W. B. Coley, "Henry Fielding and the Two Walpoles," *PQ*, 45 (1966), 157–178.

5. Miller, *Essays*, p. 3; Martin C. Battestin with Ruthe R. Battestin, *Henry Fielding: A Life* (1989), p. 318.

Northey, *née* Vyner, married; and Major Fairfax, Andrew Ducarel, D.C.L., Nathaniel Gundry, K.C., William Harbord (*olim* Morden), John Probyn (*olim* Hopkins), Samuel Henry Pont, Recorder of Cambridge, and Henry Morgan Byndloss of the Middle, erstwhile of the Inner, Temple, all have names, addresses and distinctions postdating Walpole's fall.[6]

For these fourteen subscribers, at least, and probably for others, subscription continued into 1742 and even 1743; as late as 14 February 1743, Fielding was still pleading in the *Daily Advertiser* with "all such as have dispos'd of any Receipts, and have not yet sent in the Names of the Subscribers" to send them in by the end of the month. None of this seriously challenges the received dating, of course, since only fourteen of Fielding's 427 subscriptions can be dated. Nevertheless, the names of the subscribers in the list are *prima facie* the names on Fielding's receipts; there is no evidence that he ever went back and updated them. The Earl of Lichfield—if, as I suppose, he is the same earl who subscribed for Sarah Fielding's *Familiar Letters between the Characters of David Simple*—signed on less than two months before publication; Walpole presumably subscribed after his creation as Earl of Orford, on 6 Feb. 1742.

The numerous errors in the names of subscribers indeed suggest that the receipts received little editing, apart from their alphabetical and social arrangement. "Henry Byndhass, Esq; of the Middle Temple" can only be our distorted friend Byndloss; and Adrian Ducarel, both of whose brothers subscribed, masquerades as "Adrian Duterel, Esq;" as Ruthe Battestin kindly pointed out to me. The last names of "Peter Kelewick, Esq;" and "E. Lauchert, Esq;" are quite unrecorded, and (with some assistance from the "Edward Lambert, *Esq;*" who subscribed for Sarah Fielding's *Familiar Letters*) I do not doubt that they should be *Kekewick* (of the Middle Temple and Lincoln's Inn) and *Lambert* (Deputy Recorder of Salisbury).

Fielding, who rarely gives any addresses, lists seventy-five subscribers as "of" one of the four Inns of Court, to provide rhetorical "proof" of the professional support he celebrated in the Introduction to the *Miscellanies*. The "proof" is somewhat tendentious, to be sure. The Inns housed many laymen during the eighteenth century, among them Samuel Johnson, and even businesses, like the bookstore of Thomas Waller, Fielding's publisher; nevertheless, all but three of the seventy-five subscribers are identifiably lawyers. "J. Beach, Esq;" "John Manton, Esq;" and "Lewis Innys, Esq;" indeed, all "of the Inner Temple," are not to be found in the registers of any Inn, the lists of legal personnel in the *Magnæ Britanniæ Notitia*, nor the rather less complete lists of attorneys that were maintained by Act of Parliament from 1729. And yet Fielding apparently supposed they were lawyers, or meant them to be taken as such.

Are "J. Beach," "John Manton," and "Lewis Innys" laymen, then, or

---

6. Details of the biography of the subscribers, and their identification, await my edition of the list, scheduled for publication in the Wesleyan Edition of vol. 3 of Fielding's *Miscellanies*.

unreliably recorded lawyers? On the one hand, I have not found any very plausible lay candidates for these names. A John Beech Esq; died at Richmond on 12 May 1766, but I have no evidence that he ever lived in the Inner Temple; a Mr. Manton quitted his Inner Temple chambers in 1777, leaving the rent in arrears, but I do not know his first name or whether he was renting them thirty-four years earlier; and Lewis Innes, a Scotch Catholic, died in Paris in 1738, making his way into the *DNB*, but not, I think, into Fielding's list. On the other hand, the Registers of the Inner Temple provide three closely similar names that might easily have been confused with those of the subscribers: Lewis Jones, John Martin, and Thomas Beach. The subscribers' address is a more reliable indicator of their identity here than the record of their names.

The easiest explanation of these errors is that Fielding or the compositor misread the receipts, perhaps misled by a one-stroke capital *T* such as Fielding himself wrote, or a secretary *e*, common in eighteenth-century lawyers' hands. "J. Beach, Esq;", indeed, reappears four years later without a legal address among the subscribers to Sarah Fielding's *Familiar Letters;* at least I assume it is the same man, and that she omitted his address, as she omitted Edward Hooper's, for the simple reason that she saw no advantage for her enterprise in parading their professional association. Beach's abbreviated Christian name certainly suggests that neither Henry nor his sister recognized his identity, even though, intriguingly, it appears that his father had sold some woods at West Ashton (Wilts.) to their uncle, George Fielding, so that their families may have been acquainted.

The detours of solicitation surely encouraged such errors. Historically, Fielding's list descends from the receipts sent in by his friends, in a variety of hands, as well as from those he wrote out himself. As he confessed in the Introduction, he owed "not a tenth Part" of the subscriptions to his "own Interest" (*Misc.* I, 13), and the identity of these friends of friends might well elude him. The careful arrangement and artful typography of the list argue that the compositor worked from a fair copy, and not directly from the receipts themselves. The repeated misreadings of *e* as *i* ("Briton," "Bidford," "Nathaneil," "Percival," and "Woodmancie") or as *u* ("Duvall" and "Murlott") are both attributable to a secretary *e*; since these errors have no clear personal, geographical or professional association in common, they support the conjecture that the compositor's copy was in a single hand—presumably Fielding's, though the evidence is hardly conclusive.[7] One should add, of course, that his direct acquaintance with his subscriber is no guarantee of accuracy. Both he and Sarah misreport their subscriber Richard Draper as

7. "Duvall" is rightly "Davall", but was probably written "Devall", as he appears in Sarah's subscription list. The secretary features of Fielding's hand, apparent in his *c* and *e*, are probably attributable to his legal training: cf. Mr. B's description of good Mr. Longman's hand, "Don't you see by the Settness of some of these Letters, and a little Secretary Cut here and there, especially in that *c* and that *r*, that it is the Hand of a Person bred in the Law-way?" (Samuel Richardson, *Pamela*, ed. T. C. Duncan Eaves and Ben D. Kimpel [1971], p. 229). Unfortunately, a number of Fielding's solicitors were also lawyers.

"Thomas Draper, Esq; Serjeant at Law." One is irresistibly reminded of the aphasia that perplexes Fielding's naming of his characters and his citation of his authorities, and which regularly led him to address Robert Butcher, with whom he corresponded in 1748–49, as "Richard."[8] Serjeant Draper's subscription is very likely one that Henry solicited in person, and passed on to his sister.

Because his list is exceptionally laconic, the names are peculiarly liable to distortion and difficult to identify with certainty. The subscribers are not in general represented by their legal signatures, but by social designations that assume their physical presence for full intelligibility. David Garrick is plain "Mr. Garrick," as he might appear in a cast or a playbill; Richard Grenville is "——— Greenville, Esq;" reflecting the usual pronunciation of his name. His first name is probably omitted as a mark of distinction for the eldest son, whereas his younger brothers appear as "James Greenville, Esq;" and "George Greenville, Esq;".[9] Phonetic spellings, like "Massam" for Masham, and "Guernier" for Garnier are not uncommon, though contemporaries perhaps found them less confusing than I have. "Mrs." denotes both married women and spinsters, but the spinsters are normally distinguished by the addition of their Christian names: "Mrs. Elizabeth Adams" is certainly single, whereas "Mrs. Hooper" may only be presumed to be married (in her case, wrongly). Thus the record provides ample room for ambiguity. Fortunately, I have found no evidence of pseudonymous, fictive, or jocular entries, as in some other lists.[10]

Besides misreadings (as I charitably suppose them), there are actual errors of fact, and omissions of essential data in Fielding's list. "Thomas"—or rather Richard—Draper is the most striking, but we may also wonder at "The Hon. William Leweson, Esq;" evidently a phonetic representation of the MP William Leveson-Gower, shorn of the second half of his name. The entry for Abraham Elton fails to note the baronetcy he received on 20 October 1742; and at least four of Fielding's subscribers died before publication, unnoticed in the list. The first of these virtual readers to die is Capt. Christopher Garey, who had been out of the realm since mid-October 1740 on Admiral Vernon's West Indian expedition and died on 2 February 1741, shortly before the

8. *Miscellanies by Henry Fielding, Esq; Volume Two*, ed. Bertrand A. Goldgar and Hugh Amory (1993), p. 165, n. 4 (hereafter *Misc.* II); M. C. with R. R. Battestin, "Fielding, Bedford, and the Westminster Election of 1749," *Eighteenth-Century Studies*, 11 (1978), 143–185, at p. 176.

9. R. W. Chapman, *Names, Designations & Appellations* (1936). Fielding must have known Grenville, perhaps even from his Eton years, and social habit would have encouraged the abbreviation even though authors willingly expanded entries on better knowledge. A. C. Elias Jr. kindly drew my attention to a cancel in the subscription list to Mary Barber's *Poems* (1734), which expands some last-name entries to their fuller forms; and cf. the same phenomenon in Vida's *Poemata* (1722–23), discussed by B. N. Gerrard, "Post-impression Correction in British Books Printed During the Eighteenth Century," Ph.D. Thesis (Monash University), 1993, pp. 195–196.

10. Cf. "Mrs. Ann Admirer," who appears among the subscribers to the *Spectator*, ed. D. F. Bond (1965), I, lxxxix, n. 2; or "Miss Fanny Hill," who subscribed to Samuel Derrick's *Collection of Original Poems* (1755).

siege of Cartagena, over two years before publication of the *Miscellanies,* and a year before our earliest record of subscriptions. The rest—Thomas Ashby, the Hon. Sir Michael Newton, and the eccentric Col. Richard Pierson, whose body lay forty days in state and—all died in 1743.

My identification of "Major Garey," as he appears in the list, may be questioned, since it seems to impugn the received dating for the opening of subscription. Christopher is unmistakably denoted by this entry, however, despite the discrepancy in his rank: army officers are reliably recorded, the records have been thoroughly studied and indexed by Charles Dalton, and Philip Gery, the only major who might conceivably qualify, died in 1736. Hence I doubt that an unidentified "Major Garey"—or Gary, Gery, Gerry, Geary, or Gearie—is still lurking about the staff officers of George II's army, unknown to history; and in any case, there is no other indication that subscription opened so early. I rather suppose that a friend of Garey's may have signed him up, before news of his death had reached England,[11] and that he received a brevet rank before embarking on the Caribbean campaign. Thus —whether "Major Garey" is unidentified, a vicarious entry by one of his friends, or an authorial invention to vary and enliven the social composition of the list—I see no need to question the received dating. The 4th Baron Berkeley of Stratton, William Hillman Sr., Alderman of Salisbury, the 1st Duke of Roxburghe, and the 3rd Earl of Radnor all died in early 1741, and were succeeded by heirs who answer equally well to their descriptions in the list. In such cases, I have identified the subscribers as the heirs, reducing Fielding's extinct subscribers to a minimum.

Accuracy of identification depends not just on the fullness and correctness of the record, but also on the completeness and adequacy of my reference sources. I have run the list against such standard references as Musgrave's *Obituary,* the *DNB,* the *Complete Peerage,* Burke's *Landed Gentry,* the county histories, registers of schools, universities, and Inns of Court, and wills in the Probate Court of Canterbury. Some of the classes in Fielding's list— particularly merchants, attorneys, and, of course, women—are poorly recorded in these references, but their bias is more serious for the names they do record. If we can match a subscriber in any one of these sources, there is an enormous incentive to look no further for possible homonyms. An author with a good biography, like Fielding, will thus seem to be more successful in dunning his friends and relations, and eighteenth-century merchants, if they were better represented in the *DNB,* might take a more serious interest in the arts.

Fielding's list is arranged, like many others, in a social hierarchy, but unlike most of them, he makes a firm distinction between the Esquires and the Misters. The fabric of this distinction was already wearing thin, as the College of Arms had made no visitations since the seventeenth century, but

11. For parallels, cf. Pat Rogers, "Pope and His Subscribers," *Publishing History,* 3 (1978), [7]–36, at p. 10 and n. 15; and David Foxon, *Pope and the Early Eighteenth-Century Book Trade,* rev. and ed. by J. McLaverty (1991), p. 62.

Fielding, whose own title to Esquire was insecure, took it seriously. His usage occasionally stumbles, as we might expect: "Mr." Alexander Thistlethwaite's family had lived at Winterslow (Wilts.) since the sixteenth century; "Mr. Henry Alcroft" is otherwise styled "Henry Allcraft, Esq;" in a monumental inscription; "Mr. Thomas Poldon" is the son and heir of Job Polden, Esquire; "Mr. Edward Clerke" seems to be a Wiltshire JP; and a "Mr." John Fawkner—probably the MP John Falconer—intrudes, anomalously, among the Esquires of Fielding's list. Nevertheless, these occasional mistakes scarcely argue that Fielding was wrong wherever the possibility arises, and indeed, his opinion of his subscribers' quality is clearly stated, apart from the ambiguous Mr. Fawkner, and generally correct, so far as I can judge it. Most of the Misters, for example, turn out to be attorneys, surgeons, booksellers, or actors, and even if they were armigerous, like Giles Taylor, they claimed no higher rank than "gentleman." Hence I accept the general accuracy of the distinction, in default of strong evidence to the contrary. "Hesiod" Cooke, for example, invariably subscribes himself "Mr. Cooke," and Pope dismissed him as the son of a Muggletonian innkeeper; still, like Miller and the Battestins, I think he qualifies as the subscriber "Thomas Cooke, Esq;." He was a personal friend of Fielding's, a member of Jonathan Tyers's "Club of Wits," all of whom subscribed for the *Miscellanies,* and the promoter of an edition of Plautus, for which Fielding subscribed in his turn—as "Esq;" to be sure.

Where I am defeated by the poverty of the descriptions or the richness of my sources, I have made a number of more or less plausible assumptions to resolve the ambiguities. I assume that names which reappear as subscribers to Sarah Fielding's *Familiar Letters* denote the same person, since I suppose that Henry or his friends helped his sister gather subscriptions: as I have already remarked, two subscribers appear in the same erroneous forms in both lists, but in general, Sarah's is more correct, or fuller. I have also favored candidates who have biographical connections with Sarah's subscribers. Finally, I have surveyed a sample of 100 lists appearing in books published in London, Cambridge, and Oxford between 1739 and 1749, and in ambiguous cases, I have favored candidates with a demonstrable habit of subscribing.

A few examples will illustrate the application of these assumptions. Miller, followed by Martin Battestin, accepts the manager of Drury Lane (1696–1774) as the subscriber "Mr. Lacy," but the manager was "Esquire," as he is styled in his will, and as Fielding, at least, should certainly have been aware. A likelier candidate is the homonymous James Lacy (d. 1750), an attorney of Bishop's Walton (Hants.), persuasively associated by his profession and location with many other subscribers. Such connections, which fit the subscriber into a general "profile," seem to me more reliable than vague biographical associations, since by Fielding's own confession, his acquaintance with his subscribers was limited. Like Johnson's Shakespeare, Fielding's *Miscellanies* was largely promoted by the author's friends.[12]

12. J. D. Fleeman, "Johnson's *Shakespeare*: The Progress of a Subscription," in *Writers,*

Hence I also question the identification of "Mr. Carey" with the poet and composer Henry Carey, hesitatingly proposed by Miller, and adopted by Battestin.[13] The poet hanged himself on 5 October 1743, leaving three young children and his pregnant wife "destitute of any provision."[14] He and his wife (whom Battestin also proposes as a subscriber) could scarcely have afforded to lay out two guineas on Fielding's *Miscellanies*, I believe; nor did Fielding himself, who was equally distressed, subscribe in his turn for Carey's *Dramatick Works*, published in August 1743. Miller's hesitation is thus abundantly justified. My co-editor, Bert Goldgar, however, with his unrivalled instinct for the contemporary scene, suggested the surgeon Squire Carey (his real name, not a title). Carey's medical clients included Fielding's patron, George Dodington, and the Prince of Wales (both subscribers), and his sympathy with their politics appears in his subscription to Henry Brooke's play, *Gustavus Vasa*. My judgment here is necessarily tentative. Most of the possible Carys, Careys, and Carews are Esquires; the only plausible Misters I know of are the surgeon and the poet; and of these, the surgeon seems easily the most eligible. He has no other known connection with Fielding, indeed, but he is satisfyingly connected with the subscription process, as we may picture it, and he makes an interesting addition to the large medical contingent among Fielding's subscribers.

Some four contemporary divines qualify for the subscriber listed as "The Reverend Mr. Goddard." I was initially attracted by John Goddard, Rector of Wreningham (Norf.), the only Etonian, for this is a strongly represented group among Fielding's subscribers. Nevertheless, he never subscribed for other books during my sample period, and I have therefore plumped for Peter Stephen Goddard, an active subscriber and the only Reverend Goddard to subscribe for secular literature. Finally, I could never have identified "——— Wyndham Esq;" as William Wyndham of Dinton (Wilts.) if a "Mrs. Wyndham of Dinton" had not appeared among Sarah's subscribers. I have since learned from Professor Thomas Lockwood that his name appears in a manuscript cast to the Bodleian copy of a Franglais version of Fielding's *Tom Thumb*.[15]

By these specious expedients, I have "identified" all but sixteen of Fielding's subscribers. Five of these identifications controvert Miller and the Battestins; six require substantive emendations of the text; and in thirty instances, an alternative, less plausible identification might also be proposed. Thus a total of fifty-seven subscribers, or about 13%, are either unidentified or more or less questionable, and I would double this figure to allow for sim-

---

Books and Trade, ed. O M Brack, Jr. (New York: AMS Press [forthcoming]); who kindly allowed me to read his contribution in proof.

13. Miller, *Essays*, p. 25; Battestins, p. 371.

14. The best biography of Carey is Roger Fiske's article in the *New Grove Dictionary of Music*; the quotation is from *A Biographical Dictionary of Actors . . . and other Stage Personnel in London, 1660–1800*, by P. H. Highfill, Jr., K. A. Burnim, and E. A. Langhans, v. 3 (1975), 60.

15. Call no.: Don e 126(1).

ple ignorance, the blind operation of assumptions, and the inadequacy of my sources. I have tried to explain the limitations of my research and the methods behind my conclusions, but I despair of indicating the degree of doubt appropriate to every individual case.

Even if my conjectures were infallible, moreover, I could not be as confident as some other students of subscription lists that they form a "precise readership," "unusually prompt purchasers," and the like.[16] The list only shows that 427 historical people advanced a sum of money for a copy or copies of the *Miscellanies*, or had such sums advanced on their behalf. Nothing in the list proves that they ever paid the second half of their subscription, much less that they ever read their copies if they did. What on earth could Prince Frederick have done with fifteen royal-paper copies or Sir Robert Walpole with ten? And why does not a single one of their copies seem to have survived? Indeed, no copy of the *Miscellanies* appears in the sale-catalogues of any subscriber's library down to and including Garrick's in 1823. The 1st Marquess of Buckingham, on his marriage to Mary Elizabeth Nugent in 1775, was the rightful heir of eight subscribers: his great-uncle and great-aunt the Cobhams, his uncle Richard, 2nd Earl Temple, his father, George Grenville and his mother, Elizabeth Wyndham, his in-laws the Nugents, and finally George Bubb Dodington, whose property, including his house at Eastbury in Dorset, had passed to the 2nd Earl Temple, were all subscribers, and their ten ordinary-paper copies and three royal-paper copies should have descended to him, together with their titles and the family estate at Stowe. But did these subscribers ever take delivery? There was no copy of the *Miscellanies* in the sales of the Stowe library in 1849 and 1921. There is no copy in the bequest of the Marquess's brother Thomas Grenville, which he left to the British Library in 1846.

Of those copies that still survive today, I can locate a total of only three with evidence of the subscriber's ownership—all, as it happens, on royal paper—as opposed to eight of both sorts that have the signatures or ex-libris of eighteenth-century nonsubscribers. We too easily assume that subscribers took their books: 75% of one poor author's list defaulted, Keith Maslen notes, and this may or may not have been exceptional.[17] If fully 300 of the 658 subscribers for the first volume (1729) of Oldmixon's *History* failed to subscribe for the second (1735), it seems a fair conjecture that many of them had little interest in possessing either.[18] In a much better-studied group of subscriptions, by Dr. Johnson, only one in five titles to which he subscribed

16. W. A. Speck, "Politicians, Peers and Publication by Subscription, 1700–50," in Isabel Rivers (ed.), *Books and Their Readers in Eighteenth-Century England* (1982), pp. 47–68, at p. 65; Pat Rogers, "Book Subscriptions Among the Augustans," *TLS* (15 Dec. 1972), p. 1539.

17. K. I. D. Maslen, "Book Subscription Lists," *TLS* (29 Sep. 1972), p. 1157, citing Castiglione's *The Courtier* (1729). Of the 113 who subscribed in advance to Edmund Morgan's *A Complete History of Algiers* (1728–29), "very few" took delivery, according to W. A. Speck, "Politicians," p. 50; and cf. the case of Blomefield's *Norfolk*, described by David A. Stoker (ed.), *The Correspondence of the Reverend Francis Blomefield (1705–52)* (Norwich: Norfolk Record Soc., 1992), pp. 46–55, esp. p. 53.

18. Rogers, "Book Subscriptions."

resurfaces in the sales catalogue of his library.[19] About 46% of the *Miscellanies* subscribed-for were never delivered, if the survivors are any indication; since some subscribers called for multiple copies, we cannot determine on this evidence how many defaulted altogether, but some such there surely were.

Certainly, as Michael Treadwell and others have shown,[20] subscribers for multiple copies occasionally took fewer than they had paid for, treating the overplus as a genteel form of patronage; others may have regarded their advance as a form of charity. Fielding illustrates the attitude in *Amelia*, where a hack writer solicits a guinea from Colonel James, "which was double the sum mentioned in the Receipt" (VIII.5). Both parties consider this to be the end of the transaction, though Fielding reflects severely on the hack's dishonesty, in never intending to publish, and on the Colonel's cynicism, in not caring whether he ever would.

Nevertheless, Fielding only singles out an abuse of what must have been common practice. Around 1740, an "F. Blyth," whom I take to be the Discalced Carmelite, once more proposed his *Poems on Various Subjects*, this time at full price (a half guinea) on delivery. "The Author's Reason for requiring no Money, for the future, till the Work be deliver'd," he explained in his new prospectus, "is to avoid being suspected (by such as are unacquainted with him) to be of the Number of Those, who make a Trade of taxing PUBLICK SPIRIT for Works they never design to publish."[21] Unhappily, as some of my readers will have guessed, his *Poems* were never printed —but perhaps his subscribers did not greatly care. Laetitia Pilkington, who proposed her *Memoirs* in the 1740s at 5 shillings down, and 5 on delivery, smugly reported that she often had "the good Fortune to have a Guinea Subscription, for Gentlemen seldom send me any smaller Coin."[22] Did these overly generous gentlemen also expect to lay down a further five shillings on publication? In Pilkington's account, as in Fielding's, they would have been hard put to it to prove how much they had actually advanced. Evidently, she provided her guinea subscribers with only a single receipt, entitling them to a single copy, for her list, at any rate, does not abound in subscriptions for four copies, as we might otherwise expect. Like Fielding's hack (though she, at least, eventually published her book), she simply pocketed the difference, and the transaction was closed on either side.

Early eighteenth-century subscribers had generally acquired their copies at a discount from the publication price,[23] but by Fielding's day, they paid

19. Donald D. Eddy and J. D. Fleeman, "A preliminary Handlist of Books to which Dr. Samuel Johnson Subscribed," *Studies in Bibliography*, 46 (1993), 187–220.

20. "Book Subscription Lists": correspondence by Paul J. Korshin and Michael Treadwell, in *TLS*, 23 June 1972, p. 719 and 7 July, 1972, p. 777; Foxon, *Pope*, p. 62; and Rogers, "Pope and His Subscribers," p. 13.

21. *Book Prospectuses before 1801 in the John Johnson Collection*, ed. J. P. Feather (1976) (italic reversed).

22. *The Third and Last Volume of the Memoirs of Mrs. Laetitia Pilkington* (1754), p. 121. A. C. Elias, Jr., kindly brought this reference to my attention.

23. Cf. the prospectuses reprinted in *The Term Catalogues*, ed. Edward Arber (London, 1903), III, 47, 118, 132, etc.

a surcharge of 55%, merely for the pleasure of seeing their names in print. "Hesiod" Cooke coolly defended this racket in his preface to a long-running but never completed translation of Plautus:

[T]he two principal Complaints which have been made against publishing [by subscription] are, that the Delays of Publication are generally too tedious, and that Subscribers purchase the Books at a dearer Rate than they are afterwards sold for: this may often be the Case; but I always looked on subscribing as promoting more than merely buying a Work of Merit, as having a Regard to the Advantage of the Author more than making a lucrative Bargain. . . .[24]

At the sale of Fielding's library in 1755, Cooke repurchased his friend's copy of Plautus: conceivably, he valued the sentimental association, but Cooke was remarkably hard-headed, not to say cynical, about his project, and I suspect that he was in hopes of a second premium.[25] By such means, the number of Cooke's subscribers might eventually have exceeded the number of copies printed.

Twenty days after the subscribers' copies of the *Miscellanies* were ready, Andrew Millar advertised a "second edition" for only fifteen shillings, bound. This is merely the first edition with a new title page, and without the list of subscribers; but in about two years, perhaps when "second edition" title pages ran out, Millar also advertised the original edition for the same low price: James Thomson did not subscribe, yet he had a first edition by 1749. Presumably Millar took the copies printed in excess of subscriptions, plus any called-for but never delivered. If we assume the probably over-generous norm of one copy per subscriber and two per married couple, the subscribers took 149 out of the 250 royal-paper and 316 out of the 1,000 ordinary-paper copies. This estimate roughly agrees with the Bowyer Paper Ledger, which shows that Bowyer had delivered no more than 160 royal-paper copies and 258 ordinary-paper copies of the "first edition" by 17 September 1743, some five months after publication.[26] This left Millar an ample supply, and indeed his successors still had copies for sale thirty-two years later.[27] Subscribers no doubt financed the *Miscellanies*, but they were greatly out-numbered by subsequent purchasers, and their weight in any account of the work's reception and readership must be gauged accordingly.[28]

24. *The Comedys of Plautus* [pt. 1: Amphitryon] (1746).

25. *Sale Catalogues of Libraries of Eminent Persons*, ed. A. N. L. Munby (hereafter *SCLEP*) 7 (1973), 123–158 (lot 53); and cf. Arthur Sherbo, " 'Hesiod' Cooke and The Subscription Game," *SB*, 41 (1988), 267–270. Pope devised a similar scheme, recounted by Foxon, *Pope*, p. 62.

26. *The Bowyer Ledgers*, ed. Keith Maslen and John Lancaster (1991), fiche P 1049; this document will be analyzed in more detail in the Textual Introduction to Vol. 3 of the Wesleyan Edition of the *Miscellanies*.

27. *SCLEP*, 1 (1971), 47–66, at p. 55 (lot 1). T. Cadell, *A Catalogue of Approved English Books in Several Branches of Useful and Ornamental Literature* (1775), p. 26 (Cambridge Univ. Lib., call no. Munby d. 19³); T. Becket, *Catalogue of Foreign Books Imported, and English Books Printed for and Sold by, T. Becket and P. A. de Hondt* (1773), p. 174 (Cambridge Univ. Lib., call no. Munby d. 141).

28. The degree to which subscription publishing was a joint venture between the author and the bookseller has often been underestimated by scholars. See, however, William M.

II
THE TEXTUAL IMPLICATIONS OF THE LIST

Fielding, famously, compared his writing to a banquet laid out for his readers, and we might consider the lower orders in his list as folk who have come for a power lunch at a posh restaurant, less concerned for what they eat and drink than for their visible association with Prince Frederick and the nobility, at the better tables. Everyone is looking at everyone else, and an informed observer may note many gradations of decorum in the number and quality of their orders. Royal-paper copies are about an inch taller, twice as thick, cost twice as much as the ordinary paper, and do not enjoy the normal trade discount of seven copies for the price of six.[29] The stiff paper and extra weight made for awkward reading, but that was not the point; the conspicuous size and expense advertised the subscriber's status. Even today, the visitor to Sir Robert Walpole's residence at Houghton Hall may readily see why he was known as the Great Man; some god, one feels, inserted a tube into an ordinary library and blew.

To avoid the taint of trade, multiple subscriptions are normally expressed in royal-paper units, and in the ordinary paper rarely rise above two or three copies. When a bookseller like Andrew Millar or Edward Easton subscribes for a single copy, he acts on his own account, as a friend, for he cannot hope to profit from the excessive advance price. Otherwise, like Robert Dodsley or James Leake, he will subscribe in multiples of six ordinary copies, pocketing the seventh as a reward for his solicitations. The bookseller like John Peele, who takes ten royal-paper copies, could expect neither commercial nor social advantage from his subscription; we may thus infer that he is acting for an armigerous client. Ralph Allen, indeed, subscribed in secret for the requisite sum,[30] and since only three other subscribers took so many royal-paper copies, it is likely enough that this is his subscription.

Conversely, subscriptions for multiple copies on ordinary paper, how-

Sale, Jr., *Samuel Richardson: Master Printer* (1950), pp. 108–117, where, with some regularity, the number of copies printed substantially exceeds subscriptions; Keith Maslen, "Printing for the Author: From the Bowyer Printing Ledgers, 1710–1775," *The Library*, 5th ser., 27 (1972), 302–309; and David McKitterick, *A History of the Cambridge University Press* (1992–   ), I, 377f.

29. R. M. Wiles, *Serial Publication in England before 1750* (1957), pp. 186–187; Wallis, "Book Subscription Lists," p. 262; Graham Pollard, "The English Market for Printed Books," *Publishing History*, 4 (1978), [7]–48, at pp. 15–16. The discount may not have been as uniform as Pollard implies, and it may be significant that Fielding's advertisement of 5 June 1742 does not specifically mention it, but the size of the booksellers' subscriptions is highly suggestive.

30. *Correspondence of Alexander Pope*, ed. G. Sherburn (1956), IV, 452: "Fielding has sent the Books you subscribd for to the Hand I employd in conveying the 20 ll. to him"; the close coincidence with "Peele's" exceptionally large subscription is irresistible, and the discrepancy may easily be explained by the fact that the nominal value of a guinea was a pound (there being no coin worth exactly £1). Fleeman, "Johnson's *Shakespeare*," provides parallels, where receipts are made out for "£1," though the subscription calls for a guinea.

ever suitable for people in the trade, look mean or odd in a gentleman. Did Bubb Dodington gape after a free copy, when he subscribed for six? W. L. Cross supposed that Charles Fleetwood distributed his twenty copies among the players of Drury Lane,[31] but it seems improbable. Had he waited until after publication, he might have acquired one more copy for £7 10s. less, and in any case, he was bilking the actors of their wages, and could hardly have fobbed off their demands with free copies of the *Miscellanies*.[32] The likeliest explanation is that Dodington and Fleetwood's "copies" merely represent receipts on which they had paid the advance, but had failed to dispose of. Had they been acting on their own accounts, they might have enjoyed more social *éclat* for exactly the same outlay, after all, by taking half the number of copies, but in the royal paper.

Apart from Peele, no male subscriber below the rank of Esquire presumes to take the royal paper, but women wear their paper with a difference. "Esquire" and "Mister" have no feminine equivalents: Kitty Clive, the daughter of Irish gentry, has the same precedence as Peg Woffington, whose father was a bricklayer. Gender replaces birth: wives defer to their husbands' subscriptions, even when, like Lady Anne Strode, they are of nobler birth, or like the Duchess of Bedford, notorious viragos; Kitty may take a royal-paper copy, and yet Peg does not, because she would not make her ordinary-paper lover, Garrick, look cheap. When only the wife subscribes, her husband thus implicitly joins in her subscription. Fielding celebrates both the Richmonds, for example, one for his generosity, the other for the whiteness of her breasts, but only the Duchess subscribed, which Miller found "strange." Perhaps he would not have found it "strange" if only the Duke had subscribed, but in any case I cannot share his perplexity: surely her generous subscription (12 guineas) recognized both obligations.[33]

Such queries and conjectures were doubtless part of the pleasures and pains of subscribing and invest the list with the intense, narrow interest of a society column, but Fielding also introduces the subscribers into the *Miscellanies* itself. In the Introduction, he acclaims the professional recognition conferred by his numerous lawyer subscribers; in the text he compliments nineteen subscribers by name, and obliquely flatters many others. Celebrating the beautiful and modest "*Seraphina*" in a *Journey from This World to the Next*, for example, he noted that "A particular Lady of Quality is meant here; but every Lady of Quality, or no Quality, are welcome to apply the Character to themselves."[34] In a rather more restricted compliment, the portrait of the patriotic King Spirit, destined long to reign, is surely intended

31. Wilbur L. Cross, *The History of Henry Fielding* (1918), I, 382.

32. Judith Milhous and Robert D. Hume, "The Drury Lane Actors' Rebellion of 1743," *Theatre Journal*, 42 (1990), 57–80.

33. *The Complete Peerage*, by G. E. C[okayne]., ed. Vicary Gibbs et al. (1910–40), X, 839, n. e; noting that her marriage (at 13) "was merely a bargain to cancel a gambling debt" between their fathers. It seems to have been an exceptionally happy one, nevertheless.

34. *Misc.* II, 12, n. *.

for Prince Fred, as Thomas R. Cleary has pointed out.[35] Consider, too, Vicary Gibbs's amusing account of the politics of the subscriber Edward Seymour, later Duke of Somerset, who was "presumably a Whig, but his aversion to the risks of small-pox . . .—which became a mania in later life— prevented him from attending crucial divisions in the House of Lords." Is he a candidate for the gentle satire on the narrator's travelling companion in *A Journey from This World to the Next,* who still dreads smallpox, even after death?[36] And finally, when the narrator encounters a physician in the City of Diseases, "whose Countenance had in it something more pleasing than ordinary,"[37] how did Dr. Barker, Dr. Bedford, Dr. Baker, Dr. Bostock, Dr. Brewster, Dr. Hoadly, Dr. Harrington, Dr. Pile, Dr. Wasey and Dr. Wilmot, all of them subscribers, respond? Did they mentally compare countenances?

Fielding also seems to have dealt out compliments with his left hand, however. The prime example, of course, is the applicability of his portrait of Jonathan Wild to Sir Robert Walpole, first proposed by Thomas Keightley in 1858.[38] Yet if Walpole, with his exceptionally large subscription, is truly part of the text, is such a sustained attack credible? Could we suppose that Squire Allworthy, who, for all his too-obvious virtues, has numerous comic flaws, is a covert satire on George Lyttelton? If *Jonathan Wild* had not become detached from the *Miscellanies* and its subscribers, I question whether Keightley's theory would ever have seemed quite so pat. "In the panegyrical Part of this Work," Fielding cautiously notes, "some particular Person is always meant, but in the satirical no body,"[39] but few have quite believed him.

Despite this textualization of the list, its leading scholars have approached it as raw data, of primarily statistical significance. The names are reduced to an index of a single aspect of the subscriber's life, like politics; the "missing persons" may become more significant than those who subscribed; and the social presence, weight and weave of the entire list is ignored in favor of minorities who ought not to have subscribed, but did. That is what statistics is all about—synecdoche; but I propose to read the list mimetically, as metaphor. It is neither randomly generated nor complete. We are entirely ignorant of those who declined to subscribe; the data on those who did are ruinously defective; and the defects can only be filled in with unproven assumptions. Mathematics continues to work its magic on this unreliable data, however, with uncanny results.[40]

35. *Misc.* II, 26–28; Thomas R. Cleary, *Henry Fielding: Political Writer* (Waterloo, Ont., 1984), p. 189.

36. *Complete Peerage,* XII, pt. 1, p. 83, n. d.; *Misc.* II, 11.

37. *Misc.* II, 18.

38. Thomas Keightley, "On the Life and Writings of Henry Fielding," *Fraser's Magazine,* 57 (1858), 1–13, 205–217, 762–763.

39. *Misc.* II, 15, n. *.

40. Cf. also John Barnard, "Dryden, Tonson, and Subscriptions for the 1697 *Virgil,*" *PBSA,* 57 (1963), 129–151; *The Spectator,* ed. D. F. Bond, I, lxxxviii–lxxxix; and Pat Rogers,

Thus, Fielding attracted few literary subscribers, as Miller has shown—indeed, fewer than Miller supposed. By my reckoning, Mallet, Garrick and Cooke, all of them personal friends, are the only professional authors, eked out by amateurs like Lyttelton, Charles Hanbury-Williams, Bubb Dodington, and Lord Chesterfield, whom Miller rather unfairly dismisses as a "scribbling peer." Pope, Thomson, Horace Walpole and Sterne, indeed, purchased copies, though they do not appear in the list; Richardson and Cibber had personal grievances against Fielding; and in 1743 Swift was deep in senile dementia, and Samuel Johnson in poverty.[41] Nevertheless, even with these allowances, we may note the absence of the Wartons, Akenside, Collins and Shenstone, of the Pre-Romantics; Edward Young, Lady Mary Wortley Montagu, the Uptons and either Whitehead, of the Augustans; Lewis Theobald, James Ralph and a host of Grubs and Dunces. "It would appear," Miller concludes, "that the publication of the *Miscellanies* was not greeted as a literary event: the majority of subscribers seem rather to represent political or professional or merely personal connections."[42]

The evidence is curiously inconclusive, however: were any of this unlikely crew of absentees ever asked? and what influence did they actually wield? None of them subscribed for Conyers Middleton's *Life of Cicero*, yet it went through eight London editions between 1741 and 1764. The *Dictionary of the English Language* was a literary event, though Johnson dedicated it, however grudgingly, to a "scribbling peer." As the *Dunciad* might suggest, professional writers were not exactly at the center of the literary scene; political, social and "merely personal" connections had always mattered far more. By isolating the list from its text, and indeed from the values of its historical moment, Miller seriously mistakes its literary function. Fielding's opinion of the relative importance of his subscribers should be clear from their arrangement, and his editor may find a guilty satisfaction in the knowledge that the women and Misters whose identity so often eludes him didn't really count.

The political composition of the list would seem to offer a more realistic subject for analysis: subscribers were patrons, and one might expect authors to defer to their political views. There were other, equally powerful factors at work beside politics, however, like family and friendship (often at several removes), so that subscriptions were rarely a strictly party affair: Brooke's *Gustavus Vasa* was a notable exception. W. A. Speck's survey of 500 lists

"Pope and His Subscribers," for other statistical or quasi-statistical analyses of subscription lists.

41. Johnson's only likely subscriptions around this period are to Brooke's *Gustavus Vasa* (only 5s.), Lediard's continuation of Rapin's *History of England* ([1735]-37), and Chambers' *Cyclopædia*, 4th ed. (1741), the last two published in six-penny numbers.

42. Miller, *Essays*, p. 25. Some of these absentees may have subscribed, but failed to appear in the list: cf. the case noted by Charles Ryskamp, " 'Epigrams I more especially delight in': The Receipts for Pope's *Iliad*," *PULC*, 24 (1962–63), 36–38. A more extreme case is Catherine Jemmat's, who claimed that the printer had omitted "upwards of 150 Names besides making many other Errors throughout the List" in her *Miscellanies* (1766) (cited by Gerrard, "Post-impression Correction," p. 54).

published between 1710 and 1740 discloses only ten in which there seems to be any positive correlation between the party of the subscribers and that of the author.[43] The admixture of Administration lions with Opposition lambs among Fielding's subscribers, then, should have come as no surprise, but scholars, as usual, have sought for more interesting explanations. "How does one account for the name of the Duke of Devonshire, one of Walpole's most loyal supporters," wonders Miller, "or the Duke of St. Albans, or Earl Cholmondeley (Walpole's brother-in-law), the Earl of Pembroke, Lord Cornwallis, or General Churchill?" And he finds the solution in Martin Battestin's account of Fielding's "changing politics."[44]

Battestin proposed that the Walpolian subscriptions rewarded Fielding's withdrawal from his party in 1741, culminating in his sendup of their efforts in *The Opposition: A Vision*. The list may thus be broken down into archeologically distinct components, the Administration stratum presumably overlaying and folding alphabetically into the originally pure substratum of the Opposition. This conjecture parallels a textual theory that goes back to Aurélien Digeon's thesis of 1923, by which the Opposition rhetoric that repeatedly surfaces in the *Miscellanies* is explained as a "survival" from an earlier stage of composition.[45] In particular, Digeon posits an earlier version of *Jonathan Wild* (an Ur-*Wild*, as we may dub it), and Battestin conjectures that the suppression of this version in 1740 was another reason for Walpole's generosity. Both Battestin's and Digeon's theories have been criticized, though the critic, like Thomas R. Cleary, may accept one, while rejecting the other; and I believe that together, they still enjoy a scholarly consensus today.[46]

43. Speck, "Politicians." MPs appear in 147 of the 500 lists, 94 of which show a "real association" between the politics of the MPs and the author; Fielding's list (45 Whig, 20 Tory MPs, as of publication on 7 Apr. 1743) would qualify as a 95th, by Speck's criteria. Of these 94 lists, only ten showed a partisan majority: 6 Whig (two of them for the same work), 1 Tory, 2 Administration, 1 Opposition. In the remaining 84 lists, Speck simply claims that "none had an inexplicable bias towards an alliance of government Whigs and Tories." In short, Administration and Opposition Whigs regularly joined in subscribing for each other's ventures. See also P. J. Wallis, *The Social Index (Newcastle*, 1978), pp. 39–40, distinguishing Whig and Tory subscriptions by a numerical figure (rev. [sceptically] by T. H. Howard-Hill, *The Library*, 6th ser., 2 [1980], 247–249).

Both Speck and Wallis rely on the PHIBB data-base (announced for publication on CD ROM, Apr. 1994). This indexes the raw data of the original lists, not the personal identities underlying the various homo-/allo-/pseudonyms, which must be controlled retrospectively, without the benefit of their historical context. The data thus correlates more readily with the fairly stable political ideologies of the period, than with its rapidly changing political combinatons; and, indeed, with the House of Commons than with the Lords (where many MPs from time to time continued their politics and their subscriptions under different names). The evaluation of the data, then, even with (or because of?) this powerful tool, is somewhat delicate, as Wallis's anxious qualifications, though not his figures, make clear.

44. Miller, *Essays*, p. 28; Martin C. Battestin, "Fielding's Changing Politics and *Joseph Andrews*," *PQ*, 39 (1960), 39–55.

45. Aurélien Digeon, *Les romans de Fielding* (Paris, 1923).

46. For a careful review of Battestin's theory and W. B. Coley's objections, see Bertrand A. Goldgar, *Walpole and the Wits* (1976), who accepts it; as does Brian McCrea, *Henry Fielding and the Politics of Mid-Eighteenth Century England* (1981), p. 98; Cleary,

I shall confine my comments here to their implications for the subscriptions of Walpole and his party.

We do not need to go back to 1740 to explain Walpole's subscription. The far more substantial, timely and solidly attested service that Fielding had rendered in *The Opposition: A Vision* adequately "explains" the Prime Minister's generosity, if any explanation is needed. If the Prime Minister had actually hoped to silence the Ur-*Wild*, why did he finally forward its publication (unchanged, by Digeon's account, apart from the addition of Heartfree's story) with an exceptionally generous subscription? And if Fielding actually published satire on Walpole in 1743, he must have had his reasons; it seems excessively ingenious to suppose that it somehow "survived" unchanged from 1740, despite his "changing politics." Or if the satire is in fact conscious, how had his politics actually changed? The allegation that Fielding suppressed the Ur-*Wild* is not only unnecessary but also insufficient to explain the Prime Minister's subscription. Walpole, at least, the only person in any position to judge, evidently saw no connection between the work he allegedly silenced, and the one to which he subscribed.

The analysis of the political tendency of Fielding's list, moreover, is circular, because the vast majority of the subscriptions are hopelessly undatable. We can sort the Whigs from the Tories (in so far as this distinction was still meaningful in 1743), but apart from a few Jacobites, whose opposition was constitutional, which subscribers belonged to which Oppositions, and which to which Administrations, is simply beyond conjecture. Did the Prince of Wales subscribe before Walpole's fall or after it? before, of course, if his subscription expressed Opposition solidarity; Opposition, of course, if he subscribed before; but there is no proof of either premise. Miller and Battestin reckoned the subscribers' politics as of 1741, when the two sides were sharply polarized. Fielding was still garnering subscriptions in 1742–43, however, when the political gamut was broader. The problem of Fielding's "Walpolian" subscribers dissolves, once Walpole's Administration ceases to be the central issue. The passions that he raised did not immediately subside with the death of his Administration, of course, but they were diverted and overlaid by political maneuver.

Between 1742 and 1743, such leading subscribers as Walpole, Pulteney, the Prince of Wales and Chesterfield were engaged in a political dance, whose figures changed from moment to moment. Even those like Winnington or Newcastle, who maintained places in the Administration, had very different games to play before and after Walpole's fall. "We shall not all die," sighed

Henry Fielding, pp. 140–162, accepts Digeon's theory, but not Battestin's; Robert D. Hume, *Henry Fielding and the London Theatre, 1728–1737* (1988) follows Cleary, but does not specifically address the later period. Digeon's theory is cogently attacked by Hollis Rinehart, "The Role of Walpole in Fielding's *Jonathan Wild*," *English Studies in Canada*, 5 (1979), 420–431, and Roy Bennis Friedman, "Fielding's *The Life of Mr. Jonathan Wild the Great*: A Textual and Critical Study," Ph.D. Thesis (City University of New York), 1982; but they are still a minority.

one old-timer as he tendered his resignation, "but be all changed."[47] Pulteney and Carteret, with the help of the Prince of Wales, triumphed over the Old Administration and the Old Opposition alike. The "Broad Bottom" coalition of 1744 was the natural product of the mutual disappointment of these two factions: four of the former Opposition—Chesterfield, Bedford, Lyttelton and Dodington—would ultimately join two "loyal" Walpolians and a Jacobite—Devonshire, Newcastle, and Sir John Hynde Cotton, whose enormous backside gave piquancy to the new group's nickname.[48] All of them subscribed to the *Miscellanies*, and if Fielding's politics changed, so did those of his subscribers. The list is not a poll on the ambivalence of Fielding's political loyalties, then; we may doubt that his subscribers ever expected the constancy of a hired pen from a gentleman who set his name to the title page; and we do not need textual crutches to explain their individualistic politics and supple principles, which were neither better nor worse than his.

If the Opposition and Administration Whig factions and the Tories are evenly represented in Fielding's list, then, one might conclude that it is *ipso facto* non-partisan; but whatever the politics of the list, its rhetorical appeal abides, transparent despite scholarly troubling. In all its order and variety, descending from Prince Frederick through the multiple orders of the nobility, ladies before gents, to a wide range of ever less distinguished commoners, Fielding's list projects a powerful impression of English society at large: *mores hominum multorum vidit, et urbes*, we may well exclaim. Society as it actually was was something else, of course: in 427 mostly masculine, armigerous names, any child can see that certain elements are over- or under-represented. Nevertheless, if one can only read the list mimetically, and not statistically, it amply satisfies neoclassical criteria of generality, and contemporary theories of virtual representation.

In a notable departure from bibliographic precedent, Fielding mustered his subscribers before the Introduction to the *Miscellanies*, in the same large type, thus assimilating them to dedicatees. Before this place, on the title page, he, "Henry Fielding, Esq;" now reassumes his proper name and rank after six years of professional anonymity; no longer the proletarian "Capt. Hercules Vinegar," he may now rise above the dust and toil of politics; and as parties to his undertaking, he impleads his 427 subscribers, in order of social precedence. The reality of this spectacular performance was perhaps suspect from the start, but that should not make us overlook its virtues. As his editor, I will correct the compositor's mistakes; I will conform the order of names to the social hierarchy that Fielding intended; I will upgrade Mr. John Fawkner to Esquire. The list of subscribers—or "Subscrebers", as the compositor would have it—is not a document, to be copied letter by letter,

47. *The Yale Edition of Horace Walpole's Correspondence*, ed. W. S. Lewis et al., 17 (1954), 333.

48. Cf. the article on Cotton in Romney Sedgwick, *The House of Commons, 1715–1754* (1970); and *Catalogue of Political and Personal Satires / British Museum, Dept. of Prints and Drawings*; comp. F. G. Stephens and Edward Hawkins (1877), no. 2613.

but an integral part of Fielding's work. I cannot, alas, print it where it belongs, in proper dignity of type at the head of vol. 1. It will appear in nine-point type at the end of vol. 3 of the Wesleyan Edition of the *Miscellanies*, followed by my identifications in eight points. The virtual reality of Fielding's list pales before mine, which should be virtually invisible.

EIGHTEENTH-CENTURY AUTHORS AND THE ABUSE OF THE FRANKING SYSTEM

by

JAMES E. TIERNEY

ALTHOUGH it is well known that the English franking privilege was much abused during the eighteenth century, very little specific evidence has come forward to show the extent to which literary figures illegally used the free postage accorded government officers and members of Parliament. Howard Robinson has called our attention to the infringements on the privilege by both Samuel Johnson and Horace Walpole, pointing to the occasions when Johnson requested Mrs. Thrale to have her husband frank their correspondence and when Walpole franked letters for his friends George Montagu and the Rev. William Cole.[1] However, little else has reached print.

The present essay, by drawing upon the correspondence of the mid-eighteenth-century London bookseller Robert Dodsley, will add a number of otherwise law-abiding authors to the list of those who winked at the prescriptions of the franking privilege by employing franks for their private correspondence. On the broader scale, it should also become clear that the illegal employment of franks during the period had come to be accepted, actually expected, even by those to whom the privilege was specifically

---

1. *The British Post Office. A History* (1948), pp. 117–118. For Johnson, for instance, see his letter to Mrs. Thrale on 7 November 1779 in the Hyde Edition of *The Letters of Samuel Johnson*, ed. Bruce Redford (1992–94), III, 210. Her husband, Henry Thrale (1728?–81), was M.P. for Southwark at the time. For Montagu, see his letter to Walpole on 17 November 1761, in *Horace Walpole's Correspondence with George Montagu*, ed. W. S. Lewis and A. Dayle Wallace (1941) I, 402; for Cole, see his letter to Walpole on 11 February 1764 in *Horace Walpole's Correspondence with the Rev. William Cole*, ed. W. S. Lewis and A. Dayle Wallace (1937), I, 59.

For some of the following general notions on the history of franking, I rely on (besides Robinson) George Brumel, *A Short Account of the Franking System in the Post Office: 1652–1840* (Bournemouth: Bournemouth Guardian, Ltd., 1936); Kenneth Ellis, *The Post Office in the Eighteenth Century* (1958); and J. C. Hemmeon, *The History of the British Post Office* (1912).

granted in law. In fact, the evidence will suggest that, during the 1740s and 1750s, the illegal use of franks had risen to such proportions that it was threatening to become an established English custom.

I

To begin, it would be helpful to recall briefly some of the major developments in both the law and practice of franking prior to, and concurrent with, the period under consideration. Franking had originated with Cromwell's government. In 1652, the Council of State ordered that ". . . all public packets on extraordinary dispatches, letters of members of Parliament and Council of State, secretaries, clerks, or officers employed in public service under them, or their committees, or in any other service of public concernment, shall be carried free. . . ."[2] Extended into the Restoration, the privilege was noticeably abused, as reflected in a Royal Warrant on 4 March 1693: ". . . the King has suffered great prejudice in the Post Office Revenue by the free carriage of letters and packets which ought to have been paid for."[3] In response to the abuse, this warrant restricted free carriage to the two principal Secretaries of State, the Secretary of Scotland, the Secretary in Holland, and the earl of Portland; two days later members of Parliament were accorded the privilege, but only during the session and forty days before and after. In addition, to forestall further abuse, members were required to write their names and to give the impression of their seals in a book provided for the purpose. A few months later, the privilege was further extended to the Treasury Lords, the Secretary of War, and the Secretary of the Admiralty.

These prescriptions, however, proved ineffective in constraining abuses, which continued to proliferate into the eighteenth century. Typical abuses were of several kinds: enclosure of private letters within franked packets by authorized persons; forging of members' names by constituents without complaint from the former; letters sent from the country to be re-addressed for delivery under members' signatures; letters directed to be sent under a privileged person's name to a City coffee house where it would be picked up by the intended recipient; the inclusion of private letters within newspaper packets that had been franked by a privileged person.

In 1715, complaints from the Postmasters-General prompted the House of Commons to enact further stipulations: franks on letters and packets were to be written in the hand of the privileged person; a letter would pass free only if a member was actually residing in the place to which the letter was addressed; a member was forbidden to frank a newspaper unless it was entirely in print (no letter enclosed).[4]

---

2. *Calendar of State Papers, Domestic Series, 1651–1652*, ed. Mary Anne Everett Green (1877), p. 507.
3. *Calendar of Treasury Books*, comp. William A. Shaw (1935) Vol. X, Pt. 1, pp. 79, 82.
4. *Journal of the House of Commons, 1714–1718*, p. 303.

The ongoing anxieties of Postmasters-General were reflected in the reported losses to the King's revenue as a result of franked material, both legal and illegal. For instance, from Lady Day (25 March) 1716 to the same day of the following year, the government audit office reported losses to revenue of £18,471 as a result of franking by the King's ministers and an additional £237 as the loss from M.P.'s franking.[5]

Despite continuing government clarifications regarding persons entitled to the franking privilege and warnings to violators, the illegal use of franks proceeded to escalate through the first three decades of the eighteenth century. Finally, reported annual losses to revenue of £36,864 during the period 1730–1733 prompted the House of Commons to undertake its own investigation of the problem in 1735. Various Post Office officials were summoned to testify on the manner and extent of the misuse of franks. Although Edward Cave, a supervisor of franks, provided elaborate evidence of false franking (notably, M.P.'s franking of letters not concerned with their business and non-privileged persons' use of blank franks supplied by members), the House became irate when it learned of Cave's methods of discovering and dealing with illegal franks. He reported that when he knew a member was not actually residing at the address on a letter, he charged the letter with postage. More distressing to the House, however, was Cave's method of detecting fraudulent franks: examining all franked letters by candlelight.[6]

Ironically, the principal effect of the investigation was the enactment of restrictions on the Post Office rather than measures directed at curing the franking problem. The House passed a Resolution forbidding the tactics employed by Cave, regarding them as infringements on members' privacy and privilege.[7] When the Postmasters-General complained to the Treasury (who set policy for the Post Office) that they were now prevented from protecting the King's revenue by this new restriction, they were told to obey the House's Resolution.[8]

Four years after George III had surrendered the Post Office revenue in favor of a Civil List settlement in 1760, Parliament passed an act, giving sanction to this longstanding privilege and repeating the principal points of the original royal proclamation. However, it put some "teeth" into the new act by including an elaborate set of regulations against abuses, and, among them, one stipulating that anyone found illegally avoiding postage would be guilty of felony and liable to transportation for seven years.[9] Initially, the act significantly reduced the illegal use of franks, but, shortly after, when the

5. *Calendar of Treasury Books January-December 1717*, Vol. XXI, Pt. 1 (1960), p. ccclxvii.

6. *Journal of the House of Commons, 1732–1737*, p. 463.

7. *Journal of the House of Commons, 1732–1737*, p. 476.

8. As Ellis notes (pp. 39–40), despite the Treasury's setting policy for the Post Office, its attitude toward franking had always differed from that of the Post Office: whereas the Treasury was always anxious to protect the privilege, the Post Office regularly sought to curtail it.

9. 4 George III, c. 24.

privilege was extended to other persons, the regulations were relaxed, and the old abuses returned in legion.

II

It is from the nineteen-year period preceding 1764—a time of lax government control—that the relevant Dodsley correspondence presented below originates. Evidence of specific franking abuses in this correspondence derives from twenty-three separate letters written by eleven different persons, including Dodsley himself. An additional fourteen letters show the bookseller actually franking his own letters. The former originate from a variety of places, including Aberdeen, Bath, Birmingham, Carlisle, Durham, and Nottingham. Mostly regular correspondents, the writers include the printer John Baskerville; John "Estimate" Brown; John Gilbert Cooper, a prolific miscellaneous writer; the poet John Dyer; David Fordyce, professor of moral philosophy at Aberdeen; Richard Graves, author of *The Spiritual Quixote*; John Scott Hylton, a numismatist from Hales-Owen; Robert Lowth, the grammarian and future bishop of London; William "Pliny" Melmoth; and the poet William Shenstone.

Not all of the instances are *de facto* violations of the franking privilege, but where they are not, it is clear that the writers, short of counterfeiting a signature, would not hesitate to so infringe. Generally the abuses are of three types: the endorsement by M.P.s of letters or packets that have nothing to do with their own business but franked as a favor to a friend; letters or packets sent to a local M.P., who, upon reception, franked his friend/neighbor's mail; and, perhaps the most notorious of all, the circulation and use of blank but franked sheets.

Five letters from Dodsley's correspondents solely concerned with the writers' literary interests or productions (and not at all with an M.P.'s business) are either franked by an M.P. or request that favor of Dodsley. Two of John Gilbert Cooper's letters, written from Derby on 18 February 1747 and from Leicester on 23 September 1749, are franked by Borlace Warren, M.P. for Nottingham (1713–15, 1727–47), and by George Wrighte, M.P. for Leicester (1727–66), respectively.[10] The first is wholly concerned with essays that Cooper encloses for Dodsley's fortnightly *Museum: or Literary and Historical Register* (1746–47); the second is taken up with directions for indexing the author's soon-to-be-published *Life of Socrates* (1749). Another letter on 16 January 1749 asks Dodsley to send Thomas Seward's pamphlet *The Conformity between Popery and Paganism illustrated* in a frank, thereby calling upon the bookseller to supply the free postage.[11] A similar favor is begged of Dodsley by John Brown on 8 November 1746, only he would like *two* pam-

10. Bodleian Library, MS Eng. Misc. d. 174, ff. 27–29; 45–46. Printed in *The Correspondence of Robert Dodsley, 1733–1764*, ed. James E. Tierney (1989), pp. 110–111, 129–130. All subsequent references to this edition will be indicated simply by *Correspondence*.

11. Bodleian Library, MS Eng. Misc. d. 174, f. 37. *Correspondence*, p. 127.

phlets—Nathaniel Cotton's *Fireside* and the "Surprising History of a late long Administration" by "Titus Livius, jr."—sent in a frank.[12] (Franked pieces were not to exceed two ounces.) Finally, David Fordyce's letter from Aberdeen on 11 February 1748 has nothing to do with the endorser, William Grant, M.P. for Elgin, but inquires at length about Fordyce's manuscript for *The Elements of Moral Philosophy*, which he had recently submitted to Dodsley.[13]

The franking of Dodsley's own letters, upon receipt, was assured in two further letters from Cooper. On 7 April 1746, he directs Dodsley to send every number of the *Museum* to the Hon. John Stanhope, Lord of the Admiralty, at Alderman Frances's in Derby, "where I shall receive it without any post charge."[14] On 9 December 1749, he enjoins Dodsley to send him "in two Separate covers (for I'm afraid one will weigh above two ounces) the last *Monthly Review* [containing a review of Cooper's *Life of Socrates*], directed, for Wrightson Mundy Esqr Membr of Parlt. at John Gilbert Cooper's in Leicester, which expedient will save me the expense of carriage, & you two franks."[15]

If one can generalize from the bulk of evidence found in the correspondence, the most common abuse of the franking privilege consisted of the wholesale endorsing of blank sheets by privileged persons for the use of their friends. The earliest instance, found in a Cooper letter on 15 November 1746, shows the author promising Dodsley another two papers for his *Museum* "as soon as I can procure franks." Apparently he did more than keep his word, for, in a letter of the following 11 February, he is reminding Dodsley that "about two months ago I sent you some franks of Mr Warren's," thereby allowing the bookseller to respond to his many queries free of charge.[16]

John Baskerville, the Birmingham printer, implicitly reveals the extent and common acceptance of the abuse in the conclusion of his letter to Dodsley on 19 October 1752.[17] There he suggests to the bookseller, whose shop in Pall Mall was near to the Houses of Parliament, that "As you are [in] the Land of Franks: half a Doz. would do me a particular pleasure, As a good Many things not worth a groat might be communicated by Yr Most obedt hble Servt." A similar impression of Bath's seasonal "resources" is conveyed by Richard Graves when writing on 30 September 1756.[18] Graves hopes "to get some Franks when our Season comes in." From another quarter, John Scott Hylton of Hales-Owen, near Birmingham, complains in a letter of 6 December 1757 that "Lord Dudley's death [5th Baron Dudley] has put an

12. Bodleian Library, MS Toynbee d. 19, f. 7. *Correspondence*, pp. 104–105.

13. Simon Gratz Collection, Case 11, Box 6, The Historical Society of Pennsylvania. *Correspondence*, pp. 121–122.

14. Bodleian Library, MS Eng. Misc. d. 174, f. 9. *Correspondence*, p. 95.

15. Bodleian Library, MS Eng. Misc. d. 174, f. 47. *Correspondence*, p. 131.

16. Bodleian Library, MS Eng. Misc. d. 174, ff. 19–[21]; 23–25. *Correspondence*, pp. 105–106; 109–110.

17. Butler Library, Columbia University. *Correspondence*, pp. 145–146.

18. Somerset County Record Office, DD/SK, 28/1,2. *Correspondence*, pp. 240–241.

end to all Franks with me."[19] Four months later, providing Dodsley with a lengthy account of his ailing neighbor William Shenstone, Hylton resorts to a frank "found . . . in Mr: Shenstone's pocket Book, which I stole for you," adding: "I wish I could procure some and then I should write with greater Satisfaction to you, than to make you pay postage for my incorrect scrawl."[20] The availability of franks seems so common that, when temporarily unavailable, Dodsley's correspondents thought twice about writing.

Obviously Shenstone himself made regular use of franks to cover his personal letters, and from whatever source he could procure them. Dodsley's response to the poet in a letter of 19 September 1758 implicitly acknowledges the free flow of franks that did not even require the user to procure them directly from a friend, or even be acquainted with his benefactor: "As to Franks, you could not have ask'd at a worse time, as I have no body in Town to apply to: however I have enclos'd three, & will send You more as soon as I have an opportunity of getting any."[21] Shenstone had revealed a reliance upon franks for his personal correspondence even earlier. On 21 December of the previous year, when sending Dodsley corrections for poems to be included in Volumes 5 and 6 of a *Collection of Poems by Several Hands*, Shenstone says he believes he will write again tomorrow, for which he has "reserv'd my *only* Frank."[22] Still another request for a supply of franks comes from William Melmoth on 3 July 1760.[23] Although missing, Dodsley's response was probably little different from that to Shenstone, for Parliament, of course, did not sit during the summer months.

Another seven allusions in the correspondence implicitly acknowledge the casual circulation of franked sheets among non-privileged persons, but, for the most part, they consist of simple apologies to Dodsley for momentarily lacking franks to cover letters, thereby requiring the bookseller to pay the post. Three such letters come from Richard Graves, on 10 October 1757, 21 May 1763, and 6 January 1764.[24] John Dyer the poet is responsible for another letter on 12 May 1757; John Scott Hylton, for one on 9 February 1758; and Robert Lowth, for one on 9 June 1758.[25] Finally, another such apology appears in Dodsley's own letter on 9 December 1758, a brief piece hastily dashed off to Shenstone amidst the excitement surrounding the performance of Dodsley's tragedy *Cleone* at Drury Lane.[26]

19. Humanities Research Center, University of Texas at Austin, Robert Dodsley/Recipient 1/Bound, ff. 13–16. *Correspondence*, pp. 315–316.

20. Humanities Research Center, University of Texas at Austin, Robert Dodsley/Recipient 1/Bound, ff. 33–36. *Correspondence*, pp. 348–350.

21. British Library, Add. MS. 28,959, ff. 103–104. *Correspondence*, pp. 372–374.

22. British Library, Add. MS. 28,959, ff. 87–88. *Correspondence*, pp. 319–321.

23. British Library, Add. MS. 35,338, f. 12. *Correspondence*, pp. 442–443.

24. Somerset County Record Office, DD/SK, 28/1, 7; 15; 79. *Correspondence*, pp. 293–294, 474–475, 482.

25. *Correspondence*, p. 280; Humanities Research Center, University of Texas at Austin, Robert Dodsley/Recipient 1/Bound, ff. 25–28 (*Correspondence*, pp. 339–341); British Library, Add. MS. 35,339, ff. 23–24 (*Correspondence*, pp. 361–362).

26. British Library, Add. MS. 28,959, ff. 110–111. *Correspondence*, p. 385.

III

Surely the most perplexing use of franks in the correspondence involves a series of fourteen letters Dodsley wrote to Shenstone and which he franked himself. On the cover of each of these letters appears, in the bookseller's hand, "R. Dodsley *free.*" The letters come midway in Dodsley's lengthy correspondence with Shenstone, covering a period of almost two years; that is, from September 1753 through July 1755.[27]

By what authority Dodsley presumed to endorse these letters escapes detection. However, it is reasonable to assume that Dodsley's endorsements do not reflect an infringement on the franking privilege. First of all, such a blatant abuse of franks, because it would amount to arrogant defiance of the law, does not fit the character of the mild-mannered, law-abiding bookseller. Moreover, as evident throughout his correspondence, Dodsley was keen to protect his business reputation, which, at the time of these letters, was rising to its zenith. As London's premiere publisher of *belles lettres*, he certainly would not have jeopardized his business for the paltry pence to be saved in this brief series of letters. Clearly, an explanation must be found within the prescriptions of the law, or at least within accepted custom. Unfortunately, nothing we know of Dodsley affords a certain explanation. No record, for instance, shows Dodsley to have held any of the offices or to have served in a secretarial capacity to any of the offices accorded the franking privilege. We are left to speculate.

One possible explanation derives from a Dodsley business activity of the time, the publishing of periodicals. David Foxon has suggested that perhaps Dodsley had gained the privilege from the Post Office Clerks of the Road, who officially franked newspapers sent into the provinces. The Clerks, Foxon notes, employed numerous agents in London to collect, wrap, and frank these papers. Dodsley, as the publisher of the weekly periodical *The World* (January, 1753–December, 1756) and as a shareholder (at least since 1747) in the most influential newspaper currently being sent into the country, the *London Evening Post*, might have been so employed.[28] If Foxon is correct, perhaps Dodsley had loosely construed the privilege of franking as extending to his private letters—an understanding that might well fit the current liberal interpretation of the franking privilege. On the other hand, if such was the case, one might question why Dodsley suddenly discontinued the practice in mid-1755 when the forementioned publications continued to be issued. No new government investigation of franking abuses seems to have occurred in that year, nor were there any new restrictions on persons entitled to the privilege.

Dodsley does seem to have come to the government's attention in late 1754 or early 1755 when the *London Evening Post* carried a series of scurrilous attacks on the Rev. Richard Blacow and probably also when, in July 1755, the paper's printer, Richard Nutt, was imprisoned for printing a libel

27. British Library, Add. MS. 28,959, ff. 12–48. *Correspondence*, pp. 156–205, passim.
28. In a letter to the author from David Foxon, Emeritus, Oxford University.

on the government. Sensitive to the government's concern regarding the *Post's* activities, Dodsley, when queried about his role in the Blacow affair by a friend in government, responded by offering to sell his share in the news-paper.[29] That the government's displeasure might have played a role in Dods-ley's failure to frank after July 1755 is a possibility, of course, but it does not explain the grounds on which he took up the practice, to begin with.

Another possible explanation for Dodsley's franking activity arises from a practice that would become, in short time, a prescription of the law of franking; namely, that Dodsley had been appointed by a privileged person to endorse letters on the latter's behalf. One prescription of the Act of 1763 allowed ministers to appoint others to frank their letters, on the condition that the names of such proxies be registered with the Postmaster-General. Those sending letters were to sign their names on the outside and themselves write the address.[30] Although this extension of the privilege does not of-ficially become law until eleven years after Dodsley's initial frank, it is quite possible that the *practice* had originated much earlier than the date of legal sanction, that the law merely codified what had been the accepted custom for some time. It is unlikely that such a prescription would have been enacted if there had not been some such pressure to legitimize it.

If such had been the case, Dodsley would certainly have been in line for such an appointment, for he had some close friends in the Ministry during these years, friends who would have been agreeable to such an arrangement. A likely benefactor in this case would have been his friend George Lord Lyttleton, significantly both a Lord of the Treasury and Shenstone's neigh-bor at Hagley. Moreover, as Lyttelton's bookseller, Dodsley had already put two of Lyttleton's works through several editions.[31] No doubt the author would have been sympathetic to Dodsley's postal expenses during years when he carried on an extensive correspondence with Shenstone regarding the preparation of Volume 4 of his *Collection of Poems* (1755). In fact, Lyttelton might have served as one of the bookseller's advisors on the publication. Also significant, as mentioned earlier, it was the Treasury that controlled the op-eration of the Post Office, appointing the Postmaster General, setting its rates, and generally determining its policy. Dodsley could not have wanted a friend in a more appropriate place.

Even these fortuitous links, however, and the potential extension of the franking privilege they suggest do not fully correspond with the peculiar circumstances of Dodsley's franking activity. During the period in question (September, 1753 to July, 1755), Dodsley's extant letters (38 pieces, *in toto*) show no other instances of franking than when writing to Shenstone.[32] Did

29. *Correspondence*, pp. 182–185.

30. 4 George III c.24.

31. Lyttelton's *Discourse on Providence* (1747) passed through three editions within its first year; his *Observations on the Conversion and Apostleship of St. Paul* had reached a fifth edition by 1754.

32. On 26 August 1751, John Gilbert Cooper wrote to Dodsley: "I recd about three days ago a letter from an unknown hand, which was directed & frank'd by you . . ." (Bodleian Ms. Eng Misc, d. 174, f. 61; *Correspondence*, p. 140). It is not absolutely clear whether Cooper

Dodsley enjoy a general franking privilege or had his free postage, by some special arrangement, been limited to the letters sent to Shenstone. Especially curious, one letter to Shenstone in the midst of this series—that on 24 January 1755—had been franked not by Dodsley but by John Harris, M.P. for Devon.[33] Again, the question looms: why did Dodsley discontinue the practice in mid-1755? From this point, the number of his letters to Shenstone increases, and Lyttelton continued as a lord of the Treasury. In effect, this series of frankings by Dodsley defies certain explanation; it has no known precedent.

IV

Important for the history of franking during the eighteenth century is the single impression emerging from the foregoing evidence; namely, that notable, law-abiding citizens, despite the illegality, could openly and regularly use franks for private purposes and be supported in the practice by those who were officially accorded the privilege. Such common and casual usage suggests that the practice was universally accepted, even expected. In several instances, it appears that franks were passed about openly, much like modern grocer coupons. Certainly the writers of these letters do not seem to imagine themselves guilty of anything untoward, for none of their allusions to the acquisition or use of franks hints of conscious covert or fraudulent behavior. The origin of the franks was readily acknowledged, the letters were posted in the usual manner, and those to Dodsley sent directly to his shop, not to some intermediate place to cover the trail. Significantly, all of the correspondents were respectable and respected gentlemen: four of them were clergymen, one a professor, and one a future bishop of London. Dodsley himself enjoyed an enviable reputation as a major London bookseller.

By extension, it seems reasonable to assume that the liberal use of franks by this coterie of literary personalities was reflected in the practice of society as a whole. Surely other booksellers and their authors indulged in the practice. In fact, one cannot imagine Dodsley's having skirted the law unless he had felt supported by the custom of common usage. Likewise there is no reason to limit the observation to relations between booksellers and their authors. Surely the world of politics, for instance, with its vested interest in outlying constituencies, swelled the ranks of likely users. The full story, however, remains to be told. Study of other collections of extant holograph letters from the period would doubtless afford additional evidence. The interpretation of the evidence, however, will probably depend on conquering the uncatalogued resources of the British Post Office archives.

means that Dodsley *personally* franked the letter or whether he is saying that the bookseller procured a frank to cover the postage. Since the Dodsley letter to which Cooper refers is missing, first-hand evidence is lacking. Given the isolated circumstances of the "frank"— two years before Dodsley's franks begin to appear, and addressed to someone other than Shenstone—it is impossible to conclude whether or not Dodsley's franking actually dates from 1751.

33. BL Add. MS. 28,959, f. 24; *Correspondence*, pp. 191–192.

THE PRELIMINARIES TO DR. JOHNSON'S *DICTIONARY*:
AUTHORIAL REVISIONS AND THE ESTABLISHMENT
OF THE TEXTS

by

GWIN J. KOLB AND ROBERT DEMARIA, JR.*

As IS true for the editors of many other works, determining authorial revisions and establishing the texts were two of the principal duties we faced as editors of the preliminaries to Dr. Johnson's *Dictionary of the English Language*—chiefly the Preface, the History of the English Language, and the Grammar of the English Tongue. Fortunately, early in our research we learned that our tasks had been notably aided by the findings of previous investigators, specifically, W. R. Keast (in his "The Preface to *A Dictionary of the English Language*: Johnson's Revision and the Establishment of the Text"), Arthur Sherbo (in his "1773: The Year of Revision"), and Daisuke Nagashima (in his *Johnson the Philologist*).[1]

I

PREFACE: ALTERATIONS IN SECOND AND FOURTH EDITIONS

Keast initially collated the first four London folio editions of the Preface, all published during Johnson's lifetime (1755; 1755 again, set from the first edition and revised by Johnson; 1765, set from the second edition and unrevised; and 1773, set from the *first* edition and revised by Johnson). In his essay, he records, with his individual assessments, virtually all the variants, substantive and accidental, in the second and fourth editions. At the end, making clear his concurrence, which we share, with the Greg-Bowers theory of copy-text, he sums up: "Future editors must . . . adopt the text of the first edition as their copy-text and introduce into it the two sets of Johnsonian revisions from the second and fourth editions, together with such changes in

* We express our warmest thanks to Ruth A. Kolb and Blake Weathersby for their fundamental assistance in the preparation of this article. Gwin Kolb also expresses his lasting gratitude to the Beinecke Library (Yale University) for the award, during the fall of 1993, of the Frederick and Marion Pottle Fellowship, which enabled him to collect some of the data contained herein.

1. Keast, *Studies in Bibliography*, 5 (1952–53), 129–146; Sherbo, *Eighteenth-Century Studies*, 7 (1973–74), 18–39, esp. 39, 29–33; Nagashima, [Hirakata, Osaka, Japan]: The Intercultural Research Institute, Kansai University of Foreign Studies, 1988, pp. 20, 35–36, 146–148. References below are identified in the text by authors' names and page numbers. See also Paul Fussell, "A Note on Samuel Johnson and the Rise of Accentual Prosodic Theory," *Philological Quarterly*, 33 (1954), 431–433.

the accidentals from these texts as seem necessary for correctness or consistency" (p. 146).

Examining anew editions one through four as well as the "proprietors'" fifth (1784), sixth (1785), and seventh (1785), the latter for possible rectification of errors, we have arrived at the same general conclusion, although our estimate of variants has differed from Keast's in two instances. Specifically, we have accepted sixty-three of Keast's suggested readings, including his emendation of *fall* for *full* in paragraph 45; but we have rejected his choice of *betwixt* rather than *between* in paragraph 15 (we have found *betwixt* neither elsewhere in the Preface nor in the *Plan of a Dictionary*, the History, the Grammar, and Johnson's letters) and his emendation of *semi* for *fair* in paragraph 38 (we have adopted *far*, proposed by the reviewer of the *Dictionary* in the *Monthly Review*, 12 [1755], 300, n. 14). Moreover, we have (1) made decisions on three variants about which Keast was undecided (pp. 130, 131); (2) selected the replacement in paragraph 26 of a semi-colon for a comma (after "language") which appears in the second, third, and fourth editions and which Keast overlooked; and (3) recorded twelve accidental variants which appear only in the third edition, unrevised, to repeat, by Johnson.

II
GRAMMAR: ALTERATIONS IN THIRD EDITION

Sherbo's essay, much less inclusive than Keast's, concentrates on Johnson's revisions for his fourth edition (1773) of Shakespeare's plays (of which George Steevens was a collaborator) and for the fourth folio edition (also 1773) of his *Dictionary*. But Sherbo mentions (p. 19) that in the third edition of the *Dictionary* Johnson, surely reacting to John Wilkes's witty remark on the mistake, modified his original comment, in the Grammar, about the letter *H* to read: "It seldom, perhaps never, *except in compounded words*, begins any but the first syllable" (our italics). His principal subject being Johnson's revisions in 1773, Sherbo says nothing else about authorial changes in the 1765 version of the Grammar.

However, our collation of the entire text reveals that Johnson did not revise the Grammar in the second edition but that he altered it in the third edition more often than anyone has ever pointed out. For example, of the thirty-three substantive variants originating in this edition, twenty-three can be confidently labeled "authorial." Fifteen of the twenty-three are additions which divide the Grammar into parts and sections—namely, "PART I. Of ORTHOGRAPHY." (with three roman section numbers), "PART II." (with six roman section numbers), "PART III.", and "PART IV." (with two roman section numbers) (sigs. L1^r, L1^v, L2^v, M1^r, M1^v, N1^r, N2^r, and N2^v). Four more are also additions—three the identifications of authors of quoted passages on sig. O1^r ("*Pope*.", Elijah "*Fenton*.", and David "*Lewis*."), the fourth an entire sentence following that on sig. L2^r ending in "as *frosty winter*"

("Yet I am of opinion that both *w* and *y* are always vowels, because they cannot after a vowel be used with the sound which is supposed to make them consonants"). The four remaining authorial revisions consist of clarifications or corrections in as many statements: (1) "None of the small consonants have a double form, except ſ, *s*" is altered to "None of the consonants have a double form, except the small ſ, *s*" (sig. L1ʳ); (2) as pointed out above, the assertion that the letter *H* "seldom, perhaps never, begins any but the first syllable . . ." becomes "seldom, perhaps never, except in compounded words, begins . . ." (sig. L2ʳ); (3) "But it may be observed of *y* as of *w*, that it follows a vowel without any hiatus, as *rosy youth*" is changed to "It may . . . *youth, but yet that it cannot be sounded after a vowel*" (sig. L2ᵛ); and (4) in the sentence "The verse of twelve lines, called an *Alexandrine*, is now only used to diversify heroick lines," "twelve lines" is corrected to "twelve syllables" (sig. O1ʳ). We have adopted all the revisions in this group except two, the identification of the author David "*Lewis*," which was expanded to "*Lewis to Pope*" in the fourth edition (see below) and (3) above, which was superseded by Johnson's revision in the fourth edition (see below).

The rest of the substantive alterations can be divided into the four which we think Johnson probably made and the six which he possibly made. The first of the former group changes "gradation" to "gradations" in the sentence reading, in part, "In treating on the letters, I shall not . . . enquire into the original of their form . . . ; nor into the properties and gradation of sounds . . ." (sig. L1ʳ). "Gradations," denoting plurality and diversity, clearly describes human sounds more accurately than does the singular "gradation," as the accompanying term "properties" evinces. And Johnson seems the plausible cause of the shift, although a careful compositor or proof corrector cannot be entirely ruled out. Likewise, the "as" inserted after "consonant" in the phrase "is a consonant, as *ye, young*" (sigs. L2ʳ–L2ᵛ) and that inserted after "*ain*" in the phrase "except words in *ain*, as *cértain*" (sig. N2ᵛ) are likely authorial additions, although, again, another person might have been responsible for them. The same comment applies to the correct replacement of "*hung*" by "*stunk*" in the original sequence of "*drunk, sunk, shrunk, hung, come*" (sig. M2ᵛ). We have adopted all these variants.

The last group of changes could have been made, we conclude, either by Johnson or by another person. The first is the deletion of the superfluous "it" in the sentence on sig. L1ᵛ originally beginning "*F*, . . . , it is numbered. . . ." We have adopted this correction. The next three consist of alterations from the plural to the singular form of verbs—"*Wr* imply" to "implies," "*Sw* imply" to "implies," and "*C1* denote" to "denotes" (sig. N1ᵛ). An examination of the context immediately reveals the reason for the change: to achieve conformity between the number of the verbs and that of neighboring comparable verbs. However, since, as we note below, the fourth edition of the Grammar contains the plural form of all the verbs just described, we have chosen the same form for our text. The fifth variant, occurring too in the fourth edition, corrects the letters "*ly*" to "*ty*" in the sentence "Words ending in *ly* have their accent on the antepenult, as *pusillanimity, activity*" (sig. N2ᵛ). We have adopted this correction. Added to the beginning of line 4 ("Shall that holy fire") of Michael Drayton's "An Ode Written in the Peake" (sig. N2ᵛ), the word "Or" is the final member of this group. Johnson or someone else, we surmise, noticing that the line, unlike the others in the poem, lacks six syllables, and not consulting an independent text, proceeded to regularize the line by prefixing the "Or" (cf. the two appearances of "Or" in the last stanza). But we have retained the five-syllable line (also in the fourth edition) because it occurs in all early editions of Drayton's poem, including that (1748) from which Johnson drew illustrative passages in the *Dictionary*.[2]

Besides the thirty-three substantive differences, the third folio edition of the Grammar contains thirty-seven accidental variations from both its predecessors and its successor, two only from its predecessors, and one only from its successor. Twenty-three of these are changes in punctuation, eight in spelling, four in accent marks, three in italics, one in the location of a sentence, and one in the position of a word. We have accepted two of the alterations in punctuation: (1) On sig. L1ᵛ, the single sentence reading in part: "*C*, . . . , never ends a word; therefore we write *stick, block,* . . . , in such words *C* is now mute" becomes two sentences by the replacement of a period for the comma immediately preceding the phrase "in such words"; Johnson seems to us the probable source of the change. (2) On sig. L2ᵛ, the period following the sentence beginning "Had he written" and concluding "appeared thus" (succeeded by four lines of poetry) is changed to a colon (i. e., "thus:"); since the same change occurs in the fourth edition, Johnson might have been the cause of it. The remaining twenty-one variants in punctuation are either manifestly improper or less suitable to their contexts than their alternatives in the first, second, and fourth editions.

We have adopted two of the changes in spelling. (1) On sig. M1ʳ, below the line of poetry ending "noble savage ran" (Dryden's *Conquest of Granada*, Part I, l. 1.209), "*Dryd.*" is expanded to "*Dryden*," which, possibly Johnson's revision, harmonizes with "*Milton*" located directly above (and below a passage from *Paradise Lost*, I, ll. 1–3). (2) On sig. O1ʳ, in the line of poetry beginning "Fairest piece" (Edmund Waller's "To Zelinda," l. 1), "welform'd" becomes "well-form'd," the same spelling as that in the wordlist of Johnson's *Dictionary*, where Waller's line is cited under *well* (adverb, sense 13). The other six variants are either errors or less preferable than their alternatives.

On sig. N2ᵛ, in the sentence beginning "1. Of dissyllables," an accent mark is correctly placed above "*fáirer*," thereby correcting a mistake in the first, second, and fourth editions. Similarly, in the sentence beginning "4. All dissyllables" accent marks are correctly placed above "*cránny*," "*lábour*," and "*fávour*," thus remedying an omission in the first, second, and fourth editions. Johnson might have been responsible for all these changes, which we have adopted.

On the other hand, we have accepted none of the remaining groups of

---

2. See W. B. C. Watkins, *Johnson and English Poetry Before 1660* (Princeton, 1936), pp. 99–101. The 1748 edition of Drayton's works is item 356 in the *Sale Catalogue* of Johnson's library (ed. J. D. Fleeman [Victoria, B. C., 1975], pp. 43, 99).

accidental variants in the third edition. The first three changes diverge from the pattern of italicizing evident in the first, second, and fourth editions. Forming the fourth difference, a short sentence is transferred—inadvertently, we assume—from its proper location, as evidenced by the context, to the end of the next paragraph. And the final difference—the location of the name of an author—is superseded by the location of the same word in the fourth edition.

III

GRAMMAR: ALTERATIONS IN FOURTH EDITION

The fourth edition of the Grammar, set, like the Preface, from the first edition, contains seventy-seven substantive, and one hundred and forty-two accidental, variants from the first, second, and third editions. Of the former group, Sherbo cites (pp. 19, 20, 29–33) thirty-four, which are starred below. Nagashima counts (p. 146) a total of twenty-seven, excluding the addition of the names of the ten poets whose lines are quoted in the section on Prosody (sigs. N2ʳ–O1ʳ), and he reproduces (pp. 147–148) two variants—a revision of a phrase (see below) and one addition to the text (see below). Neither he nor Sherbo mentions the accidental differences in the fourth edition.

The substantive variants can be divided into fifty additions and twenty-seven revisions (including omissions). The additions range from whole paragraphs and sentences through parts of sentences to single words. Since Johnson's hand is clearly discernible in most of them and consonant with the small remainder, we have admitted all of these additions into our text. Arranged sequentially from the beginning to the end of the Grammar, they are:

(1) "Saxon" and below "Saxon" two columns of the capital and small letters of the "Saxon" alphabet (sig. a1ʳ); a similar list, it should be pointed out, appears at the end of the Grammar in editions one through eight (1756–86) of the abridged *Dictionary*

(2) "and consequently able to pronounce the letters, of which I teach the pronunciation;" in the sentence beginning "I consider" (*ibid.*)

(3) "as in *věx, pěrplexity*" in the sentence beginning "It is always short" (sig. a1ᵛ)

(4) "in his *Remains*" in the sentence beginning "Camden" (*ibid.*)

(5) "This faintness of sound is found when *e* separates a mute from a liquid, as in *rotten*; or follows a mute and liquid, as in *cattle*.", forming a new paragraph after the sentence ending in "*lucre*" (*ibid.*)

(6) "*Many* is pronounced as if it were written *manny*.", forming a new paragraph after the sentence ending in "*frog*" (*ibid.*)

(7) "having no determinate sound," after the letter "*C*," which also begins the sentence (*ibid.*)

(8) "to which may be added *Egypt* and" after "*gingle*" and before "*gypsy*" in the sentence beginning "G before" (sig. a2ʳ)

(9) "It sometimes begins middle or final syllables in words compounded, as *blockhead*; or derived from the Latin, as *comprehended*," forming a new paragraph after the sentence beginning "It seldom" (*ibid.*); see also the revision above

(10) "because *sc* is sounded like *s*, as in *scene*" after "*sceptick*" in the sentence beginning "K has" (*ibid.*)

(11) "in modern pronunciation" following "sound" in the sentence beginning "It is used" (*ibid.*)

(12) *"stripe"* added between *"stramen"* and *"sventura"* in the sentence beginning *"Σβέννυμι"* (*ibid.*)

(13) "words ending in *ty*," added after "from" and before "as" in the sentence beginning *"Ti* before" (*ibid.*)

(14) "and in" after "compounds;" and before *"that"* in the sentence beginning "The sound" (*ibid.*)

*(15) "The chief argument by which *w* and *y* appear to be always vowels is, that the sounds which they are supposed to have as consonants, cannot be uttered after a vowel, like that of all other consonants; thus we say, *tu, ut; do, odd*; but in *wed, dew*, the two sounds of *w* have no resemblance of each other," forming a new paragraph after the sentence ending in *"rosy youth"* (*ibid.*)

*(16) "The English language has properly no dialects; the stile of writers has no professed diversity in the use of words, or of their flexions, and terminations, nor differs but by different degrees of skill or care. The oral diction is uniform in no spacious country, but has less variation in England than in most other nations of equal extent. The language of the northern counties retains many words now out of use, but which are commonly of the genuine Teutonick race, and is uttered with a pronunciation which now seems harsh and rough, but was probably used by our ancestors. The northern speech is therefore not barbarous but obsolete. The speech in the western provinces seems to differ from the general diction rather by a depraved pronunciation, than by any real difference which letters would express," forming a new paragraph after the sentence ending in "have followed them" (sig. a2ᵛ)

*(17) *"An* or *a* can only be joined with a singular, the correspondent plural is the noun without an article, as *I want a pen, I want pens:* or with the pronominal adjective *some*, as *I want* some *pens*," forming a new paragraph after *"Shakespeare"* (sig. b1ʳ)

*(18) "Dr. Lowth, on the other part, supposes the possessive pronouns *mine* and *thine* to be genitive cases," added after the sentence ending in "Latin genitive" (*ibid.*)

(19) "for the most part" after "have" and before "no genitives" in the sentence beginning "Plurals ending" (*ibid.*)

*(20) "They would commonly produce a troublesome ambiguity, as *the Lord's house* may be the *house of Lords*, or *the house of* a *Lord*. Besides that the mark of elision is improper, for in *the Lords' house* nothing is cut off.

Some English substantives, like those of many other languages, change their termination as they express different sexes, as *prince, princess; actor, actress; lion, lioness; hero, heroines*. To these mentioned by Dr. Lowth may be added *arbitress, poetess, chauntress, duchess, tigress, governess, tutress, peeress, authoress, traytress*, and perhaps others. Of these variable terminations we have only a sufficient number to make us feel our want, for when we say of a woman that she is a *philosopher*, an *astronomer*, a *builder*, a *weaver*, a *dancer*, we perceive an impropriety in the termination which we cannot avoid; but we can say that she is an *architect*, a *botanist*, a *student*, because these terminations have not annexed to them the notion of sex. In words which the necessities of life are often requiring, the sex is distinguished not by different terminations but by different names, as a *bull*, a *cow*; a *horse*, a *mare*; *equus, equa*; a *cock*, a *hen*; and sometimes by pronouns prefixed, as *a* he-*goat, a* she-*goat*," appearing after the sentence ending in "against them" (*ibid.*); this addition (partly) quoted by Nagashima

(21) *"some"* added to the sentence ending in "the *same*" (sig. b1ᵛ)

*(22) "as, *thy* house is larger than *mine*, but *my* garden is more spacious than *thine*" added to the sentence ending in "substantive preceding" (*ibid.*)

*(23) *"they*, when *they* is the plural of *it*," after "likewise of" and before "and are" in the sentence beginning *"Their* and" (*ibid.*)

*(24) "At least it was common to say, the man *which*, though I remember no example of, the thing *who*" after the sentence ending in "anciently confounded" (sig. b1ᵛ)

(25) *"or hath"* after *"he has"* and before "had" in the line beginning *"Sing.*" and under the *"Compound Preterite"* form of the verb *to have* (sig. b2ʳ)

*(26) "This, by custom at least, appears more easy than the other form of expressing the same sense by a negative adverb after the verb, *I like her, but* love *her* not" after the sentence beginning "It is frequently" (sig. b2ᵛ)

*(27) "of former times" after "purer writers" and before "after if" in the sentence beginning "It is used" (*ibid.*)

(28) *"till* or *until"* after *"before"* and before *"whether"* in the same sentence identified above (*ibid.*)

*(29) *"Wrote* however may be used in poetry; at least if we allow any authority to poets, who, in the exultation of genius, think themselves perhaps intitled to trample on grammarians," after the sentence ending in *"The book is* wrote" (*ibid.*)

(30) "and" after *"worshipful,"* and before *"to worship"* in the sentence beginning "Thus *worship"* (sig. c1ᵛ)

*(31) "made by *beating* different bodies into one mass" after "for food," in the sentence beginning "There are in English" (*ibid.*)

(32) "θυγατήρ" after "πορθμός" and before "μεγαλος" in the sentence beginning "It is certain" (sigs. c1ᵛ–c2ʳ)

(33) "We should therefore say *dispútable, indispútable,* rather than *disputable, indisputable;* and *advertisement* rather than *advértisement"* after the sentence beginning "16." and ending in *"commúnicableness"* (sig. c2ᵛ)

*(34) "The variations necessary to pleasure belong to the art of poetry, not the rules of grammar" after the sentence beginning "In all" and ending in "observed" (sig. d1ʳ)

*(35) *"Walton's Angler."* below the line of poetry "Are but toys" (*ibid.*)

*(36) *"Old Ballad."* below the line of poetry "Lovers felt annoy" (*ibid.*)

*(37) *"Waller."* below the line of poetry ending in "your haughty birth" (*ibid.*)

*(38) "The measures of twelve and fourteen syllables, were often mingled by our old poets, sometimes in alternate lines, and sometimes in alternate couplets" after the line of poetry ending in "distract" (*ibid.*)

*(39) *"Lewis to Pope."* below the line of poetry ending in "see" (*ibid.*)

*(40) "Beneath this tomb an infant lies
    To earth whose body lent,
    Hereafter shall more glorious rise,
    But not more innocent.
    When the Archangel's trump shall blow,
    And souls to bodies join,
    What crowds shall wish their lives below
    Had been as short as thine.
Wesley." below *"Lewis to Pope"* (*ibid.*)

*(41) "Dr. *Pope."* below the line of poetry ending in "awáy" (*ibid.*)

*(42) "Dr. *Pope."* below the line of poetry ending in "proúd" (*ibid.*)

*(43) "When présent, we lóve, and when ábsent agrée" below "Dr. *Pope."* in the addition listed above (*ibid.*)

*(44) *"Dryden."* below the line of poetry ending in "mé" (*ibid.*)

(45) " 'Tis the divinity that stirs *within us,"* below the sentence ending in "measure" (*ibid.*)

*(46) *"Addison."* below the line of poetry ending in "man" (*ibid.*)

*(47) *"Prior."* below the line of poetry ending in "abounded" (*ibid.*)

*(48) *"Glover."* below the line of poetry ending in "alone" (*ibid.*)

*(49) *"Gay."* below the line of poetry ending in "reclin'd" (*ibid.*)

*(50) *"Ballad."* below the line of poetry ending in "right" (*ibid.*).

Like the additions, the twenty-seven revisions (including omissions) strike us, with one exception, as obviously authorial or else consistent with Johnson's mode of composition. Therefore we have admitted all of them save one into our text. Listed in the same order as the additions, they are:

(1) "disquisition" substituted for "view" in the sentence beginning "I consider the English" (sig. a1ʳ)

(2) "*metre*" omitted from the sentence ending originally in "*participle, metre, lucre*" (sig. a1ᵛ)

(3) "consonant" omitted from the phrase reading originally "*w* consonant, as" in the sentence beginning "It coalesces with" (*ibid.*)

(4) "*geld*" substituted for "*gold*" in the phrase reading originally "*gear, gold, geese*" in the sentence beginning "G before *e* is soft" (sig. a2ʳ)

*(5) "perhaps never" omitted from the sentence beginning originally "[H] seldom, perhaps never, begins" (*ibid.*); see Johnson's revisions above

(6) "*snipe*" substituted for "*strife*" between "*smell*" and "*space*" in the sentence beginning "Σβέννυμι, scatter" (*ibid.*)

(7) "and" substituted for "the" in the phrase reading originally "The learned, the sagacious Wallis," which also begins the sentence (sig. b1ʳ); this change noted by Nagashima

*(8) "*Do* and *did* are thus used only for the present and simple preterite" substituted for the original sentence "*Do* is thus used only in the simple tenses" (sig. b2ᵛ)

(9) "*wend*, the participle is *gone*" substituted for the original phrase "*wend*, and the participle *gone*" in the sentence beginning "Yet from *flee*" (sig. c1ʳ)

(10) "*indecent*" substituted for "*indecency*" in the phrase reading originally "*indecency, inelegant, improper*" in the sentence beginning "In borrowing adjectives" (*ibid.*)

(11) "will not suffer *h* to be twice repeated" substituted for "prevails, lest *h* should be twice repeated" in the sentence beginning "These should rather" (sig. c1ᵛ)

(12) "*batter*" substituted for "*butter*" in the phrase reading originally "*to batter, butter*" in the sentence beginning "There are in English" (*ibid.*); see the related addition above

(13) "imply" substituted for "implies" in the sentence reading originally "*Sn* usually implies" (*ibid.*)

(14) "denote" substituted for "denotes" in the phrase reading originally "*sn* denotes *nasus*" in the sentence beginning "But as if from" (*ibid.*)

(15) "imply" substituted for "implies" in the sentence beginning originally "*Bl* implies" (*ibid.*)

(16) "imply" substituted for "implies" in the sentence beginning originally "*St* in like manner implies" (*ibid.*)

(17) "denote" substituted for "denotes" in the phrase reading originally "*st* denotes" in the sentence beginning "In all these" (*ibid.*)

(18) "imply" substituted for "implies" in the sentence beginning originally "*Thr* implies" (*ibid.*)

(19) "imply" substituted for "implies" in the sentence beginning originally "*Sp* implies" (*ibid.*)

(20) "denote" substituted for "denotes" in the sentence beginning originally "*Sl* denotes" (*ibid.*)

(21) "indicate" substituted for "indicates" in the sentence beginning originally "And so likewise . . . indicates" (*ibid.*)

*(22) "*path, pfad*," omitted from the phrase reading originally "as *path, pfad, ax*" in the sentence beginning "It is certain" (sigs. c1ᵛ–c2ʳ)

(23) "*heal*" omitted from the phrase reading originally "*whole, heal*, from" in the same sentence identified above (*ibid.*)

(24) "πα[τso]" omitted from the phrase reading originally "from πα[τ]os, αξίνη" in the same sentence identified above (*ibid.*)

(25) "εἰλέω" omitted from the same sentence identified above and ending originally in "ὅλος, εἰλέω" (*ibid.*)

(26) "neglected" substituted for "omitted" in the sentence beginning "Wallis therefore has" (sig. c2ᵛ)

(27) The single revision we have not adopted is the erroneous "in" rather than

"into" (occurring in the first, second, and third editions) in the phrase *"sc* in *sh"* in the sentence beginning "The contractions may" (sig. c2^r).

Of the one hundred and forty-two accidental variants in the fourth edition of the Grammar, one hundred and twenty-nine concern punctuation, four spelling, three italics, two accent marks, two word order, one capitalization, and one a symbol for the letter *r*. We have adopted one hundred and twenty-two changes in punctuation, although we recognize that some of them may have been made by a compositor or a proof corrector rather than Johnson. Four of the remainder are patent mistakes (the first, second, and third editions all contain the correct marks); two more are less suitable to their contexts than are their counterparts; and the last one, like the rejected variants in spelling noted below, diverges from that in the edition of Michael Drayton's poems Johnson used in compiling the *Dictionary*. We have accepted one variant (a correction) in spelling; the rest, like the rejected punctuation mark noted above, depart from the text of Drayton's poems Johnson used in preparing the *Dictionary*. Finally, we have adopted all three variants in italics (one probably authorial, the other two corrections), one accent mark (a correction, the second being an error), the two in word order (one almost certainly authorial, the other possibly so), the one in capitalization (probably authorial), and the character for the letter *r* (almost certainly authorial).

IV

GRAMMAR: ALTERATIONS IN OTHER EDITIONS, AND EMENDATIONS

Selecting as modifications of our first edition copy-text those substantive and accidental variants in the third and fourth editions of the Grammar assuredly or probably or possibly authorial has been the most difficult part of our textual responsibilities, and we are keenly aware that our choices sometimes rest on very slender evidence. On the other hand, detecting the certain or relative rightness of assorted competing variants in the first, second (unrevised), fifth (1784, unrevised), sixth (1785), and seventh (1785) editions presented fewer problems. Eight of the seventeen substantive selections from the first edition (all also in the fourth edition and five in the third) were replaced by incorrect readings in the second edition; another four names of works and authors and two names of works (all six also in the fourth edition) were reduced to authors' names; and three verbs were reduced from the plural (all also in the fourth edition) to the singular number. Of the fifty-four accidentals chosen from the first edition (thirty-two punctuation, eighteen spelling, one accent, one italics, one capitalization, and one the position of a sentence), we have judged twenty-six to be correct readings, twenty-eight preferable (usually owing to their certain or putative adherence to Johnson's copy-texts for quoted passages) to their alternatives.

Although unrevised, the second edition of the Grammar has supplied our text with (1) nine substantive readings—eight corrections of mistakes in the first edition and an expansion of the initial "B." to "Ben" (sig. M1ᵛ), which also appears in the third and fourth editions; and (2) twenty accidentals, which correct a variety of slips. Likewise, the fifth edition has added four more correct readings—two substantive, two accidental—to our text. And our collation of the sixth edition has increased the number of correct readings by three—two substantive and one accidental. We found nothing more in the seventh edition.

Of the preliminaries to the unabridged (folio) *Dictionary*, only the Grammar appears in at least the first seven editions of the "proprietors' " abridged (octavo) version. Our collation showed that the first octavo edition (1756) of the Grammar was set from the first folio edition, the second octavo (1760) from the first, the third (1766) from the third folio edition, the fourth (1770) from the third octavo, the fifth (1773) from the fourth octavo, the sixth (1778) from the fourth folio edition, and the seventh (1783) from the sixth octavo. Our collation also revealed no signs of authorial revisions in any of the octavo editions of the Grammar.

Lastly, in the formation of our text, we have emended the text of the Grammar by altering three words. On sig. c2ʳ, in the phrase "apex, *a piece*; peak, *pike*; zophorus, *freese*," "*a piece*" has been changed to "*apice*," which appears in John Wallis's *Grammatica linguae Anglicanae* (fourth edition 1674), from which Johnson drew the phrase and numerous other parts of his Grammar.[3] Also on sig. c2ʳ, in the phrase "so in *scapha* [rightly "scapha" in the fifth edition], *skiff, skip*," "*skip*" has been changed to "*ship*," the proper translation, along with *skiff*, of the Latin *scapha*; *ship* also occurs, it should be noted, in Wallis's Grammar. Again on sig. c2ʳ, in the phrase "and *spell, a messenger*, from *epistola*," "messenger" has been altered to "message," the correct translation of Wallis's "nuncium."

Neither in the Grammar nor in the History have we emended the passages—a great many in the History—which Johnson quotes from other writers. But wherever mistakes obstruct a reader's comprehension of the text we have supplied correct readings in our textual notes.

V

HISTORY: ALTERATIONS IN FOURTH EDITION

Our collation of the "proprietors' " first seven editions of the unabridged *Dictionary* revealed that Johnson (slightly) revised only the fourth edition of his History of the English Language. Four substantive changes in this edition are certainly authorial: (1) the phrase "mixed in considerable numbers with the *Saxons* without" is altered to "mixed with another in considerable numbers without" (sig. D1ʳ); (2) "and has been twice published" is expanded to "and having been twice published before, has been lately reprinted at Ox-

---

3. See Allen Reddick, *The Making of Johnson's "Dictionary," 1746-1773* (Cambridge, 1990), p. 74 (cited below as "Reddick"); James H. Sledd and Gwin J. Kolb, *Dr. Johnson's "Dictionary": Essays in the Biography of a Book* (Chicago, 1955), pp. 17-18, 209 nn. 44, 49.

ford, under the inspection of Mr. *Lye,* the editor of *Junius*" *(ibid.)*; (3) in the next sentence, "both descended" becomes "both have descended" *(ibid.)*; and (4) in the sentence beginning "*Dryden,* who mistakes . . . and, in confidence" is changed to "*Dryden,* who, mistaking . . . , in confidence" (sig. F1^v). In his article, Sherbo records (pp. 28–29) the second of these alterations; in his study, Nagashima records (pp. 35–36) the first, second, and fourth, as well as two variants in punctuation which we have not adopted in our text.[4]

Besides accepting these four variants from the fourth edition, we have retained fourteen substantive readings in the first edition which were corrupted in the second (ten), third (three), and fourth (one) editions: (1) "On þis. . . . eorl of Albamar þe þe king" (sig. E1^v) instead of "Albamar þe king" (2nd ed.); (2) "changes of its own forms and terminations" (sig. E2^r) instead of "changes of its own form and terminations" (2nd ed.); (3) "kynz Alfred to ys wylle" (sig. E2^v) instead of "in ys wylle" (3rd ed.) in the line of poetry beginning "To þe kynz;" (4) "And that that men gon upward" (sig. F1^r) instead of "than that men" (4th ed.); (5) "thei ben 31500 myles" (sig. F1^v) instead of "thei ben 315000 myles" (2nd ed.); (6) "I that . . . am compelled to fele" (sig. F2^r) instead of "and compelled" (3rd ed.); (7) "Alas Alas how . . . : and yet refusythe" *(ibid.)* instead of "add yet refusythe" (2nd ed.); (8) "But I . . . was amasyd or astonyed" (sig. F2^v) instead of "amasyd and astonyed" (2nd ed.); (9) "This . . . knight had ben" (sig. G1^v) instead of "knight hath ben" (2nd ed.); (10) "Of the works . . . it was necessary" (sig. G2^v) instead of "is was necessary" (3rd ed.); (11) "Hee was . . . for the suretie or encrease" (sig. I1^r) instead of "suretie and encrease" (2nd ed.); (12) "For whom . . . som by writing and secret messengers" (sig. I2^r) instead of "writing or secret messengers" (2nd ed.); (13) "Vnto whiche . . . king aunswered" (sig. I2^v) instead of "sting aunswered" (2nd ed.); (14) "Long was . . . Lucke" *(ibid.)* instead of "Luke" (2nd ed.). Lastly, we have adopted one substantive correction in the second ("being diffused among those classes" [sig. G2^v] instead of "being disused among"), third, and fourth editions; and one appearing only in the third edition, the insertion of "not" between "does" and "allow" in the clause "which the paucity of books does not allow" (sig. F2^r).

According to our collation, the number of accidental variants in the first four editions of the History totals two hundred and twenty-nine. Of this number, one hundred and fifty-eight concern spelling, sixty-four concern punctuation, six capitalization, and one italics. We have retained one hundred and fifty first-edition spellings, all of words in quoted passages, which we have checked against their originals whenever possible. We have also accepted five second-edition corrections of misspellings in quoted passages, two fourth-edition spellings (one possibly authorial, the other a correction of a mistake in a quoted passage), and one third-edition spelling, which, since it also appears in the fourth edition, is possibly authorial. Again, we have retained fifty-one first-edition versions of punctuation in quoted passages

---

4. Nagashima also records (p. 36) another substantive variant, which, however, appears earlier in the second edition of the History (see below).

and five in Johnson's own prose; and have admitted six second-edition versions in quoted passages plus two corrections in Johnson's prose. Likewise, we have retained six first-edition versions of capitalization in quoted passages and have adopted one second-edition use of italics in a quoted passage.

VI
Preface to Abridged Edition and Advertisement to Fourth Edition

In addition to the Preface, the Grammar, and the History, two other short pieces fall under the heading of "preliminaries" to Johnson's *Dictionary*—the "Preface" to the abridged (octavo) version and the "Advertisement" to the fourth folio edition. As indicated above, seven editions of the former appeared in Johnson's lifetime. Our collation of all of them disclosed only one small substantive variant and seven equally small accidental differences: nothing to suggest any kind of authorial revision or the need for any emendation. Therefore we have retained first-edition readings throughout the text.

As also noted above, the fifth, sixth, and seventh editions of the "proprietors' " unabridged *Dictionary* were published in 1784 and 1785. Our collation of the three printings of the "Advertisement" turned up no substantive, and only six accidental, variants and no evidence of textual corruption. Consequently, we have retained everywhere the original readings in the fourth edition.

VII
Summary

In conclusion, we append brief assorted comments which largely restate or extend remarks running the risk of being overlooked amid the mass of details forming the body of this article. Johnson revised the second and fourth editions of the Preface to his unabridged *Dictionary*, the third and fourth editions of his Grammar, and the fourth edition of his History. We can offer an explanation for only the alterations in the fourth edition—namely, Johnson's agreement with the bookseller proprietors (apparently arrived at in 1771) to revise the fourth, which was published early in 1773 (Reddick, pp. 89-90, 170). Neither the changes made in the preliminaries to that edition nor those made earlier in the second and third editions exhibit constant examination and care. It is obvious, for example, that Johnson spent little time indeed scrutinizing the passages in the History which he borrowed from other authors. Keast's generalizations about the revisions in the Preface apply equally well to the companion pieces: without exception Johnson's revisions "were rather casual performances, not at all like his thorough-going work on the *Rambler*. He evidently read rapidly through the text[s], mending or improving where something happened to catch his eye" (p. 145).

Yet these actions, occasional though they were, possess considerable interest and value. They show a brilliant writer in the process of re-composition, and they increase one's knowledge of the making of the preliminaries—the first a truly noble pronouncement, the other two meriting scholarly attention —to the greatest one-man dictionary of English ever published. By including in our first-edition copy-texts certain, probable, and possible authorial revisions, along with other substantive and accidental variants deemed necessary for correctness and consistency, we have provided for our reader a fuller, more accurate rendering of the preliminaries than has hitherto been available.

TEXTUAL TRANSFORMATIONS: *THE MEMOIRS OF MARTINUS SCRIBLERUS* IN JOHNSON'S *DICTIONARY*

by

ANNE MCDERMOTT

JOHNSON's *Dictionary* is such a large and complex work, and so time-consuming to analyse manually,[1] that scholars and critics have tended to rely on Johnson's own comments in the *Plan* and the Preface about his methods, procedures and objectives. His reasons for the inclusion of the vast number of illustrative quotations have been taken to be broadly those he states:[2] to

1. The texts of the first and fourth editions of the *Dictionary* have been entered into an electronic database by Rom-Data Corporation Ltd. in association with the University of Birmingham in preparation for publication of the text as a CD-ROM. This is the first stage in The Johnson Dictionary Project which will eventually see the publication of a critical edition of Johnson's *Dictionary*. Access to this database makes some searches easier and more reliable (although see notes 10 and 22 for qualifications of this), but for the most part my searches have only confirmed what other scholars have found. Gwin and Ruth Kolb called their samplings 'narrow' and 'unscientific', allowing them only 'tentative generalizations', but the pattern of deletions they noticed is repeated with great regularity ('The Selection and Use of the Illustrative Quotations in Dr. Johnson's *Dictionary*', in *New Aspects of Lexicography: Literary Criticism, Intellectual History, and Social Change*, ed. Howard D. Weinbrot [1972], 61–72). Allen Reddick's researches have revealed the process by which these deletions occurred in his examination of the manuscript materials and analysis of Johnson's revisions to the quoted passages (*The Making of Johnson's Dictionary 1746–1773* [1990]).

2. 'In citing authorities, on which the credit of every part of this work must depend, it will be proper to observe some obvious rules, such as of preferring writers of the first reputation to those of an inferior rank, of noting the quotations with accuracy, and of selecting, when it can be conveniently done, such sentences, as, besides their immediate use, may give pleasure or instruction by conveying some elegance of language, or some precept of prudence, or piety' (*The Plan of a Dictionary of the English Language* [1747], 30–31); 'When I first collected these authorities, I was desirous that every quotation should be useful to some other end than the illustration of a word; I therefore extracted from philosophers principles of science; from historians remarkable facts; from chymists complete processes; from divines striking exhortations; and from poets beautiful descriptions' (Preface, par. 57).

provide authority for his definitions by examples of usage in the best writers; to offer instruction by extracting passages which explain technical terms or philosophical concepts; to promote religion and morality by quoting from pious writers and excluding those, such as Hobbes and Samuel Clarke, whose moral principles or religious views were dangerous or unorthodox;[3] or simply to 'intersperse with verdure and flowers the dusty desarts of barren philology' by including passages which are poetically beautiful. But does the textual evidence support Johnson's claims? To answer this question it is necessary to examine the source texts in detail, noting the editions Johnson used, any changes he may have made to the text, and the context of the original passage. In order to test his claims more fully, I have chosen to examine his quotations from *The Memoirs of Martinus Scriblerus*, a text which seems to run directly counter to Johnson's stated principles of selection and about which he is subsequently scornful and dismissive.

Though Johnson confesses that 'Many quotations serve no other purpose, than that of proving the bare existence of words', most critics have found other, ideological reasons for the selection of particular texts, following Johnson's hint that 'I was desirous that every quotation should be useful to some other end than the illustration of a word'. While it is broadly true that the majority of source texts in the *Dictionary* fulfil his criteria of being 'pleasing or useful', some appear to be neither and so raise the possibility of an unstated, unacknowledged principle of selection in operation. Where a text is quoted only once there is a strong *prima facie* case for assuming that he probably got the quotation from a secondary source,[4] but there are some texts which are

3. 'When I published my Dictionary, I might have quoted *Hobbes* as an authority in language . . . but I scorned, sir, to quote him at all; because I did not like his principles' (Conversation with Thomas Tyers, *The Early Biographies of Samuel Johnson*, ed. O M Brack, Jr., and Robert E. Kelley [1974], 82). Dr. William Adams wrote in a letter to Boswell that Johnson 'had made it a rule not to admit Dr. Clarke's name in his Dictionary' because of Clarke's anti-Trinitarian views, but he adds 'This, however, wore off' (*Boswell's Life of Johnson*, ed. G. B. Hill, rev. L. F. Powell, 6 vols. [1934–64], IV, 416, n. 2). The name 'Clarke' appears 41 times in the *Dictionary*, but most of these are probably from John Clarke's *A New Grammar of the Latine Tongue* (1733) or *An Introduction to the Making of Latin* (1740). However, under the word 'justification', the second definition, 'Deliverance by pardon from sins past', has the name Clarke against it, with no quotation, and this may well be taken from Samuel Clarke. Hester Thrale notes Johnson's expression of a general principle that 'he never would give Shaftesbury Chubb or any wicked Writer's Authority for a Word, lest it should send People to look in a Book that might injure them forever' (*Thraliana*, ed. Katherine Balderston [1951], 34).

4. There are many examples of Johnson using a secondary source in the *Dictionary*. W. R. Keast has found perhaps the most dramatic in showing that Johnson's quotations from *Clarissa* are in fact from *A Collection . . . of Moral and Instructive Sentiments* selected from the novel by Solomon Lowe and included as an appendix to Vol. VII of the fourth edition of *Clarissa*, 1751 (*Studies in Philology*, 54 [July 1957], 429–439). Arthur Sherbo pointed out that a quotation which is cited in the *Dictionary* simply as 'Old Comedy' is, in fact, taken from a note by George Steevens in his revised edition of Johnson's Shakespeare ('1773: The Year of Revision', *Eighteenth-Century Studies*, 7 [1973], 18–39); I am grateful to Dr. G. W. Nicholls for the additional information that this quotation is from John Day's *Law-Trickes, or, Who Would have Thought It* and is quoted in the Johnson-Steevens edition of Shakespeare (1773), II, 321, n. 8. There are many other examples of the same phenomenon,

quoted frequently enough to exclude this possibility and which yet do not seem to qualify for inclusion according to Johnson's declared criteria. The *Memoirs*, jointly written by the members of the Scriblerus Club, Pope, Swift, Gay, Arbuthnot, Parnell and Harley, is quoted 146 times in the first edition and 143 times in the fourth, providing sufficient evidence against which to measure Johnson's principles of selection, yet it is a text which one might have expected Johnson to exclude, whether on the grounds of moral propriety or literary merit.

This text, like many other Scriblerian pieces, was considered rather vulgar in places; so much so that when Bishop Warburton published his edition in 1751 he omitted the Double Mistress episode, considering it as too indecent even for robust eighteenth-century taste. There is no evidence available of what Johnson thought of Warburton's edition, but he was generally in sympathy with Warburton's views and thought highly of his scholarship. In addition, Johnson expresses a low opinion of the *Memoirs* on literary grounds in his Life of Pope: 'If the whole [of the Scriblerus project] may be estimated by this specimen, . . . the want of more will not be much lamented' and he comments that 'it has been little read, or when read has been forgotten, as no man could be wiser, better, or merrier, by remembering it'.[5] All this is fairly damning and if it were not for the inclusion of the text in the *Dictionary*, no question would arise about Johnson's view of the work. As it is, the evidence provided by the *Dictionary* quotations needs to be carefully examined. It is, of course, always possible that Johnson changed his view of the *Memoirs* in the intervening years between publication of the first edition of the *Dictionary* in 1755 and the composition of his Life of Pope in 1780, but in the absence of any evidence for this, one is left with certain questions to consider. How far can one establish Johnson's view of a text from its frequency and manner of quotation in the *Dictionary*? Is it possible to reconcile that evidence with other available evidence about Johnson's view of a text? Is there textual evidence available in the changes which he makes to the quotations which might provide clues to Johnson's intentions?

Evidence about Johnson's general view of the *Memoirs* can be pieced together from various sources. Though he calls it a 'joint production of three great writers' in his Life of Pope, he evidently thought that Swift could not have written it, and indeed he credits Arbuthnot with the major share, 'with a few touches perhaps by Pope'. His reasons for excluding Swift are related to his generally low opinion of him as a writer, reflected in the relatively short length of his Life of Swift. 'In the Poetical Works of Dr. Swift,' he writes, 'there is not much upon which the critick can exercise his powers'.[6] According to Johnson, his defect lies in his style which is smooth, easy and clear without dazzling: 'he excites neither surprise nor admiration'. It is a suitable style for expressing new thoughts, which depend on clarity, but not for attracting

and I think it highly likely that where a text is quoted only once, the source will be a footnote to a text Johnson was already marking up, rather than the original text itself.

5. Life of Pope, *The Lives of the English Poets*, ed. G. B. Hill, 3 vols. (1905), III, 182.
6. Life of Swift, *Lives of the Poets*, III, 65.

attention to old, universal truths, which are known already. Since moral truths are, according to Johnson's view, all of this latter kind, Swift's could not be a style suitable for moral purposes.

But his criticisms go deeper than this, for he thinks Swift's writings lack thought, which is why he is reluctant to believe that Swift wrote *A Tale of a Tub*: 'it has so much more thinking, more knowledge, more power, more colour, than any of the works which are indisputably his'. And, crucially in terms of the Scriblerus project, he thinks that Swift's wit is inferior: 'Swift is clear, but he is shallow. In coarse humour, he is inferior to Arbuthnot; in delicate humour, he is inferior to Addison'.[7] All of this, whether true or not, suggests reasons why Johnson might exclude Swift's name from the citations to the *Memoirs* in the *Dictionary*. The form of the citation is most often given as 'Arbuthnot and Pope' or some abbreviation of this, significantly giving the precedence to Arbuthnot, but occasionally it appears as just 'Arbuthnot'. The reason for this cannot simply be shortage of space for the full citation because the name often appears as the only word on a line.[8]

Johnson's high opinion of Arbuthnot is attested by Boswell: 'I think Dr. Arbuthnot the first man among them [the eminent writers of Queen Anne's reign]. He was the most universal genius, being an excellent physician, a man of deep learning, and a man of much humour' (*Life*, I, 425). This opinion may come as a surprise to literary scholars who are used to thinking of Pope and Swift as the brightest stars in that particular firmament. Arbuthnot is also credited as being 'a wit, who, in the crowd of life, retained and discovered a noble ardour of religious zeal',[9] so it seems probable that his works would qualify as 'pleasing and useful' according to Johnson's criteria. Seven of his works (including the *Memoirs*) are quoted in the *Dictionary* and he is quoted approximately 2000 times, which puts him in the middle rank according to frequency of citation.[10]

It should come as no surprise that Johnson admired Arbuthnot. He was a scholar and a medical man who was instrumental in initiating developments in medical practice, such as the study of the effects of diet on the human body. He was also a religious and deeply moral man who was popular and evidently

---

7. Boswell's 'Journal of a Tour to the Hebrides' in *Boswell's Life of Johnson*, V, 44.

8. I have counted 26 instances in the first edition and 28 instances in the fourth edition of the citation appearing as just 'Arbuthnot'. In two cases, under 'MISCARRY' and 'SELF', the citation appears as 'Pope and Arbuthnot', and in one case, under 'MONSTROSITY', the citation appears as 'Pope and Arbuthnot' in the first edition but as 'Arbuthnot and Pope' in the fourth.

9. Life of Pope, *Lives of the Poets*, III, 177.

10. Arbuthnot is quoted 1955 times in the first edition and 1986 times in the fourth edition. These figures may not be strictly accurate, and are likely to be conservative, since I have only counted citations in which his name appears; citations in which the title only is given (e.g. 'Mart. Scrib.') are not included. The other six works quoted are *Tables of the Ancient Coins, Weights and Measures* . . . (1727); *The History of John Bull* (1712/1727); *An Essay Concerning the Nature of Aliments* (1731); *An Essay Concerning the Effects of Air on Human Bodies* (1733); *Practical Rules of Diet* (1732) and *The Art of Political Lying* (1712). *The History of John Bull* appeared in the second volume of Benjamin Motte's *Miscellanies*, a text which Johnson used for many of his quotations from Pope. See below, n. 29.

much loved. The puzzling thing is why Johnson apparently thought so little of a work which he credited mainly to Arbuthnot. Perhaps the answer has something to do with his attitude to the particular kind of satire practised by the Scriblerians.

Despite twice imitating Juvenalian satires in verse, and in spite of some elements of satire evident in other works such as his periodical essays, Johnson was not much in sympathy with the form as it was practised by the Scriblerians. He saw satire as primarily a *moral* form of writing, an emphasis shown in his *Dictionary* definition: 'A poem in which wickedness or folly is censured'. He then adds a comment which may suggest a reason why Pope and Swift did not always please him in their use of the form: 'Proper *satire* is distinguished, by the generality of the reflections, from a *lampoon* which is aimed against a particular person; but they are too frequently confounded'. Lampoon retains the disapproval and abuse of satire, but lacks the moral element. As Johnson pithily phrases it in his definition of 'lampoon', it is 'censure written not to reform but to vex'. Johnson regarded satire as primarily a useful rather than a pleasing form: 'All truth is valuable, and satirical criticism may be considered as useful when it rectifies error and improves judgement',[11] and an indication of his priorities is present in his criticism of Gay's *Beggar's Opera* on the ground that 'The play . . . was plainly written only to divert, without any moral purpose'.[12] Johnson viewed the Scriblerians as thinking of satire especially as entertainment and as regarding ridicule as a legitimate means to that end, whereas for him the purpose of satire is always to instruct and ridicule is only legitimate if it achieves that end.

For Johnson, satire degenerates into mere lampoon if there is no universal applicability of its censure in the interests of moral reformation, and there is plenty of evidence that Johnson thought of Pope's use of the form in this way. In the first place, he suspected Pope's motives were those of revenge and self-importance, rather than a desire to improve morals: 'He was not likely to have been ever of opinion that the dread of his satire would countervail the love of power or of money; he pleased himself with being important and formidable, and gratified sometimes his pride, and sometimes his resentment . . .'. Secondly, he thought much of Pope's satirical writing was aimed at targets which it was beneath him to notice. He should have ignored Cibber's attacks on him because answering them made them respectable: 'Cibber had nothing to lose. . . . Silence only could have made him despicable'; and by arbitrarily changing the main target of *The Dunciad* from Theobald to Cibber, Pope compounded the fault by making his satire seem random: 'he reduced himself to the insignificance of his own magpye, who from his cage calls cuckold at a venture'.[13]

Johnson was never emotionally attracted to attacks in print as a form of revenge on his enemies. His way of dealing with printed abuse was either to

11. Life of Pope, *Lives of the Poets*, III, 242.
12. Life of Gay, *Lives of the Poets*, II, 278.
13. Life of Pope, *Lives of the Poets*, III, 181, 186, 187.

ignore it or to welcome it as a sign that his own writing had had its effect.[14] This form of writing for personal vengeance would, in any case, have a short life, because the target of the attack would be unknown to future generations and they could have no interest in the dispute. This has been the fate, in Johnson's view, of Pope's invectives against Hervey in his poems and letters: to 'a cool reader of the present time' they exhibit 'nothing but tedious malignity'.[15] A telling example of his views on this matter is his judgement on *Three Hours After Marriage*, which he speculates was jointly written by Pope, Arbuthnot and Gay. In it these writers satirise Dr John Woodward, a geologist and physician who had a great interest in fossils. This was a man, in Johnson's view, 'not really or justly contemptible' and he calls their satire an 'outrage'.[16] Woodward is also targeted in the *Memoirs*, presumably to Johnson's further disapproval.

One might think that Johnson would be sympathetic to some of the aims of the Scriblerus Club. Its overall purpose was to satirise the various follies of the learned world, and Martinus Scriblerus was intended to exemplify every learned folly from medical quackery to absurd scientific experimentation. Johnson's portrait of Quisquilius, the virtuoso, in Rambler 82 is obviously drawn from the same model. He collects rarities with an obsession which allows no time for consideration of their significance or intrinsic worth, and finally spends or is tricked out of his entire fortune on this activity so that he is forced to sell the collection he spent so much time amassing.

But in the very next issue of *The Rambler* Johnson warns that while it is not easy to 'forbear some sallies of merriment' when faced with virtuosi who spend their lives and their fortunes investigating 'questions, of which, without visible inconvenience, the world may expire in ignorance', yet these are men who are engaged in harmless activity and are pursuing 'innocent curiosity'. Their activities, which seem contemptibly minute and trivial, may ultimately contribute to the sum of human knowledge, 'for all that is great was at first little'. The only censure which Johnson offers is that these men of ability have enlisted in 'the secondary class of learning' and avoided the 'drudgery of meditation', but as far as broader moral considerations go, they 'cannot be said to be wholly useless'.[17] Johnson's ridicule is always tempered by tolerance and sympathy for his victim. We are always aware of a sense of common humanity, and though we may not share the particular weakness which is being satirised, Johnson makes us feel that we all have equivalent temptations to which we are susceptible. Though there is room for amusement and gentle mockery, there is none of that sense of intellectual and moral superiority that there is in the Scriblerians.

14. He seems to have welcomed attack for his political pamphlets and was disappointed by the reaction to *Taxation no Tyranny*: 'I think I have not been attacked enough for it. Attack is the re-action; I never think I have hit hard, unless it rebounds', and his general view was that 'the worst thing you can do to an authour is to be silent as to his works' (*Boswell's Life of Johnson*, II, 335; III, 375).

15. Life of Pope, *Lives of the Poets*, III, 179.

16. Life of Gay, *Lives of the Poets*, II, 271–272.

17. Rambler 83, The Yale Edition of the Works of Samuel Johnson, vol. IV, *The Rambler*, ed. W. J. Bate and Albrecht B. Strauss (1969), 70–76.

On the other hand, Johnson had some sympathy with the tradition of burlesque exemplified in works such as *Don Quixote* and *Hudibras*, and there are traces of this tradition in the *Memoirs*.[18] Johnson thought that the *Memoirs* were not original, for 'besides its general resemblance to *Don Quixote*, there will be found in it particular imitations of the *History of Mr. Ouffle*'.[19] Charles Kerby-Miller, in his splendid edition of the *Memoirs*, identifies this as a 'curious and now almost forgotten work by the Abbé Laurent Bordelon', first published in Paris in 1710, but comments: 'that [the Scriblerians] derived any significant amount of literary inspiration from its turgid pages is difficult to believe'. Bordelon's work is 'a slight and episodic narrative' in which the hero, a man of 'boundless credulity who has spent a great part of his life reading books on magic, witchcraft, astrology, and various superstitious practices', commits various follies. The learning in the work is immense, so that 'the footnotes total almost two-thirds of the whole work'.[20] *Hudibras* is a similar kind of work. There is a loose narrative framework holding everything together, but the digressions into learned matters of sectarian religious disputes, arcane issues in logic, metaphysics and philosophy, alchemy, witchcraft and astrology have marked similarities with parts of the *Memoirs*.

Johnson was, though, of a different age and temperament from the Scriblerians and was not likely to be inspired by the same burlesque models as they. He was himself an accomplished scholar and was not so apt to see the futility of modern learning. He writes frequently about the vanity of learning from the point of view of its failure to bring happiness or contentment, and he would have appreciated the section in Burton's *Anatomy of Melancholy* which deals with the misery of scholars, but he did not see the pursuit of learning as in itself a futile endeavour, however small the addition to human knowledge. He was very fond of chemical experiments which he performed as a pastime and he recommends to Susannah Thrale, a young girl of fourteen, that she should go to see Herschel's telescope because the acquisition of learning is itself of intrinsic value:

What he has to show is indeed a long way off, and perhaps concerns us but little, but all truth is valuable and all knowledge is pleasing in its first effects, and may be subsequently useful. . . . Take therefore all opportunities of learning that offer themselves, however remote the matter may be from common life or common conversation. Look in Herschel's telescope; go into a chymist's laboratory; if you see a manufacturer at work, remark his operations.[21]

18. *Don Quixote* was one of only three books (*Robinson Crusoe* and *Pilgrim's Progress* being the other two) which Johnson thought 'wished longer by its readers' (*Johnsonian Miscellanies*, ed. G. B. Hill, 2 vols. [1897], I, 332). *Hudibras* is mentioned in the *Dictionary* citations 739 times in the first edition.
19. Life of Pope, *Lives of the Poets*, III, 182.
20. *The Memoirs of the Extraordinary Life, Works, and Discoveries of Martinus Scriblerus*, ed. Charles Kerby-Miller (1950), 69–70. All quotations from the *Memoirs* are taken from this edition.
21. Letter to Susannah Thrale, 25 March 1784 (*The Letters of Samuel Johnson*, The Hyde Edition, ed. Bruce Redford, 5 vols. [1992–94], IV, 301–302).

The enthusiasm for all kinds of learning here is the same as that which drove
the encyclopédistes to include mechanical processes in their *Encyclopédie*
along with more traditional forms of learning. As Johnson remarked to Boswell on another occasion, 'All knowledge is of itself of some value. There is
nothing so minute or so inconsiderable, that I would not rather know it than
not' (*Life*, II, 357).

All this is a long way from the satire contained within *The Memoirs of
Martinus Scriblerus*. Its combination of personal abuse, lack of distinct moral
direction, and ridicule of kinds of learning which to Johnson were not at all
ridiculous would have made it, in his eyes, an ephemeral, insubstantial sort
of work, a venting of spleen against paper targets. Yet much of this is true of
other Scriblerian texts which nonetheless appear in the *Dictionary* with sufficent regularity to suggest that these deficiencies presented no great obstacle
to their status as authorities. Pope and Swift are both criticised by Johnson
for having 'an unnatural delight in ideas physically impure', yet both *Gulliver's Travels* and *The Dunciad* appear fairly frequently in the *Dictionary*.
It may be significant, though, that there is in each case a substantial reduction
in frequency of quotation in the fourth edition.[22] The revisions to the *Dictionary*, carried out just six years before the publication of *The Lives of the
Poets*, may have caused Johnson to reassess the judgement of these works which
led him to include so many quotations in the first edition.

If frequency of citation is to be the test, no such reassessment can be
suggested in the case of the *Memoirs*, for Johnson omits just three quotations
from the fourth edition.[23] So why does Johnson quote so frequently from this
Scriblerian text? One possible reason is that the text has many obscure and
unusual words in it arising from the satirical treatment of pedants with their
love of technical terms. The words which might qualify for inclusion under

22. *Gulliver's Travels* is cited 99 times in the first edition and 44 times in the fourth;
The Dunciad is cited 162 times in the first edition and 90 times in the fourth. Again,
though, I have only counted citations in which the title itself appears. I have not noticed
quotations from either of these texts in which the title is not given, but there may be some.
23. In the first edition the text is quoted under abductor, abortion, administer, aduncity,
apple woman, arid, as, bachelor, bestiality, bigamy, billet, birdcage. bite, bobcherry, brow-
beat, burst, catamountain, chicanery, chirographist, christening, chromatick, clasp, cock,
cockmatch, compile, confidant, constrictor, contain, contentation, coquette, court-day, crack-
brained, cradle, cringe, cudgel, dead, decompound, disinclination, duck, duenna, effossion,
embolus, enervate, enrapt, enthymeme, extensor, fatner, fence, file, flexor, fluid, football,
gavot, gymnastick, handydandy, hebetate, heedlessly, hermaphrodite, hotcockles, hydraulick,
hysterick, incapacitate, incontinently, incrust, indignant, individuality, inhale, intort, in-
trust, jackal, judgment, lame, lighthouse, longitude, lovetoy, lyre, make, manacle, mantiger,
marble, microscopical, minor, miscarry, monstrosity, moor, murrey, musick, new, nonentity,
nozle, numskull, ogle, ostrich, parish, pathognomonick, percussion, physiognomist, piazza,
pineal, porcupine, potbelly, pout, prizefighter, punster, puppetshow, push, puss, quill, quoit,
retreat, river-god, robustness, roe, salacious, saraband, satin, seal, seat, self, sesquipedalian,
show, sigh, skylight, spirit, spleened, squall, stammer, state, straddle, suction, swift, tennis,
tour, trade-wind, troglodyte, tune, uncoif, undismayed, ungently, universal, vectitation,
vice, whirligig, wilderness, womanly, yonder. In the fourth edition the quotations under
billet, new, and sigh are omitted. Very few of the quotations are altered or even condensed
further in the fourth edition, though this is a common practice with other texts.

this principle are: abductor, aduncity, chicanery, chirographist, chromatick, constrictor, contentation, effossion, embolus, enthymeme, extensor, flexor, hebetate, hermaphrodite, hydraulick, pathognomonick, physiognomist, pineal, sesquipedalian, troglodyte and vectitation.[24] Of these twenty-one 'hard words' which are quoted in the *Dictionary*, twelve are unaccompanied by quotations from other texts to illustrate the definition, suggesting the rarity of most of these words.[25] This would seem to support the notion that quotations from the *Memoirs* are included because Johnson could not find these obscure words elsewhere, but it is difficult to draw a hard and fast rule here. Some words in the *Memoirs* are obscure and unusual (e.g. arietation) and appear in the *Dictionary*, but Johnson does not use the quotation from the *Memoirs* to illustrate them. On the other hand, the vast majority of the quotations which do appear are neither obscure nor technical terms, but perfectly ordinary words which he could have found in any text.

An alternative explanation might be that the *Memoirs* were first printed in *The Works of Alexander Pope, in Prose. Vol. II.* in 1741 and continued to be published as part of Pope's works. The implications of this arrangement might simultaneously raise the work in the public esteem, by suggesting it was the work of the major poet of the day, and damage its reputation by burying it among the poet's minor prose writing. Johnson may have been attracted to the piece because of its associations with Pope, from whom he quotes extensively in the *Dictionary*,[26] but we know that he was not convinced of Pope's major role in the writing of the Memoirs when he came to write his Life of Pope, for he credits him there with only 'a few touches'.

Another possible explanation is similarly excluded. Bishop Warburton published an edition of Pope's works in 1751 which contained the *Memoirs*, and we know that Johnson had a very high opinion of Warburton, so it would not be unnatural for him to quote from this edition. He used Warburton's edition of Shakespeare for the most part as the base text for his own edition of Shakespeare and for quotations from Shakespeare in the *Dictionary*,[27] and Warburton's version of the text of the *Memoirs* would have had the apparent advantage of omitting the most vulgar parts of the text, including the Double Mistress episode. It is to the inadequacies of Warburton's edition that Charles Kerby-Miller in his edition attributes Johnson's 'sweeping and ill-considered

24. There are others which are unusual but not technical or scientific: bobcherry, catamountain, gavot, handydandy, hotcockles, mantiger, murrey, porcupine, saraband.

25. The twelve words are abductor, aduncity, chicanery, chirographist, chromatick, constrictor, effossion, embolus, flexor, pineal, troglodyte and vectitation.

26. He quotes from Pope approximately 4000 times in the first edition and 4150 times in the fourth edition. This compares with approximately 17500/17700 for Shakespeare; 11400/11500 for Dryden; 6200/7000 for Milton; 4350/4450 for Addison and 3200/3300 for Swift. These figures are not absolutely reliable for the reasons given (see notes 10 and 22).

27. But see Arthur M. Eastman, 'The Texts from which Johnson Printed his Shakespeare', *JEGP*, 49 (1950), 182–191, for evidence that Johnson occasionally used Theobald's 1757 edition as base text for his edition of Shakespeare, and Anne McDermott, 'The Defining Language: Johnson's *Dictionary* and Shakespeare's *Macbeth*', *RES*, n.s. 44 (November 1993), 521–538, for evidence that Johnson occasionally departed from Warburton's text in his *Dictionary* quotations.

judgment of the piece' (66). But the fact is that Johnson did not use Warburton's edition in quoting from the text in the *Dictionary*, and there is no evidence that he based his opinion on that edition.

In a detailed and informative article for *Review of English Studies*, Treadwell Ruml II discusses the evidence concerning the texts of Pope's works which Johnson knew when collecting authorities for the *Dictionary*.[28] In some cases he conflated two versions of the same passage from different editions, possibly because he was quoting from memory, but more frequently the variations from the received scholarly text stem from Johnson's use of a variant text. It seems that Warburton's edition probably appeared too late for him to use, since by 1751 Johnson had already marked up most of the illustrative passages he intended to include as authorities. There are some exceptions to this rule, but Ruml reports that in no case has he found a reading in the *Dictionary* text of Pope that first appeared in Warburton's edition. From the evidence of textual variants in the quotations he examines, Ruml draws the interesting conclusion that Johnson used different editions of Pope's works for different poems.[29] The evidence seems very complex and it is not always possible, as Ruml concedes, to determine whether what appears to be a textual variation may not be just a coincidence arising from errors of memory or transcription, but it does seem clear that identifying Johnson's exact source is no simple matter.

Ruml suggests that Johnson used the first 1742 octavo issue of the *Works, Vol. III, Part II* (Griffith No. 566) for quotations from the *Memoirs*, and some readings support this view. The most obvious is the following passage: 'The Cretans wisely forbid their servants Gymnasticks, as well as Arms; and yet your modern Footmen exercise themselves daily in the *Jaculum* at the corner of *Hyde Park*, whilst their enervated Lords are softly lolling in their chariots (a species of Vectitation seldom us'd among the Ancients, except by old men)'. This quotation appears, variously abbreviated, under ENERVATE, GYMNASTICK and VECTITATION, and in each case the word 'softly' is included, a word omitted in every edition other than the first 1742 octavo. Other readings which point to this edition are quoted under BILLET ('carrying' instead of 'carry'); CONTENTATION ('whereof a cut' instead of 'a cut of which'); FATNER ('the wind was at West' instead of 'the wind was West'); HEEDLESSLY ('whilst' instead of 'while').

There is, however, one reading which points to a different edition. Under BOBCHERRY the following passage is quoted: 'We shall only instance one of the most useful and instructive, *Bob-cherry*, which teaches at once two noble Virtues, Constancy and Patience; the first in adhering to the pursuit of one end,

---

28. Treadwell Ruml II, 'The Younger Johnson's Texts of Pope', *RES*, n.s. 36 (1985), 180–198.

29. Ruml suggests that Johnson probably used the fourth edition of Lintot's *Miscellany* (1722); Motte's *Miscellanies* (possibly the 1733 edition); the 1736–43 edition of *Works, Vol. I*; the 1736 *Works, Vol. III*; the 1738 *Works, Vol. II, Part II*; the first octavo issue of *Works, Vol. III, Part II*; the 1740 or 1743 *Works, Vol. II, Parts I and II*; and the 1743 Pope-Warburton edition as the major sources of his quotations.

the latter in bearing a disappointment'. Johnson quotes the passage from 'Bob-cherry' onwards, but where the 1742 octavo edition has 'Constancy and Patience', the *Dictionary* quotation has 'patience and constancy'. This is a reading which appears in the folio and quarto 1741 editions of the *Works, Vol. II*, but it is not necessarily evidence that Johnson used that edition. This may be one of those coincidences where memory has intruded or the passage has been mistranscribed. It is hard to believe that Johnson preferred this reading because it makes a nonsense of what follows (adhering to an end can only be an example of constancy, and bearing a disappointment can only be an example of patience), and it was clearly a mistake in the earlier editions.

I have found examples of variations in the text quoted in the *Dictionary* which correspond to none of the published editions of the *Memoirs*. The following passage is quoted under BIRDCAGE, PERCUSSION, VICE and WHIRLIGIG: 'For example, he found that *Marbles* taught him *Percussion* and the *Laws of Motion*; *Nut-crackers* the use of the *Leaver*; *Swinging* on the ends of a Board, the *Balance*; *Bottle-screws*, the *Vice*; *Whirligigs* the *Axis* and *Peritrochia*; *Bird-cages*, the *Pully*; and *Tops* the *Centrifugal* motion'. Under BIRDCAGE Johnson has 'centrifugal force' instead of 'centrifugal motion', yet under PERCUSSION, where this particular part of the passage is also quoted, he has 'centrifugal motion'. Thinking that this might be an example of a familiar phrase suggesting itself in place of a less familiar, I searched the *Dictionary* for the word 'centrifugal' and found that, apart from these two quotations from the *Memoirs*, the word only appears twice, and one of these instances is under CENTRIFUGAL itself. Both here in a quotation from Dr. George Cheyne and under SPIRTLE in a quotation from William Derham 'centrifugal' is associated with the word 'force' rather than 'motion'. This seems to conform to what has been called by linguists 'the idiom principle', whereby 'a language user has available to him or her a large number of semi-preconstructed phrases that constitute single choices, even though they might appear to be analysable into segments'.[30] 'Centrifugal force' was probably such a 'semi-preconstructed phrase' for Johnson, so that when he read the word 'centrifugal', he automatically supplied the word 'force' as its collocate, thereby misreading the original text.

Most of the variations in the text which appear in the *Dictionary* are changes to the spelling. When Johnson alters words, he does so for the most part to make them conform to the spelling he adopts in the headword. For example, under HYDRAULICK the spellings of 'hydraulic', 'chemical' and 'elastic' are changed to 'hydraulick', 'chymical' and 'elastick'. It is interesting to note in this example that none of the changes which Johnson made in an attempt to 'fix orthography' was finally adopted into the language. One curious example is the quotation under BESTIALITY in which the word 'centre' is spelled 'center' by Johnson, but he adopts the former spelling in the headword list. The two spellings appear in roughly equal numbers in each edition ('centre' 137 times in the first edition and 112 in the fourth, as against

---

30. John Sinclair, *Corpus, Concordance, Collocation* (1991), 110.

'center' 112 times in the first edition and 96 times in the fourth), and not all the occurrences of the spelling 'center' are in quotations. In the first edition approximately 24% of the occurrences of 'center' are in Johnson's own prose, and, interestingly, his definition of SEMIDIAMETER contains both spellings within the one sentence. This suggests that the spelling of the word was unstable at that time.

One example in which Johnson makes his views clear is under CHIROGRAPHIST where he quotes the following passage: 'Let the Physiognomists examine his features; let the Chirographers behold his Palm; but above all let us consult for the calculation of his Nativity'. Johnson has 'chirographist' in place of 'chirographer', but he notes the improper usage of this word: 'This word is used in the following passage, I think improperly, for one that tells fortunes, by examining the hand; the true word is *chirosophist* or *chiromancer*'. CHIROGRAPHER is included as a headword with the definition: 'He that exercises or professes the act or business of writing'. Here, too, is an example of Johnson spelling a word (phisiognomists) differently from the way it appears both in the source text and in his own headword list (where it is spelled 'physiognomist').

Johnson offers 'physiognomick' and 'physiognomonick' as alternatives in the headword list, but he offers no similar alternative for 'pathognomonick'. The only quotation to appear as an illustration for this word is from the *Memoirs*, but he changes the original spelling of 'pathognomick'. The reason for his preference here may be etymological since he gives the Greek source as παθογνωμονικὸς, but the same is true of 'physiognomick' which he allows as an alternative.

Another example of Johnson changing the spelling of a word occurs in the passage quoted under PUSS: 'I will permit my son to play at *Apodidiascinda*, which can be no other than our Puss in a Corner'. This whole chapter in the *Memoirs* is heavily dependent on Julius Pollux' *Onomasticon*, the famous encyclopedia of Greek culture. Kerby-Miller suggests that it was probably known to the Scriblerians in the Amsterdam edition of 1706, and it is possible that Johnson also knew this edition because he spells the game 'apodidrascinda', the same way as Pollux.

The most frequently occurring type of change to the text is a simple editorial amendment to the syntax, declensions or parts of speech in order to make the abbreviated and condensed passage grammatical. The general sense of the original passage is not changed. A straightforward example of this kind of alteration appears under PORCUPINE, where this original passage from the *Memoirs*:

Near these was placed, of two Cubits high, the black Prince of Monomotapa; by whose side were seen the glaring Cat-a-mountain, the quill-darting Porcupine, and the Man-mimicking Manteger

is amended in the quotation to:

By the black prince of Monomotapa's side were the glaring cat-a-mountain and the quill-darting *porcupine*.

Another case in which changes are made to the text is in the hyphenation of words, so that sometimes he represents hyphenated words as single words (e.g. 'hotcockles' for 'hot-cockles'), and at other times he represents single words or hyphenated words as two separate words (e.g. no body). The interesting thing here is that all of the examples in which hyphenation is removed appear in that form as headwords in the *Dictionary*: browbeaten, greyhound, handydandy, hotcockles, lighthouses, numskulls, and puppetshow. The exception is cudgel-playing, which appears under Fence as a single word and under Cudgel as hyphenated, but which is not itself included as a headword. On the other hand, of the hyphenated words which are represented as two separate words (bomb vessels, mad men, no body, quill darting, tennis court), the only three to appear in the headword list are represented as hyphenated (Bomb-vessel) or as single words (Madman and Nobody). Hyphens are notoriously tricky with wide variations in practice, and mistranscription or misreading by the printer are always possibilities that cannot be discounted.

It is less easy to dismiss or explain the more substantial changes which Johnson makes to the text. One puzzling example is the part of the passage cited earlier that is quoted under Vice and Whirligig: 'For example, he found that *Marbles* taught him *Percussion* and the *Laws of Motion*; *Nut-crackers* the use of the *Leaver*; *Swinging* on the ends of a Board, the *Balance*; *Bottle-screws*, the *Vice*; *Whirligigs* the *Axis* and *Peritrochia*; *Bird-cages*; the *Pully*; and *Tops* the *Centrifugal* motion'. In both quotations the phrase 'axis and peritrochia' is altered to 'axis in peritrochio', but I am unable to suggest an explanation for this. This is not the reading of any of the editions up to 1742 and 'peritrochia/peritrochio' does not appear as a headword in the *Dictionary*.

Two other examples of substantial changes are more readily explained. The following passage from the *Memoirs* (suitably abbreviated) appears under Universal: 'Cornelius told him that he was a lying Rascal; that an *Universale* was not the object of imagination, and that there was no such thing in reality, or a *parte Rei*'. The context of the passage makes it clear that the target of the satire is philosophers who speak of abstract ideas or concepts; when asked if he can frame the idea of a universal Lord Mayor, Crambe replies that he can conceive of one 'not only without his Horse, Gown, and Gold Chain, but even without Stature, Feature, Colour, Hands, Head, Feet, or any Body', to which Cornelius gives the above response. A universal is an abstract idea or concept supposed to be common to all members of a class, and as such it has no empirical substance or reality, so it cannot be 'imagined' (pictured in the mind) in the way Crambe pretends.

Johnson may not have fully comprehended the meaning of the passage, because the quotation in the *Dictionary* under Universal omits the crucial 'not' and asserts that 'An universal was the object of imagination, and there was no such thing in reality'. Johnson may have assumed that the contrast was intended to be between imagination and reality, a common dichotomy, whereas, in this context, the imagination can only image something which has empirical existence in reality, and so it cannot be applied to universals. The definition which Johnson gives: 'Not particular; comprising all particulars' does not hint at the broader meaning and is, in any case, confusing because he is defining a noun adjectivally.

The other example shows Johnson acting more deliberately and confidently. Under STRADDLE he quotes from the chapter on the Case of a Nobleman: 'Let him surprize the Beauty he adores at a disadvantage; survey himself naked, divested of artificial charms, and he will find himself a forked, stradling Animal, with bandy legs, a short neck, a dun hide, and a pot-belly'. The humour of this passage in the original text is that the disease the young nobleman is suffering from is diagnosed as self-love, and looking at himself naked in a mirror is the recommended cure. But the passage also has echoes of more serious texts such as *King Lear*: 'Unaccommodated man is no more but such a poor, bare, forked animal as thou art'.[31] Johnson deliberately enhances this effect by changing 'him' to 'man' in the quotation in the *Dictionary* and condensing the passage so that it reads: 'Let man survey himself, divested of artificial charms, and he will find himself a forked stradling animal, with bandy legs'. The original text has been transformed into a statement about the human condition and effectively lost its humour.

This loss of satirical edge is a more general effect applying to many of the quoted passages in the *Dictionary*. Taken out of their original context, it becomes impossible to read some passages with the irony they possess in the source text. An example of this is a passage quoted under ABORTION, in which Cornelius is the butt of many satirical jokes about his anxiety over the birth of his offspring: 'His Wife miscarried; but as the Abortion proved only a female Foetus, he comforted himself, that, had it arrived to perfection, it would not have answer'd his account; his heart being wholly fixed upon the learned sex'. In the first edition, under ABORTION, the whole passage up to 'account' is quoted in full, but, without the contextual material of the remainder of the chapter, it can be read with a serious tone and without recognizing the humour of the original text. The effect is even more pronounced in the fourth edition where the quotation ends at 'himself'.

Another example of this effect is contained in the passage quoted under HEEDLESSLY: 'Consider also by how small Limits the Duty and the Trespass is divided, lest, whilst ye discharge the duty of Matrimony, ye heedlessly slide into the sin of Adultery'. The passage is intended to be comic. Martinus Scriblerus and Prince Ebn-Hai-Paw-Waw of Monomotapa have fallen in love with the Siamese twins Lindamira and Indamora. Many jokes are made of Martin's courtship of Lindamira, including the fact that Indamora is really in love with Martin and jealous of her sister, but if she breaks up their relationship she will also lose Martin. Finally the case between Martin and the Prince is decided at law, with an opportunity for jokes at the expense of the judicial system, where the Judge decides that Martin and the Prince may both marry, but that they must 'lie in bed each on the side of his own wife', and he then adds the warning contained in the passage quoted above.

31. *King Lear*: The Folio Text, III. iv. 100–102, *The Complete Works of Shakespeare*, ed. Stanley Wells and Gary Taylor (1988).

Not only is the satirical humour lost, but the passage reads entirely differently in the *Dictionary*: 'Whilst ye discharge the duty of matrimony, ye heedlessly slide into sin'. It has become a rebuke aimed at those who allow the thoughts to be polluted even whilst engaged in the lawful 'duty of matrimony'. It also changes the meaning of the word 'heedlessly' from the suggestion of carelessness in the original to something indicative of *moral* negligence. The interesting point to note from both these examples is that a text can be changed in the *Dictionary* even if the wording remains exactly as it does in the original, because the *Dictionary* provides it with a context entirely different from the source text.

If it were not for certain evidence to the contrary, one might be tempted to account for Johnson's inclusion of quotations from the indecent Double Mistress episode and from the following Case at Law[32] by demonstrating that in the *Dictionary* they are no longer vulgar because of the change of context or because Johnson condenses them in the same way as he does the quotation under HEEDLESSLY. But, in fact, some of them retain the hint of impropriety that they have in the original, and, in any case, Johnson does not need to look in these two chapters to find indecent material. For example, under 'duenna' he quotes the following passage from the Introduction to the Reader: 'I felt the ardour of my passion increase as the season advanced, till in the month of July I could no longer contain. I bribed her *duenna*, was admitted to the bath, saw her undress'd and the wonder displayed'. Here rarity of examples may be one explanation why this passage is included, since it is the sole illustration for the word, but, nonetheless, Johnson could have edited the quotation so that it was not quite so sexually powerful. An abbreviated version of this same quotation appears under CONTAIN as: "I felt the ardour of my passion increase till I could no longer contain'.

Turning again to the question of whether we can rely on Johnson's statements about his reasons for choosing certain texts as authorities in preference to others, one is forced to conclude that his standards of morality were not so rigid as to exclude entertaining and humorous texts which might have slightly vulgar contents, and he was not above quoting the indecent passages from those texts. We cannot, I think, ignore his comment to Hester Thrale that he would never quote 'any wicked Writer's Authority for a Word, lest it should send People to look in a Book that might injure them forever',[33] but it seems that he excluded quotations from texts which were doctrinally suspect or which contained moral *theories* which were dubious or misleading in his view. Texts which one might regard as indecent rather than immoral seem not to have troubled him overmuch. As for the literary merit of the *Memoirs*, I think we can only assume that Johnson did not have such a low opinion of it in the years when he was marking up texts for the *Dictionary* as he developed later on. He declares that he intends to quote from the best writers

---

32. He quotes from the Double Mistress episode 19 times and from the following chapter on the Process at Law 12 times.

33. See note 3 above.

and he adheres to this principle more or less steadily, with the odd exception in favour of personal friends or particular favourite writers. *The Memoirs of Martinus Scriblerus* seems to have been regarded by Johnson as having sufficent status to be quoted unproblematically as an authority in the *Dictionary*, and he evidently did not have a radical change of view about the text when he came to make revisions for the fourth edition.

RICHARD HURD'S EDITIONS OF HORACE AND THE BOWYER LEDGERS

by

Donald D. Eddy

Richard Hurd (1720–1808) is a familiar figure to students of the literature and times of eighteenth-century England. As a Fellow of Emmanuel College, Cambridge, for more than twenty years, his circle of friends included John Brown, Thomas Gray, William Mason, William Whitehead, Sir Edward Littleton, Henry Hubbard, Thomas Balguy, and Dr. William Heberden. In the 1750s he developed close friendships with William Warburton and Ralph Allen. Through his own considerable merits as well as the active assistance of Warburton and Charles Yorke, he was promoted steadily in the church until he was made Bishop of Worcester in 1781, a position he retained until his death.

The See of the Bishop of Worcester was (and is) Hartlebury Castle, an ancient house in a lovely valley a few miles south of Kidderminster. When Hurd arrived there in July of 1781, he immediately decided to add a library to the house. Finished in 1782, it is a long room at the back of the house, overlooking the valley. It is spacious and beautiful, housing 3040 titles in some 5,000 volumes. The well-oiled leather bindings gleam in the light, and the oil portraits of Warburton and Pope—as well as books from both their libraries—and the Gainsborough portrait of Hurd provide an ideal setting in which to study eighteenth-century books. This investigator was delighted to do so, and he thanks the Bishop of Worcester for the privilege.

Hurd's academic and clerical careers were helped greatly by the large number and high quality of his writings. Beginning with his first book, an edition of Horace's *Ars Poetica* in 1749, more than two dozen editions of his various writings were printed in London by William Bowyer the younger (1699–1777). This is a fortunate coincidence for any present investigator, because Bowyer's printing records still exist, have recently been well edited and published, and present a unique source of additional information about many of Hurd's writings (see note).

This paper has three objectives. It is the beginning of a bibliography of the writings of Richard Hurd. (The Bowyer ledgers show that Hurd's editions of Horace are the only work which he chose to have printed with both regular and large paper copies, and this seemed sufficient reason for beginning the bibliography by examining them.) It will provide some examples of ways that printing ledgers can give us both bibliographical and biographical information about an author's writings. Finally, it inevitably raises questions about certain aspects of the book trade—the use of illustrations, and large paper copies; relationships among author, publisher, and printer; and even the tangled problem of shared printing.

In the last paragraph of his introduction to the *Ars Poetica* of 1749, Hurd mentions several Italian critics whose methods he chooses not to follow. Instead, he says, "I chuse therefore to rest on the *single* authority of a great author, who hath not disdained to comment a like piece of a late critical poet. What was indeed the amusement of his pen, becomes, it must be owned, the *labour* of inferior writers. Yet, on these unequal terms, it can be no discredit to have aim'd at some resemblance of one of the least of those *merits*, which shed their united honours on the name of the illustrious *friend* and *commentator* of Mr. POPE" (p. xv). This fulsome praise of Warburton, a man Hurd had never met, had its intended effect. The book was published May 27, 1749 (see below), and Hurd at once sent Warburton a copy—a large paper copy, presumably stitched in marbled paper, since there was no time to have it bound. Warburton, in his earliest known letter to Hurd, dated June 1, 1749, thanked him for the book and added, "I tell you, with all sincerity, I think the Notes one of the most masterly pieces of criticism that ever was written . . . I wish it was in my power to make a suitable acknowledgment for my obligations" (see *Letters from a late eminent Prelate to one of his Friends.* 2d ed. [1809], 1–2—cited hereafter as "Letters"). Warburton returned the compliment when his nine-volume edition of *The Works of Alexander Pope* was published on June 18, 1751 (*Daily Advertiser; General Advertiser*). In the *Essay on Criticism* Pope has a passage beginning "But where's the man . . ." (lines 632 ff.) describing the characteristics of an ideal critic; and in his note on this passage Warburton says, "And indeed the discovery of him, if it could be made, would be but an invidious business. I will venture no farther than to name the piece of Criticism in which these marks may be found. It is intitled, *Q. Hor. Fl. Ars Poetica, with an English Commentary and Notes*" (I, 202). Hurd had just published his edition of the *Epistola ad Augustum* the previous month—on May 21, 1751 (see below)—so he had to wait until 1753 to dedicate to Warburton the second volume of his new edition of Horace. Friendship flourished amid the mutual admiration.

As Hurd progressed in his editing of the Epistle to Augustus, two things became increasingly apparent. His interest in Horace was primarily in his critical writings, so he felt that his editorial work would be finished when it was published in the spring of 1751. As he commented in the Advertisement of the book, "It will, further, be observed, that these two pieces make a complete edition of Horace's CRITICAL, that is to say, the best and most exquisite of *all* his writings" (p. iv). At the same time he was interested in writing and publishing critical essays on other topics. Throughout 1750 he was writing and showing to Warburton drafts of his "Discourse on Poetical Imitation," the first of a group of essays which he later always referred to as "Dissertations." In a letter to Hurd dated April 21, 1750, Warburton commented that "I am glad the discourse on imitation is advancing. If the Commentary on the Ars Poetica and the Epistle to Augustus and that discourse will altogether make a just volume, I think they should do so. If they will not, I think the discourse should not be published alone. Pamphlets are soon forgotten; and this should be conveyed to posterity" (*Letters*, 49). As usual, Hurd followed his advice; the Discourse was printed with the Epistle to Augustus in 1751, and one more "dissertation" was added to each of the next three editions. The second edition of Hurd's Horace of 1753 added the dissertation "On the Provinces of the Several Species of Dramatic Poetry"; the third edition (1757) added "A Letter to Mr. Mason; On the Marks of Imitation"; and the fourth (1766) added "A Dissertation on the Idea of Universal Poetry." The third and fourth of these dissertations were also reprinted and published separately at the same time their respective editions of Horace were published. The fifth and final edition (1776) was merely a reprint of the 1766 edition.

These editions, plus a Dublin reprint and a German translation, make a total of ten works which are listed below in chronological order. I mark with an asterisk those copies I have examined personally. I am deeply grateful to all those librarians who have answered patiently my questions about copies I have not examined. In most instances the reader will find some additional copies of these editions listed in NUC or ESTC.

Note: The citation "Bowyer Ledgers" refers to *The Bowyer Ledgers*, edited by Keith Maslen and John Lancaster (London: The Bibliographical Society; New York: The Bibliographical Society of America, 1991). Whenever a reference is followed merely by a number, it refers to an entry in the Chronological Checklist, which constitutes the bulk of the printed book. When the number is preceded by a "B," it refers to the number in the microfiche edition of Ledger B (Grolier Club Library 19474). When the number is preceded by a "P," it refers to the number in the microfiche edition of the Paper Stock Ledger (Bodley MS.don.b.4).

Throughout this paper I am indebted to Edwine Montague Martz, *Bishop Hurd as Critic*, unpublished Ph.D dissertation, Yale University, 1939—hereafter cited as "Martz."

RICHARD HURD'S EDITIONS OF HORACE

I. 1749 (ESTC ID: T046134). First Edition.

Q. HORATII FLACCI / ARS POETICA. [red] / EPISTOLA ad PISONES. / With an English / COMMENTARY [red] / AND / NOTES. [red] /

LONDON, [red] / Printed by *W. Bowyer*, / And sold by R. Dodsley in Pall-mall, and / M. Cooper in Paternoster-Row. / MDCCXLIX. [red]

Collation: 8⁰: a⁸ B–K⁸ L² = 82 leaves = 164 pages.
Contents: Page *i* title, *ii* blank, iii–xv Introduction, *xvi* blank, *1* 2–32 *Ars Poetica*, *33* special title "Notes on the Art of Poetry," *34* blank, *35* Preface, *36* blank, *37*–148 text. Page 57 misnumbered 75.
Press figures: 25–1, 50–1, 77–1, 91–1, 98–1, 121–3, 132–4, 143–3.
Size of an uncut copy: None examined.
Number of copies printed: Bowyer Ledgers #3556: 480 copies on demy and 20 copies on royal paper (26 May 49).
Date of publication: Saturday, May 27, 1749 (*London Evening-Post*). On Tuesday, May 23, the same newspaper advertised that "Next Thursday will be publish'd" the *Ars Poetica*, but the "This Day is publish'd" advertisement did not appear until Saturday, May 27. The book also was advertised on Friday, June 2, 1749, in the *General Advertiser*. N.B. These are strange advertisements, for they list no author, price, format, or bindings. In its review, the *Monthly Review* (see note 3, below) lists the price of the book as 3s.
    William Warburton wrote to Richard Hurd on June 1, 1749, saying, "I received the favour of your edition of Horace's Art of Poetry: for which I beg leave to make my best acknowledgments" (*Letters*, 1).
Illustrations: Page *1* has an engraving of the Muses, signed "F. Hayman inv. & del.", "C. Grignion Sculp." (see Figure 1).
Copies: Regular (demy) paper copies: *Bodleian Library 2 copies: Godw. Pamph. 2094 (10) and Vet. A4e. 497 (2); Brown (ex libris Charles Townsend) PA 6393 E6 1749 Foster Collection [I thank the Coordinator of Readers' Services, Jean Rainwater, for describing this copy for me]; *Hartlebury Castle Lf6 (1); *Harvard (Houghton) *78–1291; Indiana (Lilly) PA 6393 E6H9 1749 [I thank the Head of Public Services, Joel Silver, for describing this copy for me]; *Jesus College, Cambridge H.14.68 (1); Northwestern 871 H5 Ohu [I thank the Curator of Special Collections, R. Russell Maylone, for describing this copy for me]; *Princeton PTT 2865 .311 .249; *Yale Gnh6 B749.
    Royal paper copies: *British Library 76.e.4; Free Library of Philadelphia 1749M629 [I thank the Reference Librarian, Karen Lightner, for describing this copy for me]; *Hartlebury Castle Lf10 (1). (See note 2, below.)
Notes: 1. The watermark of the royal paper, seen clearly only in the Hartlebury Castle copy which although trimmed measures 22.0 x 13.0 cm., is a fleur-de-lis over a shield with the Strasbourg bend, over LVG. For a sketch of this watermark, see Edward Heawood, *Watermarks mainly of the 17th and 18th Centuries* (1950, repr. 1981), no. 106—hereafter cited as "Heawood"; also see W. A. Churchill, *Watermarks in Paper in Holland, England, France, etc., in the XVII and XVIII Centuries and their Interconnection* (1935, repr. 1965), no. 434. The three elements of this watermark are also reproduced in Philip Gaskell, *A New Introduction to Bibliography* (1972), 68—hereafter cited as "Gaskell."
    LVG are the initials of Lubertus van Gerrevink, the owner of the Egmond mill near Hoef in North Holland. He had his initials registered as a trademark in paper in 1726 (see Churchill, p. 40). [When I see this paper used in a book, I am apt to think of it as "Large & Very Good" paper.]
    The regular paper copies have no visible watermark.
    2. The British Library copy is bound in full white vellum with the remains of a gilt morocco label on the spine. Both covers are gilt-stamped with the seal of King George the Third. All edges are cut, but the page measures 20.6 x 12.7 cm. The copy in the Free Library of Philadelphia is 21.2 cm. tall. Both of these copies show the edge of a star or sun as watermark, so this may be a variant (or quite different) paper used for large copies. In any case, enough of some watermark may be seen in the margins to classify these two—very hesitantly—as trimmed royal paper copies.

3. This volume was reviewed very favorably in the *Monthly Review:* "The ingenious author of this commentary and notes, has with great judgment and accuracy cleared the sense, ascertained the scope and purpose, and pointed out the connexion of the several parts of this celebrated epistle" (*Monthly Review* 1 [Aug. 1749], 277). This is the opening sentence of the fine review written by Dr. William Rose (1719?–86); for confirmation of his authorship, see Benjamin Christie Nangle, *The Monthly Review First Series 1749–1789 Indexes of Contributors and Articles* (1934), #2052—hereafter cited as "Nangle."

II. 1751 (ESTC ID: T046141). First Edition. One Horatian Epistle and one dissertation.

Q. HORATII FLACCI / EPISTOLA [red] / AD / AUGUSTUM. / With an English / Commentary and Notes. [red] / To which is added, / A DISCOURSE / CONCERNING / POETICAL IMITATION. [red] / [rule] / By the AUTHOR of the COMMENTARY, &c. / on the Epistle to the PISOS. / [rule] / LONDON, [red] / Printed for *W. Thurlbourn* in Cambridge. / And sold by *R. Dodsley* in Pall-mall; *J. Beecroft* in Lom-/bard Street; and *M. Cooper* in Paternoster-Row. / [rule] / M DCC LI. [red]

Collation: 8°: A² B–O⁸ = 106 leaves = 212 pages.
Contents: Page *i* title, *ii* blank, iii–iv Advertisement, *1* 2–27 text, *28* blank, *29* special title "Notes on the Epistle to Augustus," *30* Advertisement, *31*–106 text, *107* special title "A Discourse on Poetical Imitation," *108* blank, 109–207 text, *208* blank.
Press figures: 11–5, 22–1, 36–1, 50–1, 66–1, 112–4, 123–3 or none, 144–1, 160–1 or none, 173–4, 192–1 or none, 204–3.
Size of an uncut copy: None examined.
Number of copies printed: Bowyer Ledgers #3684: 500 copies on demy and 26 copies on royal paper (16 May 51).
Date of publication: Tuesday, May 21, 1751 (*General Evening Post*). In its issue of Saturday, May 18, 1751 the same newspaper advertised that "Next Tuesday will be published" the *Epistola ad Augustum*, and accordingly the "This Day was published" notice appeared in the issue of Tuesday, May 21. N.B. Once again this advertisement seems strange, for it lists no author's name, price, format, or bindings.
Illustrations: Page *1* has an engraving of the head of Augustus, signed "WS" (see Figure 2).
Copies: Regular (demy) paper copies: *Bodleian Library 3 copies: Vet. A4e. 497(1), Godw. Pamph. 2095(4), and Montagu 257; *British Library 11355.ff.4; Chicago PA 6393 .E75H9 1751 Rare [I thank the Rare Books Coordinator, Willard J. Pugh, for describing this copy for me]; *Cornell; *Hartlebury Castle Lf6(2); *Harvard (Houghton) *78–1292; *Jesus College, Cambridge A/G.9.30; McMaster B14650 [I thank the Archives Cataloguer, Renu Barrett, for describing this copy for me]; Northwestern Horace H961 1751 [I thank the Curator of Special Collections, R. Russell Maylone, for describing this copy for me]; *Princeton 2865 .331 .251; *Yale Gnh6 ea751; *D. D. Eddy.
    Royal paper copies: *Hartlebury Castle Lf10(2).
Note: The watermark of the royal paper, seen clearly only in the Hartlebury Castle copy which although trimmed measures 22.0 x 13.0 cm., is a fleur-de-lis over a shield with the Strasbourg bend, over LVG (see Heawood 106). This is the same large paper used in Hurd's 1749 *Ars Poetica*, and the two works are bound together in the volume at Richard Hurd's library at Hartlebury Castle. The regular paper copies have no visible watermark.

III. 1753 (ESTC ID: T150243). The two Horatian Epistles and two dissertations.

Volume I. Edition title page.
Q. HORATII FLACCI / EPISTOLAE / AD / PISONES, / ET / AUGUSTUM: / With an ENGLISH / COMMENTARY and NOTES. / To which are added / TWO DISSERTATIONS: / THE ONE, / On the PROVINCES of the several Species / of DRAMATIC POETRY; / THE OTHER, / ON POETICAL IMITATION. / [rule] / IN TWO VOLUMES. / [rule] / The SECOND EDITION, Corrected and Enlarged. / [rule] / *LONDON:*/ Printed for W. THURLBOURNE, at *Cambridge*; / and sold by R. DODSLEY, in *Pall-mall*; / J. BEECROFT, in *Lombard-street*; and / M. COOPER, in *Pater-noster-Row.* / [rule] / MDCCLIII.

Volume I. Volume title page.
Q. HORATII FLACCI / ARS POETICA, / EPISTOLA ad PISONES: / With an ENGLISH / COMMENTARY and NOTES. / To which is added / A DISSERTATION concerning the PROVINCES / of the several Species of the DRAMA. / [rule] / VOL. I. / [rule] / *LONDON:* / Printed for W. THURLBOURNE at *Cambridge*; / And sold by R. DODSLEY, in *Pall-mall*; / J. BEACROFT, [*sic*] in *Lombard-street*, and / M. COOPER, in *Pater-noster-Row.* / [rule] / MDCCLIII.

Collation: 8°: π⁴ A–S⁸ T⁴ = 152 leaves = 304 pages.
Contents: π1ʳ edition title page, π1ᵛ blank, π2ʳ volume title page, π2ᵛ blank, π3ʳ Dedication to Sir Edward Littleton, π3ᵛ blank, π4ʳ "VOL. I," π4ᵛ blank, pages iii–xvi Introduction, *1* 2–34 text of Ars Poetica, *35* section title, *36* blank, *37* Preface to the Notes, *38* blank, *39*–216 Notes of the Art of Poetry, *217* section title, *218* blank, *219* Contents, *220* blank, *221*–280 A Dissertation on the several Provinces of the Drama, *281* Errata, *282* blank. Page 272 misnumbered 472. In two copies (British Library and Emmanuel College, Cambridge), page 16 is misnumbered 6.
Press figures: ix–3, 12–1, 15–3, 29–1, 48–2, 60–3, 72–4, 84–1, 110–2, 127–1, 141–4, 161–4, 177–4, 180–4, 210–3, 214–5 or none, 242–1, 246–1, 273–4.

Volume II. Title page.
Q. HORATII FLACCI / EPISTOLA / AD / AUGUSTUM. / With an ENGLISH / COMMENTARY and NOTES. / To which is added / A DISCOURSE / CONCERNING / POETICAL IMITATION. / [rule] / VOL. II. / [double rule] / [short rule] / M.DCC.LIII.

Collation: 8°: a⁸ A–Q⁸ = 136 leaves = 272 pages.
Contents: Page *i* title, *ii* blank, *iii* iv–xv Dedication to William Warburton, dated 29 March 1753, *xvi* blank, *1* 2–27 text of Epistola ad Augustum, *28* blank, *29* section title, *30* Advertisement, *31*–113 Notes on the Epistle to Augustus, *114* blank, *115* section title, *116* blank, 117–231 A Discourse on Poetical Imitation, *232* blank, *233*–253 Index to the Two Volumes, *254* blank, *255* Errata, *256* blank. Page 121 is misnumbered 112. In the British Library copy, page 73 is misnumbered 7.
Press figures: None.
Size of an uncut copy: None examined.
Number of copies printed: Bowyer Ledgers #3800: 730 copies on crown and 20 copies on medium royal paper (29 Mar. 53)

Date of publication: Presumably it was published shortly after printing was completed on March 29. In April, 1753 William Warburton wrote to Richard Hurd saying, "I received this evening your most kind present of the Commentary on Horace" (*Letters*, 133). In its review, the *Monthly Review* (see note 4, below) lists the price of these two volumes as 7s. 2d.

Illustrations: In Vol. I, page *1* has an engraving of the Muses, signed F. Hayman inv. & del., C. Grignion Sculp. In Vol. II, page *1* has an engraving of the head of Augustus, signed WS. These are the same plates used in the 1749 and 1751 editions.

Copies: Regular (crown) paper copies: *Bodleian Library 2 copies: Godw. subt. 280–281 and Vet. A5f. 1652–3 (lacking leaves π1 and π4 in Vol. I); Brown PA 6393 E4 1753 Foster Collection [I thank the Coordinator of Readers' Services, Jean Rainwater, for describing this copy for me]; *Cambridge University Library 2 copies: 7706.d.93,94 (lacking leaves π1 and π4 in Vol. I) and Ely.d.696 (Vol. II only present); Chicago 2 copies: PA 6393 .E2 1753 Rare (c. 1, Vol. I only present; c. 2, Vol. I lacks dedication leaf) [I thank the Rare Books Coordinator, Willard J. Pugh, for describing these copies for me]; Free Library of Philadelphia 1753M653 [I thank the Reference Librarian, Karen Lightner, for describing this copy for me]; *Harvard (Widener) Lh8 565; *Princeton 2865 .331 .253; *Yale Gnh6 B753.

Royal paper copies: *British Library 11385.f.17 (lacks leaf π4 in Vol. I); *Emmanuel College, Cambridge 328.4.64–65.

Notes: 1. The watermark of the royal paper is a crowned shield containing a fleur-de-lis, over LVG (see Heawood 1743; Gaskell, 68, Fig. 29). The regular paper copies have no visible watermark.

2. The two royal paper copies are exceedingly handsome. Both volumes of the British Library copy are bound in full straight-grain red morocco and have all edges gilt. Both front and rear covers have gilt supra libros with the front covers adding the motto "Deus alit me" and the script initials "TW." This copy belonged to the Rev. Theodore Williams, who died in 1826 and whose library was sold at auction on April 5 and 23, 1827.

The second copy is much more significant because it was the gift of Richard Hurd to one of his colleagues at Emmanuel College. The first volume contains the note "The Gift of ye Author (in Sheets) to H. Hubbard Eman. Coll. (Binding 2 Vols. 3s 6d)." This was Henry Hubbard (1708–78), who had been a Fellow of Emmanuel College since 1732; for an accurate, brief account of him, see John Venn (1834–1923). *Alumni Cantabrigienses . . .,* 10 v. (1922–54) Part I, Vol. II, p. 422. When Richard Hurd matriculated at Emmanuel in 1735, "he was happy in receiving the countenance, and in being permitted to attend the Lectures, of that excellent Tutor, Mr. Henry Hubbard, although he had been admitted under another person"; see Hurd's own list "Some occurrences in my Life" as printed in *The Correspondence of Richard Hurd & William Mason,* ed. E. H. Pearce and L. Whibley (1932) xxvi—hereafter cited as "Hurd-Mason Correspondence."

3. It is probably not wise to make generalizations based on the few copies thus far examined. However, all of the regular paper copies examined have horizontal chain lines throughout both volumes, and both of the royal paper copies examined have vertical chain lines throughout both volumes. If this holds true as more copies are seen, it will be an easy way to differentiate between regular and royal paper copies, even in closely trimmed volumes.

Of course, there are also differences in thickness of the two papers. In the royal paper copy in the British Library, for example, the sheets of Vol. I measure 2.7 cm. thick; while in the regular paper copy in Cambridge University Library, the sheets of Vol. I measure 1.9 cm. thick. In comparing the same copies of Vol. II, the British Library copy measures 2.2 cm. versus 1.7 cm. in the Cambridge copy. Such comparisons are made with due diffidence, for an unpressed book in sheets bulks much, much larger than a copy of the same book which has been heavily pressed during several rebindings.

4. Dr. William Rose (1719?–86) again wrote a long and highly laudatory re-

view article in the *Monthly Review* 9 (July 1753), 11–33; see Nangle, #2055.

5. Two printers were involved in printing this edition. According to his ledgers (B544, P1094), William Bowyer printed only Vol. I. Thurlbourne had the second volume composed and printed at Cambridge University Press; in the Cambridge University Library Archives, see Cambridge University Press Minutes Book (Min. VI. 1*, p. 88), listing as copies "730 & 20 Fine." Volume I has all the usual Bowyer press figures; Volume II has none. For a discussion of this edition, see below under the heading "Shared Printing."

IV. 1757 (ESTC ID: T149881). The two Horatian Epistles and three dissertations.

Volume I. Edition title page.
Q. HORATII FLACCI / EPISTOLAE / AD / PISONES, / ET / AUGUSTUM: / With an ENGLISH / COMMENTARY and NOTES. / To which are added, / TWO DISSERTATIONS; / The one, on the PROVINCES of the DRAMA: / The other, on POETICAL IMITATION: / AND / A LETTER to Mr. MASON. / [rule] / In TWO VOLUMES. / [rule] / The THIRD EDITION, Corrected and Enlarged. / [rule] / *CAMBRIDGE*, / Printed for W. THURLBOURN & J. WOODYER; and / sold by R. DODSLEY in Pall-mall, J. BEECROFT and / M. COOPER in Pater-noster Row, London. / [rule] / M DCC LVII.

Volume I. Volume title page.
Q. HORATII FLACCI / ARS POETICA, / EPISTOLA ad PISONES: / With an ENGLISH / COMMENTARY and NOTES. / To which is added / A DISSERTATION / Concerning the PROVINCES of the several / Species of the DRAMA. / [rule] / VOL. I. / [double rule] / *CAMBRIDGE*, / Printed for W. THURLBOURN & J. WOODYER. / [rule] / M DCC LVII.

Collation: 8°: π4 A–U⁸ = 164 leaves = 328 pages.
Contents: π1ʳ edition title page, π1ᵛ blank, π2ʳ volume title page, π2ᵛ blank, pages *i* ii–iii Dedication to Sir Edward Littleton, signed "Cambridge, 21 June 1757," *iv* blank, iii [*sic*]–xvi Introduction, *1* 2–34, *35–36* 39 [*sic*]–242 *243–246* 247–308 text. Page 225 is correctly numbered in the Bodleian and Cambridge University Library copies; it is unnumbered in all other copies examined. Other pages misnumbered as above.
Press figures: 86–4.

Volume II. Title page.
Q. HORATII FLACCI / EPISTOLA / AD / AUGUSTUM: / With an ENGLISH / COMMENTARY and NOTES. / To which are added, / A DISCOURSE / CONCERNING / POETICAL IMITATION; / AND / A LETTER to Mr. MASON. / [rule] / VOL. II. / [double rule] / *CAMBRIDGE*, / Printed for W. THURLBOURN & J. WOODYER. / [rule] / M DCC LVII.

Collation: a⁸ A–T⁸ = 160 leaves = 320 pages.
Contents: Page *i* volume title page, *ii* blank, *iii* iv–xv Dedication to the Rev. Mr. Warburton, signed "Cambridge, 29 March, 1753," *xvi* blank, *1* 2–27 text, *28* blank, *29* section title, *30* blank, 31–101 text, *102* blank, *103* section title, *104*

blank, 105–207 text, *208* blank, *1* title page to A Letter to Mr. Mason. . . . *2* blank, 3 [misnumbered 1] 4–76 text, dated on p. 76: "15 August 1757," 77–*96* Index to the Two Volumes. In the Letter to Mr. Mason . . ., page *3* is misnumbered 1 and 67 is misnumbered 76 in all copies. In the course of printing, page 190 slowly lost its first digit: in three copies examined it is correctly numbered, in four other copies it is numbered ^{1}90, and in another five copies it is misnumbered 90.

Press figures: 13–4 or none, 31–4, 43–4, 66–2, 91–4, 166–4, 178–3, 206–4, ^{2}10–4, ^{2}22–1 or none, ^{2}26–2, ^{2}79–2.

Size of an uncut copy: Regular (small) paper copy, 19.8 x 12.5 cm. (Cornell copy, in blue wrappers).

Number of copies printed: Unknown; but since 750 copies of the second edition had been printed four years earlier, it is probably safe to assume that this edition was at least that large. Keep in mind that the next printing—the fourth edition of 1766—was printed in 1000 copies. Volume II of this edition was printed at Cambridge University Press, and the colophon on the last page reads: "CAMBRIDGE, / Printed by J. Bentham Printer to the University. / [rule] / M DCC LVII." Joseph Bentham presumably printed this work for Thurlbourne and Woodyer on his "private account," so since it was not a publication of Cambridge University Press there is no record of it among the archives of the Press in Cambridge University Library. There is no record of this edition in the Bowyer ledgers, nor are there any decorative initials or ornaments of any kind in either volume to help in identifying the printer.

Date of publication: Although the last piece in Vol. II is dated 15 August 1757, at least a few printed copies were available immediately afterwards. In a letter to Thomas Gray dated August 16, 1757, Hurd states that "The Letter to Mason is printed off, and I shall send you a copy very soon to Dodsley's" (Hurd-Mason Correspondence, 36–37). In a letter to Hurd dated September 12, 1757, William Warburton says that "I have received your new Edition.—Your additional notes, and new pieces, are admirable" (*Letters*, 253).

Illustrations: In Vol. I, page *1* has an engraving of the Muses, signed F. Hayman inv. & del., C. Grignion Sculp. In Vol. II, page *1* has an engraving of the head of Augustus, signed WS. These are the same engravings found in the previous editions.

Copies: Regular (small) paper copies: *British Library 1578/2836; *Cambridge University Library 4 copies: Adv. d. 75. 6–7, Ely d. 697–698, Keynes R. 3. 15–16 (ex libris Edward Gibbon Esq.), and X. 5. 80–81; *Cornell; University of Florida at Gainesville 871 H5e 1756 [*sic*]; Free Library of Philadelphia 1757M680 [I thank the Reference Librarian, Karen Lightner, for describing this copy for me]; *Jesus College, Cambridge MK. 3. 1–2; Northwestern Horace H961 1757 [I thank the Curator of Special Collections, R. Russell Maylone, for describing this copy for me]; *Yale Gnh6 b753b; *D. D. Eddy.

Large paper copies: *Bodleian Library Vet. A5e. 2067, 2068.

Notes: 1. The watermark of the regular paper copies is best seen in the uncut copy at Cornell; it has a watermark of a fleur-de-lis over the initials "IV" (see Heawood 1540; Gaskell, 68).

2. The Bodleian copy is handsomely bound in speckled calf with double labels, the covers and spines ornately gilt, and all edges gilt. Both volumes contain the ex libris of Sir Edward Littleton Bart., so this is a dedication copy. Although both volumes were so heavily trimmed in binding that only traces of a watermark are visible, yet both measure 20.6 x 13.0 cm. and so are slightly larger than the uncut small paper copy at Cornell.

The University of Florida copy is bound similarly to the Bodleian copy, except that its edges are not gilt. Both of its volumes also contain the ex libris of Sir Edward Littleton Bart., so it appears that Richard Hurd sent attractively bound sets of both the large and small paper copies to the dedicatee. In binding, the pages of both volumes of the Florida copy were trimmed to 18.0 cm. in height. [I am grateful to the University of Florida Library Curator of Rare Books,

Miss Carmen Hurff, for giving me an accurate description of these volumes.]

"At Cambridge [Hurd] formed a close friendship with his pupil and old schoolfellow, Sir Edward Littleton, bart." *(DNB)*. Littleton was admitted to Emmanuel College as a nobleman on April 20, 1744, and he received his M.A. in 1746; see Venn, *Alumni Cantabrigienses*, Part I, Vol. III, p. 92.

V. 1757 (ESTC ID: T068159)

A/ LETTER / TO / Mr. *MASON*; / ON THE / MARKS of IMITATION. / [rule] [quotation from Malherbe] / [double rule] / *CAMBRIDGE:* / Printed for W. THURLBOURN & J. WOODYER; and / sold by R. DODSLEY in Pall-mall, J. BEECROFT and / M. COOPER in Pater-noster Row, London. / [rule] / M DCC LVII.

Collation: 8°: A–E^8 = 40 leaves = 80 pages.
Contents: Page *1* title, *2* blank, *3–76* text, *77–80* Advertisements for "Books printed for and sold by W. Thurlbourn and J. Woodyer, in Cambridge." Page 58 misnumbered 85.
Press figures: 26–1, 34–1, 58 [misnumbered 85]–3, 68–1.
Size of an uncut copy: None examined.
Number of copies printed: Unknown. Although this is a different edition from the one included in the 1757 edition of Hurd's Horace, it was presumably printed at approximately the same time at Cambridge University Press.
Date of publication: Again citing Hurd's letter to Thomas Gray (see above), at least some printed copies were available on August 16, 1757.
Illustrations: None.
Copies: *Bodleian Library 2 copies: Godw. Pamph. 105(1) and Godw. Pamph. 1860 (16); *British Library 11825.b.29(1); *Cambridge University Library Yorke. d. 630 (3); *Cornell (lacking pp.77–80); *Princeton 2865 .331 .253(2); *Yale Had 21 g757h; *D. D. Eddy (ex libris R. W. Chapman).
Note: Owen Ruffhead (1723–69) praised this book highly in a long review article in the *Monthly Review* 18 (Feb. 1758), 114–125; see Nangle, #2457. The price is listed as 1s.

VI. 1766 (ESTC ID: T046143). The two Horatian Epistles and four dissertations.

Volume I.

Q. HORATII FLACCI / EPISTOLAE / AD / PISONES, / ET / AUGUSTUM: / WITH AN ENGLISH / COMMENTARY AND NOTES: / TO WHICH ARE ADDED / CRITICAL DISSERTATIONS. / BY THE / REVEREND MR. HURD. / IN THREE VOLUMES. / THE FOURTH EDITION, / CORRECTED AND ENLARGED. / VOL. I. / LONDON, / PRINTED FOR A. MILLAR, IN THE STRAND; / AND W. THURLBOURN AND J. WOODYER, / AT CAMBRIDGE. MDCCLXVI.

Collation: 8°: a^4 b1(=T4) A–S^8 T^4(–T4=b1) = 152 leaves = 304 pages.
Contents: Page *i* title page, *ii* blank, *iii* Contents, *iv* blank, *v–ix* Dedication to Sir Edward Littleton, Bart., *x* blank, ^{2}*i–xvi* Introduction, *1–36* text, *37* section title, *38* blank, *39–277* text, *278* blank.
Press figures: vii–1 or none, ^{2}iv–1, 2–4, 13–2, 22–2 or none, 34–2, 41–4, 52–1, 58–4,

70–4, 76–1, 84–4, 98–2, 123–1, 140–4, 156–4, 164–1, 175–4, 182–1, 194–2, 212–2, 240–1, 270–4, 276–2.

Volume II.

[Title identical with Vol. I, but deleting "IN THREE VOLUMES" and reading "VOL. II."]

Collation: 8°: a⁸ b² B–Q⁸ R⁴ = 134 leaves = 268 pages.
Contents: Page *i* title, *ii* blank, iii–xix Dedication to William Warburton, *xx* blank, 1–32 text, *33* section title, *34* blank, 35–131 text, *132* blank, *133* section title, *134* blank, 135–161 text, *162* blank, 163–247 text, *248* blank.
Press figures: xi–2 or none, 11–1, 28–1, 42–4, 59–4, 68–4, 92–2, 105–1, 124–4, 139–4, 146–1, 173–2, 174–3, 185–2, 186–2, 203–2, 222–2, 233–4, 242–1.

Volume III.

[Title identical with Vol. I. but deleting "IN THREE VOLUMES" and reading "VOL. III."]

Collation: 8°: *A*1 B–R⁸ S⁴ *T*1 = 134 leaves = 268 pages.
Contents: *A*1ʳ title page, *A*1ᵛ blank, 1–240 text, 241–265 Index, *266* blank.
Press figures: 9–2, 18–2, 38–2, 57–2, 70–1, 94–1, 100–3, 106–1, 121–2, 136–2, 153–2, 169–2, 184–2, 190–4, 205–2, 210–1, 234–4, 242–3, 249–2, 262–3, 264–2.
Size of an uncut copy: None examined.
Number of copies printed: Bowyer Ledgers #4608: 1000 copies (6 May 66).
Date of publication: Thursday, May 15, 1766 (*Public Advertiser*). "This Day is published, Elegantly printed on a fine Writing-Paper, in Three Volumes, Duodecimo [*sic*], Price bound 9s. A new Edition (being the Fourth) corrected and enlarged . . . By the Rev. Mr. Hurd, Preacher to the Honourable Society of Lincoln's-Inn. . . ." On May 6, the day printing was completed, the *Public Advertiser* carried its first "Speedily will be published . . ." notice.
Illustrations: None.
Copies: *Bodleian Library Montagu 252–254; *British Library 237.l. 21–23; *Cornell; Free Library of Philadelphia 1766M713 [I thank the Reference Librarian, Karen Lightner, for describing this copy for me]; *Hartlebury Castle Bb 24–26; *Harvard (Houghton) Lh8 .567* (see note 2, below); *Jesus College, Cambridge F. 5. 22–24; *Princeton PTT 2865 .331 .266 (Vol. II lacks signature Q); *Yale Gnh6 b753c; *D. D. Eddy.
Notes: 1. The paper used has vertical chain lines throughout all copies examined but has no visible watermarks. No copies were printed on large paper.

2. Hurd was made "Preacher of Lincoln's Inn, on the recommendation of Mr. Charles Yorke, &c., November 6, 1765" (Hurd-Mason Correspondence, xxvii); and when the fourth edition of his Horace was published the following spring, Hurd was happy to include his name and new title in the newspaper advertisements (see above). Also residing at Lincoln's Inn at that time was Thomas Hollis, who presented to the Harvard College Library a set of the three volumes of this edition of Hurd's Horace, the copy listed above. The volumes were bound by John Shove of London and have his characteristic tool in the center of each cover. Each volume also contains the college bookplate engraved by Nathaniel Hurd of Boston, filled out in manuscript "The Gift of Thomas Hollis, of Lincoln's Inn, London." For pictures of Shove's binding tool and Hurd's bookplate, see W. H. Bond, *Thomas Hollis of Lincoln's Inn: A Whig and his Books* (1990), 54–55, 89–90.

3. This edition apparently contains Hurd's final thoughts about his edition of Horace. "A manuscript in Hartlebury Library, in the handwriting of Hurd's nephew, reveals the Bishop's directions concerning the collected edition of his

works: . . . Horace & the Critical Dissertations [are to be] printed from the 4th Edition in 1766" (Martz, p. 587).

VII. 1766 (ESTC ID: No58848)

A / DISSERTATION / ON THE / IDEA / OF / UNIVERSAL POETRY. / [ornament] / LONDON, / Printed for A. MILLAR, in *The Strand.* / MDCCLXVI.

Collation: 8°: A–B⁸ = 16 leaves = 32 pages.
Contents: Page *1* title, *2* blank, *3* 4–29 text, *30–32* blank.
Press figures: None.
Size of an uncut copy: None examined.
Number of copies printed: 250. "Used for 2 sheets No. 250 1 [ream]; Dd to Mr Millar the Pamphlet No. 250" (Bowyer Ledgers P1221).
Date of publication: Friday, May 30, 1766 (*Daily Advertiser*). In the month of May, 1766, none of the advertisements for the fourth edition of Hurd's Horace in either the *Daily Advertiser* or the *Public Advertiser* mentioned any separate reprint of the "Dissertation" until the notice in the *Daily Advertiser* of May 30 added: "Note: The above Dissertation on Universal Poetry may be had separately, Price 6d."
Illustrations: None.
Copies: *Emmanuel College, Cambridge 331.3.65 (3) [I thank the Sub-librarian, Rhiannon Jones, for initially describing this copy for me]; Folger Shakespeare Library PN 1055 H9 Cage, lacking final blank leaf B8 [I thank the Reference Librarian, Georgianna Ziegler, for describing this copy for me]; University of Kansas B 4569, lacking final blank leaf B8 [I thank the Associate Special Collections Librarian, Richard W. Clement, for describing this copy for me].

VIII. 1768 (ESTC ID: T187173)

Volume I.
Q. HORATII FLACCI / EPISTOLAE / AD / PISONES, / ET / AUGUSTUM: / WITH AN ENGLISH / COMMENTARY AND NOTES: / TO WHICH ARE ADDED / CRITICAL DISSERTATIONS. / BY THE / REVEREND MR. HURD. / IN TWO VOLUMES. / THE FIFTH EDITION, / CORRECTED AND ENLARGED. / VOL. I. / *DUBLIN:* / PRINTED BY SARAH STRINGER, UNDER DICK'S / COFFEE-HOUSE IN SKINNER-ROW. / [rule] / M,DCC,LXVIII.

Collation: 12°: a⁴ A–I¹² 2a⁶ [between I11 and I12] K–N¹² O1 = 167 leaves = 334 pages. ²a2 missigned a3.
Contents: Page *i* title, *ii* blank, iii Contents, *iv* blank, v–viii Dedication to Sir Edward Littleton, ²i–xiv Introduction, 1–32 text, *33* section title, *34* blank, 35–198 text, *199* section title, *200* blank, ³i–xi Dedication to William Warburton, *xii* blank, 201–229 text, *230* blank, *231* section title, *232* blank, 233–299 text, *300* blank.
Press figures: None.

Volume II.
[Title page same as Vol. I, except: . . . VOL. II. / DUBLIN : / . . .]

Collation: 12°: A1 B–L¹² M⁸ = 129 leaves = 258 pages.
Contents: A1ʳ title, A1ᵛ blank, pages 1–75 text, *76* blank, 77–240 text, 241–256 Index.
Press figures: None.

Size of an uncut copy: None examined.
Number of copies printed: Unknown.
Illustrations: None.
Copies: *Bodleian Library Montagu 255, 256; University of North Carolina at Chapel Hill PA 6393 .E75 1768 [I thank Dr. Charles McNamara for describing this copy for me]; *Yale Gnh6 b753e.
Note: The paper used has horizontal chain lines throughout the copies examined and has no visible watermarks.

IX. 1772 Translation into German by Johann Joachim Eschenburg, 1743–1820.

Volume I.

Horazens / Episteln an die Pisonen / und / an den Augustus / [rule] / mit / Kommentar und Anmerkungen / nebst / einigen kritischen Abhandlungen / von / R. Hurd. / [rule] / Aus dem Englishen uebersetzt / und / mit eigenen Anmerkungen begleitet / von / Johann Joachim Eschenburg. / [rule] / Erster Band. / [rule] / Leipzig / bey Engelhart Benjamin Schwickert 1772.

Collation: 8°: π1(=2C8?) A–2B⁸ 2C⁸ (–2C8) 2D² = 210 leaves = 420 pages.
Contents: π1ʳ title, π1ᵛ blank, pages 1–54 text, *55* section title, *56* blank, *57* 58–246 text, *247* section title, *248* blank, *249* 250–292 text, *293* section title, *294* blank, *295* 296–418 text.

Volume II.
[Title identical with Vol. I, except for reading "Zweyter Band."]

Collation: π1(=U8?) A–T⁸ U⁸ (–U8) X²
Contents: π1ʳ title, π1ᵛ blank, *1* section title, *2* blank, *3* 4–24 text, *25* section title, *26* blank, *27* 28–94 text, *95* section title, *96* blank, *97* 98–214 text, *215* section title, *216* blank, *217* 218–321 text, *322* list of errata.
Size of an uncut copy: 21.5 x 13.5 cm. (Princeton copy, top edge lightly trimmed and gilt, the other edges uncut).
Copies: *British Library 11385. c. 26; Illinois (Champaign-Urbana) 871 H5a .huG [I thank the Curator of Rare Books, N. Frederick Nash, for describing this copy for me]; Northwestern Horace H961 1772 [I thank the Curator of Special Collections, R. Russell Maylone, for describing this copy for me]; *Princeton PTT 2865 .311 .272.
Notes: 1. The entire book, both text and title pages, is set in Fraktur.
   2. Again I thank Fred Nash for locating in Illinois two more copies of this elusive translation: DePaul University Library and Bethany Northern Baptist Seminary Library.

X. 1776 (ESTC ID: T046144)

Volume I.
Q. HORATII FLACCI / EPISTOLAE / AD / PISONES, / ET / AUGUSTUM: / WITH AN ENGLISH / COMMENTARY AND NOTES: / TO WHICH ARE ADDED / CRITICAL DISSERTATIONS. / BY THE / REVEREND MR. HURD. / IN THREE VOLUMES. / THE FIFTH EDITION, / CORRECTED AND ENLARGED. / VOL. I. /

LONDON, / PRINTED BY W. BOWYER AND J. NICHOLS: / FOR
T. CADELL, IN THE STRAND; AND / J. WOODYER, AT
CAMBRIDGE. / MDCCLXXVI.

Collation: 8°: a1–5 A–S⁸ T1–3(=a6–8?) = 152 leaves = 304 pages.
Contents: Page *i* title page, *ii* blank, iii Contents, *iv* blank, v–ix Dedication to Sir
   Edward Lyttelton, *x* blank, ²i–xvi Introduction, 1–36 text, *37* section title, *38*
   blank, 39–277 text, *278* blank. In some copies, page 82 not numbered; in the
   Princeton copy, 82 and the NO of the headline NOTES are both lacking; in the
   Harvard and Northwestern copies, 82 and NOT are lacking.
Press figures: vi–1, viii–2 or none, ²ii–5, 6–7, 9–3, 26–4, 34–6, 56–5, 62–1, 79–7, 92–4,
   94–1, 111–4, 126–2, 141–3, 143–2, 146–1, 168–2, 190–1, 205–7, 207–4, 221–1, 223–7,
   239–2, 248–5, 264–5, 270–3.

Volume II.
[Title same as Vol. I, except for deleting "IN THREE VOLUMES" and reading "VOL. II." instead of "VOL. I."]

Collation: 8°: a⁸ b² B–Q⁸ R⁴ = 134 leaves = 268 pages.
Contents: Page *i* title page, *ii* blank, iii–xix Dedication to Warburton, *xx* blank, 1–32
   text, *33* section title, *34* blank, 35–131 text, *132* blank, *133* section title, *134* blank,
   135–161 text, *162* blank, 163–247 text, *248* blank. In approximately half the copies
   examined, the inner forme of signature L is mis-impressed and misnumbered;
   see note 2, below.
Press figures: x–6, xiii–4, 14–4, 25–7, 48–6, 54–6, 61–2, 68–5, 75–1, 91–1, 107–5, 127–4,
   143–7, 158–1, 172–3, 185–4, 187–3, 200–6, 223–1, 245–7.

Volume III.
[Title same as Vol. I, except for deleting "IN THREE VOLUMES" and reading "VOL. III." instead of "VOL. I."]

Collation: 8°: A1 B–R⁸ S⁴ T1 = 134 leaves = 268 pages.
Contents: A1ʳ title page, A1ᵛ blank, pages 1–240 text, 241–265 Index, *266* Advertise-
   ments for three works of Hurd published by T. Cadell. Page 176 misnumbered 76.
Press figures: 2–6, 27–5, 42–2, 50–5, 79–4, 89–5, 110–2, 121–4, 127–2, 134–1, 150–1,
   170–2, 191–7, 194–1, 222–5, 236–2, 238–1, 254–6, 263–3.
Size of an uncut copy: None examined.
Number of copies printed: Unknown; see Bowyer Ledgers #5095.
Illustrations: None.
Copies: *Bodleian Library 29764 e. 7–9; *British Library 1002. h. 16–18; *Cambridge
   University Library Nn. 34. 36–38; *Cornell; Free Library of Philadelphia 1776
   M744 [I thank the Reference Librarian, Karen Lightner, for describing this copy
   for me]; *Hartlebury Castle Bb 13–15; *Harvard (Widener) Lh8 .569; North-
   western Horace H961 1776 [I thank the Curator of Special Collections, R. Russell Maylone, for describing this copy for me]; *Princeton PTT 2865 .331 .276;
   *St. John's College, Cambridge H. 12. 8–10; *Trinity College, Cambridge Z. 14.
   44–46; *D. D. Eddy 2 copies.
Notes: 1. The watermark is a fleur-de-lis in the paper used in all copies. There are
   no royal paper copies.
      2. In Volume II, signature L (pages 145–160) exists in two states: in the first,
   the inner forme was mis-impressed and page 160 in the outer forme was misnumbered 164; thus the page numbers of the signature read 145, 150, 151, 148,
   149, 146, 147, 152, 153, 158, 159, 156, 157, 154, 155, and 164. Copies of this first
   state are: Bodleian Library, British Library, Cornell, Free Library of Philadelphia, Northwestern, Princeton, St. John's College, Cambridge, and D. D. Eddy

copy 1. In the second state, all of the pages are correctly impressed and page 160 is correctly numbered; copies: Cambridge University Library, Hartlebury Castle, Harvard, Trinity College, Cambridge, and D. D. Eddy copy 2.

COMMENTS, SPECULATIONS, AND QUESTIONS
THE ENGRAVINGS

In the editions of 1749, 1753, and 1757, the first page of the *Ars Poetica* has an attractive engraving of two Muses, seated, with three satyrs playing and dancing in the background. The female figure on the viewer's left represents Thalia, the Muse of comedy and bucolic poetry. In her right hand she holds the smiling mask of comedy and in her left a flute. Next to her, holding a lyre, is Erato, the Muse who presided over lyric and amatory poetry (see Figure 1).

Q. HORATII FLACCI

ARS POETICA

EPISTOLA AD PISONES.

Figure 1. From entry I (1749), p. *1*. (Reproduced, by permission, from The Robert W. Patterson Collection of Horace. Rare Books Division. Department of Rare Books and Special Collections. Princeton University Libraries.)

This plate was designed and drawn by Francis Hayman (?1708–76) and engraved by Charles Grignion (1721–1810). By the middle of the eighteenth century, these two men were perhaps the most popular artists producing copperplates for book illustrations in London. In the early 1740s Hayman relied upon Gravelot (1669–1773) as his engraver, but after Gravelot departed for

France in 1745 Hayman turned increasingly to Grignion. In 1749 Hayman had a busy year, for it saw the publication of Thomas Newton's famous edition of *Paradise Lost* with all of Hayman's full-page illustrations as well as three different editions of Horace, including Hurd's; see, for example, Hanns Hammelmann, *Book Illustrators in Eighteenth-century England* (1975), 49–55.

Who was responsible for hiring these artists for a book by an almost unknown writer? Hurd's only previous work was a pamphlet issued by Mary Cooper in 1746, so this was to be the first book by the young Fellow of Emmanuel College, Cambridge. The imprint of this 1749 book is somewhat unusual, for it lists the names of the printer and booksellers but no publisher (see note 1). Fortunately, William Bowyer's ledger B487 shows that William Thurlbourne of Cambridge was responsible for ordering and paying for the entire work. It is logical that Hurd would have turned to Thurlbourne for advice, for by 1749 Thurlbourne had been a leading bookseller and publisher in Cambridge for twenty-five years. Why, then, did Thurlbourne not include his name on the imprint as publisher? Perhaps we may speculate that although Thurlbourne paid Bowyer the complete bill of £25:10:3 (for paper, printing, binding the fine copies, advertising, and 3s. "for working the plate"), yet Thurlbourne may have been acting merely as an agent for Hurd, who was responsible for paying the bills. It was certainly not uncommon at that time for authors to have to pay for the production of their early books (see note 2). In this case Thurlbourne may have left his name off the imprint—and out of the newspaper advertisements—since, technically, he was not the publisher. Therefore, since William Bowyer was directly responsible for all aspects of producing the book, he may have hired Hayman and Grignion; or, as an old professional in the book trade, Thurlbourne may have requested those artists from Bowyer; or, since he may have been paying for it all, Hurd may have requested them on the advice of his good friend William Mason, whose *Musaeus* had been illustrated by Hayman and Grignion in 1747.

In the editions of 1751, 1753, and 1757, the first page of the *Epistola ad Augustum* contains a left-facing head of Augustus Caesar, surrounded by an inscription "DIVVS AVGVSTVS PATER" (see Figure 2). Under the plate are the initials "WS," but the identity of this engraver remains conjectural. Whoever he was, the center of his engraving—that is, everything inside the circle, including the lettering—is an extremely close copy of John Pine's engraving in his celebrated edition of Horace; see *Quinti Horatii Flacci Opera* (Londini: Aeneis Tabulis Incidit Johannes Pine, 1733), I, 21.

William Thurlbourne was clearly the publisher of the 1751 edition, yet some costs were still passed on to "Mr Hurd of Emanuel" according to William Bowyer's printing ledgers. On April 16 (and 20), 1751, there were charges of 3s. 6d. "for working at Rolling Press the Head of Horace [*sic*]" and 5s. "for advertising twice" (ledgers B487 and B544). From a financial point of view, the *Ars Poetica* of 1749 and the *Epistola ad Augustum* of 1751 are similar in many ways: both were printed by Bowyer for Thurlbourne, both have title pages printed in red and black, and both have only one copperplate engraving; yet the 1751 should have been the more expensive book to

Q. HORATII FLACCI

EPISTOLA AD AUGUSTUM.

Figure 2. From entry II (1751), p. *1*. (Reproduced, by permission, from General Collections. Princeton University Libraries.)

produce, for it has three more sheets of text than the 1749 and 26 more copies were printed. Thurlbourne was charged £25:10:3 for the 1749 (as noted above) and £17:17:2 for the 1751 edition, with the main differences being in the costs for paper: the bill for the 1749 included £7:13:0 for ten reams of Demy at 15s. each and 11s. 3d. for nine quires of Royal at 1s. 3d. per quire, while the bill for the 1751 edition does not mention any costs for paper. We may presume that Thurlbourne was billed for the paper used, either separately or by including the costs in other Thurlbourne accounts; but the amount does not seem to be identified in the Bowyer ledgers.

Perhaps a more meaningful comparison, however, is in the prices Bowyer charged per sheet of printing. Of the 500 copies of the 1749 edition, there were "10 sheets & 1/4 with Title red equal to 11 Sheets at 24s. per Sheet" (B487). Of the 526 copies of the 1751 edition, there were "13 Sheets & 1/4 and Title red equal to 14 Sheets . . . at 24s. per sheet" (B544). Of the 750 copies of the 1753 edition, Bowyer printed "vol. I. 19 sheets . . . at 22s. per sheet" (B544); for Vol. II of this same edition, Thurlbourne was charged 20s. 9d. per sheet at Cambridge University Press (Minute Book Min. VI. 1*, p. 88). There are no price records for the later editions of Hurd's Horace, but surely the 1000 copies of the 52 1/2 sheets Bowyer printed for Millar for the 1766 edition would have been priced at a much lower rate. Examining other entries in the Bowyer ledgers at this period amply confirms the general maxim of business: when comparing similar types of work, the larger the quantity ordered the lower the cost per unit.

There is no listing in these detailed ledgers of the expenses of buying the copperplates and having them engraved, so we will probably never learn the difference in cost between a plate done by Hayman and Grignion and one by the presumably less expensive WS. But regardless of the costs, who would normally have paid for the engravings in a book, and who owned them and controlled their use in later editions? In the case of Hurd's Horace, each plate was used in its first printing for 500 or so copies, a second printing in 1753 of 750 copies, and a third printing in 1757 of presumably 750 or more copies. Any copperplate may show signs of wear after 2000 or more impressions; and Thurlbourne, who presumably controlled all the editions through 1757, may well have scrapped the plates after the Cambridge edition of that year. In any case, when Andrew Millar had Bowyer print 1000 copies of the fourth edition in 1766, the plates were probably too worn to print that many more copies and Millar did not care to have new ones made, so no plates were used. When the fifth edition was published ten years later, Cadell also omitted any plates.

Notes: 1. In this context the term "publisher" means the person responsible for paying the costs of producing the book, and whose name in the imprint usually was preceded by "Printed for." One says "usually" because it was the normal practice among the major figures in the London book trade, but one excludes booksellers such as "the Coopers, who are recognized retailers with no likely financial share in many smaller works stated on the title-page to have been printed for them"; see Keith Maslen, *An Early London Printing House at Work: Studies in the Bowyer Ledgers* (New York: The Bibliographical Society of America, 1993), 101—hereafter cited as "Maslen." One can only agree when Maslen argues that "imprints were not meant to reveal the background of a commercial transaction, and therefore may seriously mislead the modern scholar who reads them too literally" (p. 101); but, to paraphrase Pope, what can we reason but from what we see on the printed pages before us?

2. Regardless of their imprints, books printed for the author were common. The Bowyer ledgers indicate that "from 1710 to 1773 at least 315 separately published works large and small are charged to 160 or so gentlemen" (Maslen, 98). In this group, the largest number were clergymen, and one of the most common types of books they produced was editions of the classics (Maslen, 104). The young Reverend Mr. Hurd, with his editions of Horace, was a good example. After all—a bookseller might wonder—how many editions, translations, and imitations of Horace could the London public be expected to buy in any year? Hurd was the exception to such gloomy predictions, for his editions received critical acclaim and sold relatively well.

THE ROYAL PAPER COPIES

Today it is not unusual for popular authors to have their works published not only in hardcover and paperback trade editions but also in limited editions, numbered and signed by the author. This practice, as such, does not seem to have been normal—if it happened at all—in eighteenth-century England. In some instances all copies of an edition were numbered and signed by the author—e.g., John Angell's *Stenography: or, Short-hand improved* of 1758. In other cases all copies of an edition were signed by the author—e.g., John Payne's *New Tables of Interest* of 1758, or Christopher Smart's *A Song to David* of 1763. But what purchasers of books usually had to pay extra money for were those copies printed on large (or fine, or Royal) paper, whether these were normal trade or subscription editions. Pope's *Iliad*, of course, was issued simultaneously in two formats and four different grades and quality of paper, each at a considerably different price. At a time in the booktrade when the cost of paper normally represented two-thirds of the cost of producing a book, the public paid—and paid extra—for those fewer copies of an edition printed on higher quality paper. It was not uncommon, however, for an author to have a small number of Royal paper copies printed for his personal use.

Like many academics before and since his time, Richard Hurd tried to advance his career by having his writings published and then distributing copies to everyone who might be helpful to him. An excellent example of this practice is a small pamphlet which Hurd paid Bowyer to print for him in 1751 at exactly the same time Bowyer was printing Hurd's edition of the *Epistola ad Augustum*. Entitled *The Opinion of an eminent Lawyer, concerning the Right of Appeal from the Vice-Chancellor of Cambridge, to the Senate . . .*, its imprint states accurately that it was "London, Printed, and Sold by M. Cooper . . ." thus reflecting the lack of any named publisher. Astonishingly, Hurd paid for printing three editions of this little piece in the months of May, June, and July of 1751—£4:10:0 for each edition—but apparently it was worth his while to distribute the pamphlet widely. Of the 250 copies of the first edition, 100 copies, stitched, were sent to Thurlbourne in Cambridge; Cooper took 80 copies, "not stitched," for London; six copies were sent "to the Author"; and Hurd had the remaining 64 copies "Stitched in Marble paper" at the cost of 2d. each and sent "To the Judges & other presents" (see Bowyer Ledgers B487, B564, and P1074). All the copies of this pamphlet were printed on ordinary paper; but with his early editions of Horace, Hurd had 20 or 26 copies of each edition printed on Royal paper and distributed to friends and persons of potential influence.

Of the *Ars Poetica* of 1749, Hurd paid £1:11:6 to have the twenty Royal paper copies printed and another 2s. 6d. to have them "sew'd in Marble paper" (Bowyer Ledgers B487, P1067). Of the 1751 *Epistola ad Augustum*, Bowyer printed 26 copies on "Large [paper] with marg[ins] opened"—that is, the type was reimposed with wider margins in order to accomodate better the large paper—and of these, twelve copies were sent to Thurlbourne, presumably for Hurd's use. Of the remaining fourteen, three were "bound & gilt" at 2s. each and sent to the Bishop of Norwich, Mr. [Ralph] Allen, and to the Honble. Charles Yorke; the other eleven were "sewed in Marble" for the total cost of 3s. 8d. and sent to the "Ld. Bishop of London, Mr. Tho. Villers, Honble. George Littleton, Dr. Tunstal, Dr. Heberden, Mr. Warburton, Mr. Whitehead, Dr. Askew, Mr. Mason, Mr. Morris, and the Revd. Mr. Barnard" (Bowyer Ledgers B544, P1084).

Of the 1753 edition of Horace in two volumes, twenty copies were printed on Royal paper (Bowyer Ledgers B544, P1094). The ledgers do not record any distribution list for this edition, but we do know that Hurd presented one large paper copy in sheets to Henry Hubbard of Emmanuel College (see above). Of the 1757 edition we have no statistics of printing, since this was printed, at least in part, by Joseph Bentham in Cambridge instead of William Bowyer. We know, however, that Hurd continued his custom of having some copies printed on Royal paper; for he had one such copy handsomely bound and presented to the dedicatee, Sir Edward Littleton, and another (in marbled paper?) was sent to William Warburton (see above).

Thus, of the editions of 1749 through 1757, apparently all large paper copies were reserved for Hurd's personal use and none were offered for sale. All editions later than 1757 were printed uniformly without any large or fine paper copies.

SHARED PRINTING

Shared printing—that is, simultaneous collaboration in producing a work by two or more printing houses—is one of the most puzzling and difficult problems facing any investigator. Many of these problems cannot be answered beyond speculation because of the lack of hard evidence and information. In recent decades, however, enough evidence has become available for us to realize that shared printing was quite common in English printing shops in the seventeenth and eighteenth centuries; and the printing ledgers indicate that the Bowyers, for instance, shared with various colleagues the printing of a total of 685 works between 1710 and 1777 (Maslen, 153). As one might suspect, it is much easier to share the printing of previously printed works rather than first printings which involve splitting up an author's manuscript, and the ledgers show that it is much more common. Nor is it always large or multi-volume works which get shared: Bowyer printed seven editions of John Brown's *Estimate* in 1757–58, printing all of the first, sixth, and seventh editions but no more than half of the fourteen sheets of the other four editions. Since such a practice obviously complicated the working life of printers, why did they do it? The reasons are varied and practical. Any well organized shop has its work scheduled as far ahead as possible, so depending upon the work load any new job order may be shared with other shops if it is to be finished in a reasonable time. Authors who are engaged in hot pamphlet warfare, for example, may demand that their pieces be printed immediately, and so the work is shared. Anyone paying the bills, author or publisher, can demand any printer or printers he chooses. Finally, many printers were members of the Company of Stationers and as such they regularly shared work with other members, especially in such jobs as printing almanacs.

With eighteenth-century books it is often difficult to see whether a work was produced by shared printing merely by examining the finished product. Therefore an investigator is always grateful for any external evidence which may prove relevant, and in the case of the second edition of Hurd's Horace in 1753 there is such evidence. Richard Hurd wrote a letter to William Bowyer dated Cambridge February 14, 1752, saying in part:

. . . Dr. Chapman, you see, has published an answer to the *Opinion*, of which I shall scarce think it worth my while to take any notice. But would it not be proper to take the opportunity of advertising again the Opinion, that you may try to get off the remainder of the third edition.——I have considered your proposal about Horace, and cannot bate a farthing of what I mentioned in my last. We Authors, you know, have always some excuse to comfort ourselves for our books not selling. One reason at least for the Epistle to Augustus not going off was, I think, Thurlbourn's neglect to advertise it properly when it was published. I happened to be abroad at that time, and he is apt to be very careless. I have lately met with some of my own friends who never observed it in the papers till the other day, when it was advertised more carefully. You say, if you purchased the edition, you should expect to have *the right of the copy absolute.* I suppose you only mean the right of the copy of 750; that is, of this edition. Pray let me have your final answer as soon as possible. What I propose is to have the new edition printed off directly, so as to be finished at the farthest this summer; though I would not publish it till the edition of the Epistle to Augustus be sold off. And, as I am sensible, as you say, of the difference betwixt a piece of dry criticism and a novel, I should not insist on the payment of the 40*l.* till a year after the time of publication, if that would make any difference. But, if I part with the copy for less than this sum, I think myself obliged in honour to let Mr. Thurlbourne have it, against whom I have no complaint, but that as he grows old he grows lazy. . . . I am, Sir, your humble servant, R. Hurd. (See note)

Clearly Bowyer did not intend to pay £40 for the right merely to print and sell one edition, so it is reasonable to suppose that Hurd finally sold his copyright to Thurlbourne for some smaller amount. When the new edition was printed and delivered late in March of 1753, William Bowyer—as noted above—was the printer of only the first volume, and Thurlbourne had the second volume printed at Cambridge University Press. As Bowyer wryly remarked on a later occasion, "Of two Volumes, the removing away one to another Printer is a crust I have been forced to devour all my life" (*Literary Anecdotes,* 2:388).

Besides our sympathizing with Bowyer in his dealings with an inexperienced and demanding young author, we are left bemused by the complexities of working out the shared printing of these two volumes. In the days before telephones and fax machines, who was responsible for coordinating the printshops to use not merely paper of equivalent quality but the same paper for all small paper copies and the same paper for all large paper copies? Who determined the fonts of type, and who decided that no ornaments of any kind would be used? Who arranged such fine details of printing as the fact that all the Royal paper copies would be printed with vertical chain lines and the ordinary paper copies with horizontal chain lines? Why, we may ask, did not Thurlbourne merely turn over the entire project to Bowyer? We will probably not be able to answer these questions until we discover the correspondence between Thurlbourne and Bowyer, so we are left with the mere fact that at some time after February, 1752, it was considered necessary or desirable to share the printing of these volumes.

Note: John Nichols (1745–1826), *Literary Anecdotes of the eighteenth-century . . .,* 9 vols. (1812–16), 2:230–31—hereafter cited as "Literary Anecdotes." Hurd, of course, was overly optimistic about selling the remaining copies of the third edition of the *Opinion*; finally, in 1759 he ordered Bowyer to burn the remaining copies (*Literary Anecdotes,* 6:511 [misnumbered 611]). It was ungracious, to say the least, for Hurd to criticize Thurlbourne about the advertising for the Epistle to Augustus, since Hurd paid the bill for it and Bowyer's records show how many times it was advertised and in what newspapers. Perhaps he did not know that Bowyer kept such records.

More than sixty years ago the Bodleian Library bought Bowyer's Paper Stock Ledger, and most of the remaining Bowyer ledgers were uncovered at the Grolier Club thirty years ago; but it was not until 1991 that the scholarly efforts of Keith Maslen and John Lancaster were finally published. Their work in letterpress and microfiche makes the Bowyer ledgers fully accessible for the first time; and when Professor Patricia Hernlund finishes her work on the ledgers of William Strahan, we will have available the records of the two major printers in eighteenth-century England. All scholars in the field are truly grateful for such work, for it enables us to base our interpretations and speculations on their solidly grounded facts.

FROM THE BISHOP OF GLOUCESTER TO LORD HAILES: THE CORRESPONDENCE OF WILLIAM WARBURTON AND DAVID DALRYMPLE

by

Donald W. Nichol

WILLIAM WARBURTON, Bishop of Gloucester (1698–1779), and David Dalrymple, 3rd Bart. Lord Hailes (1726–92), carried on a lengthy correspondence from 1762 to 1776 touching on antiquarian, bibliographical, historical, legal and philological matters. The letters have in recent years become accessible to scholars through the acquisition of the New Hailes collection by the National Library of Scotland.[1] Unfortunately, only one side of this correspondence—Warburton's—is known to survive. Warburton's scarcely noted interest in Scottish life, literature and culture is made abundant here. His letters pass comment on subjects as diverse as James Beattie and the Edinburgh professoriat, the Berean sect, copyright litigation, the Douglas cause, the Foulis press, the origin of words like 'Pipowers' and 'sallet,' and various printing specimens for Dalrymple's books.

In 1762 Warburton was in his mid-sixties, although his literary disputes were not yet over. Warburton had risen to the height of his clerical career with his consecration as Bishop of Gloucester in 1760. His series of seven letters in *The History of the Works of the Learned* in 1738 defending Alexander Pope's *An Essay on Man* from the attacks of the Swiss theologian Jean Pierre de Crousaz had brought him into the poet's influential sphere in the

1. I am grateful to the Trustees of the National Library of Scotland for permission to print the text of these letters. Olive Geddes and Dr. Brian Hillyard of the NLS, Dr. John Cairns of the University of Edinburgh and William Barker of Memorial University have offered much helpful advice.

early 1740s. Through Pope, Warburton met the Prior Park benefactor, Ralph Allen, whose niece, Gertrude Tucker, Warburton married in 1746. Warburton's editions of Shakespeare (1747) and Pope (1751) were widely attacked. In the 1750s, Warburton had been embroiled in the controversies surrounding deism and naturalism expounded by Henry St. John, Lord Bolingbroke, and David Hume. Shortly after his correspondence with Dalrymple commenced, Warburton was ridiculed by John Wilkes in the obscene parody, *An Essay on Woman*, which rocked the House of Lords on 15 November 1763; but this scandal was soon overshadowed by the furor over number 45 of Wilkes' *North Briton*, which was declared a seditious libel against George III by the House of Commons.

Twenty-eight years Warburton's junior, Dalrymple had been admitted to the Faculty of Advocates in 1748. Dalrymple was raised to the Bench as Lord Hailes in 1766 and appointed a Lord of the Justiciary in 1776.[2] This eminent Scottish biographer, historian, judge and editor sent Warburton a copy of *Memorials and Letters Relating to the History of Britain in the Reign of James I* in the spring of 1762. On the same date as his first known letter to Dalrymple, Warburton sent the following note to the London bookseller Thomas Becket which suggests that Dalrymple was a stranger to him: 'I beg you would direct the inclosed to Mr Dalrimple who it seems is now Sr David Dalrimple. but as I neither know his titles nor address, I have left the direction to you and have franked it, because I suppose it is to go by the post' (Historical Society of Pennsylvania: Gratz Collection). Warburton's enclosure was very likely his first letter below.[3] Becket may well have brought the correspondents together: he published Sir John Dalrymple's *The Appeal to Reason to the People of England, on the Present State of Parties in the Nation* in 1763. On the other hand, the Edinburgh-born London bookseller Andrew Millar may have provided the link: Millar published both Warburton's and Pope's works from 1755 to 1769 as well as John Dalrymple's popular *An Essay towards a General History of Feudal Property in Great Britain*, which ran to four editions from 1757 to 1759.

2. For an account of Dalrymple's literary journalism, see Robert Hay Carnie, 'Lord Hailes's Contributions to Contemporary Magazines', *Studies in Bibliography*, 9 (1957), 233–244. See also Professor Carnie's series of 'Lord Hailes's Notes on Johnson's "Lives of the Poets"', *Notes and Queries*, 201 (1956), 73–75, 106–108, 174–176, 343–346, 486–489. Although not made explicit in these letters, Dalrymple shared with Warburton an interest in the text of Shakespeare. In 'Lord Hailes, Shakespeare Critic', *Shakespeare Quarterly*, 40 (1989), 175–185, Arthur Sherbo reproduced Dalrymple's 1786 *Edinburgh Magazine* article, 'Critical Remarks on the late Editions of SHAKESPEARE's Plays'. Published seven years after Warburton's death under the *nom de plume* of Lucius, Dalrymple took Warburton to task over offering twenty-two illustrative quotations where two would have sufficed, resulting in 'superfluous anxiety' (177).

3. Oddly, Warburton's two letters of 9 May 1762 would appear to come from his two residences: Prior Park ('P.P.'), near Bath, and Grosvenor Square, London. The most probable explanation is that Warburton sent his first letter to Dalrymple from Prior Park via Becket and put down Grosvenor Square as the address to which Dalrymple should reply. (On April 17, he sent a letter to Thomas Newton from Prior Park and on July 28 he sent another to John Nourse from Gloucester.)

David Dalrymple sought Warburton's advice on the publication of *An Account of the Preservation of King Charles II, with his Letters* (1766), *Memorials and Letters Relating to the History of Britain in the Reign of Charles I* (1766) and *Annals of Scotland from Malcolm Canmore to Robert I* (1776). Warburton and Dalrymple shared passionate interests in antiquarian and contemporary books. With Dalrymple, Warburton felt he could let loose his collar and be on familiar terms, although they did not always see eye to eye: in 1774, Dalrymple and Warburton evidently took opposing sides in the great literary property debate. Warburton, who as the main copyright-holder of Pope's works had a strong financial incentive for preserving monopolies, put forward his case in the anonymous 1747 pamphlet, *A Letter from an Author to a Member of Parliament concerning Literary Property*. Dalrymple inclined towards the prevailing view that monopolies held by small groups of mainly London-based booksellers were untenable. In the arguments over the case of Hinton v. Donaldson (the result of which led Donaldson to victory in the precedent-setting case against Becket in the House of Lords), *The Decision of the Court of Session, Upon the Question of Literary Property*, compiled by James Boswell (Edinburgh: Printed by James Donaldson, for Alexander Donaldson, 1774), Dalrymple referred to his correspondent in defense of Donaldson: 'in the opinion of *The Sages in St. Paul's Church Yard*, Stackhouse is no less an original author than Hooker or Warburton' (p. 8).

Unfortunately, Warburton did not live long enough to see Dalrymple's *Disquisitions concerning the Antiquities of the Christian Church* (1783). Warburton's last known letter to Dalrymple, dated 29 February 1776, acknowledged his receipt of a volume of the *Annals of Scotland* and 'an elegant edition of Languet's Epistles'. His only son, named after Ralph Allen, died of consumption in 1775, and Warburton, who never completely recovered from the shock, died on 7 June 1779. Almost a year after the bishop's death, Warburton's widow drew up a list of his manuscripts for Richard Hurd, his literary executor and editor. Bishop Hurd, translated to Worcester in 1781, acquired Warburton's collection for his new library in Hartlebury Castle; Pope's library had been more or less re-united when Warburton inherited Ralph Allen's library in 1764. On 3 May 1780, Gertrude Warburton sent Hurd a letter along with her inventory from Prior Park, which might explain what happened to the letters Dalrymple sent to Warburton:

> Your Lordship will favour me by letting me know what part of the Papers you wish to see, & what part of them you wd. advise me to burn. The poor Bishop himself destroyd numbers of Letters & other papers before his Death. It may be right to return Lord Mansfields Letters, the only one of his Correspondents now alive, except Dalrymple. (Hartlebury Castle: Hurd MS. 16, ff.10–11)

Under the heading '*Letters to the Bishop*', she included 'Ld. Mansfield 2 or 3 dozen', but all that appears under Warburton's other surviving Scottish correspondent is: 'Dalrymple, relating to his Work, the Annals of Scotland'. Pope's old friend and Warburton's legal adviser, William Murray, Lord Mansfield, whose library was destroyed in the Gordon Riots of June 1780, died in 1793. The extent of Warburton's burning of his own manuscripts is unknown, as is any subsequent destruction. None of the papers listed in Gertrude Warburton's inventory is known to survive at Prior Park or Hartlebury Castle. According to Robert M. Ryley, approximately one thousand letters to and from Warburton survive (*William Warburton*, 1984, p. 91). Warburton may have inadvertently lost or destroyed his letters from Dalrymple.

Notes: The following twenty-six letters have been transcribed as closely as modern fonts will allow. Warburton's use of capitals, superscribed letters, punctuation, paragraph indents and spelling have all been preserved. Where deletions are still legible, they have been given as strike-throughs. Suffixes denoting ordinal numbers generally appear as a swirl which I have rendered as a small circumflex. I have silently corrected "it's" where "its" is appropriate, but have preserved spelling idiosyncrasies (e.g. "knowlege" and "acknowlege"). Square brackets are used for editorial insertions; carets denote Warburton's interpolations. Two letters, both sent from Gloucester, dated 7 May and 20 June 1774 (old reference number: Acc. 7228/18, ff.167–168 and 169–170) have gone missing, presumed stolen, between the editor's cataloguing and transcribing of this correspondence. For further light on Warburton's papers and controversies, see *Pope's Literary Legacy: the Book-Trade Correspondence of William Warburton and John Knapton with other letters and related documents (1744–1780)*, ed. Donald W. Nichol (Oxford Bibliographical Society, ns XXIII, 1992). The following short forms have been adopted:

Gaskell	Philip Gaskell, *A Bibliography of the Foulis Press*, 2nd ed., Winchester: St. Paul's Bibliographies, 1986
G.S. [in letters]	Grosvenor Square, London
NLS	National Library of Scotland
P.P.	Prior Park

Letter 1   9 May 1762   NLS: MS 25295, ff. 120–121

Grosvenor Square
May 9ˆ 1762

Sir

    I had the honour to receive, by your order, a small but very choice collection of Original Letters; for which I beg leave to return you my best thanks.[4] I hope we shall have many following Vols from you, of the same kind. This is a species of Literature that equally delights men of the best taste & those of no taste at all; I mean, true Critics & true Antiquarians. But it is a field in which the former only should Labour, or we shall continue to have, what we have had so much of hitherto, the weeds collected instead of the Corn.

I have the honour to be,
Sir, your very obliged & faithfull

4. David Dalrymple, *Memorials and Letters Relating to the History of Britain in the Reign of James the First* (Glasgow, 1762); Gaskell 405.

humble Servant
W. Gloucester

[f.121 blank]

Letter 2   6 March 1764   NLS: MS 25295, ff. 122–123

Grosvenor Square March 16ˣ 1764

Good Sir,

I have the honour of yours of the 12ˣ. this evening.

Mr Hales of Eaton[5] was one of the most enlarged thinkers of his time: and tho', in his stile, he had not (like Chillingworth) got above the quaint pedantry of the age of James the 1st, at a time when good writers were growing ashamed of it, and the coming troubles shook it all off, and nature & simplicity of expression regained their rights, to paint the turbulent passions of a new set of actors on the public Scene; yet, with regard to his matter, neither Chillingworth nor any other excelled him, either in extent of knowlege, in accuracy of judgment, or in brilliancy of wit. And how much his talents struck the public fancy may be seen by this trifling circumstance. The editors of the 4° Ed. of his Sermons & letters, have put a celebrated comparison of his, on the subject of controversial Divinity, into picture, to ornament the frontispiece of the title page.[6]

On the whole, I think nothing more worthy of a learned age than an elegant and compleat edition of this great Man's writings. But whether this age be worthy of them is another question, as being but little intitled to the above appelation. However this I am pretty sure of, that it will stand a better chance of good reception in coming from the north, than if printed here; not only on account of the superior execution of the printer's part, but from our opinion of the literature of the north: for amidst this rage of Faction in dep[r]eciating North Britain, I meet with few but who do justice to its Learning. I will leave you to judge in what condition Letters are here at present, when I tell you, that the London Booksellers assure me, that while the English translation of Hugo Grotius's book *of the truth of Christian Religion*[7] is in constant sale amongst the Clergy they never [matter deleted] ₐsellₐ a Latin

5. John Hales (1584–1656). Dalrymple sought Warburton's advice in preparation for publication of his edition of *The Works of the Ever Memorable Mr. John Hales of Eaton*, 3 vols. (Glasgow, 1765); Gaskell 443.

6. The frontispiece of Hales's *Golden Remains* (London, 1659), containing his sermons and letters, depicts two figures: one is Reason wearing a crown, holding a compass, with a finger pointing towards his head; the other is Revelation dressed like a monk, holding a Bible, with a finger pointing towards the sky. The panel below them is a cave scene with miners and devils. The motto reads: 'Controversers of the Times like Spirits in the Mineralls with all their labor nothing is don [sic]'.

7. Hugo de Groot (1583–1645). His *De veritate religionis christianæ* was translated by John Clarke as *The Truth of the Christian Religion*, 4th ed. (London, 1743; 5th ed. 1754). The NLS has an interleaved copy of de Groot's *In questionis redacti de jure belli ac Paris*, lib. III (1688), inscribed 'Dav. Dalrymple, April 4 1746' in quarto (NLS: MSS 25331–2). William Lauder also translated some of de Groot's works, in connection with the Milton controversy, in 1752.

one. But Hales's works are happily in English. And I am such a zealot for having the memory of our best English writers of the golden ages of literature revived by new Editions of their works, that the Bp of Clonfert in Ireland,[8] a grandson of the famous Cumberland, just now applying to me for my opinion of the propriety of a new Edition of his Grandfather's incomparable book *de Legibus naturæ*,[9] a copy of which he put into my hands corrected by his Father in Law, Dr Bentley, that I encouraged him, (who sought only his Grandfather's honour) to reprint it, tho' written in very barbarous latin. You see, Sir, my fondness for these Heros of happier times makes my judgment not to be depended on as to ye success of a new Edition of Hales's works. one thing only I am assured of, that you could not make a nobler present to the Public, how little soever its futility may deserve it. I shall always be proud in being honoured with your commands, and am,

Sir, with the truest regard
& esteem, your most Obedient
& faithfull humble Servant
W. Gloucester

Letter 3   28 March 1764   NLS: MS 25295, ff. 124–125

Grosvenor Square March 28 1764

Worthy Sir,

I have the honour of yours of the 23ˆ The specimen is very elegant.

I have not Hales's Sermons by me, and so do not know to what he predicates, *eo dulciùs quo secretiùs*.[10] But the subject determines the sense. If he says it of *devotion*, then the sense is, that the more secret & sequestered the acts of it are, the more rapturous they become. if he says it of the spiritual sense of Scripture (as the subject of the sermon would make one think) then I suppose it means, the profounder you dive into the Sacred Writer's meaning, the more delightfull & wonderfull you find it.

The, Coli Deos sanctè magis quam scitè,[11] I suppose means, *worship* rather in the simple purity of a pious mind, than with the studied elegance of pomp

8. Denison Cumberland (1705/6–74), Bishop of Clonfert (1763), translated to Kilmore (1772), was the grandson of Richard Cumberland, Bishop of Peterborough, and father of the playwright by the same name. Denison Cumberland's wife, Joanna, whom he married in 1728, was the daughter of Richard Bentley.

9. Richard Cumberland, *De legibus naturæ disquisitio philosophica* (1672). This was reprinted (London, 1701; Dublin, 1720) and translated by John Maxwell as *A Treatise of the Laws of Nature* (London, 1727) and by John Towers as *A Philosophical Enquiry into the Laws of Nature* (Dublin, 1750 [1751]). The edition proposed here does not seem to have materialized.

10. '*eo dulciùs quo secretiùs*': the Latin phrase occurs in John Hales' sermon, '2 Pet. 3. 16.', in *Golden Remains*, p. 1: see 30 March 1764. Dalrymple translated the full passage as: "except those internal and sweet lessons of divine inspiration, where truth speaks without words or writing, and where the more secret the information the more delightful" (2: 2).

11. 'Coli Deos sanctè magis quam scitè': *Golden Remains*, p. 7. "The Gods ought to be worshipped, not curiously, but in the simplicity of a pious mind" (2: 12–13).

& magnificence—This, if the external act of worship be meant. But if, by *cole*, the context leads you to understand the *Contemplation* of the Deity, than [*sic*] the meaning must be, search not too curiously into the Divine nature but approach it with reverence & a pious mind.

Des Maizeaux a french Refugé well known in the republic of Letters 30 or 40 years ago wrote the life of Mr J. Hales in the manner of one of Bayle's lives, in a very thin 8°.[12] it is curiously written and I suppose would not be improper to prefix to a compleat Ed^n.

There is a miserable & enormous heap of stuff, called *Biographia Brit.* for the composition of which, the undertaking Booksellers called from the way side the lame & the blind &c. yet it suited the People & preserved some little credit with others by means of Mr Cambel a man of sense & industry who has written much for the Booksellers and composed some few lives in this Collection.[13] I suppose Hales's life may be found in it, probably transcribed from Des Maizeaux.[14]

Fowlis of Glascow[15] is an excellent printer but often when the type & paper are excellent he deforms the Edition by too narrow a margin, & a disproportioned letter. I think the success of this Ed^n, (especially in England, where we are more struck with circumstances than essentials) will depend much on the elegance of the Edition.

> I have the honour to be
> Sir your very faithfull and
> Obedient humble Servant
> W. Gloucester

Letter 4   30 March 1764   NLS: MS 25295, ff. 126–127

Sir

I have got, since I sent my last, Hales's sermons, & I find, that *eo dulcius* is a kind of fanatical speech of Fulgentius[16] concerning inspiration and means that *where Truth speaks without the use of speech or writing, there, the more secret the information is, the more delightfull.* Sancti magis quam scite[17] I see is to be understood in the second sense I gave it, of not *inquiring with too*

---

12. Pierre Des Maizeaux, *An Historical and Critical Account of the Life and Writings of the Ever-memorable Mr. John Hales, fellow of Eton College* (London, 1719). Pierre Bayle's *Dictionnaire historique et critique* (1695–97) was the model for many British biographies, including *Biographia Britannica*.

13. John Campbell (1708–75) was a contributor to the first edition of *Biographia Britannica* (1747–66) under the general editorship of William Oldys. Campbell's lives are signed E and X. Previously, he had compiled *Lives of the Admirals*, 4 vols. (London, 1742–44).

14. The biography of John Hales appears in volume 4 of *Biographia Britannica* (1757), pp. 2481–90, signed 'P' for Philip Nichols; Des Maizeaux's 1719 biography is cited.

15. I.e., Robert Foulis.

16. Fulgentius (468–533), the anti-Arian Bishop of Ruspe in Numidia: see 28 March 1768.

17. See note 11 above.

*much curiosity into divine matters, but receiving them as they are delivered
in the simplicity of a pious mind.*

Sir your most obedient
humble Servant
W. Gloucester

G.S. March 30 1764
[f.127 blank]

Letter 5   13 October 1764   NLS: MS 25295, ff. 128–129

Prior Park near Bath
Octr 13ˆ 1764

Dear Sir,

I received the honour of yours of the 1st inst. yesterday at this place. I think the printers have advised right as to the size of Hales's Edition.[18] The cheapness of it will invite purchasers in the North and the elegance of it will make it sought after, here.

The *testimonies of Authors* is certainly right.[19] I have not had an opportunity, as I remember, of giving the Character of Mr Hales in any of my Writings.

You did not in any of your Letters, as I remember, speak of your declining to republish Hales's life by Des Maiseaux; at the same time I never supposed you had any such intention: for I think of the man just as you do—a miserable Refugeé, who with a very moderate share of Learning & of parts, fled from persecution in France, to propogate infidelity in England. What I meant by recommending his life of Hales to your perusal, as likewise Dr Birche's, in the *general Dictionary*[20] was to furnish you with materials for a new Life, which I hoped you intended: and am now very sorry to find you decline; because I am well assured it was in your power to make it both very entertaining & very instructive.

Your kind intention of inscribing the Edition to me does me great honour, & is very flattering to me; and I have nothing to add on that head but my best thanks for this distinction.[21]

I think your Motto a very good one. The pleasant account you give me of Lady Huntington's *Conciliabulum*,[22] tho' so near me, was news to me. Yet for all that, not the less likely to be true, considering her ladyship's Character, made up of simplicity & mistaken piety. The Methodists have had her, tho' a

18. The Hales edition was printed in small octavo.
19. Dalrymple prefixed the edition with testimonies from the Earl of Clarendon, Lord Say, Andrew Marvell and others.
20. Thomas Birch wrote most of the English biographies in *General Dictionary, Historical and Critical*, 10 vols. (1734–41).
21. If Dalrymple intended to dedicate his edition of Hales to Warburton, he evidently changed his mind.
22. Selina Hastings, Countess of Huntingdon (1707–91), devoted a good deal of energy and money to Methodism; she appointed a number of its clergymen as her chaplains.

Churchwoman, as an *usufruct* for many years. It is true, she is every now & then ready to escape from them; and that is when they have drained her of her money with a more than ordinary rapacity. At those seasons she has her scruples, whether the sober propogation of the Gospel be not more usefull than this of her Zealots. And this she once confessed to me. But she always returned most cordially to them on the return of her financies [*sic*].

Your goodness to me, Sir, will make me shameless in the request I am about to make to you. You know the great value I sat [i.e. set] upon that small collection of Letters which you did me the honour to send me.[23] I lent it to my incomparable Friend, Lord Mansfield, who was so struck with the numberless curiosities that it contained, that, as he could not buy it, he would never let me have it back. I endeavoured to get another of the London Booksellers; but in vain; which forces me to beg that, if you have any copies remaining, you would favour me with one. For I set a great value on this small Collection both on account of its own intrinsic worth, & for the sake of the Collector; being with great truth,

Dear Sir, your very Affectionate
& Obliged humble Servant
W. Gloucester

Letter 6   27 May 1765   NLS: MS 25295, ff. 130–131

Prior Park near Bath
May 27ˆ 1765

Worthy Sir

I have just now received from a Bookseller in London your noble Present of Mr Hales's Works; for which I hold my selfe much indebted to you.

The Edition is extremely elegant; and will, I make no doubt, make its way where all the Author's fine parts & extensive Learning would, in a sordid garb, move heavily on. I have long mentioned to the most eminent London Booksellers the service they might likely do themselves, certainly the public, by reprinting in an elegant manner (for otherwise, in this trifling age, it is doing nothing) the best writers of the last age now almost forgotten, such as William's (*Bp* of Lincoln) fine tract *of the holy alter name & thing* Harsnet's (*ABp* of York) *detection of certain Popish Impostures*,[24] that has all the good sense, & what is more, the wit, of our most applauded Writers. Lord George Digby's & Ld Lucius Faulklands fine tracts agt Popery,[25] which ₐtwo lastₐ I

---

23. See 9 May 1762.

24. John Williams, Bishop of Lincoln (1621–41), translated to Archbishop of York (1641–50), *The Holy Table, Name & Thing* ([London?], 1637); and Samuel Harsnett (1561–1631), Archbishop of York (1629–31), *A Declaration of Egregious Popish Impostures* (London, 1603), a work from which Shakespeare borrowed devil names like 'Flibbertigibbet' and 'Modo' for Edgar's ravings on the heath as Poor Tom in *King Lear* (3.4.115, 135).

25. George Digby (1612–77), *Letters Between Ld George Digby and Sr Kenhelm Digby Kt concerning Religion* [1651]; and Lucius Cary, 2nd Viscount Faulkland (1610?–43), *A View of some Exceptions made by a Romanist* (London, 1646).

spoke of lately to Mr Millar[26] who did not seem indisposed to print them together. But nothing can be printed in London approaching to the Elegance of the Glasco printers.[27] Baskerville is much inferior to two little books I have seen from them, a *Cornelius Nepos* & a *Lucretius*.[28] If we may judge by our present set of writers the age wants some good models of Composition. For ~~they have~~ it has suffered such as are so to slip out of the minds & memory of men.

I have the honour to be, Sir,
Your very obliged & very obedi-
-ent humble Servant
W. Gloucester

[f.131 blank]

Letter 7　　　　　　16 June 1765　　　NLS: MS 25295, ff. 132–133

Prior Park June 16ˆ 1765

Sir

I have the honour of your obliging Letter of the 6ᴬ. *Bp* William's Tract is full of good learning & wit & very worthy to be reprinted, & the more as the original Edition is miserably printed. I will take care to write to Oxford, Cambridge and London to get a transcript of all the papers you mark out, and as soon as they come to my hands will send them to you.

I am Sir, with great esteem
your very obedient humble
Servᵗ
W. Gloucester

[f.133 blank]

Letter 8　　　　　　24 June 1765　　　NLS: MS 25295, ff. 134–135

Prior Park June 24ˆ 1765

Dear Sir

I wrote to the Master of Sᵗ John's in Cambridge, to the Master of Pembroke in Oxford and to Dʳ Birch in London.[29] I have inclosed their three

26. Andrew Millar, Warburton's bookseller.

27. Robert and Andrew Foulis.

28. *Cornelii Nepotis excellentium imperatorum vitae* (*Lives of the Emperors*) (1761; Gaskell 397), and *De rerum naturae* (1759; Gaskell 370), were both printed in Glasgow by Robert and Andrew Foulis. On 27 December 1761, Warburton wrote to Hurd: 'I think the Booksellers have an intention of employing Baskerville to print Pope in 4to; so they sent me the last Octavo to look over' (*Literary Anecdotes of the Eighteenth Century*, ed. John Nichols, 9 vols. [London, 1812–15], 5: 653). According to William Shenstone, on 16 May 1762, 'Baskerville has of late been seized with a violent Inclination to publish Hudibras, his favourite Poem, in a pompous Quarto, with an entire new sett of Cutts.—Dr Warburton has, I hear, also engaged Him to publish a Quarto Edition of Mr Pope' (*The Letters of William Shenstone*, ed. Marjorie Williams [Oxford, 1939], p. 62).

29. William Samuel Powell (1717–75) was elected master of St John's College, Cam-

answers, two of which are final & satisfactory; and the third I am sure will perform his promise effectually. When I get his transcripts, they shall be sent to you; in the mean time I would not keep you in suspence, how far I had obeyed your Commands.

I own this tract of the A.Bp. of York's[30] was always a favorite of mine; [deletion] for the wit, the good sense, and the Learning of it.—Ld Clarendon in his 4th *B. of Hist. Reb.* mentions it in this manner—*he published a Book ag^t the using those Ceremonies, in which there was much good learning, and too little gravity for a Bishop.*[31] By *too little gravity*, his Lordship means, *too much wit*. But if one considers ye nature of that trifling subject, at that time of solemn importance one shall be ready to confess that the *Bp* treated it as it deserved, and in a way [deletion] likely to reduce it to its just value; which was a thing then most to be wished.

> I am Sir with great esteem
> your very faithfull & obedient
> humble Servant
> W. Gloucester

[f.135 blank]

Letter 9   18 July 1765   NLS: MS 25295, ff. 136–137

> Prior Park July 18 1765

Sir

I have your favour of the 13^ inst. and shall be always glad to have it in my power to contribute my assistance to any of your generous & worthy schemes for the promotion of literature.

I think I have *Bp* Williams' curious book in my Library at Gloucester; and shall write thither to one of my Chaplains to look it out, and send it to Mr Millar in London; with directions to have it sent to you under the care of the Bookseller, either of Edinburgh of [i.e. or] Glasgow which you mention, as can be most commodiously & expeditiously done. One reason of the great scarcity of this fine tract was its being printed so villainously, as to tempt people rather to tear it for the most sordid uses, than to read it.

> I have the honour to be,
> with great respect, Sir
> Your very obedient & faithfull
> humble Servant W. Gloucester.

[f.137 blank]

---

bridge, on 25 January 1765 upon the death of John Newcome. John Ratcliffe (1700–75) was master of Pembroke College, Oxford, from 1739 to 1775; Thomas Birch (1705–66) was a well-known editor and compiler.

30. John Williams: see 27 May 1765.

31. The underlined quotation is to be found in Edward Hyde, Earl of Clarendon, *The History of the Rebellion and Civil Wars in England* (Oxford, 1704), 3 vols., vol. 1, p. 271. The *History* is divided into sixteen books.

Letter 10   5 April 1766   NLS: MS 25295, ff. 138–139

Grosvenor Square Apr. 5 1766

Good Sir

I have the honour of yours of the 29ˆ past. You give a very good reason for dropping your design on *Bp* Williams. I shall send you (by the care of Mʳ A. Millar) a copy of that excellent & entertaining Treatise of *Bp* Harsnet called *A Declaration of Egregious Popish impostures*,[32] for your amusemᵗ for I am sure you will read it with pleasure. It is almost slipt out of the memory & knowlege of the World. If any body amongst you thinks it worth reprinting it be open at their service. Hales I find is both too serious & too profound for this dissipated & trifling age. I shall wait with impatience for what you promise. And now Sir give me leave to congratulate with you, or rather with North Britain on your honouring the Bench of the Lords of Session. I hope I am not mistaken or that my sincere congratulations are premature. But A. Millar told me that you was the person meant in the Article of the public papers mentioning that promotion.[33]

I am Worthy Sir
Your most obedient & faithfull humble Servant
W. Gloucester
P.S. I shall beg your acceptance of the new Edition of my Book of the *Alliance*.[34]

Letter 11   23 March 1767   NLS: MS 25295, ff. 140–141

Grosvenor Square
March 23ˆ 1767

Worthy Sir

I have the honour of your very obliging Letter of the 16ˆ.

As you thought the anecdote concerning Julian curious, I fancied that the perusal of a Letter from the french Translator which I have inclosed would not be unacceptable to you. You will find that, by accident, I laid the foundation of Mʳ. de Silhouette's fortune who was the late Controller of the finances. The Duke de Noailles brought him into the Family of the late late [*sic*] Duke of Orleans where he succeed[ed] d'Argenson.[35]

32. Harsnet, *A Declaration of Egregious Popish impostures*: see 27 May 1765.
33. Millar may have read the story of Dalrymple's appointment in *The Scots Magazine*, 28 (February 1766), 111–112: 'Sir David Dalrymple of Hailes, Bt., *one of the Lords of Session*, in the room of Lord Nisbet, deceased.—*P.S.* His commission arrived at Edinburgh by express in the morning of March 4. he entered on his trials as Lord Probationer that day, and was received on the 6th, taking the title of Lord *Hailes*'.
34. *The Alliance between Church and State*, 4th ed., corrected and enlarged (London, 1766).
35. Étienne de Silhouette translated Pope's *Essay on Criticism* (1737; reprinted 1741) and *Essay on Man* (1736; reprinted 1741, 1745, 1762, 1772) in prose. Some letters between Warburton and de Silhouette are held by the Bibliothèque Nationale in Paris.

Your observations on the several passages in Julian are very just.

It is very certain that the Minister's just jealo[u]sy of the King's, & his Favorite's bias towards Popery disgusted James as much as their licence in their Pulpets, which they seem to have made a necessary part of their *Discipline.*

Nothing can be juster in [deletion] it selfe, or of more importance for the State to espouse, than your Opinion, that the Lords of Session should not interpose in a matter merely spiritual, concerning Discipline, with civil censures. The natural support of Church Discipline are church-censures such as excommunication unattended with Civil consequences. But this demand of the Assembly is the natural issue of a ˄national˄ Church, claiming *independency* on the State: a claim never at rest, till it has gained a supremacy. And indeed, for the sake of the general Society, it ought to be allowed in one, or in the other body; since an *imperium in imperio* (which is the condition of two *independent* bodies) brings on inevitable destruction to the public peace. [deletion] And indeed, this demand of the Assembly, under the name of a *Petition,* looks towards Sovereignty. The Church of Rome first began their Usurpation under the simple claim of *independency* on the State. This occasioned a great and long struggle; in which the Church, at last, came off victorious. But when they had gained this point, that, of Sovereignty was speedily & easily compassed.

The State, to prevent that confusion which two independent powers must eternally occasion, gave up the Superiority to the Church for peace sake.— The State as Protector of the National Church, has a right (in the prosecution of civil Justice) to call occasionally on the Church's aid for the inforcement of Conscience: Hence the custom (and a good one, in my opinion, it is) in the Parliament of Paris in strong presumptions of hidden fraud ˄in civil matters˄ to apply for the ArchBishop's mandate to enjoin all under pain of excommunication who have any knowlege of the affair in question, to reveal their knowlege to the Magistrate. But, for the Church, in spiritual matters, such as ecclesiastical Discipline to require the aid of the State by civil censures is I think presumptuous in the request & dangerous in the compliance. I make no doubt but our horrid Writ *de Heretico comburendo* took its begin[n]ing from as modest a request to have the aid of civil Authority to *constrain* witnesses to depose in spiritual matters. For it is an easy step from the Church's making the Civil Magistrate its *Coadjutor* to make him its *Executioner.* On the whole, Sir, I think, your opinion thus publicly delivered in your judicial capacity does you infinite honour. You do me a great deal too much, in asking mine, in a matter of which you are so great a master.

I have the honour to be, Worthy Sir,
Your most faithfull & obliged
humble Servant
W. Gloucester

P.S. You guessed shrewdly of him who threatened an answer to *Julian* here. It was one Nichols, who was convicted of stealing books, & narrowly escaped the Gallows.[36] He calls himselfe a Dr of Physic; is yet alive, and has not left off his old trade, tho' he has taken up a worse, of political pamphleteering.

Letter 12   23 April 1767   NLS: MS 25295, ff. 142–143

Grosvenor Sq. 23 Apr. 1767

My Lord

You had no need of any one to strengthen you in the rectitude of your Opinion in the point in which you was alone in the Court. It was founded in the great Principles of Right which you so fully comprehend. I communicated the matter occasionally to my two dearest & Most intimate Friends, Ld Mansfield & Mr Yorke; and they both think with you & me on this point.

I own I think the paper inclosed is a frank imposture, both from the stile & matter. It is true, that before Loyola's death the Society was well established; had spread it selfe over Europe, & had met with great opposition from Schools & Universities; but this was only on acc^t of their teaching academic Learning, cheaper & better. It was long after that they invented their commodious casuistry for the use of the Great; into whose general confidence they had not yet insinuated themselves.

I have the honour
to be My Lord Your most faithfull & Obedient
humble Servt W. Gloucester

[f.143 blank]

Letter 13   26 October 1768   NLS: MS 25295, ff. 144–145

Prior Park. Bath. Octr 26^ 1768

My Lord,

I have the honour to receive of your Lordship, a very curious Specimen of a work, which I hope you will not long delay to give the Public. I foresee it will be extremely learned & usefull. — An ingenious Person, one Mr Barrington a welch-Judge has attempted something of the same kind, on our old Statutes. It is intitled *Observations on the Ancient Statutes* 4°.[37] It is done with taste. But he is defective in the old English Language. And without

---

36. According to the account on Warburton in the *Dictionary of National Biography*, Philip Nichols stole books from Cambridge. After the proprietors of *Biographia Britannica* cancelled the leaf in the article on Smith in 1763, volume 6, part i, Nichols published *The Castrated Sheet, in the Sixth Volume of Biographia Britannica by a proprietor of that work*: see Warburton's letter to an unidentified bookseller, dated 29 January 1761, in *Pope's Literary Legacy: the Book-Trade Correspondence of William Warburton and John Knapton with other letters and related documents (1744–1780)*, ed. Donald W. Nichol, Oxford Bibliographical Society, ns XXIII, 1992, pp. 140–145.

37. Daines Barrington, *Observations on the Ancient Statutes* (London, 1766). The first edition is not to be found in the British Library or National Library of Scotland. However, the words Warburton refers to may be found in the much expanded third edition *Observations on the more Ancient Statutes, from Magna Charta to the Twenty-First of James I* (London, 1769): for example, 'sallett' (p. 307), 'pele' (p. 376), 'Pipowder' (p. 382).

that knowlege of the Antiquities of the middle Ages, and wanting in that acumen, so conspicuous in the *Specimen of Notes*.—It is full of mistakes (I presume your Lordship has the book) arising from these defects. For instance p 213. he says SALLET[38] *conveys no idea whatsoever*. Tho all our old English writers use it to signify a light head piece. I suppose from the Italian *Celata*. The fr[ench]. say *Salade* as you observe. p. 254 *pele* he supposes may signify *hair*, whereas it is the skin, with the remaining wool after it has been shorn. p. 257. he corrects the etymology of the Lawyers, concerning the *Court of Pipowers*, who derive it from *pes pulvericatus* because *pied puldreaux* ∧which∧ is the sam[e], in french signifies a *Pedler*; not reflecting on the tralatitious[39] use of words. p. 259—*puzzled the Antiquary*—all the puzzle which the *Tumuli, barrows,* or little hills at the end of Villages in England, was only this, whether they were raised for the use of Archery, and called *Butts*, or whether they were not ancient Tumuli, whose distance from each other served for the use of *archery*. p. 281. St. 3. Hen. 8—*some also* CAN no letters—he would have it CON; and so corrects it, not adverting that in the old Eng. CAN signifies to *know—to be able to do a thing*. p. 319 he supposes that because polygamy, (as he heard) was punished by an *auto de fe* in portugal, it was not a civil crime in that Kingdom. In catholic Countries Polygamy is both a Civil & Eccl: crime as it is a violation of a sacrament.—But it seems the Author has called in this Ed[n], and given the purchasers, another, which I have not seen.[40]

But to return to the *Specimen*, which I truly think admirable in its kind. I was surprised at what is said p. 8 of your Lawyers, who interpret *bruarium* fr. *Bruiere* to signify a *brewery*. The word perpetually abounds in our old Charters, and our Lawyers never took the change. The common people have done it. When I lived in Lincolnshire near the Great *Heath* there, and in the neighbourhood of a ruin called *Temple bruiere* or the *Temple on the Heath*, an old Hospitalary of the *Knights Templars*, the Common people, who had preserved the Tradition of the luxury of those Knights, [deletion] call it, *Temple Brewery*. for that they were famous for brewing the best ale in all the County

Your Lordship's justly expressed aborrence of the Writ de haretico comburendo p. 10. does honour to your station. You brand it by an ingenious comparison. Yet, it is certain, that, altho the *running or passing thro' the fire* be amongst the common *lustrations* of the ancient World, yet *the passing thro' the fire to Moloch* in Scripture, signifies a real sacrifice or immolation, being always made equivalent to [deletion] ∧those∧ other expressions—*they burnt their sons & daughters in the fire to their Gods*.—they *sacrificed their sons & daughters to Devils* and Ezekiel [deletion] uses one of these expressions to

38. 'In mediæval armour, a light globular headpiece, either with or without a visor, and without a crest, the lower part curving outwards behind', *OED*, which also gives Warburton's Italian and French derivations.

39. 'Metaphorical; not literal', Johnson, *Dictionary* (1755); 'characterized by transference; *esp.* of words or phrases, metaphorical, figurative', *Oxford English Dictionary*.

40. According to the *DNB*, Barrington bought up remaining copies of the earlier edition when the next one was ready for publication.

explain the other—*having caused their children to pass thro' the fire to devour them* XXIII.37.

In a word, my Dear Lord, let me repeat my best wishes for your health not only for your own sake, but for the sake of literature in general, and for the public justice of Scotland in particular. I have the pleasure to know that two of my most intimate Friends, the great Lawyers, Ld Mansfield and Mr Charles Yorke, have, with me, the highest opinion of your Lordship's Virtues. The latter (who always gives me what leasure he can spare) had but just left me, when the Specimen came, which would have afforded much pleasure to a man whose knowlege is universal.

While he was with me he was much busied in a morning with the Speeches of the Lords of Session in the Douglas cause in which he is to appear before us, after Christmas, for the House of Hamilton.

We both admired the elegance, the great sense, & the legal precision of Ld Hailes's speech: and I have an equal contempt for Ld Kames's. I have read the great 4° *Factum* of both Parties; and I will tell you, inter nos, my present sentiments. I think there is but a base Physical possibility that the pretended Son is the real Son of Lady Jane: and further, that had Lady Jane, by one of the perverse caprices of pregnant women, set upon contriving the means of discrediting [deletion] ₐher own Son'sₐ pretensions, she could not have done it more effectually.[41]

Let me continue my good Lord to have your esteem, and believe me to be with the truest regard, your affectionate and faithfull humble Servant

W. Gloucester

Letter 14   19 April 1769   NLS: MS 25295, ff. 146–147

G[r]osvenor Square 19^ April 1769

My dear Lord,

I am honoured with yours of the 14^ inst. and am much obliged to you for your kind enquiries concerning my health. I thank God it is now become tolerable again.

The times are truly become *miserable*; not from any *danger* of the Public, but from the *dishonour* brought upon it by these mock Patriots, without parts or virtue, the Apes of those fierce Fanatics who had both, and misused them under Charles the first, to overturn a constitution which they pretended to reform. They had a foundation to work upon, *real grievances*; These, only fictitious. Had Charles the first the advantages of George the third, of 30000 veteran troops; and a House of Commons become odious and contemptible

41. When Lady Jane Douglas (1698–1753) died, her brother, Archibald, Duke of Douglas (1694–1761), refused to acknowledge her surviving son, whose legitimacy was disputed. Shortly before his death, the Duke was persuaded to revoke his will in which he bequeathed his estates to the Hamiltons in favour of his nephew. The House of Lords had decided in favour of Douglas on 27 February 1769. See Frederick A. Pottle, *James Boswell: The Earlier Years, 1740–1769* (London, 1966), pp. 311–317, *passim*, for a discussion of the Douglas Cause, 'which has been called the greatest trial in Scottish history affecting civil status' (311–312).

to the People, he had ended the quarrel at a blow; and, instead of demanding the 5 *Members*, he had demanded the 500; and not left it to C[r]omwell to padlock up their Door. What obligations have we then to our excellent King who saves us from our selves, and shuts fast that Door of destruction of which he only has the Key. For as to the mad cry of the mob for a *Republic*, it is like that of the fifth monarchy ∧men∧, of old, for the Millenium. A Republic demands a virtuous People. But ours have neither virtue nor Religion: and so, have chosen for their head two or three [of] the most diabolic wretches upon Earth.—In a discourse written some years ago, in which I gave a history of the rise and progress of the present state of Religion amongst us occasioned by the intrigues of our Politicians, I said they would now soon have an opportunity of experiencing the truth of their favorite maxim, that Government might be easily carried on without Religion. But why do I give your Lordship the pain of saying so much on this odious subject; and with equal pain to my selfe? I know not, unless it be, that complaining in our distresses seems a kind of reliefe to them.

But it is time to come to a more agre[e]able subject. Your Lordship does wisely to withdraw your mind from this scene of horrors, on the elegant and usefull attention to that important part of History, the Ecclesiastical. I shall devour the *tract* you mention (as I do every thing of yours) with exquisite pleasure: but shall be extremely concerned if the *melancholy hours* you mention, be not those we all pass, for the Public, but rather those of a domestic kind, in the loss of some, deservedly most dear to you—But this is the appen age of Humanity, which we are all doomed to partake of.

> I have the honour to be, my Lord,
> Your Lordship's most Obedient
> and affectionate humble Servant
> W. Gloucester

Letter 15   14 June 1769   NLS: MS 25295, ff. 148–149

Grosv^r Sq. June 14^ 1769

My dear Lord,

I had the honour of your obliging Letter of the 24 of last April: and I deferred my acknowlegment for it, till I had received, & carefully read your Preface & notes; which I lately received from your Brother,[42] to whom I have carefully returned them. I read them with much pleasure & instruction. They are written with the utmost judgment & knowlege of the subject; and enlivened here & there (tho' they did not want that help) with delicate strokes of Satire & ridicule, which these miserable times will force from every generous mind.

Your Lordship & I think alike with regard to the *use* of Religion to Society, and with regard to its *truth*. With regard to its *use* Ministers of State

---

42. Dalrymple's father, Sir James, had seven sons. Warburton is likely referring to Sir John.

are (tho' with the latest) brought to see their folly in fancying they could govern, without it. All the late & present disorders proceeding from their having long contributed to the taking this curb [cub?] from the jaws of this headstrong Monster, the People.

I heartily condole with your Lordship on your domestic loss.[43] The sweet plaintive lines occasioned by this loss, would make all your friends call to mind the,

Qualis Populea mærens Philomela sub umbra Amisos queritur foetus—

> I am my Dear Lord, your
> Lordship's faithfull & affectionate
> humble Servant
> W. Gloucester

[f.149 blank]

Letter 16   2 February 1770   NLS: MS 25295, ff. 150–151

> Grosvenor Square Feb.ʸ 2 1770

My dear Lord,

On coming to Town since Christmas I found your *Historical Memorials*[44] on my Table, for which I have many thanks to return, not only for the book, but for the instruction & entertainment the reading of it have afforded me. Would Antiquarians add taste & elegance (as your Lordship has done) to industry & Learning, these studies would not only be amongst our most usefull but our most engaging enquiries.

> I have the honour to be, my
> good Lord, your Lordship's most
> faithfull & obliged humble Servant
> W. Gloucester

[f.151 blank]

Letter 17   21 February 1772   NLS: MS 25295, ff. 152–153

> Grosvenor Square Feb. 21ˆ 1772

My dear Lord,

I have this moment received the honour of your obliging Letter of the 17ˆ. I am but too sensible there is a detestable set of men crept in, into the Scotch ministry, who, as usual, are always ready to give themselves a *good name*, tho' their principles be destructive of Revelation. Whatever morals they may have, I am sure they are not Christian Morals: and, therefore, very unfit for the Ethical Chair, in a Christian Country. Scotland, I hope, may be

---

43. Dalrymple's first wife, Anne (née Brown), died giving birth to twins.

44. Dalrymple's *Historical Memorials concerning the Provincial Councils of the Scottish Clergy* (Edinburgh, 1769).

yet so called; whatever title England may deserve. Nor do I know any one so compleatly qualified for it as Mr Beatie;[45] whose books I have read with infinite pleasure; and not only I, but the most respectable of my profession, as well as of the Law; especially those two incomparable Persons who honour me with their Friendship, my Lord Mansfield, and the Late Chief Justice of the Common Pleas, 1st Earl [deletion] Wilmot. The latter of whom having lately had occasion to go to Oxford, advised the heads of Houses, to have it in their care, that all the Youth committed to their trust, should be directed to study Mr Beatie's book. It was but the other night that I had much talk with Lord Mansfield on this subject. He is truely sensible of this learned person's merit; and the service he has done to Religion and good letters, in the confutation of the Impiety and the Sceptical Nonsense of the unhappy man he confutes. I shall press his Lordship all I can to exert what interest he may have amongst those who have the disposition of this professorship in their power, in favour of Mr B[e]atie. I am glad to find it is not in the disposal of the King's Ministers ∧here.∧ For speaking of them, in favour of a clergyman of our church who is most deserving the King's notice & distinction, Ld M[ansfield]. replied, that the situation of affairs is such, that the King cannot get more than *one* out of *ten* of his own Preferments at his own disposal. I said I was glad to find his Ministers so modest, that as he was yet owned to be the Head of the English Church, they did him so much justice as to give him the *Tyth*. To be serious, I shall religiously keep your Secret: tho' I am confident my application must lose much of its force, by not being permitted to tell him th[r]ough what channel it derived.

The Anecdote in your Lordship's P.S. is a most curious one, and I am much obliged for the communication of it. The Baillifs of Glasgow acted with the dignity & good sense that does honour to a Parliament, and the Parliament of 1646 degrade themselves by sinking into the low Character of a City Baillife.

I have, my Dear Lord, the honour
to be your Lordship's most faithfull
and affectionate humble Servant
W. Gloucester

Letter 18   5 March 1772   NLS: MS 25295, f.154

Grosvenor Sq March 5 1772
My Dear Lord

I have the favour of yours of the 25^ past. I had spoken to Lord M[ansfield]. and he assured me of his inclination to serve Mr Beatie [deletion] in the manner your Lordship proposed to me, but that he has not the least

45. By 1772, James Beattie (1735–1803), the poet and professor of Moral Philosophy at Marischal College, Aberdeen University, had published *An Essay on the Nature and Immutability of Truth* (1770) and the first canto of *The Minstrel* (1771). For the popular reception of these works, see Everard H. King, *James Beattie* (Boston, 1977), pp. 24–25.

knowlege of any one of the magistrates of Edinburgh. But I am assured that
he will warmly recommend Mr Beatie in the manner you mention, on all
occasions. A Minister ∧of Religion∧ of his Character ought to be supported
by all the friends of Religion, for the sake of Religion. It has not many
such friends amongst us; perhaps fewer amongst you; certainly fewest of all
amongst those of the *bon ton*, amongst our neighbours. It will always have a
true & sober friend in your Lordship, who is so great an ornament to both
Societies, Civil & Religious.

I have the honour to be, my Dear Lord,
Your Lordship's most faithfull
and affectionate humble Servant
W. Gloucester

Letter 19   30 June 1772   NLS: MS 25295, ff. 155–156

Gloucester June 30 1772
My Dear Lord,
    The honour of your last favour of the 21^ inst. was sent me hither, into the
country. Dr Hurd will be delighted with your Lordship's opinion of his Book.[46]
His parts & learning, uncommon and extraordinary as they are, are the least
part of his merit. His moral character, the virtues of his heart and mind,
charm all his Friends.
    I will take the liberty of communicating your Letter, on the subject of
his book, to him. It will give him much pleasure to make him partaker of your
excellent remarks: in which both your learning and acumen are so conspicuous. I had the happiness of bringing him into the acquaintance of Lord
Mansfield, some time ago: with whose extraordinary qualities his Lordship
was soon so taken, as to admitt him to great intimacy with him. I will only
venture to give you a short Specimen of the D^r's Character by which you will
find how free he is from all inordinate Ambition. His Virtues were so well
known to the King & Queen, that he was ordered to be [deletion] spoken to by
Ld Holderness, last year, when the Pr[ince]. of Wales's Family was settled,
[deletion] with an offer to bear a share in his royal Highness' Education. and
as this was an affair of importance the Governor was directed to tell the D^r,
his answer was not expected immediately, but that he might take a fortnight's
time to consider of it. The D^r, after making his best ack[n]owlegments for the
honour, & said he was prepared to give an immediate & a final answer to the
proposal.—that he had just past the meridian of life, and with but indifferent
health, so that he dared not venture on so important a charge; but must beg
leave to decline the offer.—There are but few instances of a Clergyman's thus
starting [i.e. standing] aside from the high road of Preferment, when he was
so fairly entered. Your Lordship will be amongst the first to set a just value on

----

46. Richard Hurd (1720–1808), Bishop of Worcester. He delivered the first Warburton
lecture, published as, *An Introduction to the Study of the Prophecies concerning the Christian Church* (1772; 5th ed. 1788).

such a Character, and will be glad to find this age able to afford such an example.[47]

I have the honour to be, my Lord
your Lordship's most faithfull and
affectionate humble Servant
W. Gloucester

[f.156 blank]

Letter 20   26 March 1773   NLS: MS 25295, ff.157–158

Gloucester March 26ˆ 1773
My dear Lord,

I had your favour of the 18 instant; and immediately urged your request to Lord Mansfield. How it may agree with his inclination, or the present state of his court attachm[en]ts, I know not. This I am sure of, such a mark of your Opinion will be highly acceptable to him, as it is, according to the old saying, *laudari a laudato Viro*. I think, indeed, with your Lordship, that the publication of his Argument ₐwould beₐ of high importance to the public.

I have the honour to be,
my dear Lord your Lordship's
most faithfull and affectionate
humble Servant
W. Gloucester

[f.158 blank]

Letter 21   18 December 1773   NLS: MS 25295, ff.159–160

Grosvenor Square Decʳ 18 1773
Dear Sir

On coming to Town yesterday af[t]er a long absence, I had the pleasure to see for the first time, on my Table *Remarks on the history of Scotland* which you did me the honour of sending to me, full of very curious & entertaining Dissertations.[48] There are two copies sent to me, but without directions how one of them is to be desposed of, I keep both till further directions, and am,

Sir, your very obliged & faithfull
humble Servant
W. Gloucester

[f.160 blank]

---

47. The NLS also has a collection of 115 letters, dating from 28 December 1773 to 3 July 1792, from Richard Hurd, Bishop of Worcester and Warburton's editor, to Dalrymple (MS 25297), which were examined by Francis Kilvert in Bath in 1860 for his biography of Hurd. Dalrymple and Warburton shared numerous correspondents, including Thomas Balguy, Thomas Birch, John Jortin, Thomas Warton, and Charles York.

48. Dalrymple's *Remarks on the History of Scotland* (Edinburgh, 1773).

Letter 22   8 April 1774   NLS: MS 25295, ff.161–162

London April 8 1774
My dear Lord

    I have the honour of your favour of the 2ᵈ instant. And with regard to the affair of Dʳ Beatie I spoke, as you desired, to Lord Mansfield; who after expressing his highest regard to you and his good opinion of your friend, Dʳ Beatie, gave me the satisfaction to declare his opinion that the Magistrates of Edinburgh were very ~~very~~ well disposed to favour the Dʳˢ Suit, and that they will be averse to favour Professor Fergusson's request, as very unreasonable. Lᵈ Stanhope giving his Tutor four hundred pounds a year while in his Lordship's Service, and settling two hundred pounds a year for life upon him afterwards so that for the reason you give, the modesty of the Magistrates is to be commended in leaving their good dispositions to your friend, free. In the mean time Lord Mansfield promises to omit no opportunity of acquainting every one with the good opinion he had entertained of Dʳ Beatie.

    We are here no strangers to the mad opinions of the fanatics, who go under the names of methodists & Moravians; and of their rage against the ministers of the Established Church. The name of Bereans[49] which they have given themselves, I suppose because they are commended in Scripture for searching for their salvation there, is not yet known amongst us. But all in good time. Such searchers, with such interpretations they are likely to supply us with, are likely to search for what they are never likely to find.

    Your Lady's remark on the barbarians you speak of, is enough to shame the strange credulity of lying Travellers.

    The progress your Lordship tells me you have made in your Ch[r]onological History gives me much pleasure. your Lordship says true, as appears by the truths you have already favoured us with, that the paradoxes, in which your National history abounds, are not of your seeking but of your exposing, ~~with which your story abounds~~. I predict that it will be a noble work and will do great credit to the work, and honour to your selfe.

I am my good Lord with great truth,
affection & esteem your Lordship's most
faithfull and obedient servant
W. Gloucester

[f.162 blank]

Letter 23   24 April 1774[50]   NLS: MS 25295, ff.163–164

My dear Lord

    I have the pleasure of your obliging Letter of the 16 inst. I have returned

---

    49. The Bereans were a sect 'based on scripture in the Acts (xvii.11) where they of Berea are commended for searching the Scriptures to see if the things spoken by Paul were so'. The Bereans were founded by John Barclay (1734–98) of Crieff (*The Scottish National Dictionary*, vol. 1, ed. William Grant [Edinburgh, (1929)]).

    50. Two letters between this letter and the next in the present series (October 1774),

the copy of Mr Beatie's letter,[51] as thinking you might expect it or want it. It is pitty but he might be prevailed on to submit to the untoward circumstances he mentions, for the sake of the good he might do in that station.— Tho' I be just going back into the country I could not leave this place without acknowleging your last favour & rejoicing in the specimen you promise of so important a work. Ld Mansfield is much your servant. I need not tell you, my good Lord, how much I am

your Lordship's most affectionate and
faithfull humble Servant
W. Gloucester

Lond. Apr. 24 1774
[f.164 blank]

Letter 24   October 1774   NLS: MS 25295, ff.165–166

Gloucester *1744*[52]
My dear Lord

I have the honour of your historical papers No. 1, 2, 3, 4, 5, 6.[53] full of the accuracy and good sense of the former. I see nothing either in the remarks or in the stile which I am able to improve. There are two particular which struck me most, your judicious reflections on the introduction and improvement of the feudal Law in Scotland; and the history of Q Margaret.[54] I have packed up the papers carefully least you should want them back.

---

old reference numbrs Acc. 7228/18, ff. 167–168 (7 May 1774) and ff. 169–170 (20 June 1774), have recently gone missing.

51. According to Margaret Forbes in *Beattie and his Friends* (Westminster, 1904), 'Sir W[illiam]. Forbes had shown to Lord Hailes Beattie's letter of the former autumn [1773], in which the reason upon which he had chiefly dwelt for declining all thought of accepting an Edinburgh professorship was his unwillingness to be associated with those who had shown themselves hostile to him on account of his writings . . .' (p. 105).

52. Beside Warburton's error in the year, Dalrymple jotted the notes: 'Oct. 1774 scripsit imbecilli et incertâ manu, annis fractius & sui paulatium . . .' [He has written with an imbecilic hand, broken by years and by degrees . . .].

53. Specimens of Dalrymple's *Annals of Scotland*, 2 vols. (Edinburgh, 1776/79). The Advertisement to the second volume states, 'THE Author once proposed to have continued THE ANNALS OF SCOTLAND to the Restoration of James I. But there are various and invincible reasons which oblige him to terminate his Work at the accession of the House of Stewart.' Johnson also received specimens of Dalrymple's *Annals of Scotland*. See his letter to Boswell, 1 October 1774, in *The Letters of Samuel Johnson*, ed. Bruce Redford, vol. II, 1773–1776 (Princeton, 1992), p. 150. On 27 August 1775, Johnson told Boswell, 'I have now three parcels of Lord Hailes's History . . .' (p. 266) and on 10 January 1776 Johnson received the first published volume of *Annals of Scotland* (p. 284). Johnson reported receiving 'more copy' from Dalrymple on 28 June 1777 (III [1992]: 33). Boswell's *Life of Johnson*, ed. R. W. Chapman, rev. J. D. Fleeman (Oxford, 1980), is peppered with references to Dalrymple and his *Annals* (pp. 565, 567, 569, *passim*). In *The Journal of a Tour to the Hebrides* (with Samuel Johnson, *A Journey to the Western Islands of Scotland*), ed. Peter Levi (London, 1984), Boswell recorded introducing Johnson to Dalrymple in Edinburgh on 17 August 1773 (p. 181).

54. Presumably Margaret, wife of Malcolm III (m. 1070; d. 1093), mentioned in Dalrymple's *Annals*, vol. 1, pp. 12, 25, 33–41 (little is written on Margaret, daughter of Henry III and queen of Alexander III).

I have the honour to be
your Lordship's most faithfull and
attached humble Servant
W. Gloucester

[f.166 blank]

Letter 25   15 December 1774   NLS: MS 25295, ff.167–168

Gloucester 15 ∧*Decr*∧ 1774
My Dear Lord

I have the honour of your obliging letter of the 5ˆ inst: My infirmities of
ill health have kept me from London a long time and is likely to prevent my
return thither; this, & especially the parliament's taking away our literary
property[55] deprive me of the pleasure of obeying your commands; for I have
none of the books you want, and what there are left, which I have had no
curiosity to entquire [*sic*] after, are dispersed and gone from me, amongst the
trade. I regard what you want as the effect of your friendship for me & matter
of curiosity, otherwise of little worth. I am, my good Lord, your

most affectionate and faithfull humble
Servant   W. Gloucester

[f.168 blank]

Letter 26   29 February 1776[56]   NLS: MS 25295, f.169

My Dear Lord

I have recd by your favour a vol of the Annals of Scotland from the accession of Malcolm the 3ᵈ. wrote with great accuracy: & have sinc[e] been [dele-
tion] ∧favoured∧ by the same hand, for an elegant edition of Languet's Epistles.[57] I am much indebted to you for these favours, and am, my dear Lord,
your most obliged and obedient humble

Servant

W. Gloucester
Gloucester Feb. 29ˆ 1776

55. The landmark copyright case of Donaldson v. Becket went against perpetual mo-
nopoly in the House of Lords decision in 1774. Dalrymple supported the arguments for
Donaldson's case earlier in the Court of Session.

56. 1776 was a leap year.

57. Hubert Languet, *H. Langueti Epistolae ad P. Sydneium, equitem Anglum Accu-
rante D. Dalrymple* (Edinburgh, 1776).

PATCHWORK AND PIRACY:
JOHN BELL'S "CONNECTED SYSTEM OF BIOGRAPHY"
AND THE USE OF JOHNSON'S *PREFACES*

by

THOMAS F. BONNELL*

THE birth of Johnson's *Prefaces, Biographical and Critical, to the Works of the English Poets* was difficult, at once premature and overdue. An anxious set of midwives, the booksellers for whom Johnson wrote, were alarmed by John Bell, whose series of British poets from Chaucer to Churchill was projected to reach one hundred volumes. Viewing Bell's scheme as an invasion of their literary property, they had plotted to undermine it with a collection of their own, banking on Johnson's name to give them an advantage.

Timeliness was all. To facilitate dispatch, the publishers had minimized their request of Johnson, as the biographer readily confessed: "My purpose was only to have allotted to every Poet an Advertisement, like those which we find in the French Miscellanies, containing a few dates and a general character."[1] The greater hurdle, it seemed, was the printing of fifty-six volumes of poetry; to expedite this task, ten printshops were put to work.[2] The proprietors had done their best to speed things along. To their undoubted chagrin, however, Johnson ignored their scant recipe for the lives, led beyond their intention by an "honest desire of giving useful pleasure"—a process that stretched from months into years. Meanwhile, Bell enjoyed an uncontested market, his *Poets of Great Britain* steadily progressing from its commencement in 1777.[3]

Johnson's delay left the proprietors with five options, none of them appealing:

(1) To publish nothing until Johnson had finished his task. This was unacceptable because it ignored the pressing commercial problem: Bell had a product, while they still had none.

* I wish to thank David Fleeman for bringing to my notice the manuscript in the Hyde Collection to which I refer; for this and other kindnesses I am deeply grateful.

1. Samuel Johnson, "Advertisement," *Prefaces, Biographical and Critical, to the Works of the English Poets,* vols. 1–4 (London, 1779), vols. 5–10 (London, 1781), 1:v. This "Advertisement," dated 15 March 1779, supplies my next quotation, too (vi).

2. The printers of these volumes were Henry Hughs (1–8, 21, 35–36), Edward Cox (9–12, 25, 29), Richard Hett (13–16, 43, 46), J. D. Cornish (17–18), John Rivington (19, 44, 53–56), John Nichols (20, 24, 30–31, 39–42), Henry Goldney (22, 45), Henry Baldwin (23, 26–28, 37–38, 50–52), William and Andrew Strahan (32–34), and George Bigg (47–49).

3. For a record of Bell's publication, with an account of its genesis and design, see Thomas F. Bonnell, "John Bell's *Poets of Great Britain*: The 'Little Trifling Edition' Revisited," *Modern Philology* 85 (1987): 128–152.

(2) To publish the complete poetry, but withhold the prefaces until Johnson had finished. This move would have defeated their marketing scheme, reliant as it was on Johnson's name.

(3) To publish what Johnson had completed to date, binding up his prefaces with the poems they introduced, while reserving the rest of the poems for similar publication either serially as Johnson progressed or collectively when he had ended his labors. Given Johnson's uneven rate of progress, the proprietors understandably would have been reluctant to proceed dilatorily and commit themselves to an indeterminate promotional plan.

(4) To publish whatever prefaces were ready, affixing them to their respective poets (as in option 3), but also to release the rest of the poems (without prefaces), promising to sell the balance of the lives in a batch when they were ready. This course would have yielded a half-baked set of books, with some prefaces joined to the works and others detached.

(5) To publish the complete poems, along with separate volumes containing whatever prefaces Johnson had finished, with the rest of the lives to be sold in additional volumes when they were finished. This option was evidently the least objectionable. In March 1779, with only twenty-two of the fifty-two slated lives ready, the proprietors published an inchoate collection. The *Prefaces* formed four separate volumes, to which six more were added in 1781 to finish the collection. Owing to these accidents Johnson's *Prefaces* were not prefaces at all, but rather "*Appendices*, Biographical and Critical, to the Works of the English Poets."

This anomaly elicited a jibe from Bell. In 1783, upon the completion of his series, he published a triumphal letter in which he sniffed at the irregular bond between Johnson's *Prefaces* and the proprietors' collection of poems. Johnson, Bell observed, had had no real concern in the edition called "Johnson's Poets" "otherwise than in writing and compiling the four volumes of the lives, which have no reference or allusion whatever to that Edition of the Poets, more than to mine.—Nay, I will even dare him so say, that he saw even a single sheet of manuscript, or printed copy, of what is called his Edition of the Poets, before it came finished from the press."[4] It was true: the four-volume *Lives of the Most Eminent English Poets* (the 1781 reprint of the *Prefaces*) bore no clear affiliation to the *Works of the English Poets*. Nor had the original *Prefaces*—this was Bell's point. Because Johnson had paid little explicit attention to the proprietors' edition in drafting his lives, and because the lives as a result did not "own" that collection, they could with equal propriety have been attached to Bell's series as well.

The insinuation was deliberately ironic. Some of Johnson's work *had*, in fact, been incorporated into *The Poets of Great Britain*: the famous writer's words and ideas were appropriated by Bell's compilers in several of his prefaces, running the gamut from outright piracy, which cost Bell a legal scrape, to the promiscuous little borrowings that were routine in eighteenth-century hackwork. To sort this out I have tried to chart the tangle of sources

4. *Morning Post*, 3 June 1783, p. 3; the letter is dated June 2.

used in Bell's lives. My purpose in doing so is twofold: (1) to bring to light one of the earliest responses to Johnson's *Prefaces*, a practical critique or compiler's-eye view of their most enticing elements; and (2) to set this practice into perspective by cataloging the other sources which shaped Bell's prefaces.

I
"That Part Which You May Call Piracy"

The mischief began in 1779 after the proprietors, on March 31, published their fifty-six volumes of poetry with the first installment of Johnson's *Prefaces*. For a compiler seeking biographical details and critical opinion, the new source was irresistible. By August 26, the first purloined material had been printed in Edinburgh, in Bell's "Life of Sir John Denham," to accompany *The Poetical Works of Denham* when offered for sale in London on 18 December 1779.

The biographical half of the preface is a jigsaw compilation of passages from Johnson and *Biographia Britannica*. Phrases, sentences and paragraphs are spliced together without their provenance being effaced. The technique may be seen at its most intricate in the following passage. For comparison I have provided the ur-source, *Athenæ Oxonienses* (*AO*), and presented Bell's text (*JB*) phrase by phrase to show the alternate use of Johnson (*SJ*) and *Biographia Britannica* (*BB*).[5]

AO: Shortly after he was prick'd High Sheriff for *Surrey*, and made Governour of *Farnham-Castle* for the King: But he being an inexpert Soldier, soon after left that Office, and retired to his Maj. at *Oxon*, where he printed his Poem called *Cooper's-hill*:

BB: Soon after he was pricked for High-Sheriff of the county of Surrey, and made Governor of Farnham-Castle for the King. But, not being well skilled in military affairs, he soon quitted that post, and retired to his Majesty at Oxford, where he published his poem called *Cooper's Hill*.

SJ: He was after that pricked for sheriff of Surrey, and made governor of Farnham Castle for the king; but he soon resigned that charge, and retreated to Oxford, where, in 1643, he published "Cooper's Hill."

JB:	He was soon after	
	pricked for High Sheriff of the county of Surrey,	[*SJ* syntax preferred]
	having an estate at Egham in that county,	[*BB*]
	and appointed Governor of Farnham Castle;	[*BB* note (d)]
	but his skill in military fairs not being extensive,	[either source]
	he resigned that charge,	[*BB*]
		[*SJ*]

---

5. Anthony à Wood, *Athenæ Oxonienses*, 2nd ed., 2 vols. (London, 1721), 2:423; *Biographia Britannica*, 6 vols. (London, 1747–66), 3:1646; *Prefaces*, Denham 10; "The Life of Sir John Denham," *The Poetical Works of Sir John Denham* (Edinburgh, 1779), vii. I use the text of the *Prefaces*; for ease of reference, however, I cite not the original page numbers but the paragraph numbers assigned in Samuel Johnson, *Lives of the English Poets,* ed. G. B. Hill, 3 vols. (Oxford, 1905).

and went to King Charles I. then at Oxford,   [*BB*]
where, in 1643, he published Cooper's Hill.   [*SJ*]

Many passages are similarly structured, with some paraphrase but mostly fractured and reassembled quotation. Elements of Johnson pervade this section of the life; they provide the framework, while materials from *BB* are either interpolated or relegated to footnotes. Most of *SJ* 11–20 is quoted wholesale.

Where the critical section of the life begins, Bell's text becomes wholly Johnson's. With the exception of five altered phrases, one sentence deletion, the omission of a few verses in the poetical examples, and the switching of paragraphs 25 and 26, Johnson's critical discussion of Denham (*SJ* 21–42) is reprinted in full.

How word of the theft reached the proprietors is unclear. Months passed before any of the interested parties noticed, but by the end of March they had sought legal counsel to establish whether the offense was actionable. This advice in hand, several printers and booksellers met at Anderson's Coffeehouse on 27 March 1780. Calling themselves "the Committee of the Poets," they resolved as follows:

> Agreed unanimously, in Consideration of the Case laid before them, and Mr Kenyon's Opinion thereupon, that Mr Bell's printing the Life of Denham "is a plain Invasion of the Property of the Proprietors of the Lives written by Dr Johnson; and that they may have Remedy *by Bill in Equity*," that a Prosecution be immediately commenced against Mr Bell under the Direction of Mr Reed; and that the Proprietors be acquainted therewith.

Thirteen parties witnessed the resolution: Thomas Longman, George Nicol, Thomas Cadell, Thomas Evans, Lockyer Davis, Thomas Davies, John Rivington's Sons, Nathaniel Conant, John Nichols, George Robinson, Bedwell Law, Benjamin White and Robert Baldwin.[6]

Their legal help was impressive. Lloyd Kenyon was poised to receive a silk gown (on June 30), the first in a train of elevations which led to his succeeding Lord Mansfield as Chief Justice in 1788. As an equity judge his merits were "rapidity and accuracy"; perfectly versed in this branch of law, he decided cases "without any hesitation or delay."[7] Despite some failings, such as a defective manner of speech, an unprepossessing education, and a reluctance to articulate his legal principles, his judicial skill was superlative. A century later it could be said of him that "no judge who presided so long in

6. "MS Agreement of the Booksellers, 27 March 1780," in the Hyde-Adam extra-illustrated *Life of Johnson*, 3.2:111, from the Hyde Collection; quoted with the kind permission of Lady Eccles.

7. George T. Kenyon, *The Life of Lloyd, the First Lord Kenyon, Lord Chief Justice of England* (London, 1873), p. 173. This book was written to answer Lord Campbell, whose portrait of the Chief Justice was most unflattering. Nonetheless, Lord Campbell grudgingly admired Kenyon's "intuitive quickness in seeing all the bearings of the most complicated case, and his faculty of at once availing himself of all his legal resources." Campbell also was struck by the great demand for Kenyon's advice; by around 1781 he was taking in above 3000*l.* a year by answering cases. See *The Lives of the Chief Justices of England*, 3 vols. (London, 1749–57), 3:44 and 12.

the king's bench has been as seldom overruled," and that "the decisions and rulings of no judge stand in higher estimation than those of Lord Kenyon."[8]

Isaac Reed, too, was a natural choice. He was an intimate of the London literary scene, whose passion was to amplify and correct the biographical and bibliographical record of the nation. By 1780 his assistance, usually anonymous, had been vital to the notes in Nichols' *Select Collection of Poems* (4 vols., 1780), the revisions of *Biographia Britannica*, and the republication of Dodsley's *Collection of Old Plays* (6 vols., 1780), including the preface, annotations, and accounts of the playwrights.[9] More pertinent was his link to Johnson's *Prefaces*, as recalled in Boswell's summary of the help Johnson received: "But he was principally indebted to my steady friend Mr. Isaac Reed, of Staple-Inn, whose extensive and accurate knowledge of English literary History I do not express with exaggeration, when I say it is wonderful."[10] If anyone knew the exigencies of compiling lives and had faced repeatedly the practical divide between legitimate borrowing and piracy, it was Isaac Reed.

Rather than to face this formidable legal challenge and expose himself in the courts to possible penalties, Bell cut his losses. He withdrew the edition of Denham from sale, thereby avoiding an injunction or worse.[11] Changes to the book in the ensuing months tell of Bell's efforts to regroup and to salvage from the setback something of a commercial opportunity.

To retrace this bibliographical trail one needs to know a few facts about *The Poets of Great Britain.* The series was printed in Edinburgh by Gilbert Martin and sons. Its format is 18mo in sixes; the first three leaves in a gathering are signed with letters and roman numerals (for instance D, Dij, Diij). Besides an engraved series title-page and in some a frontispiece portrait, each volume contains two letterpress title-pages. Since the series consisted of reprints, and the extent of any volume was known from the outset, the compositor had no need to resort to a separate sequence of signings for the pre-

---

8. Edward Foss, *Biographia Juridica: A Biographical Dictionary of the Judges of England* (London, 1870), p. 384; and *The Dictionary of National Biography,* ed. Leslie Stephen and Sidney Lee, 22 vols. (Oxford, 1921–22), 11:30–32. Leman Thomas Rede wrote that Kenyon's "manner was ungraceful—his language uncouth, awkward, unharmonized. . . . He is in the habit of hurrying his words so disagreeably together, that his articulation is not only indistinct, but sometimes totally unintelligible. He lisps, hesitates, and occasionally stammers. . . . Yet, under all these defects (insuperable as they might be imagined) . . . he was not only heard with patience, but with attention and respect" (*Strictures on the Lives and Characters of the Most Eminent Lawyers of the Present Day* [London, 1790], pp. 98–99).

9. Arthur Sherbo, *Isaac Reed, Editorial Factotum,* ELS Monograph Series No. 45 (Victoria: University of Victoria, 1989), chapters 3 and 4. Reed's anonymity was broken when the editors of *Biographia Britannica* expressed their gratitude, naming him twice in the "Preface to the Second Edition of the Second Volume" (1780), p. viii.

10. *Boswell's Life of Johnson,* ed. G. B. Hill, rev. L. F. Powell, 6 vols. (Oxford, 1934–50), 4:37.

11. Had he lost in court, Bell could have been forced to pay a fine of one penny for every sheet in his custody, "either printed or printing, published, or exposed to sale," and to forfeit all sheets to the copyright holders, who "forthwith [would] damask, and make waste paper of them" (8 Anne, c. 19, § I).

liminaries. The single sequence begins with the title-pages ([A] and [Aij]), resulting in the first page of the prefatory life (p. [v]) being signed Aiij. On the final page of each volume was printed a colophon that reads "From the APOLLO PRESS, by the MARTINS," followed by a date. According to the colophon, the press work for *The Poetical Works of Sir John Denham* was completed on 26 August 1779.

In this volume "The Life of Sir John Denham" appeared on pp. [v]–xviii, followed by Denham's dedication "To the King" (pp. [xix]–xxii) and the poems (pp. [23]–178). With a two-page table of contents, the book came to 180 pages, or precisely five sheets of paper printed in 18mo, for a collation of A–P⁶. The paper Martin used for Denham had a crowned horn watermark with a pendant "GR," and a "J TAYLOR" countermark.¹² These are the earmarks of the book containing the pirated Johnsonian preface. The final four sheets (pp. 37–180) were never altered. What happened to the first sheet is what defines the second and third states of this edition and its subsequent re-issue.¹³

To avoid further legal action Bell withdrew the piracy from sale and laid plans for re-issuing the volume once he had obtained a revised life of Denham. As an interim measure he sold copies of the book from which the life had been cancelled. Cut out were pp. [v]–xviii, or seven leaves (A3 through

12. Closest to number 2754 in Edward Heawood, *Watermarks Mainly of the 17th and 18th Centuries* (Hilversum, 1950). As Martin imposed his pages, with three gatherings per sheet, the watermark and countermark wound up centered on the fifth leaves of each first and third gathering, with portions of the "J" sometimes visible on the second leaf in the gutter, and a fraction of the "R" appearing at the fore-edge of the second or fifth leaf of the second gathering.

13. The choice of terms between "state" and "re-issue" in the following paragraphs is no easy matter. Here are some considerations: (a) the completion of the initial print run without alterations, leading to (b) publication; (c) the interruption of sales to cancel the life, followed by (d) the renewal of sales without the life; (e) the printing of a revised life, paving the way for (f) a second resumption of sales, with the new life; and (g) the re-publication of the volume with the first sheet re-set, incorporating not only the revised life but also (h) an updated title-page, with (i) concomitant external evidence in the form of an advertisement to corroborate the public nature of the event. If time and the publisher's intention mattered most, a case could be made, once (a) and (b) had occurred, to call each new release of the book in altered form a new issue: sales of the book were halted, changes were made, and sales were then resumed. And it must be said, (c) and (d) resulted in a dramatically different book, the causes of which are known and can be documented. It might be especially tempting to call (f) a re-issue, since much "conscious planning" was required to publish the book in this form, and since the change was expressly designed to be noticed by the audience that counted most at this juncture, the lawyers. On balance, however, I defer to one of Bowers' definitions of re-issue: a book issued *"again"* in different form, the purpose of which alteration is "the stimulation of lagging sales, or a complete revival of the sale of sheets which have lost their currency." Although Bell's Denham, having truly lost its currency, was partly revived by steps (c) through (f), complete revival awaited the co-ordinated plan of (g), (h) and (i); the book at this stage may certainly be called a re-issue. The edition at stages (d) and (f), then, may be referred to as its second and third states. See Fredson Bowers, *Principles of Bibliographical Description* (Princeton, 1949), p. 66 and *passim*; and G. Thomas Tanselle, "The Bibliographical Concepts of 'Issue' and 'State,'" *Papers of the Bibliographical Society of America* 69 (1975): 17–66, esp. 46–47.

B3) from the first two gatherings.[14] Such copies constitute a second state, typographically identical to the first except for the missing life. That copies in this state were deemed saleable, their mutilation notwithstanding, is a sign of Bell's impatience before the full remedy could be implemented.

To end this predicament Bell was willing to improvise, anxious lest his regular printing arrangement with Edinburgh cause undue delay. The moment his revised text was ready, he had it printed closer to home (presumably in London) and then, inserting the fresh "Life of Sir John Denham" into the gap left by the cancels, resumed at least a limited sale of the volume.[15] Bibliographical evidence tells the story of this third state. The life is not the presswork of Gilbert Martin. Departures from the style of the Apollo Press include: a double rule above the title of the life on p. [v], a feature shared with no other preface in the *Poets*; block quotations of poetry which are flush left, not indented as in the rest of Bell's series; and Arabic instead of Roman numerals in the signings. In addition, the type is larger—a bourgeois letter with a small brevier or large minion for the block quotations, in place of the Apollo Press brevier with block quotations in pearl. The paper, too, featuring a "W" countermark, differs from any other in Bell's edition.[16] The format employed was a version of 18mo called "sixteen pages to a half sheet of eighteens," resulting in eight leaves, signed A through A4, and numbered [v]–xx.[17] As the sixteen-page life did not fit the fourteen-page gap left by the cancels ("To the King" starts on p. xix), the volume would have been spared its redundant pp. xix and xx if the new life arbitrarily had been numbered [iii]–xviii, instead of [v]–xx.[18]

This third state was a stopgap. A limited supply would have sufficed until the revision had made its way to Edinburgh and back, where Martin could

14. Had copies in this state been altered in no other way, the stubs of the five cancellanda would be visible between the second title-page and the dedication (p. [xix]). (Five, not seven, because A3 and its conjugate A4 could be removed entirely.) None that I have examined, however, fits this description. Three stubs only are present in a copy at the University of Virginia: those of B1, B2 and B3. The leaves conjugate with the title-pages (A5 and A6) were cancelled at the fold, requiring the title-pages to be pasted onto the stub of B1. Copies at Wellesley and Notre Dame betray an effort either to conceal the loss of text or to strengthen the attachment of the remaining leaves of $A and $B to the rest of the volume: the five stubs crop up, not in front of the dedication, but between pp. 24 and 25, just before the C gathering. What remains of $B was lifted up; the stubs of B1, B2 and B3 were folded back in the opposite direction; and the gathering was nestled into the middle of the A gathering. Its collation: A1–2, B4–6 [stubs B1–3 A5–6] C–P6.

15. To the best of my knowledge Bell was not yet printing for himself, as he did later on.

16. Having seen only one copy of Denham's poems in this third state, and hence only one half sheet, I do not know what watermark stood opposite the countermark.

17. The term is found in *Caleb Stower: The Printer's Grammar 1808*, English Bibliographical Sources, ed. D. F. Foxon, ser. 3, no. 4 (London, 1965), p. 182. In this case a seven-leaf or fourteen-page version of 18mo would have been more convenient, which, had it been workable, Bell presumably would have requested. I have seen nothing of the sort in the printers' manuals.

18. Technically this would have made pp. [iii] and iv redundant, but since the second title-page and its blank verso were not numbered, the glitch in pagination would have been less noticeable.

print the new text in the usual style of Bell's *Poets*. At this point it was simplest to reprint the entire first sheet, which effectively made a cancel of the first three gatherings. This new sheet from the Apollo Press defines Bell's re-issue of the Denham edition. As before, the paper bears the watermark of a crowned horn with pendant GR, but the countermark now reads "IV."[19] The text of the sixteen-page life has been followed verbatim, with changes in accidentals, but has been recast in brevier type to restore the original pagination ([v]–xviii).[20] Since the first sheet encompassed pp. [i]–36, the other features also needing to be reset were the title-pages, dedication, all of "Cooper's Hill," and the first eighteen verses of "On the Earl of Strafford's Trial and Death." The imprint was updated to 1780, to suit Bell's purpose in re-advertising the edition. These sheets were shipped to London and sewn onto the second through fifth sheets of the original 1779 stock, readying the volume for re-issue.

How many copies of Bell's Denham were affected by these changes? A survey of ESTC, OCLC, RLIN, and NUC (along with chance discoveries) yields a list of thirty copies with the 1779 imprint, and twenty-one with the 1780 imprint. Other things being equal (not always a safe assumption), this ratio would suggest that before re-issuing the edition, Bell had sold more than half of his print run. As for the relative numbers of the 1779 issue extant in its various states, my own research (in effect a random selection) may serve as a rough guide. Of the seventeen copies I have seen or questioned others about, eleven conform to the original state (with the pirated life), five to the second state (without a life), and only one to the third state (with the sixteen-page life). If representative, this sample implies a considerable sale of the original state (nearly 40% of the full print run), a far from negligible number sold in the imperfect second state (between 15% and 20% of the edition), and a fairly minimal exposure to sale of the third state.[21]

The re-issue was heralded in the *Morning Post* of 19 July 1780.[22] With his usual promotional flare Bell advertised the "New Edition" of Denham's works in the course of an open rebuke "To the FORTY BOOKSELLERS, who have so long, and impotently attempted by their combined wealth and influence, as well as by every plausible imposition on the public, which art could sug-

19. Still closest to Heawood 2754, the 1780 watermark is smaller than its 1779 look-alike, 10.0 cm from the top of the crown to the bottom of the "GR," as opposed to 11.7 cm.

20. To identify the type sizes I have relied on John Richardson, Jr., "Correlated Type Sizes and Names for the Fifteenth through Twentieth Century," *Studies in Bibliography* 43 (1990): 251–272.

21. The third state, curiously, happened to serve as the Morisons' copytext for *The Poetical Works of Sir John Denham* (Perth, 1780), as evidenced by the compositor's fidelity to the sixteen-page life. The Apollo Press printing of the revised preface differs in scores of accidentals. I wish to thank several people for lending me copies of the 1779 Denham or patiently examining the book as I questioned them over the phone: Nancy Birkrem, James Green, Samuel Huang, Gwin Kolb, Eric Nye, Richard Oram, Ruth Rogers, Eleanore Stewart, and Michael Suarez.

22. Page 3. The letter/advertisement was partially reset and then repeated on July 20 (p. 4).

gest, or malevolence devise, to suppress and to rival Bell's Edition of the Poets, or to annihilate the publisher." He trumpeted the "NEW LIFE of the Author, intended as a PARAPHRASE of that, which *is supposed to have been written*, by Dr. SAMUEL JOHNSON." By refusing to concede that his first life had been a piracy, and casting doubt on the allegation itself, Bell implied that his opponents had not dealt with him in good faith. Addressing his rivals "with contempt," he palliated his offense and improved upon hints of their fraud:

This is the first time I have had occasion, and I chearfully crave your pardon, for I have innocently offended against the legal rules of your business, *'tho not against the daily practice of yourselves*. The Life of DENHAM, which was published in my First Edition, was, it seems, *inadvertently*, and I solemnly declare, without my consent or knowledge, partly composed from that, which has *been forced upon the world* by you as the production of Dr. JOHNSON: The *Poetical* Works of the respective Poets, require not, and I flatter myself my publication of them needs not, the aid even of a JOHNSON'S name to recommend them to the favour of the world.

While the piracy of Johnson could not have been inadvertent, Bell's denial of involvement is plausible. Apart from his implicit policy of reprinting authoritative lives, where available, and otherwise the fullest warrantable compilation, there is no reason to think that he supervised this work closely, especially if it was done in Edinburgh.

As to the proprietors' "daily practice" belying their legal rules, there is a grain of truth to the charge. Publishers commonly tested their borrowing limits, though it was disingenuous to suggest that theft as extensive as the Denham piracy, and with materials so recent, was the norm. More incriminating is Bell's view of their marginal ethics in promotional matters. The whole collection *had* in fact "been forced upon the world . . . as the production of Dr. Johnson." To say these were "Johnson's Poets" was a lie, one that Johnson himself protested in characterizing the unauthorized use of his name as misleading and indecent.[23] No one could have been more keenly attuned to such marketing licence than Bell.

In closing, Bell softened his grievance, portraying himself as a responsible bookseller whose initiative had been swift and voluntary:

in justice, therefore, to my own feelings, and to prevent you any cause of detraction, I have cancelled that part which you might call piracy, as soon as I discovered it; and I have now substituted another account of the Author, equally circumstantial; and I flatter myself which will be more acceptable; comparison will convince, the perusal may instruct and entertain you.

The challenge to compare the two versions, an otherwise obligatory promotional topos, is all the more defiant because the revised life was not an overhaul. It was based on the contested text itself, the source of Bell's legal headache, and declared to be "intended as a paraphrase."

In the biographical half of the revised preface, the erstwhile quotations

---

23. See *The Letters of Samuel Johnson*, ed. Bruce Redford, 5 vols. (Princeton, 1992–94), 3:226; and *Boswell's Life of Johnson*, 4:35n.

of Johnson have been targeted for change. Witness the following revision, compared with the original sources:[24]

BB: In 1652, or thereabout, he returned into England; and, his paternal estate being greatly reduced by gaming and the Civil Wars, he was kindly entertained by the Earl of Pembroke at Wilton, and continued with that Nobleman about a year. (3:1647)

SJ: About this time, *what estate the war and the gamesters had left him was sold, by order of the parliament*; and when, in 1652, he returned to England, he was entertained by the earl of Pembroke. (16; my emphasis)

1779: Mr. Denham returned into England about the year 1652, and *what estate the Civil war and the gamesters had left him being sold by order of the Parliament*, he was kindly entertained by the Earl of Pembroke at Wilton, with whom he continued near twelve months. (x; my emphasis)

1780: About the year 1652 he returned to England; and his paternal estate being greatly reduced by gaming and the Civil wars, he was kindly entertained by the Earl of Pembroke at Wilton, with whom he resided near twelve months. (x)

The tactic is clear: Johnson's phrase (in italics) is relinquished, and the re-reviser retreats to *BB*. Obviously this kind of revision, combing through the pirated text phrase by phrase to detect and remedy the plagiarism, was possible only with Johnson and *BB* both open before the reviser.

While Johnson's preface served as a map for revision, it was also used in one instance for further, though more circumspect, borrowing. Bell's 1779 text called upon *BB* and *SJ* to recount Denham's appointment as Surveyor of the King's Buildings and his receiving the Order of the Bath. Johnson's paragraph consists of three sentences, the second of which, with two surgical transplants from *BB*, formed Bell's paragraph. The reviser duly cut away the plagiarised words, again falling back on *BB*, but could not leave the operation without grafting on Johnson's first and third sentences:

SJ: Of the next years of his life there is no account. . . . He seems now to have learned some attention to money; for Wood says, that he got by his place seven thousand pounds. (17)

1780: From this period to the Restoration, in 1660, there appears to be a chasm in the history of Denham's life. . . . He likewise now appears to have acquired a greater degree of economical prudence than he had been usually blessed with, as Wood informs us that he realized by his appointment upwards of 7000*l*. (x)

The mode of disguise here is wordiness, one of the principal means of paraphrase employed in the revision.

Verbosity could also be used to mask the retention of Johnson's verbal formulae:

24. In what follows I cite Bell's pirated text as "1779" and the revision of it as "1780." For the revision I have used *The Poetical Works of Sir John Denham* (Edinburgh, 1780), printed by the Apollo Press, rather than the earlier setting of the text by the unidentified press.

1779: He seems to have divided his studies between law and poetry; for in 1636 he translated the second book of the Æneid. (vi; *SJ* 7)

1780: During the period he had abstained from his favourite amusement, in consequence of his father's admonitions, he appears to have divided his time between the study of the law and the cultivation of his poetical talents; for in the year 1636 he translated the second book of the Æneid, which was published twenty years after, under the title of The Destruction of Troy; or, An Essay upon the second book of Virgil's Æneids [*sic*]. (vi–vii)

The core borrowing is embellished with a dependent clause in front (the needless reiteration of a previous point) and a relative clause at the end (merely the addition of a title and publication date).

If the compiler could fall back on *BB* or even Wood where the biographical outline was concerned, the critical section presented no such opportunity. There were stark alternatives to retaining Johnson's opinions: either to form an independent literary appraisal, or to abandon the section altogether. Remarkably, even under the legal scrutiny to which the revision would have been subjected, Johnson's ideas were considered fair game so long as some of the words were changed. The critical section itself was reorganized; Johnson's order of presentation was altered.[25] But the striking fact remains that Johnson's ideas survive the paraphrase.

As a measure of this retention, compare the following passage with its revision:

1779: He appears to have had, in common with all mankind, the ambition of being, upon proper occasions, a merry fellow; and, in common with most of them, to have been by nature, or by early habits, debarred from it. Nothing is less exhilerating [*sic*] than the ludicrousness of Denham. He does not fail for want of efforts: he is familiar, he is gross; but he is never merry, unless the Speech against Peace in the Close Committee be excepted. For grave burlesque, however, his imitation of Davenant shews him to have been well qualified. (xi–xii; *SJ* 22)

1780: . . . in the ludicrous he generally fails of answering the end proposed. There is nothing in this species of his poetry that excites our risibility, or that tends to exhilarate. He affects to be thought a humorous writer, but Nature seems to have debarred him from being so. When he attempts to be witty he is familiar, gross, and disgusting to a chaste imagination. In every effort he miscarries, unless we except The Speech against peace in the Close Committee, which is written with some humour. His imitation of D'Avenant, indeed, shows that he was not ill qualified for grave burlesque. (xiv)

The reviser shuffles a few sentences, alters syntax, changes a verb from active to passive voice, substitutes words and phrases, and elaborates a conceit or two. Still, the ideas and examples are unmistakably Johnson's, even many

25. See the collation below in Section III.

of the key terms. Little substance is lost in translation. The thoughts which do not survive the paraphrase—the comment about a shared human desire to be thought funny, and the glance at habit as a developmental factor—are missed for the distinctive turn of mind that they convey.

As if to offset the loss of Johnson's voice, the reviser often affects a Johnsonian style, however crudely understood. Compare these sentences from the two versions:

1779: Nothing is less exhilerating [*sic*] than the ludicrousness of Denham. (xi; *SJ* 22)

1780: There is nothing in this species of his poetry that excites our risibility, or that tends to exhilarate. (xiv)

Intent on parallelism, the reviser mimics Johnson's diction by adding a second polysyllabic, Latinate word ("risibility" to complement "exhilarate"). Too much strain goes into this stylistic elevation, as is evident in the appraisal of Denham's rhymes:

1779: . . . as exact at least as those of other poets, though now and then the reader is shifted off with what he can get. (xvii; *SJ* 39)

1780: . . . as well coupled as those of other poets; yet we may discern in many of them a manifest inattention. . . . (xiii)

The original prose is relaxed and colloquial, the revision self-conscious and ceremonious. Blind or indifferent to the energy and relative informality of Johnson's mature style, the reviser echoes the allegedly "stiff, laboured, and pedantic" style of the *Rambler* and *Dictionary* years.[26] This anachronism is audible in substitutions like these.[27]

1779	1780
got by his place (*SJ* 17)	realized by his appointment (x)
ends of his verses (xvii; *SJ* 41)	terminations of his lines (xiii)
the morality too frequent (xiii; *SJ* 29)	the morality superabundant (xv)
learned some attention to money (*SJ* 17)	acquired a greater degree of economical prudence (x)
law and poetry (vi; *SJ* 7)	the study of the law and the cultivation of his poetical talents (vi–vii)

While never amounting to a sustained imitation of "Johnsonian" prose, the stylistic preening to which the paraphrase is given comes across frequently as a bid to out-Johnson Johnson.

It is tempting to regard this mimicry also as a touch of recalcitrance. What better irreverence than to tease the lawyers who, paragraph by paragraph, would vet the revision in search of any lingering evidence of piracy? In this light even a polite commonplace takes on a sly edge:

26. This was one view of Johnson's prose in the early 1750s, attributed by Charlotte Lennox to readers who could not appreciate Johnson's "Language, because it reaches to Perfection," and who were therefore deaf to its "inimitable Beauties" (*The Female Quixote* [Oxford: World Classics, 1989], p. 253).

27. The two phrases designated solely by *SJ* paragraph numbers do not occur in Bell's 1779 life. Taken up for the first time in 1780, their handling is in line with the stylistic transformation of the earlier piracy.

1779: The strength of Denham . . . is to be found in many lines and couplets, which convey much meaning in few words, and exhibit the sentiment
with more weight than bulk. (xv; *SJ* 34)

1780: His *forte* appears to have been a mode of conveying a great deal of
meaning in few words, or of compressing (if we may be allowed the phrase)
a large quantity of sentiment into a little space. (xvii)

Under the circumstances of legal duress, the reviser's begging leave to use a
phrase might be seen as an exaggerated show of deference to the lawyers.

Bell did not forget this lesson nor the sting to his pride. When someone
published an unauthorized abridgement of a property of his, *An Apology
for the Life of George Anne Bellamy* (5 vols., 1785), he got the courts to grant
an injunction against "a publication piratically taken from another." Their
offense? Publishing "facts, and even the terms in which they were related . . .
frequently *verbatim* from the original work."[28] Bell had to bide his time
before he could finally thumb his nose at the proprietors of Johnson's *Prefaces*.
In 1793 he published a second edition of *The Poetical Works of Sir John
Denham*, attaching to it the 1779 piracy instead of the revised life of 1780.
Fourteen years had elapsed since 1779, and because Johnson had died in that
time, the copyright on his "Life of Denham" could not be renewed for another
fourteen years. So Bell had the last word. He had moved on to other concerns, however, when in 1807 Samuel Bagster and others reprinted Bell's
collection in expanded form as *The Poets of Great Britain in Sixty-One Double Volumes*. Several of Johnson's lives now were reprinted openly, among
them the "Life of Denham"—the full text this time, with Johnson's name
on the title-page and on the first page of the life.[29]

II
"Additional Materials . . . Interwove"

An image for Bell's handling of sources is provided in a footnote to "The
Life of John Philips": "This life is principally copied from Dr. Sewell's Life
of Philips: where that was found defective the additional materials will be
found either interwove in the text or thrown into marginal readings."[30] The

28. See "Bell *against* Walker and Debrett," *Brown's Chancery Cases* 452, 28 Eng. Rep.
1235.

29. I believe it is Bagster's edition to which William Prideaux Courtney and David
Nichol Smith refer when they claim that "Johnson's *Lives* were incorporated in John Bell's
The Poets of Great Britain, 109 vols." (*A Bibliography of Samuel Johnson* [Oxford, 1925],
p. 147). Had they known of any lives adopted by Bell (other than that of Savage, noted on
p. 17), they would have listed them on pp. 150–152, where they trace the reappearance of
individual lives in subsequent imprints, even where the lives are altered, excerpted, or present merely "in substance." Thus they seem, *pace* their statement, to have been unaware of
the borrowing that is my focus.

30. *The Poetical Works of John Philips* (Edinburgh, 1781), p. [v]. All subsequent citations of Bell's edition will be parenthetical: no title is needed, since all begin with *The
Poetical Works of*; the poet in question will be clear from the context; and the imprint year
of the volume corresponds with the colophon date listed for each poet in Table 1. For
poets whose works took up several volumes, only the first (with the life) is of concern.

metaphor, albeit mixed, is apt: to mend a central text, threads from other narratives are interwoven, or patches stitched into the "margins" (i.e., footnotes). The notion of an imperfect fabric, closely mended or hastily patched, captures the process of compiling Bell's lives.

Johnson's *Prefaces* afforded a ready supply of these materials, too good to pass up despite the trouble over Denham. As accident and delay would have it, there were two phases of borrowing. Had Bell kept to his projected timetable of publishing one volume per week, he would have had no chance to pilfer from Johnson, for his series would have been completed by the time Johnson appeared in print. A fire, however, having burnt the Apollo Press to the ground in 1778, Martin was unable to resume printing until mid-1779, by which time the first four volumes of the *Prefaces* had been published (31 March 1779). After ten months of printing, another delay postponed the series until the last six volumes of the *Prefaces* had appeared (15 May 1781).[31] Table 1, which charts the printing of Bell's *Poets* against the staggered publication of the *Prefaces*, shows which of Johnson's lives were used as compared with those that were "available" when Bell's compiler presumably was hunting for sources. The question was moot for Johnson's lives of Milton, Dryden, Butler, Waller and Cowley, since Bell's editions of these poets were published before Johnson's volumes containing these lives went on sale. Several of the lives in Johnson's fourth volume, however, were eligible targets. Why Pomfret and Garth failed to attract is unclear; but Denham, Hughes, and Roscommon drew the attention of Bell's compiler.

What caused a seventeen-month hiatus between April 1780 and September 1781 is a mystery. Yet the dates raise an intriguing possibility. Printing of the series faltered just when Bell would have been apprised of the lawsuit, assuming the proprietors notified him soon after their resolution of March 27. By the time Bell had sent word to Martin, the first of the two Somerville volumes would have been in the press; and with these volumes, their colophons dated April 15 and 22, the series abruptly ceased. It is not surprising that the *Poets* would be suspended while legal action was pending and until Bell could re-issue the Denham in altered form. But after July 1780, why the further delay? Was he low on capital? If so, it did not hamper *Bell's British Theatre*, which Martin went on printing during this period at a healthy pace.[32] It is just conceivable that Bell, occupying himself meanwhile with other projects, waited to resume the *Poets* until Johnson's second installment of *Prefaces* had appeared. Could an urge to nettle his rivals have gotten the better of his acumen, or could he simply have wanted to provide his compiler with a broader choice of sources? Whatever the case, the series and Bell's borrowing from Johnson resumed simultaneously with the Collins/Hammond volume, printed within four months of the release of *Prefaces*, vols.

---

31. For the dates of publication, see two articles by J. D. Fleeman, "Some Proofs of Johnson's *Prefaces to the Poets*," *The Library*, 5th ser., 17 (1962): 213n, and "The Revenue of a Writer: Samuel Johnson's Literary Earnings." *Studies in the Book Trade, in Honour of Graham Pollard* (Oxford, 1975), p. 217.

32. See Bonnell, pp. 146–147, n. 28.

TABLE 1
Bell's Use of Johnson's *Prefaces*

Poet	Vol. No. in SJ's *Prefaces*			Date Bell's "Life" Printed	Time from SJ Publication to Bell Printing	SJ *Preface* Used by Bell?		
	1779	1781	Not Included			Yes	No	Not Applicable
Milton	2			17 Aug 1776				NA
Pope		7		9 Oct 1776				NA
Dryden	3			23 Jan 1777				NA
Butler	2			3 Mar 1777				NA
Prior		6		9 Apr 1777				NA
Thomson		9		8 May 1777				NA
Gay		8		4 Jun 1777				NA
Waller	1			8 Sep 1777				NA
Young		10		22 Sep 1777				NA
Cowley	1			30 Oct 1777				NA
Spenser	—			3 Jan 1778				NA
Parnell		8		14 Mar 1778				NA
Congreve		6		4 Apr 1778				NA
Swift		8		8 Apr 1778				NA
Addison		5		8 May 1778				NA
Shenstone		10		16 May 1778				NA
[SJ's *Prefaces*, vols. 1–4, published:				31 Mar 1779]				
Churchill			—	1 Jul 1779				NA
Pomfret	4			22 Jul 1779	3 mos. 3 wks.		N	
Donne			—	29 Jul 1779				NA
Garth	4			19 Aug 1779	4 mos. 3 wks.		N	
Denham	4			26 Aug 1779	4 mos. 4 wks.	Y		
Hughes	4			2 Sep 1779	5 mos. 0 wks.	Y		
Fenton		6		16 Sep 1779				NA
Dyer		10		23 Sep 1779				NA
Lansdowne		6		27 Nov 1779				NA
Buckingham		5		22 Jan 1780				NA
Savage		9		19 Feb 1780				NA
Roscommon	4			11 Mar 1780	11 mos. 2 wks.	Y		
Mallet		10		8 Apr 1780				NA
Somerville		9		15 Apr 1780				NA
[SJ's *Prefaces*, vols. 5–10, published:				15 May 1781]				
Collins		9		15 Sep 1781	4 mos. 0 wks.	Y		
Hammond		9		15 Sep 1781	4 mos. 0 wks.	Y		
Cunningham			—	22 Sep 1781				NA
Broome		8		29 Sep 1781	4 mos. 2 wks.	Y		
King	4			6 Oct 1781	28 mos. 1 wk.		N	
Rowe		6		20 Oct 1781	5 mos. 1 wk.	Y		
Tickell		6		27 Oct 1781	5 mos. 2 wks.	Y		
Akenside		10		3 Nov 1781	5 mos. 3 wks.	Y		
Lyttelton		10		17 Nov 1781	6 mos. 0 wks.	Y		
West, G.		10		24 Nov 1781	6 mos. 1 wk.	Y		
Philips, J.	4			1 Dec 1781	30 mos. 0 wks.	Y		
Philips, A.		8		8 Dec 1781	6 mos. 3 wks.	Y		
Moore			—	15 Dec 1781				NA
Armstrong			—	22 Dec 1781				NA
Smith	4			22 Dec 1781	30 mos. 3 wks.	Y		
Watts		8		5 Jan 1782	7 mos. 3 wks.		N	
Pitt		8		25 May 1782	12 mos. 1 wk.	Y		
Gray		10		3 Aug 1782	14 mos. 3 wks.		N	
West, R.			—	3 Aug 1782				NA
Chaucer			—	7 Sep 1782				NA

5–10. This was roughly the same interval as had been required for the Denham piracy.[33]

Leaving aside the life of Savage, a separate case,[34] twenty of Johnson's lives presented Bell's compiler with an opportunity for borrowing. Fifteen were used. When not appropriated for the main narrative, they were treated as a source of threads for interweaving or snippets to be "thrown into marginal readings." If the Denham preface had not been challenged, piracy might well have been the preferred mode. Bell's life of Roscommon, printed before the legal issue had been raised, was nearly as flagrant a theft as the other, its second half taken *en bloc* from Johnson. (Even so, Bell was not forced to retract this preface, and the text was never changed.) The Denham crisis ensured that subsequent loans would consist of shorter passages, usually in lazy paraphrases which, far from disguising their origin, preserved much of Johnson's syntax and word choice. Apart from Denham and Roscommon, three other Johnsonian lives served as Bell's primary source: those of Broome, Lyttelton, and West. Strands from the accounts of Hughes, Rowe, Tickell, Ambrose Phillips, Pitt, and Akenside were interwoven into other narratives. And material for footnotes was lifted from the lives of Collins, Hammond, John Philips and Smith.

Any grain in specificity was worthwhile. At the most rudimentary level, Bell's compiler gathered key minutiae from Johnson—a missing date, birthplace, or name. In the life of Hughes, for instance, drawn mainly from William Duncombe's account of the poet, the compiler embellishes a reference to "Mr. Montague" with Johnson's epithet, "the general patron of the followers of the Muses" (vi; *SJ* 4). To the end of a lengthy paragraph in the same life the compiler tacks on this sentence: "The same year 1699 our Author produced a song on the Duke of Gloucester's birth-day" (vii; *SJ* 4). The need for this addition is symptomatic of the shortage of dates and titles that often confronted the compiler. What many earlier literary biographies lacked, ironic though it seems, is what the *Prefaces* usually provided: a firmer chronology. To this obvious task Johnson brought his fascination with the course of life, especially a writer's life, and marked with empathy the stages of his subjects' poetic careers. For example, he characteristically notes the first attempt by Ambrose Philips, with verses on the death of Queen Mary, to "solicit the notice of the world"; Bell's compiler interrupts Cibber's *Lives*

33. As Table 1 shows, Bell's borrowing from Johnson was executed in fairly short order. A four month turn-around is noteworthy, given that the process was more involved than placing a book to be pirated into a compositor's hands. Once Johnson's text reached Edinburgh, the compiler had to gather whatever other sources were wanted, and printing could go forward only after the other coordinates of the series (establishing a schedule of successive poets and collecting the pertinent editions of their poems) had been plotted. In the light of these contingencies, the attention paid to Johnson's *Prefaces* seems to have been quite prompt.

34. Bell reprinted Johnson's *Life of Savage* in 1780, more than a year before the biography was incorporated into the *Prefaces*. Copyright protection of the work, first published in 1744, had long since expired. Strictly speaking, it falls outside the pattern of Bell's borrowings from the *Prefaces*.

of the Poets (TC), his primary source, to insert this bit of intelligence ([v]; *SJ* 1).

In addition to the biographical data so easily inserted into the prefaces, Bell's compiler made little grafts of the "characters" which were a feature even in some of Johnson's shorter prefaces. Examples of this borrowing are the thumbnail sketches of Tickell (xii; *SJ* 17) and Ambrose Philips (vii; *SJ* 34).

Of highest value on the biographical side of the ledger were the anecdotes. As a companion of Collins, for instance, Johnson had seen "the guineas safe in his hand" from an advance he accepted for translating Aristotle's *Poetics*; he knew also that, the bargain never fulfilled, Collins had returned the sum. In abbreviated form (and minus the occular testimony), this anecdote becomes a footnote in Bell (ix; *SJ* 5). Johnson related a story told by Dodsley, who had sought Pope's opinion of *The Pleasures of Imagination* in manuscript: "this [is] no every-day writer," Pope advised him, a comment that finds its way via the *Prefaces* into Bell's life of Akenside (ix; *SJ* 4). In his life of Smith, Johnson tells how the unlucky poet died from taking a self-prescribed medicine against his apothecary's warning; how Addison asked Smith to write a history of the revolution; and how the poet had no part in corrupting the text of Clarendon's history. All this Johnson had on the authority of his friend Gilbert Walmsley, who had known Smith, and it winds up in Bell (vi–vii, x; *SJ* 43, 57–59, 71, 56). Firsthand knowledge of Collins, Dodsley's report of what Pope had said, conversations with an acquaintance of Smith— by these means Johnson preserved the kind of biographical detail he prized most, the volatile and evanescent impressions which are lost forever if not set down in print. In seizing upon them Bell's compiler attests to their currency and appeal.

Relative to the supply of such anecdotes, however, the *Prefaces* offered a greater fund of critical opinions. From this storehouse dozens of Johnsonian renderings were pilfered. Bell's compiler interrupts *TC*'s discussion of Rowe's *The Fair Penitent* to distill (rather awkwardly) Johnson's appraisal of the drama, "one of the most pleasing tragedies on the stage, of which it still keeps, and probably will long keep, possession, the story being of a domestick nature, the fable interesting, and the language delightful" (xiii; *SJ* 7). Johnson's critical estimate of *The Royal Convert* is also introduced: "The fable of this play is taken from dark and barbarous times, and the scene is native, being laid among our ancestors. Rhodogune is a character highly tragical, vicious with a mind that must have been truly heroick if formed to virtue" (xiv–xv; *SJ* 11). Where stronger praise is offered, Johnson's words are often quoted directly and attributed to him, as when he praises Rowe's Lucan as "one of the greatest productions of English poetry" (xviii; *SJ* 35). The approach is similar in the life of Ambrose Philips. Johnson lurks anonymously in paraphrase where the poet's "epitome of Hacket's Life of Williams has been thought destitute of spirit"; on the other hand, his epithet for *The Freethinker*, which "Dr. Johnson styles his happiest undertaking," is openly acknowledged (xvi, xvii; *SJ* 5, 28).

Some of Johnson's less favorable assessments were mitigated. The frankness in his appraisal of Tickell, for instance, was carefully excised.

SJ: Of the poems yet unmentioned the longest is *Kensington Gardens*, of which the versification is smooth and elegant, but the fiction unskilfully compounded of Grecian Deities and Gothick Fairies. Neither species of those exploded Beings could have done much, and when they are brought together, they only make each other contemptible. (17)

JB: Kensington Garden is the longest of our Author's poems. The fiction is compounded partly of Grecian deities and partly of Gothick Fairies. The versification is harmonious, and the language elegant. (viii)

The compiler overlooks the sarcasm about "exploded Beings," ignores the adverb "unskilfully," and adorns what little praise Johnson admits, pairing "language" with "versification" and promoting the versification from "smooth" to "harmonious." Johnson's dismissal of two tragedies by Ambrose Philips as being "not below mediocrity, nor above it" (35) elicits an oblique refutation. In reference to some other poems, Bell's compiler counters that "though they reach not excellence they are yet above mediocrity" (xxii). Even if commercial expedience, not conviction, is the spur to this merest of critical disagreements, as an answer to the *Prefaces* it offers an early hint of the polemical engagement that so often defined the reception of Johnson's text.

In more accomplished hands the interweaving and footnoting of Johnson might have been a seamless process. But, no doubt for reasons of haste and uncertainty, ragged edges are sometimes obvious. Where Johnson and Langhorne record different years for an event in Collins's life, Bell's text gives both (viii). More glaringly, text and footnote in the life of Smith are at war over the question of his student days at Oxford. The main narrative, copied from *TC*, lauds Smith for his talents and fails to mention his expulsion from the university. This unflattering episode, condensed out of *SJ* (30, 35–36, 40), is added in a footnote. The compiler tries lamely to mute the dissonance: "We must observe in this note, notwithstanding of what is said in the text, that the indecency of Smith's behavior" caused him to be expelled (v). Incoherently, the matter is left at that.

Confronted with a similar discrepancy, Johnson would have ruminated over the credibility of his sources. This example underscores the quality that could not be transferred to Bell's lives: a strong voice, an idiosyncratic authorial presence. In the life of John Philips, for example, Johnson corrects a mistaken attribution: "The inscription at Westminster was written, as I have heard, by Dr. *Atterbury*, though commonly given to Dr. *Freind*" (8). Bell's compiler follows the sentence word for word, but deletes the incidental "as I have heard" (xxxviii). Johnson's colloquial presence is masked in other cases with anonymous phrases like "it is said" or "we are told," substitutions which preserve the cadences of oral history but efface its authority.

More analysis is needed on this topic, but what I have done presently is enough to call attention to the compiler's unique perspective on Johnson's *Prefaces*. His assignment was to organize various sources as efficiently as possible into more or less coherent prefaces. Because this was the task faced by

Johnson, the record of what Bell's compiler selected from the *Prefaces*, and what he altered, is a critique of their practical appeal. While Johnson's reviewers went their heated ways, the utilitarian compiler identified materials that were of immediate value for adding interest or depth to his compilations. While these borrowings were neither sustained nor consistent, they comprise an important chapter in the early reception of the *Prefaces*.

III
"A Connected System of Biography"

Bell conceived of his series as a repository of English classics. Suitable to the ceremony implicit in such an undertaking, the poets were to be presented in full dress, one element of which was the prefatory life, or "biographical and critical account of each author."[35] Instead of the various and sometimes prolix formulae that had dotted eighteenth-century title-pages, Bell settled for a simple, uniform phrase: "The Life of . . . ." As no other poetic reprint series had included this feature, much less cultivated this degree of formality,[36] the credit for innovation belongs to Bell.

It was natural, Bell asserted, for readers to "wish to know something of the man who entertains and edifies [them]." This curiosity he thought had been neglected, "the lives of but few of our poets being transmitted to the public along with their writings." To remedy this defect his prefaces were meant to "convey to posterity the most authentic anecdotes relative to those eminent men, whose writings are the object of the present undertaking; and by thus forming a connected system of biography, so far as relates to this particular class of writers, bring the reader acquainted at once with the poet and the man."[37] Not only was each life to illuminate the connection between writer and human being; the lives taken as a whole were to form a literary history, a "connected system" to advance our understanding of poets and poetry.

Unlike the proprietors of *The Works of the English Poets*, Bell had too little capital to commission a famous writer to undertake a series of fifty lives; and it made no sense to get one who was not famous. Besides, as the proprietors found out, original composition brings a greater risk of delay. It was better, in Bell's mind, to stress "authentic materials"—that is, to reprint earlier lives in full, or to rely on hackwork to weave and patch together divers materials.

Table 2 categorizes the sources for Bell's lives. The taxonomy of Pat Rogers proves helpful: "single" lives indicate those published independently or prefixed to the author's works; "general" lives denote entries in universal or national dictionaries of biography; and "authorial" lives come from spe-

35. *Morning Post*, 16 May 1777, p. 1.
36. Robert and Andrew Foulis's series of English poets in pot 12mo (48 vols.; Glasgow, 1765–76), William Creech's *British Poets* (44 vols.; Edinburgh, 1773–76) and John Boyle's *English Poets* (20 vols.; Aberdeen, 1776–78).
37. Advertisement printed at the back of John Dryden, *The Spanish Fryar* (London, 1777), sig. H5^v.

cialized collections concerned exclusively with writers.[38] In Table 2 and the collations below, the following abbreviations refer to three general and three authorial sources:

AO   Anthony à Wood, *Athenæ Oxonienses,* 2nd ed., 2 vols. (London, 1721).

BB   *Biographia Britannica,* 6 vols. (London, 1747–66): vol. 1 (1747), vol. 2 (1748), vol. 3 (1750), vol. 4 (1757), vol. 5 (1760), vol. 6, part 1 (1763), vol. 6, part 2 (1766).

BD   *A New and General Biographical Dictionary,* 12 vols. (London, 1761–67).

TC   Theophilus Cibber, *The Lives of the Poets,* 5 vols. (London, 1753). "*TC*" honors the nominal author, who wrote less of the work than Robert Shiels.[39]

CP   David Erskine Baker, *A Companion to the Play-House,* 2 vols. (London, 1764).

SJ   Samuel Johnson, *Prefaces, Biographical and Critical, to the Works of the English Poets,* 10 vols. (London, 1779–81).[40]

Table 2 reveals a strong emphasis on single lives and multiple sources at the outset of the series: the first poets being more famous, single lives of them were more common; and some of these lives having a reputation of their own, Bell had promotional reasons for using them. Equally noteworthy in the later phase, once the final volumes of the *Prefaces* had been published, is the persistent recourse to Johnson.

Bell's connected system of biography is detailed below, in alphabetical order by poet. The entries will take the following form:

Source(s). Where the compiler has drawn on more than one text, the first listed is the primary source, with the others ranked in descending order of importance. Unless otherwise noted, the sources are London imprints. Note: if a text had seen more than one edition, it is virtually impossible to know which one the compiler used. For that reason it makes no sense to insist upon either first editions or the last one prior to Bell, nor to clutter the record with bibliographical details easily obtained elsewhere. I will list only the edition I used to collate Bell's text.

Collation. This record details the sources used to construct Bell's text page-

38. Pat Rogers, "Johnson's *Lives of the Poets* and the Biographic Dictionaries," *Review of English Studies* N.S. 31 (1980): 149–171, esp. p. 150. An expanded definition of "single lives" is warranted for Table 2, for I include in this category non-biographical features that perform the office of introducing the author's works. Bell's prefaces, like Johnson's, were meant to be critical as well as biographical; and because a critical notice attached to the works plays a parallel role to the single life thus situated, it makes sense to grant it the same status. This definition applies to sources connected with Armstrong, Broome, Butler, Chaucer, Dyer, Hammond, Parnell and Waller.

39. For sifting through the authorship of this work see *SJ* Hammond 1; Walter Raleigh, *Six Essays on Johnson* (Oxford, 1910), pp. 120–125; and William R. Keast, "Johnson and 'Cibber's' *Lives of the Poets,* 1753," in *Restoration and Eighteenth-Century Literature: Essays in Honor of Alan Dugald McKillop,* ed. Carroll Camden (Chicago, 1963), pp. 89–101.

40. Whether for the later borrowings the compiler might have had in hand not the *Prefaces* but *The Lives of the Most Eminent English Poets,* 4 vols. (London, 1781) is a question I have not decided.

TABLE 2
Kinds of Sources for Bell's Lives

Poet	Single Lives No. of Sources	General Lives			Authorial Lives			No. of Other Sources	No "Life" in Bell
		AO	BB	BD	TC	CP	SJ		
Milton	2							1	
Pope					TC				
Dryden			BB		TC				
Butler	2							1	
Prior	1								
Thomson	1							1	
Gay	1		BB						
Waller	3	AO	BB		TC			3	
Young	1			BD				2	
Cowley	1								
Spenser	1								
Parnell	2							2	
Congreve			BB		TC				
Swift	3							3	
Addison					TC				
Shenstone	1								
Churchill	1							1	
Pomfret	1				TC				
Donne	1								
Garth					TC				
Denham (1779)			BB				SJ		
Denham (1780)		AO	BB				SJ		
Hughes	1						SJ		
Fenton			BB		TC				
Dyer	1								
Lansdowne					TC			1	
Buckingham			BB						
Savage	1								
Roscommon					TC		SJ		
Mallet						CP			
Somerville									NL
Collins	1						SJ		
Hammond	1						SJ	*	
Cunningham								*	
Broome	1						SJ	2	
King			BB		TC				
Rowe			BB		TC		SJ		
Tickell					TC		SJ		
Akenside			BB				SJ		
Lyttelton	1						SJ	1	
West, G.							SJ		
Philips, J.	1		BB				SJ		
Philips, A.					TC		SJ		
Moore						CP		2	
Armstrong	1								
Smith					TC		SJ		
Watts	1								
Pitt					TC		SJ		
Gray	1							1	
West, R.									NL
Chaucer	1		BB						

*Bell's "Life" is original; see collation.

by-page. The term *Bell* indicates the opening page(s) of the life, expressed in Arabic or Roman numerals according to Bell's usage. (Parentheses around numerals indicate footnotes.) What follows the colon is a list of sources for those pages, with a slash mark (/) to designate each interruption. The initial *Bell* is not repeated; progress through the text, consequently, is marked by page numbers which stand alone. By contrast, the page numbers of the sources are always accompanied by a two-letter abbreviation: usually the author's initials, but where that is not possible, a two-letter abstract of the title (and where this could be confusing, the list of sources provides the abbreviation assigned it). Numerals after *SJ* refer to paragraphs; those after the other abbreviations are page numbers. A hyphen between numerals (231–233) suggests continuous copying; a comma (3, 4) represents a more selective gathering. Where *BB* is concerned, the main text is cited with numerals, the footnotes with capital letters in brackets, and marginal notes in parentheses.[41] If the numerals are missing (as in "*TC* 35 / *SJ* 11 / *TC* / *SJ*"), the compiler has returned to the last page or paragraph cited from that text. When multiple pages are listed for *Bell* (as in "vi–vii"), the first source cited supplies the text which bridges the page.

Comments. Next I note how the sources were used (reprinted, paraphrased, abridged, etc.), along with any quirks in the compilation. Parenthetical citations refer to the page numbers in *Bell*.

Acknowledgement. Where a source text is cited by Bell, however cryptically, I make a note of it. Acknowledgements within a source text—that is, to its own sources, prior to *Bell*'s compilation—are not recorded.

ADDISON. *TC* 3:305–320. *Bell* [v]–xxiii. Reprint, with two minor adjustments. *TC*, published two years before Johnson's *Dictionary*, regrets that "our language yet wants the assistance of so great a master, in fixing its standard, settling its purity, and illustrating its copiousness, or elegance"; the anachronism failed to register with the compiler (xix; *TC* 316). In the life of Roscommon, by contrast, the compiler brought up to date *TC*'s anticipation of "an English Dictionary, long expected, by Mr. Johnson" (x; 2:348).

AKENSIDE. *BB* 1:103–107 (2nd ed., 1778); and *SJ*. *Bell* [v]: *BB* 103 / *SJ* 2–3 / vi–vii: *BB* 104 / *SJ* 10 / *BB* [C], 104 / *SJ* 11 / vii–viii: *BB* 104–105 / *SJ* 13 / viii–ix: *BB* 105, [D], 105, [E] / *SJ* 14, 4 / ix–xiv: *BB* [F] / *SJ* 14, 20 / xiv–xv: *BB* [F] / *SJ* 23, 24 / xv–xvi: *BB* [G]. Quotation and paraphrase. *BB* serves as the framework; *SJ* donates some biographical details; critical assessments from *SJ* are liberally interpolated, sometimes in quotation marks. Acknowledgement: *BB* cited twice (x, xiv); *SJ* credited twice (xiv, xv).

ARMSTRONG. Untitled preface to *Miscellanies; by John Armstrong, M.D.*, 2 vols. (1770), 1:[iii]–[v]. *Bell* [v]–vi. Reprint. Called an "Advertisement," not "The Life of John Armstrong."

41. The footnotes in *BB* are granted special attention: given their length and digressive tendency, the compiler had to deliberate—whether to adopt or ignore, abbreviate or copy in full, interweave with the narrative or leave as a note. With the occasional footnotes in other sources, it is assumed they have been brought along into *Bell* and rest at the bottom of the page.

BROOME. *SJ* (Broome, Pope, and Fenton); [*OH*] *The Odyssey of Homer*, 5 vols. (1725–26); Alexander Pope, *The Works of Alexander Pope Esq.*, ed. William Warburton, 9 vols. (1751); and William Broome, "The Preface: Being an Essay on Criticism," *Poems on Several Occasions* (1727), pp. [1]–17. *Bell* [v]: *SJ* B.1, 2, 3, 4 / *SJ* P.86 / [v]–vi: *SJ* B.5 / *SJ* F.10 / *SJ* B.6 / *SJ* P.130 / (vi): *SJ* P.129, 134 / vi–vii: *SJ* B.6 / *OH* 5:260–261 / *SJ* B.6, 7 / vii–viii: *AP* 5:219 / *SJ* B.8 / *SJ* P.254 / *SJ* B.9 / (viii):*WB* 3 / ix: *SJ* B.11 / *WB* 16–17 / ix–x: *SJ* B.12–14, 15. Paraphrase, slightly abridged, with interweaving from *SJ*'s lives of Fenton and Pope, a note from *AP*, and WB's preface to his poems and postscript to his notes for *OH*.

BUCKINGHAM. *BB* 6:3653–3666. *Bell* [v]–xxviii. Reprint of body of *BB*, with footnotes [A], [F], [L], [O], [Q], [T], [X], [Z], [CC], [EE], [GG], [HH], [II] and [LL] in full, and abbreviated versions of [D], [R], [S], [BB] and [KK]. Since *BB* presents a continuous block of text, *Bell* introduces paragraph breaks. (True for lives of Chaucer and King as well.)

BUTLER. [*AL*] "The Author's Life" and [*ZG*] "Preface," *Hudibras*, 2 vols., ed. Zachary Grey (Cambridge, 1744), 1:[iv]–xiv, [i]–xxxvi; and *Genuine Remains*, 2 vols., ed. Robert Thyer (1759). *Bell* [7]–10: *AL* [iv]–viii / (10): *ZG* xxxiv / 11–14: *AL* viii–xiii / (14): *RT* 1:[i] / 15: *AL* xii–xiv / (15): *RT* 1:(145) / 16: *ZG* xxxiv. Reprint of *AL*, taken from an earlier edition of *Hudibras*,[42] along with Grey's footnotes, the epitaph from *ZG*, and two additional footnotes drawn from *RT*. *Bell* performs a tiny surgery on *AL*. "[T]here being several particular persons reflected on, which are not commonly known," the writer had cautioned, "*and some old stories and uncouth Words which want explication*, we have thought fit to do right to their memories; and . . . to explain their characters in some additional Annotations" (*AL* ix–x). The phrase I highlight was strategically omitted (*Bell* 12); it was expected that little known personages should require a footnote, but not acceptable to characterize parts of the text as old and uncouth.

CHAUCER. *BB* 2:1293–1308; and Thomas Tyrwhitt, "An Abstract of the Historical Passages of the Life of Chaucer," *The Canterbury Tales of Chaucer*, 5 vols. (1775–78), 1:xxiv–xxxvi. *Bell* [vii]–lxv: *BB* 1293–1308 / [lxvi]–lxxvi: *TT* 1:xxiv–xxxvi. Reprint of *BB*, with some interpolation of marginal notes; all the footnotes are used except [L] and [N] (on *The Testament of Love* and *The Conclusions of the Astrolabie*); from [B] and [P] the poetic stanzas are dropped. To "The Life of Geoffrey Chaucer" proper is appended *TT*. Acknowledgement: *TT* is cited by title "from Tyrwhitt's edit. 1775" ([lxvi]).

CHURCHILL. "Memoirs of the Rev. Mr. Charles Churchill," *The Annual Register* (1764), pp. 58–62; and Charles Johnstone, *Chrysal: or, The Adventures of a Guinea*, 3rd ed., 4 vols. (London, 1768), 4:90–96. *Bell* [v]–xiii: *AR* 58–62 / xiii–xxii: *CJ* 90–96. Reprint of *AR*, to which is appended the excerpt from *CJ*, introduced as "an anecdote frequently told of him" but with the following caveat: "leaving the credit due to the story, which is much to the honour of humanity, with the reader" (xiii). The sentimental anecdote recounts an act of generosity, the guinea's "master" lifting a family out of financial misery. Acknowledgement: "Chrysal, vol. I. chap. 21" (xiii), by which is meant chapter 21 of the first book in vol. IV.

COLLINS. John Langhorne, "Memoirs of the Author," *The Poetical Works of Mr. William Collins* (1771), pp. i–xv; and *SJ*. *Bell* [v]–vi: *JL* i–v / (vi): *SJ* 1 / vii–viii: *JL* v–viii / *SJ* 4 / viii–ix: *JL* viii–xi / (ix): *SJ* 4, 5 / x: *JL* xi–xiii / (x): *SJ* 5 / xi–xii: *JL* xiii–xv. Reprint of *JL*. Unable to resolve a discrepancy between *JL* and *SJ* over the

---

42. First published with the edition of 1704, it is tentatively ascribed to Sir James Astrey (*New Cambridge Bibliography of English Literature*, ed. George Watson, 5 vols. [Cambridge, 1969–77], 2:437).

year WC left Oxford for London, *Bell* adds "or 1744" (*SJ*'s guess) to *JL*'s "1743" (viii). The only other disruptions of *JL*'s text are the typographical symbols for four brief footnotes derived from *SJ*. These notes, couched in *SJ*'s words, concern the occupation of WC's father, WC's proposals for the *History of the Revival of Learning*, the advance he obtained to translate the *Poetics*, and the amount he inherited from his uncle. *Bell* uses the 1771 text of *JL*, which eliminates (from the first edition of 1765) an ad hominem attack on Andrew Millar for being "a favourer of genius, *when once it has made its way to fame*" (xi).

CONGREVE. *TC* 4:83–98; and *BB* 3:1439–1449. *Bell* [v]–xix: *TC* 83–95 / xix: *BB* [P] / xix–xx: *TC* 95, 98. Quotation. Inserted from *BB* is the inscription on Congreve's monument. What *Bell* omits from *TC* (95–97) is the poem "Of Improving the Present Time," which *TC* prints from *BB* 1447. Also deleted from *TC* are two negative opinions: after the mention that WC's pastoral elegy on the death of Queen Mary had been "extolled in the most lavish terms of admiration," *TC* adds "but which seems not to merit the incense it obtained" (xi; *TC* 88); and in summary of WC's piecemeal translations of the "Art of Love," *The Iliad*, and some epigrams, *TC* notes "in all which he was not unsuccessful, though at the same time he has been exceeded by his cotemporaries [*sic*] in the same attempts" (xv; *TC* 91).

COWLEY. Thomas Sprat, "An Account of the Life and Writings of Mr. Abraham Cowley. Written to Mr. M. Clifford," *The Works of Mr. Abraham Cowley* (1668), sigs. A1ʳ–A2ᵛ, a1ʳ–e2ᵛ. *Bell* [v]–xl. Reprint. Although *Bell* changes the title to "The Life of Abraham Cowley" (for consistency), he retains "Written to Mr. Clifford." Acknowledgement: "T. Sprat" (xl).

CUNNINGHAM. *Bell* [v]–xi. This life is largely independent of any prior account I can locate. The "Memoirs of the Late Mr. John Cunningham," *London Magazine* 42 (1773): 495–497, was surmised by Henry Morse Stephens to have been the sole authority for the lives attached to the editions of Bell, "Johnson" (1790), Cook (1795) and Chalmers (1810).[43] This is untrue, so far as it concerns *Bell*, which contains much information not available in the "Memoirs."

DENHAM (1779). *SJ*; and *BB* 3:1646–1648. *Bell* [v]: *SJ* 1–2 / *BB* 1646 / *SJ* / *BB* / *SJ* 3 / *BB* / *SJ* 4 / *BB* / *SJ* / vi: *BB* / *SJ* 5–6 / *BB* / *SJ* / *BB* / *SJ* 8 / *BB* / *SJ* 7, 9 / *BB* [A] / *SJ* / vii: *SJ* 10 / *BB* 1646, (d), 1646 / *SJ* / *BB* / *SJ* / (vii–viii): *BB* [B] / vii–viii: *SJ* 11–12 / *BB* 1646 / viii–ix: *SJ* 13, 14 / *BB* 1647 / *SJ* 14–15 / *BB* 1647, [E] / (ix): *BB* [D] / ix–x: *SJ* 15 / *BB* 1647 / *SJ* 16 / *BB* / *SJ* 17 / *BB* / *SJ* 17, 18, 19 / x–xi: *BB* / *SJ* / *BB* / *SJ* 20, 19 / *BB* 1648 / xi–xii: *SJ* 21–24, 26, 25 / xiii–xviii: *SJ* 27–42. Quotation of *SJ* with extensive interpolation from *BB*. See discussion of this piracy in Part I.

DENHAM (1780). *SJ*; *BB* 3:1646–1648; and *AO* 2:422–424. *Bell* [v]: *BB* 1646 / *AO* 422 / *BB* / *AO* / [v]–vi: *BB* / *SJ* 5 / *BB* / *AO* / *SJ* 6 / *BB* / *SJ* 8 / *AO* 423 / *SJ* / vi–vii: *SJ* 7 / *BB* [G], 1646, [A], 1646, (d), 1646 / *SJ* 10 / *BB* / *SJ* / *BB* 1646, [B] / vii–viii: *BB* / *SJ* 11, 12 / viii–ix: *BB* 1646, [C], 1646–1647, [D] / *SJ* 14 / *BB* 1747, [E] / ix–x: *SJ* 15 / *BB* 1647 / *SJ* 17 / *BB* 1647, [G] / x–xi: *SJ* 17–20 / *BB* 1648 / *AO* 424 / *BB* / xi–xii: *SJ* 21, 36–38, 36 / xiii–xiv: *SJ* 39–42 / xiv–xv: *SJ* 21–24, 26, 27, 29, 28 / xvi–xviii: *SJ* 30, 32–34, 42. Paraphrase of Denham (1779), with constant checking of (and new borrowings from) *BB* and *SJ*, including the effort to consult *AO* directly. The critical section is restructured. SJ proceeds first by genre ("descriptive, ludicrous, didactic, and sublime," though not in that order), turns to consider poetic style, and concludes by summing up the "petty faults" of JD's "first productions." *Bell* now begins with the versification, moves on through the faults, and finishes with the survey of genres. See discussion in Part I.

43. *Dictionary of National Biography*, 5:313–314.

DONNE. Izaak Walton, "The Life of Dr. John Donne," *The Lives of Dr. John Donne, Sir Henry Wotton, Mr. Richard Hooker, Mr. George Herbert* (1670), pp. [9]–88. *Bell* [v]–lxvi: *IW* 12–81. Reprint, minus "The Introduction" and three poetic tributes. IW's life, first printed in 1640, was expanded three times—in 1658, 1670 and 1675. The penultimate text, by accident or design, is copied by *Bell*. Had the final edition been used, *Bell* might have been prompted to omit one lengthy addition on the same grounds that mention of Dryden's astrology was suppressed (see next collation): the story of JD's vision of his wife, about which even IW feels it necessary to apologize. Acknowledgement: "J.W." (lxvi).

DRYDEN. *TC* 3:64–94; and *BB* 3:1749–1761. *Bell* [5]: *TC* 64 / *BB* 1749 / [5]–21: *TC* 64–74, 76–80, 82–83 / 21: *BB* 3:1760–1761 / 21–26: *TC* 83–93. Quotation. Most of *TC* has been reprinted, with short interpolations from *BB* for details of JD's family, and with some corrections, a slight re-ordering, and significant omissions. *Bell* omits six passages in *TC* that tarnish JD's reputation slightly: the mention of a distich, admitted to be "downright nonsense," which "expos'd our poet to the ridicule of the wits" (65); Burnet's character of JD, confessed to be deficient in "true resemblance" (74–76); the comment that "Mac Flecknoe" prompted Pope's *Dunciad*, "and it must be owned the latter has been more happy in the execution of his design" (76); a footnote implying that JD's translation of Virgil had been surpassed by Dodsley's (77); Dr. Trap's low estimate of JD's Virgil, with mention of Trap's own dullness (78); and a story revealing JD to be "fond of Judicial Astrology," and cautious lest anyone find out, "either thro' fear of being reckoned superstitious, or thinking it a science beneath his study" (80–82). Inexplicably, *Bell* also omits the praise of "Ode on St. Cecilia's Day" as being "justly esteemed one of the most elevated in any language" (79).

DYER. "Advertisement," *Poems. By John Dyer, L.L.B.* (1761), pp. [iii]–v. *Bell* [v]–vi. Reprint. Called "The Life of John Dyer" for conformity's sake, but nothing more than an "advertisement" with a few dates and a general character.

FENTON. *TC* 4:164–177; and *BB* 6.ii:50–52. *Bell* [v]–xvi: *TC* 164–173 / *BB* [D]. Reprint of *TC*, excluding the final bibliography and a "specimen" of EF's poetry, obviously superfluous for *Bell*. Pope's epitaph for EF is appended, taken from the life of EF included in the supplement to *BB*.

GARTH. *TC* 3:263–272. *Bell* [v]–xiv. Reprint, omitting one poetic specimen, an unflattering phrase, and a reference to Tonson's edition of SG's works.

GAY. "An Account of the Life and Writings of the Author," *The Works of Mr. John Gay*, 4 vols. (Dublin, 1770), 1:i–xvi; and *BB* 4:2182–2188. *Bell* [5]–9: *WG* i–v / (9): *BB* [I] / 9–10: *WG* v / (10): *BB* [L] / 10–11: *WG* vi / (11): *BB* [O] / 11–12: *WG* vi–vii, viii / (12): *BB* [Q], [R] / 12–18: *WG* x–xiii, xv–xvi, xv, xiv. Quotation of *WG*, slightly rearranged, with the omission of 7ovv. concerning JG's "dissatisfaction with the court" (*WG* viii–ix). To the eight (out of nine) footnotes copied from *WG*, five more are added in *Bell*, all derived from *BB*. Only one offers new data and is honestly acknowledged: "*Biogr. Brit.*" ([L]). The others are gratuitous: three are created by omitting a sentence or clause arbitrarily from *WG* and moving the same information into a footnote with phrasing from *BB* ([I], [O], and [R]); the fourth is a footnote out of the blue [Q]. Acknowledgements at second hand from *BB*'s marginal citations are made for these tidbits, their transparent purpose being to enhance the diversity of *Bell*'s sources and to magnify the compiler's seeming industry: "Cibber's *Lives of the Poets*" ([I]), "*Intelligencer*, No. III" ([O], [Q]), and "Cibber, the father, in his *Apology*, p. 144" ([R]). The attempt is farcical, however: two of the attributions (for [I] and [Q]) are mistaken; the compiler has tracked the wrong numbers into the margin.

GRAY. William Mason, "Memoirs of the Life and Writings of Mr. Gray," *The Poems of Mr. Gray* (York, 1775), pp. [1]–416. *Bell* [v]: *WM* 2, 3 / ([v]): *WM* (119) / [v]–vi:

WM 3, 12, 13, 14, 16, 15, 4–5, 39, 40, (41) / vii: *WM* 41, 40, 97, 56, 97–98, 99–102, 114, 116, (116), 116, 41 / viii: *WM* 117–118, (119), 119 / viii–ix: *WM* 120, 121, 156, 123, 124 / (ix–x): *WM* (156), 168–169 / ix–x: *WM* 157 / x–xi: *WM* [*Poems* 60][44], 155–156, 156–157, 170 / xi–xiii: *WM* 171–172, 175, 177, 179, (184), 184, 188–189, 191, 192 / xiii–xv: *WM* 193–200 / xvi: *WM* (203), 205, (205), (210), 209, 211, 221, 222, 222–223, 226, (228) / (xvi): ? / xvi–xvii: *WM* 228, 229, 230, 232–233, 235, 237–238, (258), 256, (258) / (xvii): *WM* 229 / xvii–xviii: *WM* 258–259, 292, [*Poems* (62)], 292, (293), 293, 292, 293 / xviii–xix: *WM* (293), 308, 309–318, (318), 318, 327, 328, 331–332 / xix–xx: *WM* 334, 335, 336, 337, 338, 340 / xx–xxi: *WM* 339, 341, 342, 343 / xxi–xxii: *WM* 342 / ? / 348–349 / ? / (350–351), 394 / xxii–xxiii: *WM* 395, 396 / ? / 398–399 / xxiii–xxiv: *WM* 399–400 / ? / 264, 263, (385), 384 / ? . Paraphrase of *WM*, severely abridged, using both TG's letters and WM's narrative, with interpolations from at least one additional source. Whereas the summary of epistolary content can be terse (on pp. vii and xix the substance and tone of lengthy letters is reduced to a single sentence), the rendering of WM's narrative can be prolix ("While at school, he contracted a friendship with Mr. Horace Walpole and Mr. Richard West" [*WM* 3] becomes "During the time of Mr. Gray's continuance in this abode of the Muses he contracted the strictest intimacy with two of their votaries, whose dispositions in many respects were congenial with his own" [v]). The final paragraph is a short rejoinder to "the attacks of envy and rancour," probably an allusion to *SJ*'s criticisms: "If Mr. Gray was not a poet of the first order there is no poetry existing; and if his boldest expressions be nonsense [cp. *SJ* 33], so are the best passages of Shakespeare and Milton, and the sublimest figures of divine inspiration" (xxiv).

HAMMOND. James Hammond, *Love Elegies* (1743); and *SJ. Bell* ([v]): *SJ* 3 / vi: *LE* iv, iii / vii: *LE* iii, iv, iii / ix: *LE* / x: *LE*. This collation is incomplete. Except for a few gleanings from *LE* and the footnote based on *SJ*'s information about the relationship of JH's mother to Sir Robert Walpole, this life is original to *Bell*. The writer, who knows more than can be gleaned from *SJ* or Lord Chesterfield's preface to *Love Elegies*, confesses a personal disappointment unparalleled elsewhere in Bell's *Poets*: "The writer of this Narrative hoped, about three years ago, to have drawn from [Miss Catharine Dashwood], by means of a lady her friend, a more satisfactory account; but she entreated that no questions might be asked her on so distressing a subject" (ix–x). The chance was irretrievable, for Miss Dashwood died on 17 February 1779 (vii). Acknowledgement: "Dr. Johnson informs us . . ." ([v]).

HUGHES. William Duncombe, "An Account of the Life and Writings of John Hughes, Esq.," *Poems on Several Occasions. With Some Select Essays in Prose*, 2 vols. (1735), 1:[i]–xxxvii; and *SJ. Bell* [v]: *WD* i–ii / [v]–vi: *WD* v–vi, xxix, vi / *SJ* 4 / vi–vii: *WD* vii–viii / *SJ* 4 / vii–xiii: *WD* viii–xv / *SJ* 6 / *WD* / *SJ* / *WD* / *SJ* 7 / *WD* xxix / xiii–xiv: *WD* xv–xvi / *SJ* 8 / *WD* / *SJ* 9 / *WD* / xiv–xv: *WD* xxxi, xvii–xviii / *SJ* 10 / *WD* / *SJ* / xv–xvi: *WD* / *SJ* / *WD* xxxiii / xvi–xvii: *WD* xix / *SJ* 12, 13 / xvii–xviii: *SJ* 14 / *WD* xxxvi / *SJ* 15 / xviii–xix: *WD* xxiv, ii–iii / *SJ* 16 / *WD* iii, xxv / xix–xxvi: *WD* xxxvii–xlvii. Quotation mixed with paraphrase of *WD*, rearranged, with largely verbatim interpolations from *SJ*. *WD*'s preface includes Richard Steele's essay on JH from *The Theatre* (xxxviii–xlvii), which *Bell* takes also. After *WD* had "gone thro' the first Part of [his] Design" (xxix), he retraced his steps to discuss JH's translations and prose writings; *Bell* avoids this second chronology by inserting these materials into the initial account of JH's life.

KING. *BB* 4:2850–2856; and *TC* 3:228–235. Bell [v]–vi: *BB* 2850, [B] / ([v]–vi): *BB* [A] / vi–vii: *TC* 231 / (vi–ix): *BB* [B] / viii–xx: *BB* 2850–2854 / (ix–x): *BB* [C] / (x–

---

44. In Mason's edition there are two sequences of page numbers: a bracketed series for the *Memoirs* and an unbracketed series for the poems. Here Bell's compiler inserts the text of Gray's "Sonnet on the Death of Mr. Richard West," and on p. xviii interpolates some information from Mason's footnote. All other numerals in this collation refer to the bracketed series.

xi): *BB* [D] / (xii–xiv): *BB* [E] / (xiv–xv): *BB* [F] / (xvi–xix): *BB* [G] / (xix): *BB* [H] / (xx–xxi): *BB* [K] / xxi: *TC* 229–230 / xxi–xxii: *BB* [I] / (xxii): *BB* (o) / xxii–xxv: *BB* 2854–2855 / *TC* 233 / (xxiii–xxiv): *BB* [M] / (xxiv–xxvii): *TC* 233 / xxv–xxvii: *BB* 2855 / *TC* 234 / (xxvi): *BB* [N] / xxvii–xxviii: *BB* 2855, [O]. Quotation (with a few paraphrases) of full body of *BB* and all but two footnotes ([L] and [P], which are lists of WK's works); [I] and [O] are interpolated into the body of the text. Added from *TC* are some anecdotes and WK's character.

LANSDOWNE. *TC* 4:239–249. *Bell* [v]–x: *TC* 239–243 / x–xii: *TC* 246–248 / xii–xiii: ? / xiii–xiv: *TC* / ? / *TC* 248–249. Reprint of *TC* is complete except for one gap, an exchange of verses between Lansdowne and Elizabeth Higgins. Two interpolations surface from an unidentified source.

LYTTELTON. *SJ* (Lyttelton and Gilbert West); *The Annual Register* (1774), pp. 24–29; and *The Works of George Lord Lyttelton* (1775). *Bell* [v]: *SJ* 1 / *AR* 25 / *SJ* 1–2, 4 / *AR* 26 / *SJ* / *WL* 499 / *SJ* 6 / [v]–vi: *WL* 546 / *SJ* 11 / *AR* 27 / *SJ* / *AR* 28, 27 / *SJ* 9 / *AR* / vi–vii: *WL* 549–550 / *AR* 28 / *SJ* 10 / *AR* / *SJ* / *AR* / *SJ* 13, 30, 23 / vii–viii: *WL* 514 / *SJ* 23 / viii–xi: *SJ* 24–29, 3, 16, 12 / *SJ* W.5, W.6 / xi–xii: *SJ* 12, 19, 31. Paraphrase of *SJ*, abridged, rearranged, with additional materials interwoven from *AR*, *WL* and *SJ* West. Extra details are brought to *Bell* from an unidentified source. *SJ*'s error regarding the number of GL's daughters is corrected. Two of *SJ*'s critical comments are quoted using quotation marks; other *SJ* comments are introduced with "It is said" or "We are told" (vii, xi). Acknowledgement: *SJ* cited with reference to the error and the punctuated quotations (vi, x, xi).

MALLET. *CP* 2: sig. X1ʳ (*s.v.* MALLET, David, Esq.). *Bell* [v]–vi. Quotation, with some rearrangement. Called an "Advertisement," not "The Life of David Mallet." Dated "March 1780," the lone instance in *Bell* of the date of compilation being noted.

MILTON. Elijah Fenton, "The Life of Mr. John Milton" and [*PS*] "Postscript," *Paradise Lost* (1739), pp. [vii]–xvii and [xviii]–[xx]; Thomas Newton, "The Life of Milton," *Paradise Lost* (1749), pp. i–lxi; and Jonathan Richardson, *Explanatory Notes and Remarks on Milton's Paradise Lost* (1734). *Bell* [5]–7: *EF* [vii]–viii / (7–8): *TN* vi–viii / 7–13: *EF* viii–xii / (13–14): *JR* lxvi–lxvii / 13–20: *EF* xii–xvii / 21–24: *TN* lv–lvi, lvii–lviii / *PS* xx. Reprint of *EF* (first published 1725) with additional family details from *TN*, and footnoted with letters from *TN* (Wotton on travel), and *JR* (Milton on blindness). Acknowledgement: "Elijah Fenton" (20).

MOORE. *CP* 2: sig. Y6ʳ⁻ᵛ (*s.v.* MOORE, Mr. Edward); Edward Moore, "Preface," *Poems, Fables, and Plays, by Edward Moore* (1756), pp. v–vi and 417–418; and *The World*, 4 vols. (1763). *Bell* [v]: *CP* / *EM* vi / [v]–vi: *CP* / (vi): *EM* 417 / vi–vii: *EM* vi / *CP* / vii–viii: *TW* / *CP*. Quotation of *CP* with some rearranging, plus interpolations from *EM* and information from an edition of *TW*. Acknowledgement: "Preface to the quarto edition of his works in 1756" ([v]).

PARNELL. *Poems on Several Occasions* (1770) contains three separate sources: Oliver Goldsmith, "The Life of Thomas Parnell, D.D." (pp. i–xxxv); Alexander Pope, "To the Right Honourable, Robert, Earl of Oxford and Earl Mortimer" (pp. [i]–iii); and David Hume, "Mr. Hume's Essays, page 265" (sig. π2ᵛ); and "To the Reader," *The Posthumous Works of Dr. Thomas Parnell* (Dublin, 1758), pp. [iii]–vii [*sic* for vi]. *Bell* [v]–viii: *OG* i–vi, v / viii–xvii: *OG* vi–xv, xvii / xvii: *AP* ii / xvii–xviii: *OG* xxiii, xxvi / xviii–xxi: *OG* xxv–xxviii / xxi: *DH* / *OG* xxvii / xxi–xxii: *PW* iii–iv / *OG* xxix. Paraphrase, abridged; with interpolations from *PW*, *AP*, and *DH* ("Essay on Simplicity and Refinement").

PHILIPS, Ambrose. *TC* 5:122–142; and *SJ*. *Bell* [v]: *TC* 122 / *SJ* 1 / *TC* 122, 132–133 / *SJ* 25 / [v]–vi: *TC* / vi–vii: *SJ* 30, 31, 32, 33 / *TC* 142 / *SJ* / *TC* 139 / *SJ* 34 / vii–viii: *TC* 122 / *SJ* 3 / viii–xvi: *TC* 124–131, 133–134, 132 / *SJ* 5 / *TC* / *SJ* / xvi–xvii: *TC* / *SJ* 28, 29 / *TC* 134 / *SJ* 6 / xvii–xviii: *TC* / *SJ* 35 / xviii–xx: *TC* 134–137 /

SJ 26, 27 / xx–xxii: *TC* 137–138 / *SJ* 27, 35, 4. *TC* is quoted, paraphrased, and re-arranged; poetical specimens are left out; many interpolations from *SJ*. Acknowl-edgement: "Dr. Johnson" cited for a favorable opinion (xvii).

PHILIPS, John. George Sewell, "The Life of Mr. John Philips," *Poems on Several Occasions* (Glasgow, 1763), pp. [3]–28; *BB* 5:3353–3359; and *SJ*. *Bell* [v]: *GS* [3] / *BB* 3353 / *GS* / *BB* / ([v]): *SJ* 23 / [v]–vi: *BB* / *GS* / *BB* / *SJ* 3 / vi–vii: *BB* 3353, (c) / *GS* 4 / *BB* 3353 / *GS* / *BB* / *GS* / vii–viii: *BB* / viii–xii: *GS* 4–5, 6–8 / *BB* 3354, [B] / (xii): *BB* / xii–xiii: *GS* 9 / xiii–xiv: *BB* 3359, (q), 3359, [K] / xiv–xviii: *GS* 9–14 / *BB* 3354–3355 / (xviii–xxi): *BB* [D], [E] / *SJ* 11 / xix–xxi: *GS* / *BB* 3356 / xxi–xxii: *GS* 14–15 / (xxii–xxiv): *BB* 3356, [F] / *SJ* 12 / xxii–xxvii: *GS* 15–19 / (xxvii–xxix): *BB* 3354, [I] / xxviii–xxx: *GS* 19–20 / (xxx): *SJ* 15 / xxxi: *GS* 21 / (xxxi): *SJ* 14 / xxxi–xxxiv: *GS* 21–24 / *BB* [L] / (xxxiv): *BB* (15) / xxxv: *GS* / xxxv–xxxvi: *BB* 3358 / (xxxvi): *BB* [H] / xxxvi–xxxvii: *BB* 3358 / *GS* 25 / *BB* / xxxvii–xxxviii: *GS* 26 / *SJ* 8 / *BB* / xxxviii–xl: *SJ*. Quotation of *GS* (first published in 1712) with omissions, but also with exten-sive interpolations from *BB* and many excerpts from *SJ*. The *GS* is taken from a late edition, possibly the one I cite, as evident from a footnote not found in earlier edi-tions. Acknowledgement: *BB* mentioned (xx); *SJ* credited four times (xxi, xxiv, xxx, xxxi).

PITT. *TC* 5:298–307; and *SJ*. *Bell* [v]: *TC* 298 / *SJ* 1 / [v]–vi: *TC* / *SJ* 7 / *TC* 299 / *SJ* 11 / vi–xiv: *TC* 299–307. Reprint of *TC*; a place name, a date, and Pitt's epitaph interpolated from *SJ*.

POMFRET. Philalethes, "Some Account of Mr. Pomfret, and His Writings," *Poems upon Several Occasions* (Dublin, 1726), pp. [vii]–[ix]; and *TC* 3:218–227. *Bell* [v]–vii: *PH* [vii]–[viii] / *TC* 218–219 / viii–x: *PH* [viii]–[ix]. Quotation of *PH*. *Bell* apologizes for the "short narrative, dated in the 1724, which is all we have been able to collect relative to this poet or his works" ([v]); this is not strictly true, since JP's religious char-acter is adopted from *TC*. Acknowledgement: "1724. Philalethes" (x).

POPE. *TC* 5:219–252. *Bell* [5]–46. Quotation, with minor omissions. Acknowledge-ment: "Cibber's Lives" (46).

PRIOR. Samuel Humphreys, "Some Account of the Author," *Poems on Several Oc-casions*, 2 vols. (1767), 2:[xiii]–lxxii. *Bell* [v]–xxviii: *SH* [xiii]–xxi, xxiii, xxxiv–xliii. Reprint of *SH* (first published 1733–34), with these omissions: MP's "Preamble to the Patent" for the Earl of Dorset's being created a duke; an essay by Dennis, addressed to MP, on Roman satirists; and a set of thirteen poems addressed to MP. Acknowledge-ment: *SH* cited in a separate "Advertisement" ([xlviii]).

ROSCOMMON. *TC* 2:344–353; and *SJ*. *Bell* [v]–xiii: *TC* 344–350 / xiii–xvi: *SJ* 27–39. Reprint of *TC* (itself a near copy of Johnson's biography in *Gentleman's Maga-zine* 18 [1748]: 214–217) up to the criticism of the "Essay on Translated Verse," at which point the compiler switches to *SJ* and pirates the entire section of criticism.

ROWE. *TC* 3:272–284; *BB* 5:3520–3523; and *SJ*. *Bell* [v]: *TC* 272–273 / [v]–vi: *BB* [A] / *TC* / (vi): *BB* 3520, 3522 / vi–viii: *TC* 273–274 / *BB* [B] / *TC* / (viii–x): *TC* 274–275 / *BB* [C] / ix: *SJ* 5 / ix–x: *TC* / (x): *BB* [D] / x–xi: *TC* / (xi): *BB* / xi–xii: *SJ* 5 / xii–xiii: *TC* 275, 276 / *SJ* 7 / xiii–xiv: *TC* 276–277, 279 / *SJ* 14 / *TC* 277 / xiv–xv: *SJ* 11 / *TC* 278 / *SJ* 15 / xv–xvi: *TC* 278–279 / (xvi): *TC* / xvi–xvii: *BB* 3522, [H] / (xvii): *TC* 279–280 / xvii–xviii: *BB* / *TC* 284 / *SJ* 18 / *TC* 283 / (xviii–xix): *SJ* 35 / *BB* [G] / xviii–xix: *TC* 283–284 / *BB* 3521 / xix–xx: *TC* 280 / *BB* / xx–xxi: *TC* / *BB* / *TC* 281 / *BB* 3522, [I] / xxi–xxii: *TC* / *BB* 3522 / *TC* 282 / (xxii): *BB* [K] / xxiii–xxiv: *SJ* 23–26 / xxiv–xxv: *TC* 283 / *SJ* 27 / *BB* 3522–3523, [L]. Quotation; *TC* pro-vides the framework for elaborate interweaving, *BB* and *SJ* supplying the other strands. Acknowledgement: the compiler straightens out an error committed by the "Authors of the Biographia" (vi).

SAVAGE. Samuel Johnson, "Life of Savage," *The Works of Richard Savage*, 2 vols. (1777), 1:[5]–187. *Bell* [v]–cxlvi. Reprint of *SJ* from this edition, number 77b in Clarence Tracy's "Textual Introduction" to *Life of Savage* (Oxford, 1971), p. xxiii.

SHENSTONE. Robert Dodsley, "Preface," *The Works in Verse and Prose, of William Shenstone, Esq*, 3 vols. (1764–69), 1:[i]–viii. *Bell* [v]–x. Reprint; called "Preface," as in *RD*, not "The Life of William Shenstone." Acknowledgement: "R. Dodsley" (x).

SMITH. *TC* 4:303–312; and *SJ*. *Bell* [iii]: *TC* 303 / *SJ* 28 / [iii]–v: *TC* 303–304 / (v): *SJ* 30, 35, 36, 40 / v–vi: *TC* 305–306 / (vi–vii): *SJ* 43 / vii–viii: *TC* / (viii): *SJ* 48 / viii–x: *TC* 309–311 / *SJ* 56 / *TC* / (x): *SJ* 57, 58, 59, 71, 56 / x–xii: *TC* 311–312. Quotation, with omissions; place of birth and a few anecdotal footnotes supplied by *SJ*.

SOMERVILLE. No "Life," nor is there an "Advertisement" to explain the omission.

SPENSER. John Hughes, "The Life of Mr. Edmund Spenser," *The Works of Spenser*, 6 vols. (1750), 1:[i]–xvi. *Bell* [v]–xviii. Reprint of *JH* (first published in 1715).

SWIFT. John Hawkesworth, "An Account of the Life of the Reverend Jonathan Swift, D.D., Dean of St. Patrick's, Dublin," *The Works of Dr. Jonathan Swift*, 12 vols. (1756), 1:[1]–71; Lord Orrery, *Remarks on the Life and Writings of Dr. Jonathan Swift*, 3rd ed. (1752); Deane Swift, *An Essay upon the Life, Writings, and Character, of Dr. Jonathan Swift* (1755), which includes [*AP*] "The Appendix. The Family of Swift" (separately paginated [1]–52); Laetitia Pilkington, *Memoirs*, 2 vols. (Dublin, 1748); and Samuel Johnson, *Rambler* No. 60. *Bell* [v]–vi: *SJ* 5 / *JH* 2 / *OR* 5 / *DS* 7–8 / *OR* / *DS* 7–8 / vi–vii: *JH* 2–3 / *DS* 11 / vii–viii: *JH* / *DS* 12 / viii–ix: *JH* / *AP* 35 / ix–x: *JH* 3–4 / *LP* 1:55 / *JH* / x–xi: *JH* 4–5 / *DS* 26 / xi–xii: *JH* / *DS* / *JH* 5–6 / *OR* 10 / *JH* / *OR* 5 / *JH* / xii–xiii: *OR* / *JH* / *OR* 6–7 / xiii–xiv: *JH* / *OR* / xiv–xx: *JH* 6–12 / *OR* 21 / xx–xxi: *JH* / *AP* 49 / xxi–xxiii: *JH* 12–14 / *OR* 20 / *DS* 101–102 / *OR* 21 / xxiii–xxiv: *DS* 102–103 / *OR* / xxiv–xxv: *DS* 104, 112 / xxv–xxviii: *JH* 14–16 / *DS* 87 / xxviii–xxix: *JH* / *DS* 90 / xxix–xxxiii: *JH* 16–20 / xxxiii–xxxiv: *DS* 163 / *JH* / *DS* 163–164 / *JH* / xxxiv–xxxv: *DS* 322 / xxxv–xl: *JH* 20–24 / *DS* 326 / *JH* / xl–xli: *DS* 326–327 / xli–xliv: *JH* 25–27 / *DS* 258 / xliv–lxiv: *JH* 27–41 / lxiv–lxv: *DS* 191 / lxv–lxxii: *JH* 41–46 / (lxxii–lxxiii): *DS* 93, 94–95 / lxxii–lxxxi: *JH* 46–53 / (lxxxi): *DS* (189) [*sic* for 217] / lxxxi–ciii: *JH* 53–68 / *DS* 90 / ciii–cvii: *JH* 68–71 / cviii–cx: *OR* 3–4, 213, 43–44 / cx–cxvii: *DS* 359, 360–364, 365–366, 367, 368–369, 371–373 / cxvii–cxxxiv: *LP* 1:40–48, 49, 50, 51, 52–53, 54–55, 59–60, 61–67, 72–74, 56–57, 34–35, 36–37. Quotation of *JH*, with the marginal annotations in *JH* pointing towards some but not all of the passages in *OR* and *DS* for interpolation; prefatory remarks on biography from *SJ*. Acknowledgement: *SJ, OR, DS, LP* all mentioned.

THOMSON. Patrick Murdoch, "An Account of the Life and Writings of Mr. James Thomson," *The Works of James Thomson* (1762), pp. [i]–xx; and Joseph Warton, *An Essay on the Writings and Genius of Mr. Pope* (1756). *Bell* [v]–xiv: *PM* i–ix / (xiv–xvii): *JW* 1:41–49 / xiv–xxx: *PM* ix–xx. Reprint of *PM*; long quotation in a footnote of *JW*'s critical assessment of *The Seasons*. Acknowledgement: "an ingenious and elegant writer (*Essay on the writings and genius of Pope*)" for *JW* (xiv).

TICKELL. *TC* 5:17–23; and *SJ*. *Bell* [v]: *TC* 17 / *SJ* 1 / *TC* / *SJ* 4, 14 / [v]–vi: *TC* 18 / *SJ* 14 / vi–vii: *TC* 18, 19 / *SJ* 6 / vii–viii: *TC* 20 / *SJ* 13 / *TC* / *SJ* 17 / *TC* 22 / *SJ* 9 / viii–ix: *TC* 22 / *SJ* 10 / ix–x: *TC* 22–23 / x–xii: *SJ* 10–11 / *TC* 19 / *SJ* 16 / *TC* / *SJ* / *TC* 19, 23 / *SJ* 17. Quotation and paraphrase; organization of *TC* followed, with numerous insertions from *SJ*, both of fact and critical judgment.

WALLER. Percival Stockdale, "The Life of Edmund Waller," *The Works of Edmund Waller, Esq. in Verse and Prose* (1772), pp. [i]–lxv; [*HR*] Lord Clarendon, *The History of the Rebellion and Civil Wars in England*, 3 vols. (Oxford, 1707); Lord Clarendon, *The Life of Edward Earl of Clarendon* (Oxford, 1759); Sir Bulstrode Whitelocke, *Memorials of the English Affairs* (1732); [*PR*] "Preface to the second

Part of Mr. Waller's Poems; printed in the year 1690," *The Works of Edmund Waller, Esq. in Verse and Prose* (1772), pp. 229–234; Sir Francis Atterbury, "An Account of the Life and Writings of Edmond [*sic*] Waller, Esq.," *Poems, &c. Written upon Several Occasions, and to Several Persons* (1711), pp. [i]–lxxxii; *TC* 2:240–264; *BB* 6:4099–4115; and *AO* 2:24–25. *Bell* [v]: *PS* [i], vi / *AO* 2:25 / *PS* / *FA* iii / *PS* / *FA* / *PS* vi, vii / *BB* 4099 / [v]–vi: *PS* / *AO* 2:24 / *PS* / *FA* vii / vi–vii: *PS* viii, xii, ix / *BB* 4101 / *FA* xii / *PS* xiv / *FA* / vii–viii: *PS* xiv–xv, xiv / *FA* xi / *PS* xiii / *FA* / ix: *PS* xiv, xii–xiii, xii, xxii / *TC* 245 / ix–x: *FA* xix / *BB* [L] / *PS* / *FA* xix–xx / x–xii: *PS* xxii, xxv, xxvi, xxviii, xxv–xxvi, xxx, xxxi, xxxii, xxxiii, xxxiv / xii–xiv: *BW* 70 / xiv–xxx: *HR* 2.i:247–253, 257–260 / xxx–xxxi: *PS* xlvi, (xlvii), xlvii, xlviii, li / *BB* [Y] / *PS* lii / *TC* 253 / *BB* 4111 / xxxii: *PS* lv, liii, lvi, lviii / *TC* / *PS* / *TC* / *PS* / *TC* / *PS* / xxxii–xxxiii: *PS* lx, lxi / *TC* 254 / *PS* (lxi) / *TC* / *PS* (lxi), lxii / *BB* 4113 / *PS* / xxxiii–xxxvi: *LC* 24–25 / *PS* lxiv / xxxvi–xxxvii: *PR* 229, 230 / xxxvii–xxxviii: *PS* lxv, lxiii, lxv. Quotations from *PS* serve as a frame, with *BB* guiding the compiler to almost all the other sources. Threads from *AO*, *FA*, *BB* and *TC* are interwoven; *BW*, *HR*, *LC* and *PR* are good for lengthy interpolations. Acknowledgement: specific editions are cited for *BW* (xii) and *HR* (xiv); *AO* is mentioned (vi); *PS* is cited twice (ix, xxxvii).

WATTS. "The Preface, with Some Account of the Author's Life and Character," *The Works of the Late Reverend and Learned Isaac Watts*, 6 vols. (1753), 1:iii–x. *Bell* [v]–xviii. Reprint. Acknowledgement: "Taken from the Account of Dr. Watts's Life and Character prefixed to the quarto edition of his works in six vols. printed in 1753" ([v]).

WEST, Gilbert. *SJ*. *Bell* [v]: *SJ* 1–4, 9 / [v]–vi: *SJ* 5–6, 10, 5–6. Paraphrase of *SJ*, abridged and rearranged; one judgment from *SJ* quoted. Acknowledgement: "says Dr. Johnson" for the quoted opinion (vi).

WEST, Richard. "Advertisement": "The life of Mr. West was so short, and the events of it so few, that it was judged better to insert the anecdotes which remain of this hopeful youth in the preceding account of his friend than to reserve them for a detached article" ([1]). The friend was Thomas Gray, with whose poems West's are bound.

YOUNG. *BD* 12:511–516; [*LY*] "The Life of the Rev. Dr. Edward Young," *The Works of the Author of the Night-Thoughts*, 5 vols. (1773), 5:[v]–xvi; and [*WY*] other title-specific prefaces within the 1773 edition. *Bell* [v]: *BD* 511 / [v]–vii: *BD* 511–512 / *LY* vii / vii–viii: *BD* 513 / viii–ix: *WY* 1:73 / *LY* ix–x / *BD* 514 / *LY* ix / ix–xi: *LY* x–xi, xii / *WY* 5:[3] / xii: *BD* 515 / *WY* 5:[83] / *BD* / *LY* / xii–xiii: *BD* / (xiii): *LY* (xiii) / xiii–xiv: *BD* 515–516 / xiv–xv: *LY* xv / *BD* 516 / *LY* xv–xvi. Quotation and paraphrase of *BD* (itself a reprint of "The Life of the Late Celebrated Dr. Edward Young," *The Annual Register* [1765], pp. 31–36), with interpolations from *LY*, *WY*, and at least one other source. This collation is incomplete; I have been unable to trace several passages. Acknowledgement: *LY* and *BD* are cited (ix, xii), along with "the Annals of the Drama" (ix).

Just who produced these compilations may never be known. Over the course of six years it is likely that Bell employed more than one compiler.[45] Except for the revision of Denham's life, a job which called for close supervision and was probably tackled in London, my guess is that the writers who supplied Bell's prefaces worked in or near Edinburgh. A distinct Scotticism

45. Besides, it is difficult to imagine that the writer who tracked down so many sources for Waller's life was the same one who resorted to phony footnotes in Gay's life; the two were printed one after the other (see Table 1). And the many pedestrian transcriptions are hard to square with the liquid paraphrasing in Gray's life, although there were good legal reasons for the compiler to keep his distance from Mason's prose.

crops up in several lives, one that James Beattie warned was a sure sign of North British origins. It is the insertion of the definite article in reference to a year: "in the 1713," for example, instead of "in 1713" or "in the year 1713."[46]

A Scottish identity is commensurate also with some rare and fleeting moments when the compiler turns political censor. The evidence is found in deviations from otherwise straightforward transcriptions of source material. Two cases in point involve William III. In the life of Swift, the source text accounts for one of the King's miscalculations by his being "a stranger to our constitution"; Bell's compiler rejects the inclusive pronoun and makes William "a stranger to the English constitution." In the life of Hughes, Bell's source extols at some length "The House of Nassau," a pindaric which "displays the Heroick Exploits of that Illustrious Family, than which none have ever distinguish'd themselves more eminently in Defence of the Sacred Rights and Liberties of Mankind"; the compiler, while copying the other praises of this ode, balks at the encomium.[47] Silence in place of the Williamite paean suggests a cool (if not necessarily Jacobitic) distance from the orthodox, anglocentric view of the Bloodless Revolution, and the disavowal of constitutional affiliation signals a Scottish reflex.

Only two of Bell's lives qualify as something more than compilations. Each of the lives, except for the mere reprints, is original in one sense: nowhere previously had the collated materials been joined in this fashion. But fresh information crops up in two lives, those of Hammond and Cunningham, which, interestingly, were composed consecutively (see Table 1). In the Hammond preface the veil of impersonality is dropped momentarily when the writer laments having missed a tantalizing chance at some crucial information. Another flicker of disclosure comes from the date on Mallet's life, "March 1780." Although this cryptic log, unique to Bell's prefaces, serves no obvious purpose, its relation to the date of printing (April 8 for Mallet) could indicate that the writers, rather than stockpiling prefaces for eventual use in the series, worked on the basis of a timely delivery, supplying the work close to when it was called for at the printing house.

No single pattern accounts for all the prefaces. They range from straightforward reprints to compilations spliced together phrase by phrase. At times one source is used to footnote another, as when a single excerpt from Warton's *Essay* runs its course beneath the otherwise uninterrupted reprint of Murdoch's life of Thomson; in other cases, as in the life of Waller, the sources

46. *Scoticisms, Arranged in Alphabetical Order, Designed to Correct Improprieties of Speech and Writing* (Edinburgh, 1787), p. 87. This work dates from the late 1770s, when Beattie circulated it privately amongst his students. The phrase "in the 1713" is from the preface to Hughes (xvi); other examples occur in the lives of Butler (15), Lyttelton (vi, vii), Ambrose Philips ([v], vi, xvii), John Philips (vii, xxi), Pitt (vi), Pomfret ([v]), Rowe (vi, xiv, xv, xvi), Swift (xxxv), Waller (ix, xii, xxxvi), and Young ([v]); this is not an exhaustive list.

47. John Hawkesworth, "An Account of the Life of the Reverend Jonathan Swift, D.D., Dean of St. Patrick's, Dublin," *The Works of Dr. Jonathan Swift*, 12 vols. (London, 1755), 1:8; and William Duncombe, "An Account of the Life and Writings of John Hughes, Esq.," *Poems on Several Occasions. With Some Select Essays in Prose*, 2 vols. (London, 1735), 1:viii. The affected passages in Bell's lives of Swift and Hughes fall on pp. xvi and vii respectively.

are thoroughly interwoven. Quotation outweighs paraphrase as a means of copying, and paraphrase rarely wanders far from the source text. The truth was, as Rogers points out, an "unavoidable minimum of bare fact simply had to be retailed," and Johnson himself was often restricted to "close paraphrase, diversified by elegant variations of expression" (170). Unlike Johnson, Bell's compiler in many cases made no effort.

The phrases, sentences and paragraphs from the source texts are seldom reworked for the sake of uniformity. Rarely is it necessary; the occasional effect is a bouncing back and forth between text and footnote, where careful adjustment could have produced a seamless narrative. In places, however, the effect is jarring. None of the roughness is smoothed from the *Annual Register*'s portrayal of Churchill, "this thoughtless man . . . entirely guided by his native turbulence of temper" (xiii); but in tacking on the saccharine excerpt from *Chrysal* even the compiler seems skeptical about "the credit due to the story" (xiii). There are a few incongruities as well amongst the critical judgments retrieved from disparate sources, a problem found in the life of Akenside. The authors of *BB*, Bell's main source, find fault with Akenside's odes, but are willing to grant that "still there is in them a noble vein of poetry, united with manly sense, and applied to excellent purposes" ([F]). Johnson, on the other hand, Bell's complementary source, offers no palliatives: "Of his odes nothing favourable can be said" (*SJ* 23). Rather than try to reconcile the difference, the compiler quotes them both and leaves the verdict to the reader: "In this diversity of opinions the reader will determine for himself" (xiv–xv).

One potential slip never occurs. When a source directs its readers to an earlier text of the author, and where Bell's would serve just as well, the compiler always plugs Bell. In the life of Addison a reference to "Mr. Tickell's 4to. edition" is changed to "in this edition" (ix; *TC* 3:308). In place of a specimen of King's poetry served up in *BB* the compiler advises: "The reader will find it, with Dr. King's whole other poems, in this edition of his Poetical Works in two volumes" (xix; *BB* [H]). By such advertising alerts the compiler escapes the charge, with its commercial overtones, that Bell levelled at Johnson: his lives ignored the edition to which they were attached.

A recurrent impulse is for Bell's compiler to suppress uncomplimentary criticisms. It would have been unthinkable for Johnson not to speak his mind on Tickell's "Kensington Gardens," or to sanitize the passage in the manner of Bell's compiler. But then, his bluntness was a luxury the proprietors could afford. Since their initial policy was not to sell the *Prefaces* without all fifty-six volumes of poetry, they did not need to worry about anyone deciding against the purchase of Tickell's poems as a consequence of browsing through the preface. Bell enjoyed no such leverage, and conceivably may have instructed his compiler to be wary of disparaging criticisms. Why discourage a reader from enjoying the book she or he just bought (or was about to purchase), especially when the collection was being published serially and a new volume would be offered for sale the next week?

Instantly squelched was any hint that the works of a particular poet were inadequate by themselves to form a saleable commodity. With Gray, perhaps, it could be admitted that "the joint stock of both [Gray and Richard West] would hardly fill a small volume" (xii; Mason 184), but not with other poets: the intimation that Garth's "works will scarce make a moderate volume" was surgically obliterated (xiii; *TC* 3:270), and the unlordly conclusion that Roscommon's works "are not sufficient to form a small volume" was amended to read "hardly sufficient" (xi; *TC* 2:349).[48] Neither was it allowable for the shortcomings of the prefaces to be discussed, except for the customary sighs over the lack of sources or the uneventfulness of a poet's life. When Sewell wishes there were "a larger, as well as a better" critical assessment of John Philips than his own (12), Bell's compiler omits the confession from his transcription (xvii).[49]

The compiler of Young's life avoided negative comments in several ways when copying from *BD*. The following passage was a cue to omit: "[T]here is a laboured stiffness of versification; and this is the more remarkable, as Dr. Young ever took very great pains to polish and correct the harshness of his numbers" (12:512). Another tack was to discredit the source: "By certain fastidious critics they have been stigmatized as a mere string of epigrams" (viii). If an adjective was not to the compiler's liking, a more favorable one could be substituted, as when "elegance" is substituted for "terseness" (viii; 12:513). All in all, omission was simplest. When *TC* criticizes Smith's drama as too "luxuriously poetical" of language, yet monotonous of character (4:312), Bell's compiler declines the opinion (xii). And the incentive to change copytexts near the end of the life of Roscommon was sharpened by this withering summation: "The grand requisites of a poet, elevation, fire, and invention, were not given him, and for want of these, however pure his thoughts, he is a languid unentertaining writer" (*TC* 2:352–353).

It is clear why negative criticism might be shunned, less so why a facet of a poet's life should be viewed as a detraction. Nevertheless, the compiler concealed one aspect of Dryden's life. Where "preternatural intelligence" was concerned the age was, as Johnson put it, "very little inclined to favour any accounts of this kind" (Roscommon 7). Concurring, Bell's compiler shields the reader from "superstitious" incidents in the life of Dryden, passing silently over the section in *TC* dealing with the poet's astrological calculations and fears about the life of his son Charles. Having agreed with one source to portray Young as "pious but gloomy" (x), the compiler later resists the phrase "notwithstanding this gloominess of temper," retouching it to read "so far was he from gloominess of temper" (xiv; *BD* 12:516).

Yet if Bell's purpose was to gloss over passages damaging to the poet's character or reputation, it was not carried out consistently. Many passages

48. Again, it was Johnson's candor that required censorship, for *TC* was quoting his life of Roscommon from the *Gentleman's Magazine*.

49. In any event, the confession was obviated by the compiler's footnote on p. [v], which advertised that the defects in Sewell would be repaired by additions from other accounts.

eligible for deletion on that account are retained. And whereas the praise in a source text is gently heightened on occasion, this happens less often than one might expect. It was easier, on the whole, merely to copy. In one extraordinary case an encomium in the source text is toned down. The compiler of Young's life, otherwise anxious to expunge the negative, acually reins in "the writer of Dr. Young's life" for going "too great a length when he says, 'We may assign [*The Revenge*] . . . a place in the first rank of our dramatic writings'" (ix).[50]

Although a niche in Bell's market undoubtedly was occupied by neophyte book-buyers, old and young, the ambitious plan of *The Poets of Great Britain* argues against belittling its audience as Thomas Tyrwhitt did, who claimed that the engravings in Bell's edition were a decoy for young and undiscriminating purchasers.[51] The scope of the lives runs counter to the condescension aired by another work published when Bell's series began to appear, *The Beauties of Biography*, intended "for the use of Schools." Its editor asserts that most biographical entries are "too voluminous, and more circumstantial than is required for young People, who do not reap the greatest advantage from dwelling long on the same subject."[52] By that measure Bell's reader was fully adult, an impression confirmed by comparison of Bell's edition of John Philips, for instance, with two previous ones: *Poems Attempted in the Style of Milton* (1762) and *Poems on Several Occasions* (1763), published respectively by the Tonsons and the Foulis brothers. Bell reprints George Sewell's life, folding in sections from both the text and notes in *BB*, and passages from *SJ*. The earlier compilations were far simpler. Except for a single paragraph from Sewell, the Tonsons derived their account from *BB*, leaving out a few passages and all the notes but one. The Foulis brothers simply reprinted Sewell, adding only some brief notes. Both prefaces were "defective" by Bell's standard, yet were deemed suitable by one of the century's most thriving bookselling firms and perhaps the finest university printers in Britain.[53] Bell taxed his readers' attention at a higher rate: in contrast to

50. Typically enough, the writer of Young's life in 1773 was to blame only in part. His glowing endorsement was copied from *The Annual Register* (1765), p. 34, which had copied and elaborated the sentiment from *CP* 1:sig. S4r (*s.v. The Revenge*).

51. See Bonnell, p. 149.

52. *Beauties of Biography: Containing the Lives of the Most Illustrious Persons Who Have Flourished in Great Britain, France, Italy, and Other Parts of Europe. . . . Extracted from the Biographia Britannica, Baile's Dictionary, and Other Valuable Works, for the Instruction of Youth of Both Sexes*, 2 vols. (London, 1777), 1:iii. "Circumstantial" was a key evaluative term in gauging the worth of a biography; see above, where Bell promises an "account of the Author, equally circumstantial" to the pirated Denham preface he was forced to paraphrase.

53. "The Life of Mr. John Philips," *Poems Attempted in the Style of Milton. By Mr. John Philips. With a New Account of His Life and Writings* (London: Printed for R. and J. Tonson, and T. Lownds, 1762), pp. [3]-23; and "The Life of Mr. John Philips," *Poems on Several Occasions. . . . To which is added, His Life, by Mr. George Sewell* (Glasgow: Printed by Robert and Andrew Foulis, 1763), pp. [3]-28. By calling attention to their biographies on their title pages, the publishers used this feature as a selling point. Tonson's "New Account" followed the publication of Philips's life in *BB* by only two years (vol. 5, 1760).

roughly 2675 and 5450 words in the Tonson and Foulis lives, Bell's compilation ran to about 9050.[54]

The life of Gray, neither the longest nor shortest of the bunch, may serve as a final measure of Bell's investment in his prefaces. No edition, of course, could match William Mason's with its page ratio of 416:112 between preface and works.[55] Several other editions of Gray, however, published in 1774, 1775, 1776, and 1779, also joined some form of biographical preface to the poet's works. Once again, by a significant margin Bell's was the most thorough. The word count for these lives, respectively, was 1025, 850, 1450, and 1025, to Bell's 5050.[56] What is more, to the "Life of Thomas Gray" proper Bell's compiler added a copy of Gray's last will and testament, and J. Taite's poetic tribute, "The Tears of Genius." Not surprisingly in view of the options, when a life was selected to accompany Gilbert Wakefield's "classical" edition of Gray in 1786, Bell's won the palm.[57]

Even without hiring a Johnson to write his prefaces, Bell invested heavily in this feature of his edition, both materially and symbolically. The more extensive the lives, obviously, the greater the capital outlay required for printing materials (paper and ink), labor (in compiling as well as printing), and distribution (weight and bulk in shipping). Just as important as publishing a substantial preface, however, was the appearance of publishing a substantial

54. As promised, readers of Philips's life in *The Beauties of Biography* (1:178–183) were assessed the lightest tax: around 1175 words.

55. *The Poems of Mr. Gray. To which are prefixed Memoirs of His Life and Writings by W. Mason, M.A.* (York, 1775). In a later octavo edition (4 vols.; York, 1778) Mason reversed the order, giving this explanation: "The Editor, when he compiled those Memoirs, and made them the vehicle of communicating . . . so many of the Author's unpublished compositions, both in latin and english, thought, that, on account of their novelty, they ought then to take the lead. This reason ceasing, it seemed proper that such posthumous pieces should give place to what was published in his life time" (1:sig. $\pi 1^v$).

56. "The Life of Mr Gray," *Poems by Mr. Gray. To which is prefixed, An Account of His Life* (London: Sold by A. Millar, 1774?), pp. [iii]–xv; "A Short Account of the Life of Mr. Gray," *Poems by Mr. Gray. A New Edition* (Edinburgh: Printed for Alexander Donaldson, 1775), pp. [iii]–ix; "A Short Account of the Life and Writings of Mr. Gray," *Poems by Mr. Gray. A New Edition* (London: Printed for J. Murray, 1776), pp. [v]–xviii; "The Life of Mr. Gray," *Poems by Mr. Gray. With a Biographical and Critical Account of the Author* (London: Sold by R. Tomlins, J. Chandler, D. Watson, and H. Middleton, 1779), pp. [iii]–xv. The same life appears in the Millar and Tomlin editions. The life in Murray's edition was written by Gilbert Stuart, who received three guineas for the piece (William Zachs, *Without Regard to Good Manners: A Biography of Gilbert Stuart 1743–1786* [Edinburgh, 1992], p. 57).

57. Bell took Gray's will and Taite's poem from Murray's 1778 edition, to which they were newly added (pp. [xxv]–xxxii and [xxxiii]–xxxix). Wakefield copied the life and Gray's will from Bell, but not the poem; *The Poems of Mr. Gray. With Notes by Gilbert Wakefield, B.A.* (London: Printed for G. Kearsley, 1786), pp. [v]–xxii, and [xxiii]–xxvi. Wakefield viewed his edition as an "antidote" to the criticisms of Johnson, whose strictures against Gray, "under the sanction of his respectable character, might operate with malignant influence upon the public taste, and become ultimately injurious to the cause of polite literature" ("Advertisement," p. [iii]). One review of Wakefield called his edition "a classical performance" (*Gentleman's Magazine* 56 [1786]: 592); another began with the dictate, "A Classical Poet . . . ought to have a classical Commentator," and granted that Gray and Wakefield had earned these respective epithets (*Monthly Review* 76 [1787]: 505). Neither reviewer commented on the prefatory life.

preface, one in keeping with the breadth of the full undertaking. The number of pages counted; quantity became a tangible index of value. With this kind of symbolic capital tied up in his prefaces, Bell could not risk their being seen as a perfunctory gesture.

IV

Conclusion

While Bell succeeded in one of his primary objectives, that of acquainting the reader "at once with the poet and the man," it is less clear how far he progressed towards a "connected system of biography." In his prefaces there is neither a uniform biographical approach nor a consistent critical voice. As a lot they are altogether too miscellaneous.

No matter what their peculiarities and varied degrees of competence, however, these reprints and compilations gave readers a considerable body of English literary biography. If little new in the way of fact or criticism was to be discovered, Bell could not be faulted for scrimping on them. Where sources were meager, the lives were necessarily brief; otherwise the compilers sought the fullest accounts available and often supplemented these with other materials. At their worst Bell's lives were equal to the kind of "advertisement" Johnson was asked to write; at their best they approximated the most informative biographies extant of their respective subjects. Yet the question of how they stack up against Johnson's *Prefaces* or other authoritative sources, though crucial, gives way to another when the focus shifts from the compiler to the bookseller: what sort of book was Bell trying to place in his readers' hands?

Prefixing lives to cheap octavo and duodecimo volumes of poetry had been a fairly casual matter, as the editions of Philips and Gray demonstrate. Bell's model was the life-and-works formula, not of the cheap reprint, but of the complete and authoritative edition. Into his small and relatively inexpensive books Bell transplanted lives which had made their debut in folio (Cowley, Donne) and quarto (Thomson, Swift). This stately ideal exemplifies the standard attempted by Bell's series; each author was to be accorded a substantial biographical account. It was an unprecedented enterprise.

If "system," finally, is taken to mean "any complexure or combination of many things acting together," as Johnson defined the term, then the lives in Bell's edition fit the bill. Cast in the same prefatory role, together they provided the purchaser with a broad glimpse of "this particular class of writers," and by so doing contextualized the works of the British poets.

SCOTT'S COMMENTARY ON
THE JOURNAL OF A TOUR TO THE HEBRIDES
WITH SAMUEL JOHNSON

by

ANN BOWDEN and WILLIAM B. TODD

To celebrate the completion of David Fleeman's bibliography of Samuel Johnson, this essay offers, as an epilogue to that grand enterprise, a complete reprint of Sir Walter Scott's annotations on Boswell's *Tour* with Johnson in 1773. As it was once observed for Johnson, so it now appears for Scott: early notes since disregarded are occasionally more informative than later discourse.[1] Whether some or all of those now under review are also remarkable instances of Scott's "table-talk," as Lockhart suggested,[2] is a question our readers may decide on the evidence of this reprinting. Any assessment, however, should take into account the occasion for Scott's contributions, their reception by his immediate contemporaries, and finally their sporadic recurrence in certain subsequent editions.

The initial impetus was provided by John Wilson Croker who, after negotiating conditions with the publisher John Murray, asked his old friend Scott, as a final authority, for assistance particularly in elucidating the Scottish *Tour*. This work, along with other chronicles, he intended to incorporate in the *Life* itself: a radical innovation which was allowed to remain through three successive editions.[3] To Croker's enquiry Scott immediately assented 30 January 1829 in a highly evocative letter, itself providing the material for several notes and followed by numerous other communications, most of which, in one form or another, also found their way below the text.[4] Altogether, as *The Athenaeum* reported 21 August 1830, Croker eventually "obtained half

1. William B. Todd, "Concealed Editions of Samuel Johnson," *Book Collector* 2 (1953), 59–65. The notes mentioned there, forty years ago, were in the edition now identified in this report as Wright 1835 (W).

2. J. G. Lockhart, *Memoirs of the Life of Sir Walter Scott, Bart* (1837), ii.316. Immediately before and after this comment Lockhart quotes in full, as prime examples, the entries numbered below as 65, 71, 75, 76. The entire passage is repeated, unaltered, in his revised second edition (1839), iii.280–282.

3. This odd notion may not have originated with Croker. On 19 January 1829 Lockhart suggested to Murray, the editor's publisher: "Pray ask Croker whether Boswell's account of the Hebridean Tour ought not to be melted into the book. Sir Walter has many MS. annotations in his 'Boswell,' both 'Life' and 'Tour,' and will, I am sure give them with hearty good will . . ." (Samuel Smiles, *A Publisher and his Friends* [1891], ii.288).

4. The correspondence still extant is given in Herbert Grierson (ed.), *The Letters of Sir Walter Scott* (1937), xi.110–120, 151–155, 166, 196–197; xii.461–466, 468–471, 478–479. Throughout Grierson helpfully identifies in the 1831 edition (S) whatever Scott first proposed in his letters.

a volume of curious original matter from Sir Walter Scott and others of the Northern literati, respecting the visit which the Sage paid to Scotland. . . ." More precisely, Scott contributed for the *Tour* alone seventy-seven notes, all of which, though considerably less numerically than those early supplied by Boswell (116), or later by Croker (268), were generally regarded as of greater interest, both for their novelty and for the sense of immediacy they conveyed. Not contributed by Scott but relating to his own work are two other notes, first where Croker refers to "Old Mortality" (ii.300), secondly where he expresses the wish that Scott might write a history of the Pretender (iii.88).

So annotated, Croker's augmented *Life of Samuel Johnson* appeared 22 June 1831[5] and three days later was reviewed, unexceptionally, in *The Athenaeum*. In the two following weekly issues, however, this journal implicitly recognized the importance of the edition by offering its readers certain "flowers and pearls" newly discovered among the notes for the *Tour*, citing in full one comment by Cradock, fourteen by Croker, and twenty-four by Scott.[6] Thus at first Scott's commentary was widely publicized as the principal feature of the 1831 edition.

Compared to this equable, tripartite account the next survey, by T. B. Macaulay in the September *Edinburgh Review*, can only be regarded as a sustained assault, politically motivated, by a Whiggish commentator on a Tory editor. So intense and unremitting is this attack that Scott, as an innocent bystander, though praised by Macaulay on other occasions, is here totally ignored. Any allusion, however brief, would only distract the reviewer from his avowed purpose, that of "smashing" Croker. After this diatribe, the anonymous writer in the October *Westminster Review* may certainly be viewed as rather temperate, first observing that "Of the original part of the annotations the most amusing is sir[!] Walter Scott's commentary on the Scotch Tour" (page 392) and then quoting two of the notes (74, 76) already commended in *The Athenaeum*.

The last substantive and most favorable account is to be found, not surprisingly, in the November *Quarterly Review*, a Tory journal edited by Scott's son-in-law, J. G. Lockhart, the reviewer, and a journal which in years past had often accommodated contributions from both Croker and Scott. Of Scott's Boswellian annotations Lockhart is persuaded that, in future editions, they "will never be divorced from the text which they so admirably illustrate, and indeed, invest with a new interest throughout" (page 39). As memorable examples he then cites eight, three of them (34, 65, 78) not quoted

5. Since the date has not been ascertained previously (Scott thought the book was "nearly out" on 17 February [*Letters*, xi.473], but Pottle's Boswell bibliography [p. 180] cites no reference before August), it should be reported that *The Athenaeum* 18 June 1831 announced issue "on Wednesday next" (or the 22d), a date confirmed on the 23d in the *Edinburgh Evening Courant*.

6. Evidently the reviewer hastily read first the beginning and the end of the *Tour*, quoting initially in the 2 July number seventeen Scott entries (4, 8, 9, 10, 12, 19, 20, 24, 29, 33, 70, 71, 74, 75, 76, 77, 83) then on 9 July seven other entries in the middle of the text (36, 37, 42, 44, 55 with 62, 58). Two of these (42, 55) represent postscripts to previous remarks by Croker.

in the previous reviews, four selected earlier in *The Athenaeum* (12, 44, 58, 71), and one reprinted both there and in the *Westminster Review* (74). Concerning that common choice, however, relating a heated argument between Johnson and Adam Smith over David Hume, Lockhart demurs: "We must take leave to express our strongest suspicion of this story" (page 44). Doubtless the occasion for this remark, not divulged by the reviewer, arises from an anachronism hidden in this splendid anecdote.[7]

In general, later editors of Boswell's *Tour* were concerned, not to extract some of Scott's annotations as so many "pearls," nor to treasure them all (as Lockhart would recommend) as essential adjuncts, but to retain or modify them according to whatever textual apparatus they then considered appropriate. With reference to the seventy-seven *Tour* notes only (5–81) it soon appears, from our own schematic apparatus defining these entries, that the two subsequent "Crokerian" editions faithfully transmit Scott's contributions. Discounting the innumerable minor adjustments or corrections here recorded, John Wright's ten-volume 1835 edition (W) reprints all of the notes in the 1831 issue (S) excepting only item 10, where a humorous qualification is silently suppressed, and item 40, where Scott's conjectural identification is superseded by one which Wright received from Croker. These same two amendments are accepted in Croker's own compressed single-volume 1848 edition (C), which now also provides two other notes by "Walter Scott" (22, 73), these sixteen years after the author's death!

Subsequent editions again present the *Tour* in its original form as a text separate from the *Life* and thus, with few exceptions, tend to disregard the Scott material embedded in the earlier Crokerian arrangement. The first of these, Robert Carruthers' [1852] edition (RC), also reflects the further passage of time, with notes now emphasizing what is different rather than what remains the same. Consequently, among the seventy-seven occasions eliciting some comment from Scott, Carruthers indirectly reprints only two notes (24, 76), substitutes his own remarks for twenty-two others, and omits any reference whatever for the fifty-three remaining. Nonetheless, at the very time Carruthers is excluding Scott from the commentary, he is embellishing his own notes with at least sixteen allusions to that author's other work,[8] none of which was ever intended as a documentary for the *Tour*.

In sharp contrast to Carruther's studied avoidance of any relevant Scott notes, the Alexander Napier 1884 edition (AN), issued apart in a fifth volume so numbered,[9] reprints from the 1848 Croker version (C) practically all of the

7. Later editions often cite note 74 simply as a vivid portrayal and then regularly subtend a contrary argument. At the very outset, however, the *Edinburgh Literary Journal* 16 July 1831, though properly observing that Smith's letter about Hume in 1776 could not have occasioned a dispute in 1773, cogently argues for a single encounter between Smith and Johnson, not in Glasgow, but in London between November 1776 and May 1778. Scott's anecdote, then, may be right as to the subject represented to him on good authority, but wrong as to the time and place where it occurred.

8. These are entered in Carruthers' [1852] edition, pages 10, 20, 24, 27, 28, 43, 77–78, 123, 162, 167, 174, 213, 229 (2), 276, 311.

9. Pottle 96 does not make it clear that Napier's edition of the *Tour* is first printed

commentary there entered, including the two posthumous "Scott" notes (22, 73). The only significant variations are (for note 18) the adoption of Lockhart's postscript in preference to earlier comment by Croker and Scott and (for note 74) the removal of this long Johnson-Smith anecdote to an appendix for an extensive 53-line rebuttal. Both for his four-volume *Life of Johnson* and the separate *Tour to the Hebrides*, the Reverend Mr. Napier took his notes from the final Croker edition because that convenient one-volume issue —a 19th century best seller[10]—was very probably in his manse library at Holkham.

The last account to be considered is the encyclopedic edition first issued by Birkbeck Hill in 1887 and revised by L. F. Powell first in 1950, then in 1964 (H–P). Again as with the Napier issue the *Tour* appears apart in the fifth volume, and there carries Dr. Powell's assurance (page vii) that Hill had made "judicious and extensive use" of Scott's notes, as well as other references. Though this scholarly judgment should remain unchallenged, we may yet regret that among Scott's seventy-seven entries only twenty-seven are now accepted without abridgment or qualification.[11] Coincidentally the earliest reviews altogether also quote only twenty-seven notes as especially interesting, but these two selections early (1831) and late (1887–1964) report in common only fourteen commentaries as enduring the test of time (8, 24, 33, 34, 36, 37, 55, 62, 65, 70, 71, 74, 76, 78). Such a limited consensus, it will be agreed, falls quite short of Lockhart's original estimate that all of Scott was indispensable and ever inseparable from the *Tour* it elucidates.

Given this present review, our readers may now assess the significance of Scott's annotations, here all unencumbered (beyond a minimal reference) by any Boswellian text or other commentary. In the following reprint each entry is assigned a number, followed by a brief textual quotation together with its footnote indicator as given in the 1831 edition. Then after a vertical bar is represented the note to the text, this unenclosed if by Scott, enclosed in brackets if first by some other commentator. <Other necessary comment by the present writers is given in angular brackets.> Below each entry is a starred footnote collation giving volume and page references first to the three Croker editions, each signified by a single letter:

(after the *Life of Johnson*) as volume 5 in the second 1884 edition, with *Johnsoniana* then following in an unnumbered sixth volume. In the first edition, as he observes, *Johnsoniana* follows as an unnumbered fifth volume.

10. Smiles, ii.289, on the evidence of publisher Murray's files, reports that up to 1891 some 50,000 copies of Croker's editions of the *Life* (including the *Tour*) had been sold, this despite Macaulay's "smash." Even though this reckoning apparently excludes later sales of the 1835 Croker-Wright edition, continually reissued from stereotype by Bohn and others 1848–1880, Richard D. Altick accepts the partial record as sufficient for entry in his bestseller list: *The English Common Reader* (1963), p. 388. (It may be noted further that while the first Croker five-volume edition 1831, selling at £3, was not reprinted, the third single-volume edition 1848, available at one-fourth the earlier price [15 shillings], was apparently reprinted at least nine times.)

11. Two others are slightly adapted (12, 72), three are expressed indirectly (11, 14, 32), and two more (6, 58) seem to depend upon a Scott note, though without acknowledgement.

S Scott notation in 1831
W Wright, 1835
C Croker, 1848

then to the three later editions also discussed, each denoted by a double letter:

RC Robert Carruthers [1852]
AN Alexander Napier, 1884
H-P Hill-Powell, 1887–1964.

Unless noted otherwise an edition follows the one listed before: thus AN, ordinarily dependent upon C, usually precedes RC in the listing. Edition RC itself, representing only the *Tour*, is not cited for the *Life* entries before or after that work (1–4, 82–84). In our own explanation *indirect* means a partial quotation and *variant* a note entirely different from Scott's.

Annotations before the TOUR (1–4)

1] Mr. Dempster[2] | [George Dempster, of Dunnichen, secretary to the Order of the Thistle. He was a man of talents and very agreeable manners. Burns mentions him more than once with eulogy: As Mr. Dempster lived a good deal in Johnson's society, the reader may be glad to see the following slip-shod but characteristic epitaph (communicated to me by Sir Walter Scott), which he made on himself when eighty-five, though (affecting, even at that age, to look forward to a still greater longevity) he supposes himself to have lived to 93. "Pray for the soul / Of deceased George Dempster. / In his youth a great fool, / In his old age a gamester*. <CROKER>] *Gamester*, Scottice, may rhyme with Dempster. He, however, only played for trifles; indeed the whole is a mere *badinage*. W. SCOTT.
  * Si.417, Wii.184; C139 (omits all after "eulogy", thus excluding the Scott reference and postscript), AN i.324, *variant* H-P i.408–409.

2] "Very well, sir. Lord Monboddo[2] still maintains the superiority of the savage life." | [James Burnet, born in 1714, called to the Scottish bar in 1738, and advanced to be a lord of session, by the title of Lord Monboddo, in 1767, was, in private life, as well as in his literary career, a humorist; the learning and acuteness of his various works are obscured by his love of singularity and paradox. He died in 1799.—ED.] He was a devout believer in the virtues of the heroic ages and the deterioration of civilized mankind; a great contemner of luxuries, insomuch that he never used a wheel-carriage. It should be added that he was a gentleman of the most amiable disposition, and the strictest honour and integrity. WALTER SCOTT.
  * S ii.138, W iii.172, C 227, AN ii.145, H-P ii.147, 74(Scott second sentence only, edition not stated, but false reference to "i.138" [1831]).

3] He said, he never had it properly ascertained that the Scotch Highlanders and the Irish understood each other[1]. | [In Mr. Anderson's Historical Sketches ... <22 lines>. Sir Walter Scott also informs me, that "there is no doubt the languages are the same, and the difference in pronunciation and construction not very considerable. The *Erse* or *Earish* is the *Irish*; and the race called *Scots* came originally from Ulster."—ED.]
  * S ii. 149; W iii.184 (omits Croker's note and begins "There is ...."), C 231 (reinserts Croker note), AN ii.153–154; *variant* H-P ii.156.

4] I was desirous to see as much of Dr. Johnson as I could. But I first called on Goldsmith to take leave of him. The jealousy and envy, which, though possessed of many most amiable qualities, he frankly avowed, broke out violently at this interview[1]. | I wonder why Boswell so often displays a malevolent feeling towards Goldsmith? Rivalry for Johnson's good graces, perhaps. WALTER SCOTT.

* S ii.244, W iii.304, C 264 (adds 5-line postscript signed "CROKER, 1846"), AN ii.242 (Scott note only); *omitted* H-P ii.260.

Annotations for the TOUR (5–81)

5] On Saturday the 14th of August, 1773, late in the evening, I received a note from him, that he was arrived at Boyd's inn¹, at the head of the Canon-gate. | The sign of the White Horse. It continued a place from which *coaches* used to start till the end of the eighteenth century; some twelve or fifteen years ago it was a carrier's inn, and has since been held unworthy even of that occupation, and the sign is taken down. It was a base hovel. WALTER SCOTT.

* S ii.259, W iv.12 (adds 4-line note from Chambers), C 270, AN v.9; *variant* RC 9–10, *variant* H-P v.21.

6] I presented to him Mr. Robert Arbuthnot³ | Robert Arbuthnot, Esq. was secretary to the board of trustees for the encouragement of the arts and manufactures of Scotland; in this office he was succeeded by his son William, lord provost of Edinburgh when King George the Fourth visited Scotland, who was made a baronet on that occasion, and has lately died much lamented. Both father and son were accomplished gentlemen, and elegant scholars. WALTER SCOTT.

* S ii.265, W iv.19, C 272, AN v.16; *omitted* RC 13, *variant* H-P v.29 (notes Arbuthnot's position but not the office; Scott not mentioned).

7] he presented Foote to a club in the following singular manner: "This is the nephew of the gentleman who was lately hung in chains for murdering his brother¹." | [Mr. Foote's mother was the sister or Sir J. Dinely Gooddere, bart., and of Capt. Gooddere, who commanded H.M.S. Ruby, on board which, when lying in King's-road, Bristol, in January, 1741, the latter caused his brother to be forcibly carried, and there barbarously murdered. Capt Gooddere was, with two accomplices, executed for this offence in the April following. The circumstances of the case, and some other facts connected with this family, led to an opinion that Capt. Gooddere was insane; and some unhappy circumstances in Foote's life render it probable that *he* had not wholly escaped this hereditary irregularity of mind.—Ed.] Foote's first publication was a pamphlet in defence of his uncle's memory. WALTER SCOTT.

* S ii.273, W iv.27, C 274–275 (first, Croker note revised), AN v.23; *variant* RC 19, *variant* H-P v.37.

8] We went to the parliament-house² | It was on this visit to the parliament-house that Mr. Henry Erskine (brother of Lord Buchan and Lord Erskine), after being presented to Dr. Johnson by Mr. Boswell, and having made his bow, slipped a shilling into Boswell's hand, whispering that it was for the sight of his *bear*. WALTER SCOTT.

* S ii.274, W iv.31 (adds "This was the subject of a caricature"), C 275 (reads ". . . cotemporary caricature"), AN v.24–25, H-P v.39 (Scott text only, "1831"); *omitted* RC 21.

9] Mr. Maclaurin's¹ learning and talents | Mr. Maclaurin, advocate, son of the great mathematician, and afterwards a judge of session by the title of Lord Dreghorn. He wrote some indifferent English poems; but was a good Latin scholar, and a man of wit and accomplishment. His quotations from the classics were particularly apposite. In the famous case of *Knight*, which determined the right of a slave to freedom if he landed in Scotland, Maclaurin pleaded the cause of the negro. The counsel opposite was the celebrated Wight, an excellent lawyer, but of a very homely appearance, with heavy features, a blind eye, which projected from the socket, a swag belly, and a limp. To him Maclaurin applied the lines of Virgil, "Quamvis ille niger, quamvis tu candidus esses. / O formose puer, nimium ne crede colori." Mr. Maclaurin wrote an essay against the Homerick tale of "Troy divine," I believe, for the sole purpose of introducing a happy motto, "Non anni domuere decem, non mille carinae." WALTER SCOTT.

* S ii.285, W iv.43, C 279, AN v.33–34; *omitted* RC 31, *variant* H-P v.49, 471–472.

10] At supper we had Dr. Alexander Webster[1] | Dr. Alexander Webster was remarkable for the talent with which he at once supported his place in convivial society, and a high character as a leader of the strict and rigid presbyterian party in the church of Scotland, which certainly seemed to require very different qualifications. He was ever gay amid the gayest; when it once occurred to some one present to ask, what one of his Elders would think, should he see his pastor in such a merry mood.—"Think!" replied the doctor, "why he would not believe his own eyes." WALTER SCOTT.

   * S ii.286, W iv.44 (deletes "Alexander" and "which certainly . . . qualifications"), C 279, AN v.35; *variant* RC 32, *variant* H-P v.50, 472.

11] we were attended only by my man, Joseph Ritter[2] | See *ante*, vol. i. p. 49. Joseph Ritter afterwards undertook the management of the large inn at Paisley, called the Abercorn Arms, but did not succeed in that concern. WALTER SCOTT.

   * S ii.288, W iv.47, C 280, AN v.37, indirect H-P v. 53, 475 ("1831"); *omitted* RC 33.

12] Mr. Nairne[1], advocate | Mr. William Nairne, afterwards Sir William, and a judge of the court of session, by the title, made classical by Shakspeare, of Lord Dunsinnan. He was a man of scrupulous integrity. When sheriff depute of Perthshire, he found, upon reflection, that he had decided a poor man's case erroneously; and as the only remedy, supplied the litigant privately with money to carry the suit to the supreme court, where his judgment was reversed. Sir William was of the old school of manners, somewhat formal, but punctilliously well bred. WALTER SCOTT.

   * S ii.289, W iv.48, C 280, AN v.37, H-P v.53–54 (omits "made classical by Shakspeare", "1831"); *variant* RC 34.

13] There are three wells in the island, but we could not find one in the fort. There must probably have been one, though now filled up, as a garrison could not subsist without it[1]. | The remains of the fort have been removed, to assist in constructing a very useful lighthouse upon the island. WALTER SCOTT.

   * S ii.291, W iv.51, C 281, AN v.39, H-P v.55 ("1831"); *omitted* RC 35.

14] It is not improbable that it was the poem which Prior has so elegantly translated[2]. | More likely the fine epitaph on John Viscount of Dundee, translated by Dryden, and beginning *Ultime Scotarem, &c.* WALTER SCOTT.

   * S ii.293, W iv.54, C 282, AN v.41, *indirect* H-P v.58; *variant* RC 37.

15] Since the publication of Dr. Johnson's book, I find that he has been censured for not seeing here the ancient chapel of St. Rule[1] | It is very singular how they could miss seeing St. Rule's chapel, an ecclesiastical building, the most ancient, perhaps, in Great Britain. It is a square tower, which stands close by the ruins of the old cathedral. *Martin's Antiquitates Divi Andrei* are now published. WALTER SCOTT.

   * S ii.296, W iv.57 (adds 3-line note); C 283 (deletes the additional note), AN v.44; *variant* RC 39, *variant* H-P v.61.

16] One of the steeples, which he was told was in danger, he wished not to be taken down; "for," said he, "it may fall on some of the posterity of John Knox; and no great matter?!" | These towers have been repaired by the government, with a proper attention to the antiquities of the country. WALTER SCOTT.

   * S ii.298, W iv.60, C 283, AN v.46; *variant* RC 41, *omitted* H-P v.63.

17] We went and saw the church, in which is Archbishop Sharp's monument[2]. | The monument is of Italian marble. The brother of the archbishop left a sum for preserving it, which, in one unhappy year, was expended in painting it in resemblance of reality. The daubing is now removed. WALTER SCOTT.

   * S ii.300, W iv.62, C 285, AN v.47; *variant* RC 43, *variant* H-P v.65.

18] I have also written six sheets in a day of translation from the French[1]." | [This must have been the translation of Lobo . . . <4 lines>. But, as Sir W. Scott observes, "a pool is usually succeeded in a river by a current, and he may have written fast to make up lee way."—Ed.]

    * S ii.302, W iv.65 (adds five-line note initialled "J.G.L."), C 285, AN v.49 (reprints Lockhart postscript only); *omitted* RC 45, *variant* H-P v.67.

19] Miss Sharp, great grandchild of Archbishop Sharp[1] | It is very singular that Dr. Johnson, with all his episcopal partiality, should have visited Archbishop Sharp's monument, and been in company with his descendant, without making any observation on his character and melancholy death, or on the general subject of Scottish episcopacy. WALTER SCOTT.

    * S ii.303, W iv.65, C 285, AN v.49; *omitted* RC 45, *omitted* H-P v.68.

20] Unluckily the colonel said there was but this and another large tree in the county[2]. | Johnson has been unjustly abused for dwelling on the barrenness of Fife. There are good trees in many parts of that county, but the east coast along which lay Johnson's route is certainly destitute of wood, excepting young plantations. The *other* tree mentioned by Colonel Nairne is probably the Prior Letham plane, measuring in circumference at the surface nearly twenty feet, and at the setting on of the branches nineteen feet. This giant of the forest stands in a cold exposed situation, apart from every other tree. WALTER SCOTT.

    * S ii.304, W iv.67, C 285–286, AN v.51; *omitted* RC 46, *variant* H-P v.69.

21] We were not satisfied as to this colony[1]. | The Danish colony at Leuchars is a vain imagination concerning a certain fleet of Danes wrecked on Sheughy Dikes. WALTER SCOTT.

    * S ii.305, W iv.69 (adds 3-line note initialled "J.G.L."), C 286 (omits "Danish" and signs additional note "Lockhart"), AN v.52, H-P v.70–71 (reprints W text, signing it "LOCKHART (in Croker 1835)"); *omitted* RC 47.

22] harvest sport, nay stealings[2]." | [My note of this is much too short. *Brevis esse laboro, obscurus fio.* Yet as I have resolved, that *the very Journal which Dr. Johnson read* shall be presented to the public, I will not expand the text in any considerable degree, though I may occasionally supply a word to complete the sense, as I fill up the blanks of abbreviation in the writing, neither of which can be said to change the genuine Journal. One of the best critics of our age conjectures that the imperfect passage above has probably been as follows:— "In his book we have an accurate display of a nation in war, and a nation in peace; the peasant is delineated as truly as the general; nay, even harvest sport and the modes of ancient theft, are described."—BOSWELL].

    * S ii.312–313, W iv.77–78, C 289 (adds "The *critic* was probably Dr. Hugh Blair—WALTER SCOTT"), AN v.58; *omitted* RC 53 (Boswell note only), *omitted* H-P v.78–79 (after note identifies "critic" as Malone).

23] Mr. Boyd told us that it is customary for the company at Peterhead-well to make parties, and come and dine in one of the caves here[1]. | They were also used by smugglers. The path round the *Buller* is about three feet broad; so that there is little danger, though very often much fear. WALTER SCOTT.

    * S ii.334, W iv.102, C 296, AN v.76; *omitted* RC 69, *omitted* H-P v.100–101.

24] They set down dried haddocks broiled, along with our tea. I ate one; but Dr. Johnson was disgusted by the sight of them, so they were removed[1]. | A protest may be entered on the part of most Scotsmen against the doctor's taste in this particular. A Finnon haddock dried over the smoke of the sea-weed, and sprinkled with salt water during the process, acquires a relish of a very peculiar and delicate flavour, inimitable on any other coast than that of Aberdeenshire. Some of our Edinburgh philosophers tried to produce their equal in vain. I was one of a party at a dinner, where the philosophical haddocks were placed in competition with the genuine Finnon-fish. These were served without distinction whence they came; but only one gentleman, out of twelve present, espoused the cause of philosophy. WALTER SCOTT.

* S ii.343, W iv.113, C 299, AN v.84, H-P v.110 ("1831"), *indirect* RC 77 (second sentence).

25] King Duncan's monument[2]. | Duncan's monument; a huge column on the road-side near Fores, more than twenty feet high, erected in commemoration of the final retreat of the Danes from Scotland, and properly called Swene's Stone. WALTER SCOTT.

* S ii.348, W iv.120, C 301, AN v.90, H-P v.116 ("1831", adds a further reference); *variant* RC 82–83.

26] all indicate the rude times in which this castle was erected. There were here some large venerable trees[1]. | Cawder Castle, here described, has been since much damaged by fire. WALTER SCOTT.

* S ii.351, W iv.123, C 302, AN v.92; *variant* C 85–86, *variant H-P* v.119–120, 508.

27] He said he was shown it in the Herald's office, spelt fourteen different ways[2]. | Bruce, the Abyssinian traveller, found in the annals of that region a king names *Brus*, which he chooses to consider the genuine orthography of the name. This circumstance occasioned some mirth at the court of Gondar. WALTER SCOTT.

* S ii.354, W iv.129, C 303, AN v.95, H-P v.123–124 ("1831", adds a further reference); *omitted* RC 89.

28] We dined at a publick-house called the *General's Hut*[1] | It is very odd that when these roads were made there was no care taken for *Inns*. The *King's House* and the *General's Hut* are miserable places; but the project and plans were purely military. WALTER SCOTT.

* S ii.365, W iv.141, C 307, AN v.104; *variant* RC 99, *variant* H-P v.134.

29] We passed through Glensheal[1] | In 1719, Spain projected an invasion of Scotland in behalf of the *Chevalier*, and destined a great force for that purpose, under the command of the Duke of Ormond. But owing to storms, only three frigates, with three hundred or four hundred Spaniards on board, arrived in Scotland. They had with them the banished Earl of Seaforth, chief of the Mackenzies, a man of great power, exiled for his share in the rebellion in 1715. He raised a considerable body of Highlanders of his own and friendly clans, and disembarking the Spaniards, came as far as the great valley called Glensheal, in the West Highlands. General Wightman marched against them from Inverness with a few regular forces, and several of the Grants, Rosses, Munros, and other clans friendly to government. He found the insurgents in possession of a very strong pass called Strachel, from which, after a few days' skirmishing, they retired, Seaforth's party not losing a man, and the others having several slain. But the Earl of Seaforth was dangerously wounded in the shoulder, and obliged to be carried back to the ships. His clan deserted or dispersed, and the Spaniards surrendered themselves prisoners of war to General Wightman. WALTER SCOTT.

* S ii.372, W iv.149, C 309, AN v.110; *omitted* RC 106, *variant* H-P v.140, 516.

30] It is indeed pointed at the top; but one side of it is larger than the other[2] | This was hypercritical; the hill is indeed not a cone, but it is *like* one. WALTER SCOTT.

* S ii.372, W iv.150, C 309, AN v.111; *omitted* RC 106, *omitted* H-P v.141.

31] We had a considerable circle about us, men, women, and children, all M'Craas[1], Lord Seaforth's people. | The Mac Raes are an example of what sometimes occurred in the Highlands, a clan who had no chief or banner of their own, but mustered under that of another tribe. They were originally attached to the Frasers, but on occasion of an intermarriage, they were transferred to the Mackenzies, and have since mustered under Seaforth's standard. They were always, and are still, a set of bold hardy men, as much attached to the *Caberfae* (or stag's head) as the Mackenzies, to whom the standard properly belongs. WALTER SCOTT.

 * S ii.373, W iv.151, C 309, AN v.111; *variant* RC 107, *variant* H-P v.142.

32] the learned Sir James Foulis[2] | Sir James Foulis, of Collinton, Bart. was a man of an ancient family, a good scholar, and a hard student; duly imbued with a large share both of Scottish shrewdness and Scottish prejudice. His property, his income at least, was very moderate. Others might have increased it in a voyage to India, which he made in the character of a commissioner; but Sir James returned as poor as he went there. Sir James Foulis was one of the Lowlanders whom Highlanders allowed to be well skilled in the Gaelick, an acquaintance which he made late in life. WALTER SCOTT.

 * S ii.382, W iv.162, C 313, AN v.119, *indirect* H-P v.150, 518 ("1831", cites first part of last sentence only); *omitted* RC 114.

33] JOHNSON. "Let there be men to keep them clean. Your ancestors did not use to let their arms rust." | Dr. Johnson seems to have forgotten that a Highlander going armed at this period incurred the penalty of serving as a common soldier for the first, and of transportation beyond sea for a second offence. And as "for calling out his clan," twelve Highlanders and a bagpipe made a rebellion. WALTER SCOTT.

 * S ii.383, W iv.163 (adds "See Johnson's letter to Mrs. Thrale of the 23d.Sept."), C 313 (deletes additional line and adds 7-line note signed "Croker, 1846"), AN v.120, H-P v.151 (Scott text only, "1831"); *omitted* RC 115.

34] he composed the following Ode, addressed to Mrs. Thrale[1] | About fourteen years since, I landed in Sky, with a party of friends, and had the curiosity to ask what was the first idea on every one's mind at landing. All answered separately that it was this Ode. WALTER SCOTT.

 * S ii.388, W iv.168 (adds date [1829.]), C 314 (adds 17-line note), AN v. 126, H-P v.157 (Scott text only, "1831"); *omitted* RC 120.

35] a purple camblet kilt[1] | *A purple camlet kilt.*—To evade the law against the tartan dress, the Highlands used to dye their variegated plaids and kilts into blue, green, or any single colour. WALTER SCOTT.

 * S ii.393, W iv.174 (this and later entries omit redundant italic phrase), C 316, AN v.131, H-P v.162 ("1831"); *omitted* RC 125.

36] Malcolm said he would come to it[1] | The Highlanders were all well inclined to the episcopalian form, *proviso* that the right *king* was prayed for. I suppose Malcolm meant to say, "I will come to your church because you are *honest* folk;" viz. *Jacobites.* WALTER SCOTT.

 * S ii.393–394, W iv.175, C 316, AN v.131, H-P v.162 ("1831"); *omitted* RC 126.

37] every woman in the parish was welcome to take the milk from his cows, provided she did not touch them[1]. | Such spells are still believed in. A lady of property in Mull, a friend of mine, had a few years since much difficulty in rescuing from the superstitious fury of the people an old woman, who used a *charm* to injure her neighbour's cattle. It is now in my possession, and consists of feathers, parings of nails, hair, and such like trash, wrapt in a lump of clay. WALTER SCOTT.

 * S ii.395, W iv.177, C 317, AN v.132, H-P v.164 ("1831"); *variant* RC 127.

38] he could not affirm that Ossian composed all that poem as it is now published. This came pretty much to what Dr. Johnson had maintained[2] | This seems the common sense of this once furious controversy. WALTER SCOTT.

 * S ii.395, W iv.178, C 317, AN v.132; *omitted* RC 127, *variant* H-P v.164.

39] Sandie Macleod, who has at times an excessive flow of spirits, and had it now, was, in his days of absconding, known by the name of *M'Cruslick*[3] | Alexander Macleod, of Muiravenside, advocate, became extremely obnoxious to government by his zealous personal efforts to engage his chief, Macleod, and Macdonald of Sky, in the Chevalier's attempt of 1745. Had he succeeded, it would have added one-third at least to the jacobite army. Boswell has oddly described *M'Cruslick*, the being whose name was conferred upon this gentleman, as something betwixt Proteus and Don Quixote. It is the name of a species of satyr, or *esprit follet*, a sort of mountain Puck or hobgoblin, seen among the wilds and mountains, as the old Highlanders believed, sometimes mirthful, sometimes mischievous. Alexander Macleod's precarious mode of life, and variable spirits, occasioned the *soubriquet*. WALTER SCOTT.

　　* S ii.397–398, W iv.180, C 318, AN v.134, H-P v.166 ("1831"); *omitted* RC 129.

40] One of our company[2], I was told, had hurt himself by too much study, particularly of infidel metaphysicians, of which he gave a proof, on second sight being mentioned. | Probably Talisker, who had been a good deal abroad. WALTER SCOTT.

　　* S ii.399, *variant* W iv.182 ("Mr William Macpherson informs me, that the gentleman alluded to was The Laird of MacKinnon.—C<ROKER>. 1835."), C 318 (W note slightly revised), AN v.135; *omitted* RC 130, *variant* H-P v.168, 525 (full account of Mackinnon, without reference to Croker).

41] it was formerly much the custom, in these isles, to have human bones lying above ground, especially in the windows of churches[2]. | It is perhaps a Celtic custom; for I observed it in Ireland occasionally, expecially at the celebrated promontory of Mucruss, at Killarney. WALTER SCOTT.

　　* S ii.401, W iv.185, C 319 (after "at" inserts "[the ruined abbey church on]"), AN v.137; *omitted* RC 131, *omitted* H-P v.169.

42] Miss Flora Macdonald[1] | [It is stated in the account of the rebellion, published under the title of "*Ascanius*," that she was the daughter of Mr. Macdonald, a tacksman or gentleman-farmer, of Melton, in South Uist, and was, in 1746, about twenty-four years old. It is also said, that her portrait was painted in London in 1747, for Commodore Smith, in whose ship she had been brought prisoner from Scotland; but the editor has not been able to trace it. Dr. Johnson says of her to Mrs. Thrale, "She must then have been a very young lady; she is now not old; of a pleasing person, and elegant behaviour. She told me that she thought herself honoured by my visit; and I am sure that whatever regard she bestowed on me was liberally repaid. 'If thou likest her opinions, thou wilt praise her virtue.' She was carried to London, but dismissed without a trial, and came down with Malcolm Macleod, against whom sufficient evidence could not be procured. She and her husband are poor, and are going to try their fortune in America. Sic rerum volvitur orbis."—*Letters*, i. 153. They did emigrate to America; but returned to Sky, where she died on the 4th March, 1790, leaving a son, Colonel John Macdonald, now, as the Editor is informed, residing at Exeter, and a daughter, still alive in Sky, married to a Macleod, a distant relation of the *Macleod*.—ED.] It is remarkable that this distinguished lady signed her name Flory, instead of the more classical orthography. Her marriage contract, which is in my possession, bears the name spelled *Flory*. WALTER SCOTT.

　　* S ii.416–417, W iv.204 (reads 'I' for 'the Editor'), C 324 (adds "We shall see presently that she sometimes signed *Flora*.—CROKER."), AN v.150; *variant* RC 143–144, *variant* H-P v.184, 529–531 (quotes directly a portion of Johnson's letter and adds considerable biographical data).

43] She still returned to her pretty farm—rich ground—fine garden. "Madam," said Dr. Johnson, "were they in Asia, I would not leave the rock[1]." | Dunvegan well deserves the stand which was made by Dr. Johnson in its defence. Its greatest inconvenience was that of access. This had been originally obtained from the sea, by a subterranean staircase, partly arched, partly cut in the rock, which, winding up through the cliff, opened into the court of the castle. This passage, at all times very inconvenient, had been abandoned, and was ruinous. A very indifferent substitute had been made by a road, which, rising from the harbour, reached the bottom of the moat, and then ascended to the gate by a very long stair. The present chief, whom

I am happy to call my *friend*, has made a perfectly convenient and characteristic access, which gives a direct approach to the further side of the moat, in front of the castle gate, and surmounts the chasm by a drawbridge, which would have delighted *Rorie More* himself. I may add that neither Johnson nor Boswell were antiquaries, otherwise they must have remarked, amongst the *Cimelia* of Dunvegan, the fated or fairy banner, said to be given to the clan by a Banshee, and a curious drinking cup (probably), said to have belonged to the family when kings of the Isle of Man—certainly of most venerable antiquity. WALTER SCOTT.

   * S ii.445–446, W iv.239–240 (dated 1829), C 340 (without date), AN v.188; *omitted* RC 176, *omitted* H-P v.223, ii.195 (the second, cross-reference, is false).

44] it has the sea—islands—rocks—hills—a noble cascade; and when the family is again in opulence, something may be done by art[1]. | Something has indeed been, partly in the way of accommodation and ornament, partly in improvements yet more estimable, under the direction of the present beneficent Lady of Macleod. She has completely acquired the language of her husband's clan, in order to qualify herself to be their effectual benefactress. She has erected schools, which she superintends herself, to introduce among them the benefits, knowledge, and comforts of more civilized society; and a young and beautiful woman has done more for the enlarged happiness of this primitive people than had been achieved for ages before. WALTER SCOTT.

   * S ii.446, W iv.240, C 340 (after "Macleod" adds [Miss Stephenson]), AN v.189; *variant* RC 176, *omitted* H-P v.223.

45] What can the M'Craas tell about themselves a thousand years ago[1]? | "What can the M'Craas tell of themselves a thousand years ago?" More than the Doctor would suppose. I have a copy of their family history, written by Mr. John Mac Ra, minister of Dingwal, in Rosshire, in 1702. In this history, they are averred to have come over with those Fitzgeralds now holding the name of M'Kenzie, at the period of the battle of Largs, in 1263. I was indulged with a copy of the pedigree by the consent of the principal persons of the clan in 1826, and had the original in my possession for some time. It is modestly drawn up, and apparently with all the accuracy which can be expected when tradition must be necessarily much relied upon. The name was in Irish Mac Grath, softened in the Highlands into Mac Ra, Mac Corow, Mac Rae, &c.; and in the Lowlands, where the patronymic was often dropped, by the names of Crow, Craw, &c. WALTER SCOTT.

   * S ii.447–448, W iv.242, C 340, AN v.190; *omitted* RC 177, *omitted* H-P v.225, 142.

46] the late M'Leod of Hamer, who wrote a treatise on the second-sight, under the designation of "Theophilus Insulanus[2]." | The work of "Theophilus Insulanus" was written in as credulous a style as either Dr. Johnson or his biographer could have desired. WALTER SCOTT.

   * S ii.448, W iv.243, C 341, AN v.191; *omitted* RC 178, *variant* H-P v. 225.

47] we talked of the extraordinary fact of Lady Grange's being sent to St. Kilda, and confined there for several years, without any means of relief[1]. | [The true story of this lady, which happened in this century, is as frightfully romantic as if it had been the fiction of a gloomy fancy. She was the wife of one of the lords of session in Scotland, a man of the very first blood of his country. For some mysterious reasons, which have never been discovered, she was seized and carried off in the dark, she knew not by whom, and by nightly journeys was conveyed to the Highland shores, from whence she was transported by sea to the remote rock of St. Kilda, where she remained, amongst its few wild inhabitants, a forlorn prisoner, but had a constant supply of provisions, and a woman to wait on her. No inquiry was made after her, till she at last found means to convey a letter to a confidential friend, by the daughter of a Catechist, who concealed it in a clue of yarn. Information being thus obtained at Edinburgh, a ship was sent to bring her off; but intelligence of this being received, she was conveyed to Macleod's island of Herries, where she died; [but was buried, as

Macleod informs the Editor <Croker>, at Dunvegan.]—Boswell] The story of Lady Grange is well known. I have seen her Journal. She had become privy to some of the jacobite intrigues, in which her husband, Lord Grange (brother of the Earl of Mar, and a lord of session), and his family were engaged. Being on indifferent terms with her husband, she is said to have thrown out hints that she knew as much as would cost him his life. The judge probably thought of Mrs. Peachum, that it is rather an awkward state of domestic affairs when the wife has it in her power to hang the husband. Lady Grange was the more to be dreaded, as she came of a vindictive race, being the grandchild of that Chicsley of Dalry, who assassinated Sir George Lockhart, the lord president. Many persons of importance in the Highlands were concerned in removing her testimony. The notorious Lovat, with a party of his men, were the direct agents in carrying her off (see *ante*, vol.i. p. 155); and St. Kilda, belonging then to Macleod, was selected as the place of confinement. The name by which she was spoken or written of was *Corpach*, an ominous distinction, corresponding to what is called *subject* in the lecture-room of an anatomist, or *shot* in the slang of the Westport murderers. WALTER SCOTT. *<Boswell's note continued:>* In "Carstare's State Paper," we find an authentick narrative of Connor, a catholick priest, who turned protestant, being seized by some of Lord Seaforth's people, and detained prisoner in the island of Harris several years: he was fed with bread and water, and lodged in a house where he was exposed to the rains and cold. Sir James Ogilvy writes, June 18, 1667, "that the Lord Chancellor, the Lord Advocate, and himself, were to meet next day, to take effectual methods to have this redressed. Connor was then still detained."—P.310. This shows what private oppression might in the last century be practised in the Hebrides. In the same collection, the Earl of Argyle gives a picturesque account of an embassy from *the great M'Neil of Barra*, as that insular chief used to be denominated. "I received a letter yesterday from M'Neil of Barra, who lives very far off, sent by a gentleman in all formality, offering his service, which had made you laugh to see his entry. The style of his letter runs as if he were of another kingdom."—P. 643.—Boswell] It was said of M'Neil of Barra, that when he dined, his bagpipes blew a particular strain, intimating that all the world might go to dinner. WALTER SCOTT.

   * S ii.451, W iv.246–247 (for "Editor" reads "me", for "Chicsley" reads "Chiesley", and after first Scott quotation adds 3-line note from Chambers), C 341–342 (omits the Croker interjection in brackets, after "Grange" adds "(an Erskine"; thereafter reads "Chiesley" etc. as in W), AN v.193–194, H-P v.227–228 (Boswell's and Scott's notes each rendered as a single narrative, Scott's ("1831") with "Chiesley" spelling but no reference to Croker or Chalmers notes); *variant* RC 180–181 (after Boswell the further account dependent on Chalmers and other sources).

48] at one place there is a row of false cannon[1] of stone. | Dunvegan Castle is mounted with real cannon; not unnecessarily, for its situation might expose it in war to be plundered by privateers. WALTER SCOTT.

   * S ii.457, W iv.253, C 344, AN v.198; *omitted* RC 184, *variant* H-P v.233 (quotes Scott's description of Dunvegan in 1814, Lockhart iii.226; defines "false cannon" as gargoyles).

49] the Cuillin[1], a prodigious range of mountains | These picturesque mountains of Sky take their name from the ancient hero, *Cuchullin*. The name is pronounced Quillen. I wonder that Boswell nowhere mentions *Macleod's Maidens*—two or three immense stacks of rock, like the Needles at the Isle of Wight; and *Macleod's Dining-Tables*—hills which derive their name from their elevated, steep sides, and flat tops. WALTER SCOTT.

   * S ii.460, W iv.258, C 345, AN v.200–201; *omitted* RC 187, *omitted* H-P v.236.

50] Radaratoo, radarate, radara, tadara, tandore[1] | [This droll quotation, I have since found, was from a song in honour of the Earl of Essex, called *"Queen Elizabeth's Champion,"* which is preserved in a collection of Old Ballads, in three volumes published in London in different years, between 1720–1730. The full verse is as follows: <6 lines quoted> BOSWELL] The old ballad here mentioned also occurs in Mr. Evans's collection of historical ballads, published as a Supplement to Percy's Reliques, under the inspection, I believe, of William Julius Mickle, who inserted many modern imitations of the heroick ballads of his own composing. WALTER SCOTT.

    * S ii.465, W iv.263, C 346, AN v.205–206; *omitted* RC 191 (Boswell note only), *omitted* H-P v.241 (after Boswell another reference).

51] translation of an ancient poem[2]. | This account of Ossian's Poems, as published by M'Pherson, is that at which most sensible people have arrived, though there may be some difference between the plus and minus of the ancient ingredients employed by the translator. WALTER SCOTT.

    * S ii.466, W iv.264, C 347 (adds 6-line postscript), AN v.206–207; *omitted* RC 192, *omitted* H-P v.242.

52] There is a great scarcity of specie in Sky[4]. | This scarcity of cash still exists on the islands, in several of which five-shilling notes are necessarily issued to have some circulating medium. If you insist on having change, you must purchase something at a shop. WALTER SCOTT.

    * S ii.478, W iv.280, C 351, AN v.216–217, H-P v.254; *omitted* RC 200.

53] "Adventures of a Guinea[2];" | It is strange that Johnson should not have known that the "Adventures of a Guinea" was written by a namesake of his own, Charles Johnson. Being disqualified for the bar, which was his profession, by a supervening deafness, he went to India and made some fortune, which he enjoyed at home. WALTER SCOTT. <3-line Croker postscript>

    * S ii.500, W iv.307 (deletes "which he enjoyed at home" and, for the Croker postscript, substitutes another note beginning "See also Scott's Lives of the Novelists. . ."), C 359 (after "fortune" adds "and died there about 1800"; reinserts his own postscript with a preliminary sentence: "He died, says the *Biographical Dictionary*, in Bengal, about 1800."), AN v.235, H-P v.275 (reprints Scott only from the C 1848 revision, but wrongly dates this "1831"; adds a postscript); *variant* RC 218.

54] He had looked at a novel, called "The Man of the World," at Rasay, but thought there was nothing in it[1]. | Though not, perhaps, so popular as the "Man of Feeling" of the same amiable author, the "Man of the World" is a very pathetic tale. WALTER SCOTT.

    * S ii.502, W iv.309 (adds "[*The Man of the World* was published in 1773, without the name of the author.]"), C 359 (before Scott note inserts "By Henry MacKenzie" and assigns the further W line to Croker), AN v.236; *variant* RC 219, *variant* H-P v.277.

55] The truth is, he knew nothing of the danger we were in[1] | [He at least made light of it, in his letters to Mrs. Thrale. "After having been detained by storms many days at Skie, we left it, as we thought, with a fair wind; but a violent gust, which Boswell had a great mind to call a tempest, forced us into *Col*, an obscure island; on which— 'nulla campis arbor aestivâ recreatur aurâ.' "—*Letters*, vol. i. p. 167—ED.] Their risque, in a sea full of islands, was very considerable. Indeed the whole expedition was highly perilous, considering the season of the year, the precarious chance of getting sea-worthy boats, and the ignorance of the Hebrideans, who, notwithstanding the opportunities, I may say the *necessities* of their situation, are very careless and unskilful sailors. WALTER SCOTT.

    * S ii.509, W v.7, C 362, AN v.242, H-P v.283 ("1831", with preliminary note); *omitted* RC 224.

56] no intentional fasting[1], but happened just in the course of a literary life." | This was probably the same kind of *unintentional* fasting, as that which suggested to him, at an earlier period, the affecting epithet *impransus*, (*ante*, vol. i. p. 107.) WALTER SCOTT.

   * S ii.511, W v.9, C 362, AN v.243; *omitted* RC 225, *variant* H-P v.284.

57] The name is certainly Norwegian[1] | M'Swyne has an awkward sound, but the name is held to be of high antiquity, both in the Hebrides and the north of Ireland. WALTER SCOTT. <7-line Croker postscript>

   * S ii.516, W v.15, C 364, AN v.248; *omitted* RC 229, *omitted* H-P v.289.

58] verse of the song *Hatyin foam'eri*[2] | *Hatyin foam*, (see *ante*, p. 393). A very popular air in the Hebrides, written to the praise and glory of Allan of Muidartach, or Allen of Muidart, a chief of the Clanranald family. The following is a translation of it by a fair friend of mine: <cites 26 lines, the first beginning "Come, here's a pledge to young and old," WALTER SCOTT. <1-line Croker postscript>

   * S ii.516–517, W v.15–16 (after "friend of mine" adds "[the late Margaret Maclean Clephane, Marchioness of Northampton]"), C 364 (with W addition and further note on the imperfect song), AN v.248–249; *omitted* RC 229, *variant* H-P v.290 (notes a translation in S and W editions, but Scott not mentioned).

59] Dr. Johnson said, "How *the devil* can you do it[1]?" | The question which Johnson asked with such unusual warmth might have been answered "by sowing the bent, or couch-grass." WALTER SCOTT.

   * S ii.534, W v.37, C 371, AN v.264, H-P v.306 ("1831"); *variant* RC 243.

60] Flora Macdonald waited on Lady Margaret[1] | [Though her husband took arms for the house of Hanover, she was suspected of being an ardent jacobite; and, on that supposition, Flora Macdonald guided the Pretender to Mugstot.—ED.] On the subject of Lady Margaret Macdonald, it is impossible to omit an anecdote which does much honour to Frederick, Prince of Wales. By some chance Lady Margaret had been presented to the princess, who, when she learnt what share she had taken in the Chevalier's escape, hastened to excuse herself to the prince, and explain to him that she was not aware that Lady Margaret was the person who had harboured the fugitive. The prince's answer was noble: "And would *you* not have done the same, madam, had he come to you, as to her, in distress and danger? I hope—I am sure you would!" WALTER SCOTT.

   * S ii.561, W iv.330, C 326, AN v.154, H-P v.188 ("1831"); *omitted* RC 146.

61] a case[1], containing a silver spoon, knife, and fork | The case with the silver spoon, knife, and fork, given by the Chevalier to Dr. Macleod, came into the hands of Mary, Lady Clerk of Pennycuik, who intrusted me with the honourable commission of presenting them, in her ladyship's name, to his present majesty, upon his visit to Scotland. WALTER SCOTT.

   S ii.567, W iv.337 (after last word adds "in 1822"), C 239, AN v.161; *omitted* RC 152, *omitted* H-P v.195.

62] We thought of sailing about easily from island to island; and so we should, had we come at a better season[1] | This observation is very just. The time for the Hebrides was too late by a month or six weeks. I have heard those who remembered their tour express surprise they were not drowned. WALTER SCOTT.

   * S iii.7, W v.46, C 373, AN v.270, H-P v.313 ("1831"); *omitted* RC 249.

63] a man of the world[1] | M'Quarrie was hospitable to an almost romantic degree. He lived to an extreme old age. WALTER SCOTT.

   * S iii.14, W v.54, C 375, AN v.276; *omitted* RC 253, *variant* H-P v.319, 556.

64] Ulva is the only place where this custom remains[2] <of presenting a sheep to tenants upon their marriage> | This custom still continues in Ulva. WALTER SCOTT.

   * S iii.15, W v.56, C 376, AN v.278; *omitted* RC 254, *variant* H-P v.321.

65] we took boat, and proceeded to Inchkenneth[1] | Inchkenneth is a most beautiful little islet of the most verdant green, while all the neighbouring shore of Greban, as well as the large islands of Colinsay and Ulva, are as black as heath and moss can make them. But Ulva has a good anchorage, and Inchkenneth is surrounded by shoals. It is now uninhabited. The ruins of the huts, in which Dr. Johnson was received by Sir Allan M'Lean, were still to be seen, and some tatters of the paper hangings were to be seen on the walls. Sir George Onesiphorus Paul was at Inchkenneth with the same party of which I was a member. He seemed to me to suspect many of the Highland tales which he heard, but he showed most incredulity on the subject of Johnson's having been entertained in the wretched huts of which we saw the ruins. He took me aside, and conjured me to tell him the truth of the matter, "This Sir Allan," said he, "was he a *regular baronet*, or was his title such a traditional one as you find in Ireland?" I assured my excellent acquaintance that, "for my own part, I would have paid more respect to a knight of Kerry, or knight of Glynn; yet Sir Allan M'Lean was a *regular baronet* by patent;" and, having given him this information, I took the liberty of asking him, in return, whether he would not in conscience prefer the worst cell in the jail at Gloucester (which he had been very active in overlooking while the building was going on) to those exposed hovels where Johnson had been entertained by rank and beauty. He looked round the little islet, and allowed Sir Allan had some advantage in exercising ground; but in other respects he thought the compulsory tenants of Gloucester had greatly the advantage. Such was his opinion of a place, concerning which Johnson has recorded that "it wanted little which palaces could afford." WALTER SCOTT.

* S iii.16–17, W v.61–62, C 376–377 (adds 5-line note signed Croker, 1846), AN v.279, H-P v.322 ("1831", after "member" inserts Lockhart reference); *omitted* RC 256.

66] then I get up with him[1]." | This is not spoken of hare-coursing, where the game is taken or lost before the dog gets out of wind; but in chasing deer with the great Highland greyhound, *Col's* exploit is feasible enough. WALTER SCOTT.

* S iii.25, W v.66, C 379, AN v.286, H-P v.330 ("1831"); *omitted* RC 261.

67] our excellent companion *Col*[1] | Just opposite to M'Quarrie's house the boat was swamped by the intoxication of the sailors, who had partaken too largely of M'Quarrie's wonted hospitality. WALTER SCOTT. <13-line Croker postscript>

* S iii.26, W v.68–69, C 380, AN v.287, H-P v.331 ("1831", with variant postscript); *omitted* RC 262.

68] Tradition says, that a piper and twelve men once advanced into this cave, nobody can tell how far[1] | There is little room for supposing that any person ever went farther into M'Kinnon's cave than any man may now go. Johnson's admiration of it seems exaggerated. A great number of the M'Kinnons, escaping from some powerful enemy, hid themselves in this cave till they could get over to the isle of Sky. It concealed themselves and their birlings or boats, and they show M'Kinnon's harbour, M'Kinnon's dining-table, and other localities. M'Kinnon's candlestick was a fine piece of spar, destroyed by some traveller in the frantic rage for appropriation, with which tourists are sometimes animated. WALTER SCOTT.

* S iii.27, W v.70, C 380, AN v.288; *variant* RC 263, *omitted* H-P v.332.

69] I told *Lochbuy* that he was not John*ston*, but John*son*, and that he was an Englishman[1]. | Boswell totally misapprehended *Lochbuy's* meaning. There are two septs of the powerful clan of M'Donald, who are called Mac-Ian, that is, *John's-son*; and as Highlanders often translate their names when they go to the Lowlands,—as Gregorson for Mac-Gregor, Farquhar-son for Farquhar,—*Lochbuy* supposed that Dr. Johnson might be one of the Mac-Ians of Ardnamurchan, or of Glencro. Boswell's explanation was nothing to the purpose. The *Johnstons* are a clan distinguished in Scottish *border* history, and as brave as any *Highland* clan that ever wore brogues; but they lay entirely out of *Lochbuy*'s knowledge—nor was he thinking of *them*. WALTER SCOTT.

   * S iii.37, W v.82, C 383 (adds 3-line postscript signed CHAMBERS, 1846), AN v.296–297, H-P v.341–342 ("1831", thus no postscript); *variant* RC 271.

70] "Do you choose any cold sheep's head, sir?" "No, madam," said he, with a tone of surprise and anger[3]. | Begging pardon of the Doctor and his conductor, I have often seen and partaken of cold sheep's head at as good breakfast-tables as ever they sat at. This protest is something in the manner of the late Culrossie, who fought a duel for the honour of Aberdeen butter. I have passed over all the Doctor's other reproaches upon Scotland, but the sheep's head I will defend *totis veribus*. Dr. Johnson himself must have forgiven my zeal on this occasion; for if, as he says, *dinner* be the thing of which a man thinks *oftenest during the day, breakast* must be that of which he thinks *first in the morning*. WALTER SCOTT.

   * S iii.38, W v.83, C 384, AN v.297–298, H-P v.342–343 (adds 7-line postscript); *omitted* RC 271.

71] the laird could not be persuaded that he had lost his heritable jurisdiction[1]. | Sir Allan Maclean, like many Highland chiefs, was embarrassed in his private affairs, and exposed to unpleasant solicitations from attorneys, called in Scotland, *writers* (which, indeed, was the chief motive of his retiring to Inchkenneth). Upon one occasion he made a visit to a friend, then residing at Carron lodge, on the banks of the Carron, where the banks of that river are studded with pretty villas; Sir Allan, admiring the landscape, asked his friend, whom that handsome seat belonged to. "M———, the writer to the signet," was the reply. "Umph!" said Sir Allan, but not with an accent of assent, "I mean that other house." "Oh! that belongs to a very honest fellow, Jamie ———, also a writer to the signet." "Umph!" said the Highland chief of M'Lean, with more emphasis than before. "And yon smaller house?" "That belongs to a Stirling man; I forget his name, but I am sure he is a writer, too for ———." Sir Allan, who had recoiled a quarter of a circle backward at every response, now wheeled the circle entire, and turned his back on the landscape, saying, "My good friend, I must own, you have a pretty situation here; but d———n your neighbourhood." WALTER SCOTT.

   * S iii.39, W v.84, C 384, AN v.298–299, H-P v.343–344 ("1831"); *variant* RC 272.

72] I had reason to think that the Duchess of Argyle disliked me, on account of my zeal in the Douglas cause[1]. | Elizabeth Gunning, celebrated (like her sister, Lady Coventry) for her personal charms, had been previously Duchess of Hamilton, and was mother of Douglas, Duke of Hamilton, the competitor for the Douglas property with the late Lord Douglas: she was, of course, prejudiced against Boswell, who had shown all the bustling importance of his character in the Douglas cause, and it was said, I know not on what authority, that he headed the mob which broke the windows of some of the judges, and of Lord Auchinleck, his father, in particular. WALTER SCOTT.

   * S iii.48, W v.94, C 387, AN v.307, H-P v.353 ("1831" but deletes "celebrated . . . Hamilton, and"; *omitted* RC 280.

73] Et propter vitam vivendi perdere causas[1]." | [For this and the other translations to which no signature is affixed, I am indebted to the friend whose observations are mentioned in the notes, p. 313 and 501.—BOSWELL.] [Probably Dr. Hugh Blair.—ED]

   * S iii.57, W v.106 (postscript signed C[roker]), C 390 (postscript now assigned to "Walter Scott"), AN v.315; *omitted* RC 288 (Boswell note only), *omitted* H-P v.361 (Boswell note and postscript "I have little doubt that it was Malone. . . .").

74] Dr. Adam Smith[1] | Mr. Boswell has chosen to omit, for reasons which will be presently obvious, that Johnson and Adam Smith met at Glasgow; but I have been assured by Professor John Miller that they did so, and that Smith, leaving the party in which he had met Johnson, happened to come to another company where Miller was. Knowing that Smith had been in Johnson's society, they were anxious to know what had passed, and the more so as Dr. Smith's temper seemed much ruffled. At first Smith would only answer, "He's a brute—he's a brute;" but on closer examination, it appeared that Johnson no sooner saw Smith than he attacked him for some point of his famous letter on the death of Hume (*ante*, v. ii. p. 267, *n.*) Smith vindicated the truth of his statement. "What did Johnson say?" was the universal inquiry. "Why, he said," replied Smith, with the deepest impression of resentment, "he said, *you lie!*" "And what did you reply?" "I said, you are a son of a ———!" On such terms did these two great moralists meet and part, and such was the classical dialogue between two great teachers of philosophy. WALTER SCOTT.

 * S iii.65, W v.114–115, C 393 (adds 19-line postscript denying the encounter, signed CROKER, 1835), AN v.370–371 (adds 53-line addendum also denying the encounter), H-P v.369–370 ("1831", with Croker note "1835–48" and further reference to Napier); *omitted* RC 295.

75] one of the best productions of his masterly pen[1]. | Boswell himself was callous to the *contacts* of Dr. Johnson; and when telling them, always reminds one of a jockey receiving a kick from the horse which he is showing off to a customer, and is grinning with pain while he is trying to cry out, "pretty rogue—no vice—all fun." To him Johnson's rudeness was only *"pretty Fanny's way."* Dr. Robertson had a sense of good-breeding which inclined him rather to forego the benefit of Johnson's conversation than awaken his rudeness. WALTER SCOTT.

 * S iii. 66, W v.117, C 393–394, AN v.323; *variant* RC 296, *omitted* H-P v.370.

76] the transit of Johnson over the Caledonian hemisphere[1]. | Old Lord Auchinleck was an able lawyer, a good scholar, after the manner of Scotland, and highly valued his own advantages as a man of good estate and ancient family, and, moreover, he was a strict presbyterian and whig of the old Scottish cast. This did not prevent his being a terribly proud aristocrat; and great was the contempt he entertained and expressed for his son James, for the nature of his friendships and the character of the personages of whom he was *engoué* one after another. "There's nae hope for Jamie, mon," he said to a friend. "Jamie is gaen clean gyte.—What do you think, mon? He's done wi' Paoli—he's off wi' the land-louping scoundrel of a Corsican; and whose tail to you think he has pinned himself to now, mon?" Here the old judge summoned up a sneer of most sovereign contempt. "A *dominie*, mon—an auld dominie; he keeped a schūle, and cau'd it an acaadamy." Probably if this had been reported to Johnson, he would have felt it more galling, for he never much liked to think of that period of his life: it would have aggravated his dislike of Lord Auchinleck's whiggery and presbyterianism. These the old lord carried to such an unusual height, that once when a countryman came in to state some justice business, and being required to make his oath, declined to do so before his lordship, because he was not a *covenanted* magistrate. "Is that a' your objection, mon?" said the judge; "come your ways in here, and we'll baith of us tak the solemn league and covenant together." The oath was accordingly agreed and sworn to by both, and I dare say it was the last time it ever received such homage. It may be surmised how far Lord Auchinleck, such as he is here described, was likely to suit a high tory and episcopalian like Johnson. As they approached Auchinleck, Boswell conjured Johnson by all the ties of regard, and in requital of the services he had rendered him upon his tour, that he would spare two subjects in tenderness to his father's prejudices; the first related to Sir John Pringle, president of the royal society, about whom there was then some dispute current; the second concerned the general question of whig and tory. Sir John Pringle, as Boswell says, escaped, but the controversy between tory and covenanter raged with great fury, and ended in Johnson's pressing upon the old judge the question, what good Cromwell, of whom he had said something derogatory, had ever done to his country; when, after being much tortured, Lord Auchinleck at last spoke out, "God, doctor! he gart kings ken that they had a *lith* in their neck." He taught kings they had a *joint* in their necks. Jamie then set to mediating between his father and the philosopher, and availing himself of the judge's sense of hospitality, which was punctillious, reduced the debate to more order. WALTER SCOTT.

* S iii.78–79, W v.131, C 397–398, AN v.333, H-P v.382–383 (adds 21-line postscript and further reference to 569–570), *indirect* RC 305 (the conversation doubted, further extensive commentary).

77] Indeed, there have been few men whose conversation discovered more knowledge enlivened by fancy[1]. | Lord Elibank made a happy retort on Dr. Johnson's definition of oats, as the food of horses in England and of men in Scotland: "Yes," said he; "and where else will you see *such horses* and *such* men?" WALTER SCOTT.

* S iii.81, W v.136, C 399, AN v.335–336; *variant* RC 307, *omitted* H-P v.386.

78] "Nay, sir (said he), if you cannot talk better as a man, I'd have you bellow like a cow[2]." | [As I have been scrupulously exact in relating anecdotes concerning other persons, I shall not withhold any part of this story, however ludicrous. I was so successful in this boyish frolick, that the universal cry of the galleries was, "*Encore* the cow! *Encore* the cow!" In the pride of my heart I attempted imitations of some other animals, but with very inferior effect. My reverend friend, anxious for my *fame*, with an air of the utmost gravity and earnestnes, addressed me thus: "My dear sir, I would *confine* myself to the *cow!*"—BOSWELL] Blair's advice was expressed more emphatically, and with a peculiar *burr*—"*Stick to the cow*, mon!" WALTER SCOTT

* S iii.92, W v.148–149, C 402, AN v.345, H-P v.396 ("1831", with 4-line postscript); *omitted* RC 314 (Boswell's note only).

79] Mr. Braidwood told me it remained long in his school, but had been lost before I made my inquiry[1]. | [One of the best critics of our age "does not wish to prevent the admirers of the incorrect and nerveless style, which generally prevailed for a century before Dr. Johnson's energetic writings were known, from enjoying the laugh that this story may produce, in which he is very ready to join them." He, however, requests me to observe, that "my friend very properly chose a *long* word on this occasion, not, it is believed, from any predilection for polysyllables (though he certainly had a due respect for them), but in order to put Mr. Braidwood's skill to the strictest test, and to try the efficacy of his instruction by the most difficult exertion of the organs of his pupils." BOSWELL.] The *critic* was probably Dr. Blair. WALTER SCOTT.

* S iii.95, W v.152, C 403, AN v.347–348; *omitted* RC 316 (Boswell note only), *omitted* H-P v.399–400 (substitutes postscript identifying Malone.

80] A young lady[1] of quality | Probably one of the Ladies Lindsay, daughters of the Earl of Balcarres. WALTER SCOTT.

* S iii.96, W v.154 (adds "[One of these, Lady Ann Lindesay, wrote the beautiful ballad of *Auld Robin Gray*.]"), C 404 (addition signed LOCKHART), AN v.348; *omitted* RC 317, *omitted* H-P v.401, 575–576 (direct identification and further commentary).

81] I have suppressed[1] every thing which I thought could really hurt any one now living. | [Having found, on a revision of the first edition of this work, that, notwithstanding my best care, a few observations had escaped me, which arose from the instant impression, the publication of which might perhaps be considered as passing the bounds of a strict decorum, I immediately ordered that they should be omitted in the subsequent editions. I was pleased to find that they did not amount in the whole to a page. If any of the same kind are yet left, it is owing to inadvertence alone, no man being more unwilling to give pain to others than I am. . . . <11 lines> should have suppressed.—BOSWELL] [The only passages of this kind that the editor has observed are those relating to Sir Alexander Macdonald, *ante*, v. ii. p. 380, and to Mr. Tytler, *ante*, p. 83.—ED.] I believe the scribbler alluded to was William Thompson, author of the "Man in the Moon," and other satirical novels, half clever, half crazy kind of works. He was once a member of the kirk of Scotland, but being deposed by the presbytery of Auchterarder, became an author of all works in London, could seldom finish a work, on whatever subject, without giving a slap by the way to that same presbytery with the unpronounceable name. Boswell's denial of having retracted *upon compulsion* refutes what was said by Peter Pindar and others about "M'Donald's rage." WALTER SCOTT.

 * S iii.109, W v.170–171 (deletes the second, Croker note), C 408–409 (reinserts reference, now abbreviated, at the end of note), AN v.362; *variant* RC 327–328 (identifies the "scribbler" as John Wolcot), *omitted* H-P v.416 (after Boswell's note adds further commentary on Wolcot).

Annotations after the TOUR (82–84)

82] nor was he less delighted with the hospitality which he experienced in humbler life[1] | He was long remembered amongst the lower orders of Hebrideans by the title of the *Sassenach More*, the *big Englishman*. WALTER SCOTT.

 * S iii.111, W v.172, C 409, AN v.362; *omitted* RC 308, *omitted* H-P v.416.

83] order of the clans: Macdonald is first[4], Maclean second | The Macdonalds always laid claim to be placed on the right of the whole clans, and those of that tribe assign the breach of this order at Culloden as one cause of the loss of the day. The Macdonalds, placed on the left wing, refused to charge, and positively left the field unassailed and unbroken. Lord George Murray in vain endeavoured to urge them on by saying that their behaviour would make the left the right, and that he himself would take the name of Macdonald. On this subject there are some curious notices, in a very interesting journal written by one of the *seven men* of Moidart, as they were called—Macdonald of the Clanronald sept, who were the first who declared for the prince at his landing in their chief's country. It is in the Lockhart papers, vol. ii. p. 510. WALTER SCOTT.

 * S iii.112 (this letter from Johnson to Boswell, 27 November 1773, is unnumbered), W v.174 (numbered 172), C 410 (unnumbered).

84] Mr. Maclean of Torloisk in Mull[1] | Maclean of Torloisk was grandfather to the present Marchioness of Northampton. WALTER SCOTT.

 * S iii.184 (this letter from Boswell to Johnson, 18 February 1775, is unnumbered), W v.242 (numbered 206), C 433 (unnumbered).

WHOSE *MISTRESS*? THOMAS HARDY'S THEATRICAL COLLABORATION

by

PAMELA DALZIEL

HARDY scholars and others have long been familiar with the outlines of the controversy over the production of Arthur Wing Pinero's *The Squire* at the St James's Theatre on 29 December 1881. Pinero was immediately accused by several theatre critics of having plagiarized Hardy's *Far from the Madding Crowd*; in letters to the press both Hardy and his collaborator, Joseph Comyns Carr, insisted that the management of the St James's had read and rejected a dramatization of the novel that they themselves had submitted and that was, in certain respects, still closer to *The Squire*; Pinero denied all knowledge of any such adaptation and asserted that the play was 'solely the result of [his] own plan and purpose'.[1] Supporters rallied to both camps, and the argument was intermittently sustained in a number of newspapers and magazines over the next several months, kept alive by the commercial success of *The Squire* and the decision of Hardy and Carr to produce their own version of *Far from the Madding Crowd*, under that title, first in Liverpool and other provincial cities and then at the Globe Theatre in London. The two plays in fact ran head to head for several weeks in the late spring of 1882, with *Far from the Madding Crowd* faltering and falling first and *The Squire* emerging as the clear commercial victor.

Familiar as the outlines of the controversy are, it has rarely been considered in the context of Hardy's career-long interest in the theatre or of the several other instances of his entering into collaborative relationships.[2] Nor has any sustained attempt been made to engage with the one surviving textual witness, the copy of *Far from the Madding Crowd* submitted to the Lord Chamberlain's Office for licensing just prior to the play's first performance, at the Prince of Wales Theatre in Liverpool, on 27 February 1882,[3] or with the small group of surviving letters from Carr to Hardy in the Dorset County Museum.[4] Richard Little Purdy, in his *Thomas Hardy: A Bibliographical Study*, provides the fullest available account of the dramatization,[5] but his principal concern is to identify and bibliographically 'reconstruct' a printed ur-text, called *The Mistress of the Farm*, from the extensive fragments incorporated into the collaborative (and predominantly manuscript) *Far from the Madding Crowd*, which is itself only briefly referred to. Purdy acknowledged it to be 'more probable' that *The Mistress of the Farm* reflected a first collaboration between Hardy and Carr rather than Hardy's exclusive work, but by isolating it so decisively from the Hardy-Carr *Far from the Madding Crowd* within the context of a Hardy bibliography he created an exaggerated impression of the extent to which the textual stage represented by its surviving leaves was both readily distinguishable and arguably Hardyan. By giving full attention in this paper to all elements of the *Far from the Madding Crowd* manuscript as submitted to the Lord Chamberlain's Office, I hope to be able to substantiate Purdy's scrupulous but evidently reluctant suspicion about

---

1. 3 January 1882 [published 4 January] letter to the *Daily News, The Collected Letters of Sir Arthur Pinero*, ed. J. P. Wearing (1974), p. 60.

2. See, for example, *Thomas Hardy: The Excluded and Collaborative Stories*, ed. Pamela Dalziel (1992), and Thomas Hardy, *The Life and Work of Thomas Hardy*, ed. Michael Millgate (1984). There has also been some speculation as to the contributions that Hardy's first wife, Emma Hardy, may have made to his work.

3. British Library Add. MS. 53267 J; the licensing ticket of the Lord Chamberlain's Office, still attached, is dated 25 February 1882.

4. Since Hardy destroyed so much of his incoming correspondence for the years prior to 1918, these letters of Carr's must be seen as having in some sense been deliberately preserved.

5. Richard Little Purdy, *Thomas Hardy: A Bibliographical Study* (1954), pp. 28–30.

the authorship of *The Mistress of the Farm*, disentangle much more clearly than before the compositional history of the Hardy-Carr *Far from the Madding Crowd*, and establish the complexly collaborative status of the document that constitutes its unique textual witness.

One of the difficulties hampering any close investigation of the original Hardy-Carr collaboration has always been the conflicting testimony of those most immediately involved. The two principal participants told somewhat different stories in the public letters they wrote in response to the first reviews of *The Squire*, Hardy declaring in *The Times* that the managers of the St James's Theatre had had in their hands, not only 'the novel accessible to everybody', but also 'a manuscript play of my own', based on the novel but in some unspecified sense 'improved' by Carr before submission, while Carr himself recalled that he had 'prepared in collaboration with Mr. Hardy a dramatic version of his story'.[6] Many years later, in the official biography of himself that Hardy wrote for posthumous publication over his wife's name, he characterized the Liverpool production as a 'dramatization . . . prepared by Mr J. Comyns Carr some months earlier' (*Life and Work*, p. 158). Later still, Alice Carr, Comyns Carr's wife, implied in one set of memoirs that she had herself initiated a dramatization of *Far from the Madding Crowd* that her husband had then taken over, 'only keeping portions of the dialogue as I had adapted it to stage necessity',[7] while in another set she intimated that her husband was the initiator and that he and she had then carried out the task together: 'with the consent and assistance of the author we constructed a play from Thomas Hardy's book'.[8] It is small wonder that James F. Stottlar, in his account of the controversy as an episode in the history of the theatre, is forced to admit his inability to 'reconcile all of the discrepancies'.[9]

Such reconciliation may indeed be impossible. It is clear, for example, that Alice Carr's memories, demonstrably self-conflicting, were unreliable in other respects,[10] and that Hardy in old age was deliberately distancing himself from a play that was 'not sufficiently near the novel to be to [his] liking' (*Life and Work*, p. 158) and that he had no wish to see revived.[11] Responding

6. *The Times*, 2 January 1882, p. 6; they each wrote very similar letters to the *Daily News*, 2 January 1882, p. 2.

7. [Alice Carr], *J. Comyns Carr: Stray Memories* (1920), p. 83.

8. [Alice Carr], *Mrs J. Comyns Carr's Reminiscences*, ed. Eve Adams (1926), p. 76.

9. James F. Stottlar, 'Hardy vs. Pinero: Two Stage Versions of *Far from the Madding Crowd*', *Theatre Survey*, 18 (1977), 42.

10. In *Mrs J. Comyns Carr's Reminiscences* (p. 76), for example, she dates the dramatization of *Far from the Madding Crowd* later than those of two Hugh Conway novels, *Called Back* and *Dark Days*, which were produced in, respectively, 1884 and 1885.

11. Although the dramatization, as he pointed out to a French correspondent in August 1882 (*The Collected Letters of Thomas Hardy*, ed. Richard Little Purdy and Michael Millgate, 7 vols. [1978–88], i. 108), was not under his exclusive control, he was presumably in a position to negate any proposed revival. The absence of U.S. copyright protection for British authors rendered him helpless to prevent an unauthorized New York adaptation of *Far from the Madding Crowd* from being produced (under that title) in April 1882 (see Vera Liebert, '*Far from the Madding Crowd* on the American Stage', *The Colophon*, n.s. 3 (1938), 377–382), but when the British actor-manager Frank R. Benson applied in 1895 for permission to

in April 1910 to a request from the Society of Authors for a list of his dramatic works, he wrote: 'A dramatization by J. Comyns Carr of Far from the Madding Crowd was produced in 1882. I had no hand in this beyond authorizing it' (*Collected Letters*, iv. 80). And in 1926 Florence Hardy spoke of *Far from the Madding Crowd* as having been dramatized 'very badly, by Comyns Carr, and my husband says that it would have been a success if it had been done differently'.[12]

That these negative responses to the dramatization were not solely the consequence of altered aesthetic assumptions is clear from the indications in Carr's letter to Hardy of 20 January 1882 that Hardy had doubts about associating his name—and, indeed, his novel—with the production that was now being launched in opposition to *The Squire*: specifically, he wanted the authorship of the play to remain anonymous and its title to be something other than *Far from the Madding Crowd*. But Carr, recognizing that it would be advantageous to exploit the publicity generated by the *Squire* controversy, argued strenuously against such drastic measures and against an alternative suggestion of Hardy's that theatrical colleagues had found 'too circuitous and too unusual for a playbill'. He proposed instead that the play be advertised as 'Far From The Madding Crowd "adapted by J. Comyns Carr from the novel of that name in conjunction with the author Mr Thomas Hardy". I am assured [he added] that in case of failure this description would quite relieve you of responsibility' (Dorset County Museum). In the event this formula too was abandoned in favour of the thoroughly conventional 'By Thomas Hardy and J. Comyns Carr',[13] and Hardy, generously invoked by Carr in his first-night speech, found himself much mentioned in reviews and in the extensive quotations from those reviews included in the advertisements for the play which appeared in the London newspapers.[14]

In order to obtain a better understanding of Hardy's profound ambivalence about the play, and a clearer sense of the different phases and different hands involved in its composition, it is necessary to turn to the other available evidence. The Lord Chamberlain's copy of *Far from the Madding Crowd* is comprised of two notebooks, the first containing Acts I and II of the play as submitted, the second containing Act III. The first notebook, measuring 17.7 by 11.9 cm., is made up of sixty-one leaves, plus front and rear endpapers, stitched and glued together and wrapped along the spine with purple cloth tape. The gatherings are irregular, the first consisting of the front endpaper

produce a dramatic version of the novel Hardy's response was unequivocally negative (Benson to Hardy, 21 June and 15 July 1895, Dorset County Museum).

12. Letter of 11 July 1926 to Philip Ridgeway (Frederick B. Adams collection). I am grateful to Mr. Adams for generously allowing me access to his collection and to the Trustees of the Estate of the late Miss E. A. Dugdale for permission to quote from unpublished Florence Hardy and Thomas Hardy materials.

13. This was the wording adopted in the Prince of Wales programme; the Globe Theatre programme differed only in that Carr's first initial was omitted (copies of both programmes in the Richard Little Purdy Collection, Beinecke Library).

14. See, for example, *The Times*, 3 March 1882, p. 12.

(to which a leaf of rust-brown paper has been glued to form a front cover) plus the front free endpaper and two other leaves, the second of sixteen leaves, the third of seventeen leaves, the fourth of seven leaves, the fifth of four leaves, the sixth of nine leaves, the seventh of two leaves (two further leaves having been torn away), and the eighth of four leaves. The final gathering is followed by the rear free endpaper and the rear endpaper (to which another leaf of rust-brown paper has been glued to form a back cover).

The first gathering, final three gatherings, and rear endpapers are all of the same type of unruled paper, but the notebook has been disassembled and reassembled on at least one occasion and in the second through fifth gatherings the same paper has been interleaved with leaves of a printed text, each of whose pages bears the running head 'THE MISTRESS OF THE FARM.' Present are pages 19–36 of *The Mistress of the Farm*, constituting the entirety of its second act,[15] and pages 37–58, constituting the entirety of its third act. The first gathering (fos. 1–4 in the British Library foliation[16]) is in the hand of Alice Carr; the second through fifth gatherings (fos. 5–33) contain revisions in her hand and her husband's hand on both the printed (ex-*Mistress*) leaves and the facing blank leaves; the final three gatherings consist entirely of blank leaves. Evidence of Hardy's hand can be found on only a single page (fo. 14[v]), where he has struck through his own incomplete comment.

The actual text inscribed or incorporated into the first notebook terminates at the conclusion of Act II of *Far from the Madding Crowd*—corresponding closely, though by no means precisely, to the conclusion of the third act of *The Mistress of the Farm*. Act III of *Far from the Madding Crowd*, instead of occupying those available final leaves of the first notebook, was submitted to the Lord Chamberlain's Office in a separate, commercially produced notebook. Measuring 19.7 by 16.3 cm., this notebook is comprised of a single gathering of forty-eight ruled leaves stitched through the centre to the cover of red cloth over flexible card. The first twenty-six leaves (fos. 35–60) constitute a fair-copy transcription of the greater part of Act III, beginning in Carr's hand but continuing in Alice Carr's hand and then in an unidentified hand. The twenty-seventh through twenty-ninth leaves (fos. 61–63) have pasted on to them complete or fragmentary leaves torn from at least two copies of *The Mistress of the Farm*—pages 64–66 from its fourth act and one numberless fragment apparently from its first act.[17] The thirtieth leaf is blank, and the thirty-first through thirty-ninth leaves (fos. 64–72) complete the transcription of Act III—first in the same unidentified hand, then in Alice Carr's hand,

15. Although a blank leaf of notebook paper has been pasted together with the first incorporated leaf of *The Mistress of the Farm*, the printed text of p. 19, containing the opening of the second act, is in fact completely recoverable.

16. For ease of reference this foliation will be used throughout, even though it includes covers and endpapers, excludes blank leaves, and is continuous throughout the two notebooks.

17. That at least two copies of *The Mistress of the Farm* were used is clear from the presence of both p. 65 and p. 66, each of which is pasted to a separate leaf. The printed text of p. 63 was not incorporated in *Far from the Madding Crowd*, but it—as well as the text on the verso of the fragment—remains recoverable.

and finally in Carr's hand. A number of leaves in this second notebook also bear pencil comments and additions in Hardy's hand, for the most part erased, though legible still.

The segments of *The Mistress of the Farm* incorporated into these two notebooks represent all that now remains of what was clearly a complete dramatization of Hardy's novel presumably put into print[18] with a view to its submission to one or more theatrical managers. Because both the plot and dialogue of *The Mistress of the Farm* tend to conform so closely to the plot and dialogue of Hardy's novel, it is tempting to think that it could indeed be a purely Hardyan text, the unalloyed product of the first stage in the process Hardy described to William Moy Thomas, the dramatic critic of the *Daily News*, on 30 December 1881:

Some time ago I was induced to dramatize the story, which I did alone & unassisted, under the title of '*The Mistress of the Farm*—A pastoral drama.' Some time after this Mr Comyns Carr asked if I had ever thought of dramatizing the story, when I sent him the play as I had written it. He modified it in places, to suit modern stage carpentry &c, & offered it to the St James's. . . . (*Collected Letters*, i. 99)

But there is evidence indicating that both Carr and his wife were involved in the dramatization at quite an early stage and that *The Mistress of the Farm* in its printed form (as distinct from Hardy's presumed but now vanished manuscript) incorporates whatever of their suggestions Hardy agreed to accept.

Less than ideally specific is an undated letter from Carr, annotated ''80' by Hardy, in which he tells Hardy that 'We are hard at work upon your play and have some suggestions to make to you about it' (Dorset County Museum). However, in a later letter—again undated but written from Liverpool shortly after *Far from the Madding Crowd* had opened—Carr mentions valuable suggestions of a theatrically effective nature that Hardy himself had made on earlier occasions. When he speaks of Hardy's having 'proposed the total abolition of the first act', the reference must be to the abandonment of the first act of the printed *Mistress of the Farm*, which is wholly absent from the licensing copy of *Far from the Madding Crowd*, replaced there by a few pages of scene-setting and character-introducing rustic dialogue in Alice Carr's hand. But when Carr goes on to add, 'It was you also who at a much earlier date suggested that the second act should find them married' (letter of [early March 1882]; Dorset County Museum), the reference is clearly to an alteration incorporated into the printed text of *The Mistress of the Farm*, where the opening of the third act—which becomes, with the removal of the first act, Act II of *Far from the Madding Crowd*—is shortly followed, on pages 40–41 (fos. 23^v–24^r), by the entrance of Troy and Bathsheba, just returned to Weatherbury Farm following their secret marriage.

The 'suggestions' made by the Carrs at the same early stage in the history of the dramatization are impossible to reconstruct, but a possible clue is con-

18. Examination of other plays sent to the Lord Chamberlain's Office during the 1870s and 1880s suggests that this was a frequent but by no means universal practice.

tained in the letter of protest against *The Squire* that Hardy sent to *The Times*: 'Moreover, a gipsy, who does not exist in the novel, was introduced into our play, and I see that a gipsy figures in *The Squire*' (2 January 1882, p. 6). Although Hardy's phrase 'our play' is not in itself definitive, it does suggest that while Hardy himself may have sought to condense the action of the novel by omitting the role of Boldwood,[19] giving his surname to Fanny Robin, and introducing a new character, Fanny's brother Will,[20] as the instrument of revenge on Sergeant Troy, it was probably Carr who turned him into the 'mad' figure of *The Mistress of the Farm* as actually printed. Curiously, Will is nowhere identified as a gipsy in any of the printed pages that survive,[21] but if, as would appear, the version submitted to the St James's Theatre was the printed text of *The Mistress of the Farm* in its complete and unaltered form, then such a characterization of Will could have appeared in the subsequently deleted first act, or even in the list of *dramatis personae*.

According to the letter Carr wrote to Hardy immediately upon learning of the production of *The Squire*, their own play had been accepted at the St James's Theatre, managed by John Hare and William Hunter Kendal, but then 'rejected on the caprice of Mrs Kendal'—that is, Madge Kendal, the actress and wife of William Kendal (letter of [29 December 1881?]; Dorset County Museum). In his letter to the *Daily News*, Carr said that the play had been well received by Hare—who 'undertook to produce it at the St. James's Theatre, provided it was found equally acceptable to his partner'—but it was 'not favourably received by Mr. and Mrs. Kendal' (2 January 1882, p. 2). The exact details of the situation—as of the extent, if any, of Pinero's knowledge of it[22]—now seem irrecoverable, but it is not in any case difficult to imagine why *The Mistress of the Farm*, as submitted, might finally have been judged commercially unviable. That the first act was in some way awkward and tedious is sufficiently indicated by Hardy and Carr's subsequent decision to scrap it entirely, and since Troy was already dead (shot by Fanny's brother) by the end of the third act little would seem to have remained for the fourth and final act other than the slow and not especially dramatic process of Oak and Bathsheba's resumption of courtship and eventual marriage. For whatever reason, the final version of the dramatization abandoned the existing last act, found in Bathsheba's revelation of her marriage a theatrically effective conclusion to what (with the disappearance of the old first act) was now Act II, and reserved Troy's death for the penultimate event of a new final Act III

19. It is worth noting that Boldwood seems not to have been part of Hardy's original conception of the novel; see *Life and Work*, p. 97.

20. Fanny's surname, hence Will's, was subsequently changed back to 'Robin'.

21. Nor, indeed, is he identified thus anywhere in the licensing copy of *Far from the Madding Crowd*.

22. In his 5 January 1882 letter to the novelist William Black, Hardy wrote: 'as Carr was the go-between throughout I should have some difficulty in proving that conversations were reported to the management, & showing how Pinero attained his knowledge of the play. This is what is asserted in Town—that *Mrs. K.*, who was acquainted with our play, handed on the ideas to Pinero' (*Collected Letters*, i. 100–101).

that seems—apart from the few printed pages retained from *The Mistress of the Farm*—to have been completely rewritten.

The revisions to what were now Acts I and II mostly involved additions to the existing text, the excision of material at the beginning presumably mandating expansion later on, and it is of some interest that both the additions and the revisions to these acts (as contained in the first notebook) seem to have been aimed chiefly at reducing the stiffness of the dialogue, decreasing the incidence of dialect in Oak's and Bathsheba's speeches, intensifying the dialect of the more 'rustic' characters, and bringing the text of the play closer to that of the novel. One might speculate that some at least of the changes had been made or recommended by Hardy himself and were simply being transferred (chiefly by Alice Carr) to this particular copy, but a likelier explanation —especially in light of Alice Carr's later references to adapting Hardy's dialogue to stage necessities—is perhaps that, for the Carrs, the simplest and quickest way of amplifying a text that already followed the novel fairly closely was to refer back to the novel yet again.

It is not in any case certain that Hardy participated at all actively in the process of final revision, his reluctance to be too prominently associated with the production seeming symptomatic of a desire to distance himself from the possibility of further controversy that might be damaging to his essential career as a novelist.[23] However, the presence of his hand in the first notebook —albeit only on one page—does suggest that he had at least read the final version of Acts I and II, though his sole comment,[24] struck through before completion, offers no criticism, thus further suggesting that he did not have any substantial objections to the revised text, unless, of course, he articulated them in a now lost letter. With the substantially rewritten concluding act the situation was quite different, since Carr—because of time constraints, because Hardy had given him a nearly free hand, or simply because it seemed to him the only practicable procedure—did not send a copy of Act III to Hardy until it was already too late for changes to the production to be put into effect. In an undated letter written when the play was already in rehearsal, Carr confirms that things are going to plan ('We have decided as agreed between us to put the play back early in the present century') and gives reasons for the delay in supplying Hardy with the text of the new Act III: 'I should have sent you down the last act before but time so pressed that I was obliged to have the parts copied first. I have made more action in it and I think you will like

23. In the midst of the Pinero controversy, Hardy was himself accused of having plagiarized scenes in *A Laodicean* and *The Trumpet-Major* from, respectively, a *Quarterly Review* article and A. B. Longstreet's *Georgia Scenes*. The *Academy* (18 February 1882, pp. 120–121) quoted 'without comment' the parallel passages printed in the New York periodicals, the *Nation* (19 January 1882) and the *Critic* (28 January 1882). See also *Collected Letters*, i. 103–104.

24. 'honestly? he un' (fo. 14ᵛ). Hardy evidently intended to comment on the exchange between Bathsheba and Troy with respect to Fanny's lover, said to be in Troy's regiment: 'BATH.—Then you will find out for me whether he means honestly by her? TROY.—Honestly? BATH.—Yes; if he intends to marry her?'

[it] but as the actors have the parts don't alter more than you can help.'[25] It seems fair to assume from Carr's use of 'before' that this letter was in fact accompanied by the new Act III as contained in the second of the *Far from the Madding Crowd* notebooks. The implication would also seem to be that Hardy had by this time already seen and approved the alterations to Acts I and II contained in the first notebook. This sequence of events suggests a possible explanation for the slightly puzzling use of a second notebook when a considerable amount of blank space remained at the end of the first: Acts I and II, heavily dependent on the printed text of *The Mistress of the Farm*, could have been reworked relatively quickly and sent to Hardy for comment, while Act III, only minimally dependent on *The Mistress of the Farm*, required more time for its comprehensive rewriting.

What seems certain is that Hardy was deeply dissatisfied with Act III in its radically altered form, but was rendered essentially powerless—by time, distance, and theatrical inexperience—to affect the production in any significant way. His comments and suggestions—still visible on the licensing copy—evidently reached Liverpool only a few days before the opening night. Carr must himself have been under pressure from the more experienced Charles Kelly, who was playing Gabriel Oak but also acting as a stage manager, and he perhaps had less power to influence the final form of the production than Hardy imagined. The letter Carr wrote to Hardy shortly after the opening (i.e. in early March) and in response to Hardy's comments on the early reviews seems in any case to be offering for the first time an explanation of why his suggestions for the new Act III had not been adopted. Carr chiefly pleads, as in his letter sending the text of the act, the pressure of time and the fact that the actors had already learned their parts, but he also insists, in respect of particular suggestions, that they 'would have entirely dislocated the play as it stands and involved an amount of rewriting for which there was absolutely no time or opportunity' (Dorset County Museum).

Carr clearly had some grounds for arguing as he did. A fundamental change had been made between the shooting of Troy by Fanny's brother, Will, at the end of the penultimate act of *The Mistress of the Farm* and the postponement of that shooting to the end of the final act of *Far from the Madding Crowd*, the alteration requiring Act III now to begin with Bathsheba's retrospective narration of Troy's disappearance and presumed death two years earlier, on the very day of their wedding. Hardy's pencilled, erased, and then newly pencilled suggestion, 'Would it not be more natural if they had been married 2 or 3 months',[26] entirely overlooked the pains that had been taken in the preceding act to suggest that Troy and Bathsheba, though married, had not in fact spent a night together.[27] It would also (as Carr's letter

---

25. Dorset County Museum; I have supplied the period following 'first' and omitted following 'copied' an unwanted 'I' that Carr, writing in haste, failed to strike through.

26. Fo. 36. Also erased and then rewritten was the additional sentence, 'The object of making it on wedding day is plain enough but of little consequence in the circumstances' (the second 'of' was rendered as 'by' in the later version).

27. These and other precautions still did not prevent one critic from complaining:

pointed out) render absurd several of the preceding events, including Bathsheba's ruse to get Lydia out of the house and her appeal to her work-folk to remember their pledge of good will should they have cause in the future to think ill of her.

Equally problematic was Hardy's objection to a reference in Act III to Fanny Robin's suicide by drowning:[28] 'Why not died in workhouse, or hung herself in workhouse? I should much prefer keeping as near the book as possible.'[29] Again, he seems to have forgotten that Fanny's suicide and Troy's responsibility for it had been established—melodramatically and at some length—in Act II, so that Carr could with some justification respond: 'I do not myself see that anything is gained by the suggested alteration but I am quite certain that it would have involved the entire rewriting of the act [i.e. Act II] and I know of no one who has seen the play who does not find this act its best part' (letter of [early March 1882]).

Hardy's unease with the entire situation is well signalled by his preference for 'keeping as near the book as possible', and it would seem that his reading of the final act of *Far from the Madding Crowd*, reinforced by the first reviews of the Liverpool production, had given him a strong sense of the extent to which the play had departed not only from the novel but from his own control. From a description of the play in one early review it would appear that some aspects of the production may have gone even beyond the limits of the 'script' as represented by the licensing copy:

The story as told in the stage version may thus be briefly detailed:—Bathsheba [*sic*] Everdene, the young mistress of Weatherbury Farm, while secretly loved by a farmer named Gabriel Oak, with all a female's infatuation and waywardness, gives her affections to a Dragoon sergeant named Troy, a scoundrel who has already done irreparable injury to the maid Fanny Robin. During an interview between Gabriel Oak and Will Robin, the gipsy, the latter announces that Troy has seduced his sister, and he (Robin) means to be avenged on him. Gabriel attempts to pacify him, and they depart. Next the wronged girl and the faithless sergeant have an interview, which concludes with an attempt on the part of the villain to knock his victim down the village well. [The stage direction indicates only that he knocks her down.] Finally Bathsheba and her pretty maid, Lydia, enter and observe that a straw rick has taken fire, and they dispatch the rustics to put out the flames. The hero of the fire turns out to be Garbriel Oak, who is rewarded with the appointment of farm bailiff to Miss Everdene.

In the second act we find that the sergeant and Bathsheba have been clandestinely married, and almost the first act of the husband is to insist upon the dismissal of Gabriel Oak from the position of farm bailiff. This is accomplished by the heroine, who finds a pretext in the solemn warning against Troy, which Oak sees fit to address to her. Then the two men have an exciting encounter, at the end of which the wily soldier, by means of clever inuendoes, [*sic*] renders Oak as anxious to get the sergeant

'At the close of the play Mr. Carr has committed an error in allowing Bethsheba [*sic*] to seek consolation in the arms of Gabriel Oak a few minutes after the violent death of the man who, with all his faults, was still her husband' (*The Athenaeum*, 4 March 1882, p. 293).

28. This choice of means of death demonstrates once again the dominance of the suicide-by-drowning component of the Victorian myth of the fallen woman; see Lynda Nead, *Myths of Sexuality: Representations of Women in Victorian Britain* (1988).

29. Erased pencil, struck through in ink (i.e. not by Hardy himself), fo. 43ᵛ.

and his sweetheart speedily married as he was loth before to contemplate such a contingency. A climax, however, is forced on by the suicide of Troy's first victim, and the delivery of a letter to Bathesheba, accusing that utterly abandoned character of her ruin. The act concludes with a really powerful situation, in which Will Robin, the avenger, is with difficulty restrained from killing his sister's seducer, and Bathesheba, declaring that the disclosure comes too late, and that Troy is her husband, swoons away.

After the supposed lapse of two years, the third act opens with a situation in the course of which we gather that Sergeant Troy has been drowned. Bathesheba is found mourning for her husband, and still loved by her bailiff. He, hearing his name coupled with that of his mistress, decides to quit the country, and so gives her notice to leave. This she will not accept, and ends by asking him to stay, and to stay as her husband. Then comes the greatest situation of the play, for, whilst the villagers and servants are rejoicing at the news and congratulating the happy pair, Troy suddenly returns and claims his wife. She is about to follow him, when Will Robin comes on the scene and shoots him dead, whilst Bathesheba returns to the loving protection of Gabriel Oak. It will be gathered from this outline that there are several situations in the play, especially those at the close of the second and third acts, and the curtain fell on each occasion amid the most enthusiastic applause of the crowded audience.[30]

Although the play was still billed as a 'Pastoral Drama' and much of the dialogue was still recognizably close to that of the novel, the centrality now given to the role and actions of Will Robin[31] allowed one critic to pronounce that whereas Pinero in *The Squire* had achieved a genuinely 'idyllic and pastoral tone', even 'the purity and freshness of Mr. Hardy's style', Carr, on the other hand, 'with the apparent sanction of Mr. Hardy', leant 'rather to the melodramatic than to the idyllic spirit. The scent of the hay is there, but the smell of powder is stronger.'[32]

The mixed fortunes of *The Mistress of the Farm* were not such as to deter Hardy from all subsequent involvement in theatrical matters, but the experience brought him frustrations and disappointments that can hardly have been recompensed by Carr's first-night curtain speech,[33] in which he was variously reported as attributing to Hardy 'all that was original in character and plot in the play', 'all that was original in the plot or incident in the drama', or, simply, 'all the excellence of the work'.[34] Hardy knew well enough that such terminology, though no doubt generous in its intentions, nonetheless left ample room for much in the play that was not in fact his, and it is surely neither surprising nor, on his part, disingenuous that he should have

30. *The Era*, 4 March 1882, p. 8. Sketches of characters and episodes from the later Globe Theatre production appeared in the *Illustrated Sporting and Dramatic News*, 20 April 1882, p. 148.

31. One of Hardy's annotations to Act III states that 'Robin is a little too violent here & elsewhere. He should not be offensive to audience' (fo. 43).

32. *The Theatre*, 1 April 1882, p. 245; in the *Academy* review (13 May 1882, p. 348) of the London production Robin's killing of Troy is compared with Boldwood's in the novel and found to be 'a much more commonplace and melodramatic solution'.

33. Although Hardy and his wife went to Liverpool to see the production, and especially Marion Terry in the role of Bathsheba, they did not do so until after opening night (*Life and Work*, p. 158, and Carr's [early March 1882] letter to Hardy; cf. *Mrs J. Comyns Carr's Reminiscences*, p. 78).

34. *The Era*, 4 March 1882, p. 8; *Liverpool Daily Post*, 28 February 1882, p. 5; *Liverpool Mercury*, 28 February 1882, p. 6.

sought to disown the work in later years. There is perhaps a lesson here for modern students of Hardy, who may need to recognize that neither the surviving dramatization called *Far from the Madding Crowd* nor even what remains of *The Mistress of the Farm* can be viewed as other than the product of a complex revision process involving at least three hands, an intricately collaborative work with a far from automatic claim to inclusion in Hardy bibliographies.

SIGNING BY THE PAGE

by

B. J. McMullin

IT is easy to assume that in the hand-press period (and beyond) the invariable way of indicating—for members of the printing house as well as for members of the binding shop—the order in which the pages were to fall within a gathering, sheet or volume was to sign a certain number of *leaves* in each gathering; even when pagination had become all but universal the practice of signing at least the first leaf of the gathering was retained. Confirmation that the trade did use the leaf as the basis for reference lies not merely in the system itself (which may be taken to equate with foliation) but also in the practice of sometimes signing a cancellans according to the same system (i.e. by leaf) when the cancellandum was not signed—for example, actually signing cancellans $7 as '$7' in a volume signed in its original state perhaps only $1–4. Bibliographers have not only regarded leaf signatures as the trade's mechanism for keeping track of type-pages (before and after printing) but also adopted the system as the means of referring to leaves (and pages), since not all publications are foliated, paginated or columnated; that is, reference by leaf, based on the structure of the gathering, has been regarded by modern bibliographers as the only acceptable form of reference. Certainly, some bibliographers of modern books have adopted pagination as the basic system of reference, since in most books of the last two centuries pagination is correct and therefore useable. Nonetheless, most bibliographers still prefer reference by leaf—or they use a dual system—in that, for purposes of bibliographical analysis, reference by leaf relates more clearly to the structure of the volume, sheet or gathering and also copes more readily with sequences of unnumbered leaves or pages.

Concurrently, however, there has also existed within the trade a system of reference using as its base not the leaf but the *page*, a system which may in

fact be coexistent with printing from moveable type itself. Surviving manuscripts (and printed texts) which have served as printer's copy often bear
marginal references inserted in the printing house by the compositor to indicate page breaks in the typesetting.[1] The references usually take the form
of a page number and a signature, the latter denoting the gathering plus the
page within the gathering—thus '35/C3' indicates that the following page is
page number 35 in the continuous numbering and the third page in gathering C (i.e. C2^r). Such a system is intelligible and would appear to serve the
needs of compositors, although—unlike leaf signatures—having no obvious
application in the typesetting itself or in the subsequent printing and binding of the sheets. Nonetheless, in certain publications of the late seventeenth
century and the eighteenth signed by the leaf in the normal way, there may
be an occasional leaf 'signed' according to the *page* which its recto occupies
within the gathering, in the same manner that the beginnings of pages are
marked in printer's copy. This is the practice which I call 'signing by the
page', the resultant signature a 'page signature'. Thus instead of being unsigned, page $8^r may in certain circumstances be signed '$15', indicating,
that is, that the recto of that particular leaf occupies the 15th page within
the gathering. (Sometimes, too, 'p.' precedes the number, as '$ p.15'.)

The equation of number and page is obvious enough, but the rationale
for the employment of such a system in the *printed* work is not so obvious;
indeed the possible implications for the study of the trade in these two
centuries—to be considered below—are quite surprising. Given that a system
of reference to the page within the gathering *did* exist in the printing house,
perhaps its employment in printed sheets needs to be explained simply by
reference to a supposed change of procedure or to some kind of 'contamination'. On the other hand—given their apparent concentration in particular
texts and particular printing houses—it is much more likely that the appearance of page signatures within a printed volume is to be explained by
reference to a difference in purpose. If so, the purpose is not obvious to me.
The following notes are offered, therefore, not so much as a vehicle for conveying information as a request for assistance in establishing whether the
apparent implications are capable of substantiation from other sources. With
one exception, my observations are limited to publications of the Oxford
and Cambridge University Presses and the King's Printer; that I have seen
only one example of signing by the page in the work of other printers should
not at this stage be regarded as significant, though these three printing houses
were the major producers of volumes which, on present evidence, were the
most likely to contain such signatures. In the first place—again with the one
exception—all the volumes containing leaves signed by the page are without
pagination. Secondly, the vast bulk of the leaves so signed are cancellantia.

---

1. The most comprehensive discussion of the subject is Percy Simpson, *Proof-reading
in the sixteenth seventeenth and eighteenth centuries* (1935), pp. 46–109 ('Early proofs and
copy').

Although signing by the page is overwhelmingly to be associated with cancellantia, there are two other usages which I wish to illustrate before proceeding further, particularly as they highlight the major problem associated with the practice—i.e. establishing for whom they were intended, members of the booktrade or members of the public.

The first usage involves not actual signing but the employment of gathering-plus-page number as a means of internal reference, a practice patently directed to *readers* rather than to members of the trade. In its unambiguousness the usage differs from those which are the main concern of this essay; but that unambiguousness may serve to throw light on those more common instances in suggesting that they too may have been addressed to the reader. In the various volumes of congratulatory verse written by members of Cambridge University in the first half of the eighteenth century—many, if not all, without pagination—there are often lists of errata; thus in *Epicedium Cantabrigiense in serenissimum Daniæ principem Georgium* (1708), 2°, the 'ERRATA CORRIGENDA' begins: 'IN Scheda [i.e. sheet] notata I. pag.2 [i.e. I1ᵛ] lin.33. lege *perenni*.'; I1 is signed. Elsewhere—as in *Academiæ Cantabrigiensis carmina, quibus decedenti augustissimo regi Wilhelmo III. parentat; et succedenti optimis auspiciis serenissimæ reginæ Annæ gratulatur* [1702], 2°—'pag' may be omitted, thus: 'L4. lin.2. lege *profudit*', where 'L4' represents L2ᵛ; L2 is not signed.

The various collections of Cambridge congratulatory verse represented by these two examples reflect the general difficulty of referring readers to a particular point in the text when the volume itself lacks foliation, pagination or columnation and has no internal reference system (as in works such as the Bible, dictionaries and most classical texts). The Cambridge volumes are also unusual in employing *this particular* form of reference: I know of no other instances. Indeed it might be claimed that 'normally' the lack of a numbering system would have made the inclusion of an errata list impractical. For example, in his *Lytle treatise . . . against the protestacion of Robert Barnes at the tyme of his death* (London: Robert Redman, 1540; STC23209), which is a particularly late publication to be unnumbered, John Standish could only note that the courteous reader would find printer's errors on practically every leaf of his little book (like *par* for *per*), which errors should be blamed on the carelessness of the printer, not the laziness of the author—*quicquid est vicii non meæ inertiæ, sed impressoris incuriæ imputes oro*. Once books were folliated it was possible to be precise in the identification of printer's errors; the standard form of reference in errata lists in foliated volumes was 'Folio 37, page 1' for rectos and 'Folio 37, page 2' for versos—the term 'verso' itself was not available, being not found, according to the *OED*, until 1839. The two Cambridge volumes instanced here are outside the tradition—presumably dead by the beginning of the eighteenth century—in that they use signatures (not leaf or page numbers) as the basis of their references. The form of reference in the 1708 volume illustrates the general problem of referring to a page within a volume without a numbering system, that in the 1702 the additional problem of how to infer the signing of an unsigned leaf. That both references were directed to the reader seems clear.

The second usage does involve signing by the page, but, in contrast with the usage of the Cambridge volumes of congratulatory verse, it is patently directed to a member of the trade; on the face of it, however, there is no connexion with the compositorial practice of marking copy. I know of only two instances, both of them bibles, the first a London-printed Welsh bible of 1718/17, the second an Oxford-printed English bible of 1726/25.

Eighteenth-century bibles not only normally lack pagination but can also be found bound up in two (or more) volumes. Sometimes the division into two during binding is quite arbitrary, seemingly being determined by the convenience of the binder; at other times the best possible division is made, given that few books begin at the head of a recto, let alone at the head of 1^r. The two instances under consideration, however, are ones in which the point of division was determined in the printing house, not the binding shop.

In the first instance the two volumes were designed to contain (I) the Old Testament, (II) the New and (presumably) a selection from among a variety of other pieces, such as a metrical version of the Psalms and possibly the *Book of Common Prayer*, the Apocrypha, a concordance, an index, the *Companion to the altar* and other devotional pieces; the break between Old Testament and New does not coincide with the end of one gathering and the beginning of another. In the Welsh bible, *Y Bibl Cyssegr-lan*, London, by John Baskett, 1718/17, 8° (collating A–2P⁸ 2Q⁶, [NT:] ˣ2Q² 2R–3F⁸; in some exemplars the Testaments are separated by the Apocrypha, collating [a]–[i]⁸ [k]⁴), the title page to the New Testament, ˣ2Q2ʳ, is signed "Qq p.13'. The chainlines in the paper suggest that the bifolium ˣ2Q1.2 was imposed as 2Q4.5 in the last gathering of the Old Testament; unlikely though it may seem, the signing appears to have been inserted as a guide to the binder which leaves were to be detached from 2Q or, to put it another way, which were to immediately precede 2R1. The aberrant signing can have been of use only to a member of the trade, but why this particular form of signature? The answer may be connected with the fact that 'normal' practice would have been to impose the first two leaves of the New Testament as 2Q7,8, leaving the binder to cope with the four disjunct leaves which would result from a decision to bind the bible in two volumes. (Later Cambridge practice would have been to impose the two leaves as in the 1718/17 Welsh bible but to sign the first one '**Qq**'.) Even if one discounts the claim that the aberrant signing in the 1718/17 Welsh bible was determined by the possibility that it would be bound in two volumes (all the dozen or so exemplars seen, however, are actually bound in one) the fact remains that the method of signing was dictated by the need to extract from the octavo sheet the bifolium which was to be bound as a separate gathering.

In the second instance the bible was designed to be divided into two volumes of relatively equal bulk, with additions perhaps to be distributed between the two—e.g. with the prayer book preceding the Old Testament and the metrical psalms following the New. The English bible printed in

Oxford, also by John Baskett, 1726/25, 4° in eights, was designed for division after Ezra, the second volume then beginning with Nehemiah. Had the bible not been designed so as to be capable of being bound in two volumes it would have collated A–2T^8 2U^4, [Apocrypha:] A–K^8, [NT:] A–N^8 O^4; but Nehemiah begins on what would have been 2A7^r, and the two sheets constituting 2A were therefore imposed in such a way as to produce two gatherings, 2A^6 and ^{x}2A^2, the first leaf of ^{x}2A being signed '[Aa 13]'. Here the equation between signing and division into two volumes is manifest, though the reason for employing that particular form of signing remains unclear. (Again it might be noted that normal eighteenth-century Cambridge practice would have been to sign the first leaf of the bifolium '**Aa**'.)

As already indicated, however, the vast majority of leaves signed by the page are cancellantia. And of those cancellantia the vast majority are to be found in exemplars of the *Book of Common Prayer*. Cancellation was required to bring the prayer book up to date when certain events took place within the royal family, notably the death of one monarch and the accession of another, since members of the royal family are mentioned in it by name. The earliest instances I have seen are those where prayer books of the reign of Charles II are brought into the reign of James II through the insertion of cancellantia—i.e. they date from 1685+. The case of the *Book of Common Prayer* I have dealt with elsewhere;[2] suffice it to repeat here that when cancellanda were themselves unsigned the corresponding cancellantia were sometimes—though by no means invariably—signed by the page. Thus in gathering B in the 1727 Oxford 12° (signed \$1–6) in the exemplar in the State Library of New South Wales (Richardson 91), leaves 5, 8 and 10 are cancelled, the cancellantia being signed 'B5', 'B15' and 'B19'. (Note that the first cancellans is signed in the same way as its corresponding cancellandum—conventionally, by leaf; in other words, whoever was to insert the cancellantia in this edition had to be able to work within *two* systems of notation.) The incidence of cancellation did not diminish after 1727, but thereafter the practice of signing cancellantia by the page is uncommon—the last instance that I can report is in the Oxford 8° prayer book of 1762, where in three of the four exemplars seen (Bodleian, C.P. 1762 e.1(1); British Library, C.128.c.8 and 3407.b.17(1)—the fourth exemplar is National Library of Wales, OA 201) there are cancellantia at A8 and B6, signed respectively 'A15' and 'B11'.

The updated prayer books are particularly puzzling. The purpose of signing by the page is clear: it enables a cancellans to be correctly placed when the cancellandum is unsigned and the volume lacks pagination (or foliation or columnation). The first question raised by the practice is why such a system should have been employed when the trade was presumably accustomed to inserting cancellantia in volumes without pagination, as the more usual practice of not distinguishing cancellantia in any way, or of

2. 'The Book of Common Prayer and the monarchy from the Restoration to the reign of George I: some bibliographical observations', *Bibliographical Society of Australia and New Zealand Bulletin*, 5 (1981), 81–92.

marking them with nothing more than a typographic symbol, would suggest. The second question relates to the time at which the cancellation was effected, for there is an additional complication with the prayer books: whereas cancellation in general is to be seen as part of the process of creating 'ideal copy' *prior to* issue, in the case of the prayer books it appears to be part of a process carried out *after* issue. At first sight it might be assumed that cancellantia datable possibly to several years after the date in the imprint are evidence that stocks of particular editions of the prayer book remained unsold and therefore needed to be brought up to date before they could be sold. But the situation is more complex—at least to the extent that in some instances further editions in the same format had been issued by the same publisher in the intervening years. Perhaps the 'problem' is no more than a reflexion of the state of the publisher's warehouse. On the other hand— since signing cancellantia (by the leaf) was apparently never *necessary* as a guide to members of the trade and since the observed instances of this unusual form of signing cancellantia cluster in the prayer book, a work with a potentially volatile text—the system of signing by the page may be taken to suggest that it was employed as a guide to people *outside* the trade. In other words, the system of signing cancellantia by the page may be taken to suggest that it was designed as a guide for owners of prayer books who were faced with inserting cancellantia in exemplars in their possession. (I am attracted to the notion that at least *slips* were inserted by owners by the fact that they are sometimes pasted over red rules, which, I assume, were drawn *after* the sheets had been sold, though obviously before they were bound; alternatively one would have to suppose that booksellers or binders were unconcerned to have the ruling re-done at those points.) The question which this suggestion raises is: how then were cancellantia (including slips) made available to owners? Is there any evidence indicating (a) that cancellantia were *indeed* made available to owners of prayer books (and other publications?), and, if so, (b) what the mechanism for making them available was?

At this point it is proper to concede that there are various counter-arguments to the suggestion that signing cancellantia by the page was a system devised to assist *owners* of books (specifically prayer books) rather than members of the trade. In the first place cancellantia in prayer books normally appear to have been present when the volume was ploughed, and sometimes there are no obvious stubs to which an owner could have attached them. The case for cancellantia being made available to owners of prayer books is perhaps further weakened by the fact that there was no *obligation* on owners to bring their exemplars up to date other than by making manuscript emendations. The Act for the Uniformity of Publick Prayers (XIV. Carol. II), prefaced to the Restoration prayer book, provides that 'in all those Prayers, Litanies, and Collects, which do any way relate to the King, Queen, or Royal Progeny, the Names be altered and changed from time to time, and fitted to the present occasion, according to the direction of lawful Authority' (1662 folio, first edition, b3^r). Any alterations in wording were in the event authorised by an order in council (or 'warrant'), which customarily begins:

'Whereas by the late Act of Uniformity, which establisheth the Liturgy, and enacts, that no form or order of common prayer be openly used, other than what is prescribed and appointed to be used in and by the said Book; it is notwithstanding provided, that in all those prayers, litanies and collects, which do any ways relate to the King, Queen or royal progeny, the names be altered and changed from time to time, and fitted to the present occasion, according to the direction of lawful authority: it is thereupon this day ordered . . . that the following alterations be made, *viz.*' After the changes are specified the warrant customarily concludes: 'And it is further ordered, that no edition of the Book of Common Prayer be from henceforth printed, but with the aforesaid amendments; and that in the mean time, till copies of such editions may be had, all parsons, vicars and curates within the realm, do (for the preventing of mistakes) with the pen correct and amend all such prayers in their Church Books, according to the foregoing directions. . . .'[3] The lack of an explicit requirement that cancellantia be secured and inserted does not prove incontrovertibly that no such mechanism existed. On the other hand it can no doubt be assumed that booksellers or printers would regard the injunction that no edition be printed without the specified changes as requiring them to effect those same changes in unsold stocks by a process of cancellation which might include any one or a combination of slips, single-leaf and bifoliar cancellantia, or even the replacement of whole gatherings (particularly those containing the state prayers).

Furthermore, there is an advertisement in the *London Gazette* no. 2012 (26 February–2 March 1684/5) which bears on the question. It reads:[4] 'This is to give notice, that the Common-Prayer-Book in all volumes is now to be had at the King's Printing-Office, with the alterations in the forms of prayer for the King and the Royal Family, according to His Majesty's direction and command.' Charles II had died 6 February, and the separately published warrant (British Library, C.21.f.2(14)) is dated 16 February, so that the prescribed form of words was known no more than two weeks before the date of the advertisement. The advertisement may be taken to imply that new editions of the prayer book in all formats ('volumes') had been set and run off in the intervening period. Equally, however, 'alterations' may be taken to suggest that the required changes had been made to stocks of bound sheets by means of cancellation of one kind or another and to stocks of unbound sheets by supplying the binder with the necessary cancellantia. The latter interpretation could also be taken to suggest that whatever exemplars were on hand—regardless of date of original publication—were altered, thus accounting for the phenomenon noted earlier: cancellantia appearing in editions of particular formats which were not the current ones. On the other

---

3. Quoted from the warrant of 17 April 1707, which specifies the changes made necessary by the union of the crowns of England and Scotland (capitalisation made to conform to modern practice); the wording is constant from the Restoration to at least the middle of the nineteenth century. The texts were also sometimes published in the *London Gazette*.

4. Capitalisation made to conform to modern practice. The order in council itself was not published in the *Gazette*.

hand prayer books in a particular format do not always follow one another page for page, so that economies in setting cancellantia would not necessarily be available.

The speed with which the altered versions were made available suggests that they were not newly set editions but exemplars which were on hand and into which cancellantia were inserted prior to sale—i.e. whatever form of signing was employed for the cancellantia was intended as a guide to a member of the trade. But the updated prayer books seem never to be provided with new title leaves confirming their currency, an omission which is difficult to understand if the internal changes were made while the sheets were still in the printing house or the bookseller's shop. The cancellantia, then, may well have been united with the sheets after they had left the bookseller, and the form of signing them have been supplied as a guide to the owner.

There remain two further instances of signing cancellantia by the page which must be noted, since neither is a prayer book and one is apparently the work of a London trade printer, unfortunately anonymous. Though the evidence is not unambiguous, signing by the page in both instances appears on the face of it to be designed for the use of members of the trade (as part of the process of creating ideal copy), not members of the public (as a device to allow them to effect cancellation in exemplars in their possession).

The first of these additional two instances is the 1743 Oxford quarto bible, the first edition of the Bible printed by Mark and Robert Baskett since succeeding their father John as Printers to the University. Cancellation for the moment disregarded, it collates A^2 A–3P^8 3Q^4 3R^2, [NT:] ^{x}3Q^4 ^{x}3R^8 3S–4H^8 4I^2 (the first half of each gathering is signed). Of the four exemplars seen, three (British Library, 3050.ee.8(2); National Library of Wales, BS185. d43 4to; Durham University, Bamburgh Castle L.iii.7–10) contain 62 obvious cancellantia, concentrated in the first two alphabets, all signed by the page: A5 (signed 'A9'), A6 ('A11'), A7 ('A13'), B5 ('B9'), B7 ('B13'), B8 ('B15'), D6 ('D11'), D8 ('D15'), etc. In addition, in the BL exemplar I8 ('I15') is a cancel, though the leaf is integral in the other two; the texts are the same,[5] implying that a correction was made at press. The presence of the 63 cancellantia—all replacing unsigned cancellanda—is revealed by their signatures, but there is no reason to suppose that the cancellation in this volume is confined to the second halves of gatherings. Indeed, one would expect that there would be about the same number of cancellantia in the first halves of gatherings, signed in the conventional manner—i.e. as their corresponding cancellanda. Such, in fact, is probably the case: disturbances to the patterns of watermarks, chainlines and tranchefiles serve to identify a further 51 presumed cancellantia in the British Library exemplar. The fourth exemplar of the 1743 Oxford quarto (Bodleian, Bib.Eng. 1743.d.1) is quite unlike the other three, in that it is totally devoid of cancels—at least to the extent that routine

5. The NLW exemplar was compared with the 'Eighteenth Century' microfilm version of the BL exemplar.

inspection has revealed none of the accepted stigmata of cancellation—so that a textual collation of it and one of the other three would serve to identify cancellantia not otherwise identified. In passing, it might be noted that such wholesale cancellation was effected for what seem—on the evidence of the lamentable textual state of contemporary bibles—quite trivial reasons; for example, the only textual difference in G8 ('G15') is that the cancellans corrects the erroneous 'bread' (*vere* 'beard') in Leviticus xxi.5, '. . . neither shall they shave off the corner of their bread. . . .' One might readily suppose that the Baskett brothers were anxious to establish for themselves a higher reputation for accuracy than that enjoyed by their father.

Had the Bodleian exemplar not survived, there would have seemed little doubt that signing by the page in the 1743 quarto bible was a device employed for the benefit of members of the trade, that the wholesale cancellation was part of the process of creating ideal copy. The Bodleian exemplar, however, may be taken to suggest that the cancellation in the other three exemplars was not after all occasioned by the process of creating ideal copy prior to issue; indeed the existence of two 'pure' forms (without and with the cancels) could be taken to imply the reverse: that, as in the prayer books, the cancellation took place *after* the issue of at least one exemplar, that the two varieties are separated temporally.

The sole instance known to me of signing by the page in a volume produced elsewhere than in the printing house of one of the three privileged printers (though the identity of the printer is not known) is Peter Heylyn's *A Help to English history*, 'continued to the first day of November, 1773' by Paul Wright (London, printed for the Editor: and sold by [nine booksellers in London, one in Cambridge, one in Oxford, two in Chelmsford]; by most of the booksellers in the kingdom; and by the Editor, at Oakley, near Quendon, Essex. 1773.), 8°. Following the seven leaves of preliminaries, A8 (–A8), comes (in all exemplars known to me) what in its original state was a half-sheet, signed *A3.*A4.*A5.[*A6] and consisting of a List of Subscribers, without pagination and with the final page blank. (The signing of the half-sheet suggests that ideally it should have been bound after or before A3, just as the dedicatory leaf '[*D3]' is bound before D3; A3ʳ comprises a further dedication, to George III.)[6] In all but one exemplar[7] *A6 has been replaced by a leaf signed '*a7'; this form of signature can, I think, be explained only in terms of the recto of *A6 being the seventh page in the four-leaf gathering —i.e. I take it that this form of signing serves the same purpose as it does in the other volumes discussed. The purpose of the cancellation was presumably to create ideal copy by bringing the list of subscribers up to date: the effect is to add 28 names, four being incorporated in the reset T and W sequences on the recto, the remaining 24 constituting a separate sequence on the verso.

6. A further curiosity in the preliminaries is the mixture of roman and arabic in the pagination of A: [i–vi] vii 8 ix [x] 11–14 (or π[1–6] vii 8 ix [10] 11–14).

7. British Library, 291.k.28; I am indebted to Dr. Mervyn Jannetta for information about this exemplar.

This last sequence is followed—in at least the Monash University exemplar (*942 H617H.w)—by an Addenda, dated 20 April 1774, which adds the names of two further subscribers and notes that two of the original ones have been succeeded by their sons. The existence of addenda on the cancellans is puzzling and suggests that there may be an intermediate stage, without the addenda, which would have been added by putting the page to press again.[8]

Signing cancellantia by the leaf clearly reflects what is assumed to be the standard form of reference within the trade. Is there, however, a date before which signing cancellantia by the leaf is unknown? And can a reason be advanced why such a form of designating cancellantia should be introduced —admittedly not universally—when the evidence of other volumes containing cancellantia indicates that the practice was not even necessary for keeping track of them? One has to assume, I think, that signing cancellantia was a means of assisting binders in inserting them correctly, but if binders were accustomed to working within a system which pre-supposed the capacity to infer the signing of an unsigned leaf, can binders at large be assumed to have at some stage lost that capacity? Whatever the explanation, it remains that binders would still have had to be able to locate the (unsigned) cancellandum: where cancellans and cancellandum are both found bound up in a volume it is by no means always the case that the latter has been slashed to indicate its status. Incidentally, how widespread *was* slashing in any case? And how *did* the trade keep track of an undesignated cancellans when the corresponding cancellandum was not signed and the volume itself lacked pagination?

The 1743 Oxford quarto bible may well be unique: cancellation in eighteenth-century bibles is most unusual, and the system of signing cancellantia in this one may well have been taken over from the prayer books produced in the same printing house. Likewise the edition of Heylyn may be a sport. On the other hand these two instances may suggest that a detailed examination of a wider range of eighteenth-century publications would show the practice of signing by the page to be more widespread than it appears to be from the evidence now available. But whatever the extent, the question remains: why did some printers, working over a period of nearly a century and located in London, Oxford and Cambridge, sign some leaves—specifically cancellantia—by the page? If signing in this way was designed to assist members of the trade, what were the circumstances which dictated its use and why was it not universally employed (even if only in volumes lacking pagination when replacing unsigned cancellanda)? If signing in this way was designed to assist members of the public, by allowing them to correctly place cancellantia in volumes which they already owned, what was the mechanism by which they were enabled to secure such cancellantia?

8. The volume was noticed in the *Gentleman's Magazine* for June 1774 (v. 44, p. 277). A further novelty is that the cancellans carries at the foot of the recto the statement that 'This work is entered in the Hall Book of the Company of Stationers.'

Printing History and Other History

by

G. THOMAS TANSELLE*

ISTORY IS A SUBJECT ABOUT WHICH EVERYONE SEEMS TO HAVE A heated opinion, including the determination to ignore it. Fashions in the way history is approached are a product of history itself, with one set of attitudes toward the past, and the place of the past in the present, succeeding another. The study of history, or the use of history in intellectual endeavor, has periodically been out of vogue among prominent critics of the arts; but the perennial attempts to reject history, in one form or another, show how insistently present, how inescapable, history always is. To the human mind, it appears to be a ubiquitous concern, for we bring past associations to our surroundings. G. M. Trevelyan summed up this phenomenon when he mused that "once, on this earth, once, on this familiar spot of ground, walked other men and women, as actual as we are to-day, thinking their own thoughts, swayed by their own passions, but now all gone."[1] A related point was made, no less eloquently, by Noël Coward in his song "London Pride" (1941): "Cockney feet mark the beat of history. / Ev'ry street pins a memory down."[2]

Indeed, Coward's reference to "memory" may be taken as a significant enlargement of the concept of historical associationism, adding personal experience to acquired knowledge. One can bring to one's current surroundings a sense of the distant past, developed through learning the so-called facts about the occurrences that took place there over the centuries. But even if one has never been exposed to this information, or has no interest in acquiring it, one's memory is constantly at work,

* This paper was delivered as the J. Ben Lieberman Memorial Lecture of the American Printing History Association during Rare Book School at the University of Virginia, 18 July 1994. It was also delivered at the University of Toronto on 28 September 1994 as the inaugural lecture of the Toronto Centre for the Book.

1. "Autobiography of an Historian," in *An Autobiography & Other Essays* (1949), p. 13. He made a similar statement in a 1948 piece, "Stray Thoughts on History," included in the same volume: "Here, long before us, dwelt folk as real as we are to-day, now utterly vanished, as we in our turn shall vanish" (p. 82).

2. John Gielgud, in a 1993 interview reported by Mel Gussow, said "Every street in London is full of memory" (New York *Times*, 28 October 1993, p. C1).

attaching to one's immediate environment the private associations that come from previous experiences at the same place or related places. Those Cockney feet are not only treading where other feet have trod before, adding new dramas to the old ones enshrined there and making each street a deeper palimpsest; they are also retracing for the hundredth or the thousandth time their own previous routes and are weaving, ever more intricately, the web of memories of those earlier retracings. Memory causes our every activity to be laden with history—with a history, furthermore, that is constantly changing. The narrator of *Brideshead Revisited* claims that "we possess nothing certainly except the past" (Book II, sentence 2). It would be more precise, of course, to say that we possess our memories, rather than "the past"; and thus the certainty of our possession is in contrast with the uncertain, shifting nature of what is possessed.

But our engagements with our surroundings are complex transactions, in which what we bring is mixed, in varying proportions, with what we encounter. We are surrounded by what we take to be physical masses, material objects; some are products of nature, some of human artifice, but all are from the past, from some moment prior to the present one. Our individual associations and temperaments may make each of us see these entities differently; but the masses themselves—however obscurely their objective status may be identified—do seem to contribute their share in setting the associations in motion. If, as R. G. Collingwood has said, the aim of historical study is "thought" or "mental activity,"[3] our means of getting at it must nevertheless be principally the examination of physical objects; for thought is not tangible, and the thought of the past resides mainly in the artifacts it produced, since artifacts, being physical, have a chance of surviving, though perhaps in altered form, from one moment or era to another. Oral traditions, which form the other link with past thought, should be examined as well; but they may often be suspected of reflecting a greater change through the passage of time than physical objects usually undergo.

Thus one may say that the study of human history is largely the study of physical objects,[4] for the double reason that they both reflect and

---

3. *The Idea of History* (1946), pp. 305, 306. Earlier he states that the "proper task" of historians is "penetrating to the thought of the agents whose acts they are studying"; history is "the re-enactment of past thought in the historian's mind" (p. 228).

4. An historian who has made this point the basis for his approach to history is Arthur Bestor, who said that the historian "recovers the past . . . by carefully studying a group of objects or artifacts that exist in the present, and drawing logical conclusions therefrom about the particular past event which must have produced, or shaped, or at least put its mark upon these observable things"; this statement occurs in the opening paragraph of "History as Verifiable Knowledge: The Logic of Historical Inquiry and Explanation," in

stimulate thought. Some kinds of objects—that is, human artifacts—are the direct products of mental activity. And all kinds of objects—that is, natural formations as well as artifacts—not only preserve traces of what has happened to them during their existence; they also, at any given past time, constituted the inanimate environment and influenced what was being thought. Living things were of course an influence, too, but they do not survive from most past moments, except occasionally as inanimate objects. Thus the disciplines that examine the physical remains from natural forces, on the one hand, and the study of material culture, on the other, are essential underpinnings of the attempt to learn about human thought in the past. The phrase "material culture" has been widely used in anthropology and art history to refer to the examination of artifacts as the signs of human presence; but it is less often employed in this way by students of literature and general history, to whom the word "material" is more likely to signal some form of emphasis on the role of the marketplace. Yet the study of material culture in the broader meaning must be a prime activity of all who are concerned with the past.[5] Just as "history"—in the sense of "what happened"—may be supposed to exist regardless of whether it is studied, so a "material culture"—in the sense of the interrelations of thought and objects—must exist at every moment of human history. The study of it entails the examination of such objects as utensils, machines, sculptures, paintings, prints, buildings, manuscripts, printed documents, maps, and musical scores—the material evidences of mental activity. To some people, studying objects seems less glamorous or sophisticated or intellectual than studying ideas, but there cannot be a history of ideas without a history of objects.

Of the rich variety of artifacts, I wish to concentrate on one category, printed items with verbal texts, as a way of looking at material culture. These printed items—books, pamphlets, newspapers, and so-called ephemera—are certainly one of the largest classes of artifacts from the past five hundred years, and possibly the most influential class.[6] The

---

Research Methods in Librarianship: Historical and Bibliographical Methods in Library Research, ed. Rolland E. Stevens (1971), pp. 106–127.

5. A useful introduction is Jules David Prown's "Mind in Matter: An Introduction to Material Culture Theory and Method," *Winterthur Portfolio*, 17 (1982), 1–19 (with a "Selective Bibliography" on pp. 16–19). For some indication of the difficulty historians have had with this approach, see note 11 below.

6. I do not underestimate the importance of handwriting as a means of transmitting visible language; even after the advent of printing from movable types, handwriting continued, and has continued to the present, to be indispensable in conveying verbal messages from one person to another. But for a significant part of the past five centuries, printed books were the primary means for disseminating verbal works, both new and old. What I say later about the connections between texts and the physical means of their production applies equally to manuscripts.

past, as Richard Poirier says in *Poetry and Pragmatism* (1992), "still vibrates all round us in words" (p. 33); and a substantial portion of those words has been supplied to us in printed form. It is therefore surprising that the study of printed pieces as objects—which had to be manufactured, distributed, and held in readers' hands—has not generally been regarded by historians as a major branch of their field. The explanation is presumably a condescending view of manufacturing history as a mere technical specialty, along with an unexamined intuition that the course of intellectual history was not significantly affected by such technicalities. This situation has been changing over the past generation or so with the increasing influence of Lucien Febvre and Henri-Jean Martin (authors of *L'Apparition du livre* in 1958) and their followers in *histoire du livre*. The historians of this school, now working all over the world, are attempting to trace the impact of the printed word on society. Although their subject is, in one sense, the spread of ideas, their approach differs from the traditional study of intellectual history through their focus on the role of printed books in the process. To them, the geography of the printing industry, the economics of the publishing business, the systems of book distribution, the demographics of reading, and the effects of book design on the reading process are primary elements in social and intellectual history. The recent formation of a Society for the History of Authorship, Reading, and Publishing, and the fact that its first meeting was the occasion for a cover story on "book history" in the *Chronicle of Higher Education*, symbolize the extent to which this new field has captured scholarly attention. The *Chronicle* called it a "hot topic" and paraphrased Robert Darnton, one of its leading American practitioners, as saying that "the history of the book has the potential to take its place beside the history of art and the history of science."[7]

These fields have long been recognized specialties within the overarching field of History with a capital H. So have many others, of course: economic history, diplomatic history, intellectual history, cultural history, biography, the histories of literature, of music, of architecture, and so on. It is true that not long ago the history of the book would not have been seen as on a par with these inquiries; people who stated their interest as book history—and there have always been such people—would have been regarded as narrow specialists obsessed with a tangential topic. What they were doing was history, yes, but almost as far removed from real history as the work of amateur genealogists pursuing their family

7. See Karen J. Winkler, "In Electronic Age, Scholars Are Drawn to Study of Print," *Chronicle of Higher Education*, 14 July 1993, pp. A6–A8. The Society for the History of Authorship, Reading, and Publishing was founded in 1991 and has published the *SHARP Newsletter* since then; its first conference was held in New York on 9–11 June 1993 (and is reported in *Printing History*, 34 [1993], 71–101).

trees in local historical societies, courthouses, and graveyards. In fact book history, like genealogy or any other field, has never been the exclusive province of dullards or of enthusiastic but unthoughtful hobbyists; there has been good and bad work in every field. But scholarly fashion brands some areas as less intellectual, and until recently book history was one of them. Now book historians are welcomed into academic departments of history.

The development of the new kind of book history is in general, therefore, a cause for celebration. But its rise in stature has not brought about a greater appreciation of all the studies that it necessarily comprises. The history of printing and typography, which one might logically assume to be a fundamental part of book history, does not seem to have acquired greater glamour within the new approach, and one even hears disparaging hints about its narrowness. Some superb scholarship has been produced in a number of countries during the past century in the areas of the history of letterforms, of typefounding, and of printing; but there has been a tendency on the part of some of the newer book historians to associate Britain, and the English-speaking countries generally, with the study of the physical production of books, and then to contrast the French school of *histoire du livre* and its broad social concerns with a supposed English school of more strictly technological history. Although this view of the so-called English approach is unfair, the association of the English with the study of books as physical objects probably arose from the fact that they were indeed the pioneers in what is now called analytical bibliography—the analysis of the physical evidence in books for clues that reveal information about the printing process—and in the application of this information to literary study.[8]

There is an irony in the fact that this field, analytical bibliography, has never been fully understood or accepted by the more traditional printing historians. Perhaps its development in connection with the textual criticism and scholarly editing of literary works has caused it to seem a branch of literary studies. In any case, analytical bibliography has remained on the fringes of printing history, just as printing history

8. On national trends in book history, see John Feather, "Cross-Channel Currents: Historical Bibliography and *L'Histoire du Livre*," *Library*, 6th ser., 2 (1980), 1–15. A collection of essays in this field is *Books and Society in History*, ed. Kenneth E. Carpenter (1983), which includes "A Statement on the History of the Book" (signed by the participants in the 1980 conference of the Rare Books and Manuscripts Section of the Association of College and Research Libraries) and Robert Darnton's "What Is the History of Books?" (In my introduction to this volume, I attempted to show the relation of analytical bibliography to *histoire du livre*, as I also did in my Hanes Lecture, *The History of Books as a Field of Study* [1981].) A recent theoretical overview is Thomas R. Adams and Nicolas Barker's "A New Model for the Study of the Book," in *A Potencie of Life: Books in Society*, ed. Nicolas Barker (1993), pp. 5–43.

has remained peripheral to mainstream historical scholarship, even after the social history of publishing and reading entered that mainstream. The attitudes that have led to these placements, in my judgment, reflect serious misconceptions about the nature of history and of tangible verbal communication; and the historical writing that embodies these attitudes is weakened by their presence. What I wish to suggest is that printing history, far from being a bypath of historical scholarship, is actually one of its central forms; and, further, that analytical bibliography is an important technique in the pursuit of printing history. Indeed, I would venture to assert that printing history, so conceived, is an essential study for persons engaged not merely in "history" (as defined by the contents of courses in academic history departments) but in every field of scholarship.

The first step in the argument is to note that texts are affected by the printing process. This simple, but profoundly important, point has remained outside the ken of most readers (even highly perceptive ones) over the centuries. The reasons for this neglect, along with an account of the emerging interest from the mid-nineteenth century onward (at least on the part of a few scholars) in the relationship between text and object, constitute one of the most fascinating stories of intellectual history. It is largely unsung, however, because the point at its core is still not widely understood; and thus the accomplishment of that band of British scholars who were the forerunners and founders of the Bibliographical Society is not properly appreciated.[9] Yet what they set in motion was a revolution in the way we approach printed texts, a revolution still in progress and unlikely to be completed for a long time, judging from the slow pace of its inroads into entrenched patterns of thinking. (I should say, parenthetically, that any prognostication about attitudes toward printed texts in the future is likely to seem quixotic in an age full of predictions about the demise of the printed book; but of

9. The best account of the development of analytical bibliography is F. P. Wilson's "Shakespeare and the 'New Bibliography,'" in *The Bibliographical Society 1892–1942: Studies in Retrospect* (1945), pp. 76–135 (reprinted as a separate volume, edited by Helen Gardner, in 1970); the early history of the Bibliographical Society is recounted by F. C. Francis in the same voume, pp. 1–22, and by Julian Roberts in "The Bibliographical Society as a Band of Pioneers," in *Pioneers in Bibliography*, ed. Robin Myers and Michael Harris (1988), pp. 86–100. See also my "Physical Bibliography in the Twentieth Century," in *Books, Manuscripts, and the History of Medicine: Essays on the Fiftieth Anniversary of the Osler Library*, ed. Philip M. Teigen (1982), pp. 55–79, or "The Evolving Role of Bibliography, 1884–1984," in *Books and Prints, Past and Future: Papers Presented at The Grolier Club Centennial Convocation* (1984), pp. 15–31. The fullest listing of examples of bibliographical analysis is in my *Introduction to Bibliography: Seminar Syllabus* (periodically revised; see, for example, pp. 135–162 of the 1994 revision).

course I am talking about the printed texts of the past five and a half centuries, which will continue to be studied regardless of what shape is taken by written works of the twenty-first century. And the importance of studying those earlier books in their original form, rather than an electronic "reformatting," is precisely the point I wish to pursue.)[10]

The revolution instigated by the pioneers of the "New Bibliography" consisted of approaching artifacts that have words in or on them as one would approach other artifacts—treating them as objects produced by artisans skilled in particular crafts, as objects that can be studied for physical details revelatory of their own production history. These bibliographers' view was in contrast to the notion, still prevalent, that books are merely the containers of texts, which can readily be extracted without the necessity of paying much attention to the containers themselves. The approach also necessitated a recognition of the individuality of every copy, in opposition to the common assumption that copies from the same edition are identical. Examining books as objects suggests to most people an interest in the graphic arts; what is less readily understood is that an interest in the texts of books also requires the reading of physical evidence (which, because it is physical, may vary from copy to copy).

Even sophisticated historians of material culture sometimes have difficulty regarding books as just another category of artifact, for the presence of words in them tends to suggest that they can speak to us in a more direct way—in our own language, as it were.[11] When words are

10. On this general subject, see my "Reproductions and Scholarship," *Studies in Bibliography*, 42 (1989), 25–54, and "The Latest Forms of Book-Burning," *Common Knowledge*, 2.3 (Winter 1993), 172–177.

11. Jules David Prown, for example, in his important essay "Mind in Matter" (see note 5 above), unwittingly illustrates the difficulty people have had in thinking about objects containing verbal texts; when, near the end, he says that artifacts "tell us something, but facts are transmitted better by verbal documents," he is failing to recognize the physicality of visible texts or to acknowledge that such texts are artifacts themselves, requiring the same kind of examination and interpretation as other artifacts. The neglect of this point on the part of many historians has caused them to believe that verbal texts speak to them more directly than do physical objects containing no words and thus to ignore the physical aspects of "verbal documents." (The common use of the word "artifact" to refer only to objects without verbal texts reflects the mistaken assumption that "verbal documents" are in a class apart from other objects.) This line of thinking has often led historians not merely to undervalue physical evidence but actively to disparage its use. Thirty years ago John Chavis criticized this attitude in a piece for *Curator* (the magazine of the American Museum of Natural History) entitled "The Artifact and the Study of History" (7 [1964], 156–162), deploring "the willingness of the academic historian to do without the utilization of the artifact." To represent the historians' position, he summarized William B. Hesseltine's "The Challenge of the Artifact," in *The Present World of History*, ed. James H. Rodabaugh (1959): although Hesseltine recognizes that verbal documents preserve physical evidence, he thinks of it as "external" to what the text "says" and naïvely believes that one cannot determine what nonverbal objects say. Chavis contrasted this view with E. McClung

not present, one is forced (even if such texts as pictures or decorations
have been applied) to examine an object in all its physical detail in order
to "read" it. But the presence of words often lures us into believing that
our reading can be limited to the words (taken as words in a language,
not as letterforms in ink)—and, indeed, that we can receive, even while
ignoring the other physical features of the object, a more subtle and less
ambiguous message than could be conveyed without words. Whether
verbal statements are in fact more subtle and unambiguous than nonverbal ones is debatable. But that question is irrelevant to the recognition that words in books are physical, made up of inked shapes on paper;
those shapes are constituent elements in the physical objects called books,
and their precise form, selection, and arrangement are the result of a
manufacturing process, which must therefore be understood if the text
is to be understood.

When Henry Bradshaw in the nineteenth century observed a correlation between textual divisions and paper stocks (or gatherings of sheets)
in certain incunables, he was noting a connection between printing and
text;[12] so is a present-day editor who discovers that a blank-verse passage
in an Elizabethan play was set as prose at a point where the space would
not otherwise have held the pre-assigned text.[13] Some recent students of

---

Fleming's in "Early American Decorative Arts as Social Documents," *Mississippi Valley His-
torcial Review*, 45 (1958–59), 276–284: Fleming believes that the artifact is "a social document" and regrets that "the historian has tended to ignore this primary source in his pre-
occupation with printed and manuscript materials" (p. 276). Some years later Fleming
developed his point in "Artifact Study: A Proposed Model," *Winterthur Portfolio*, 9 (1974),
153–173 (in which he again laments the fact that the "use of material culture by historians
and social scientists is minimal" [p. 154]). Similarly, Henry Glassie has said, "Because of his
commitment to the primacy of print, the historian has been unable to produce an authentic history"; see "Archaeology and Folklore: Common Anxieties, Common Hopes," in
Historical Archaeology and the Importance of Material Things, ed. Leland G. Ferguson
(1979), pp. 23–35 (quotation from p. 29). It is noteworthy, however, that even these cogent
calls for greater attention to physical evidence do not explicitly place books and manuscripts in the world of artifacts. Anyone who wishes to encourage use of the physical evidence that resides in objects with verbal texts thus faces a double obstacle: not only the
neglect of physical evidence in general but also the failure to regard verbal documents as
artifacts. A notable exception to this common failure is Arthur Bestor's "History as Verifiable
Knowledge" (see note 4 above): "a document is simply a special kind of artifact. The marks
that were impressed upon it by past events are intelligible marks, produced as the result of
the operations of a mind like our own." Furthermore, Bestor effectively makes the point that
logically follows: however persuasive the verbal text may be, "the historian must not be
misled into imagining that it speaks to him with such authority as to relieve him of the
obligation of carrying out a critical and logical inquiry of his own" (pp. 108–109).

12. For an excellent account of Bradshaw's concern with the "relation of text to structure," see Paul Needham's Hanes Lecture, *The Bradshaw Method* (1988), esp. pp. 5–6, 10–12.

13. The classic examination of the Elizabethan compositors' practice of "setting by
formes" (rather than following the numerical order of the pages) is Charlton Hinman's
"Cast-Off Copy for the First Folio of Shakespeare," *Shakespeare Quarterly*, 6 (1955), 259–273.
An admirable brief treatment is provided by Peter W. M. Blayney in *The First Folio of*

fifteenth-century books have paid attention to "frisket bite," in which the frisket, meant to protect the margins from ink, slipped and covered the edge of the type page;[14] similarly, bibliographers of nineteenth-century books have noticed the loss of punctuation at right margins, now caused by wear along the edges of stereotype plates.[15] The word "not" is absent from some copies of the Shakespeare First Folio at a point (in the fifth act of *Julius Caesar*) where in other copies it is present (thus reversing the meaning of the sentence);[16] in the 1846 printing of the "Revised Edition" of Melville's *Typee*, the word "groves" occurs in some copies at a point (in Chapter 12) where other copies have "grove."[17] The variation in *Julius Caesar* resulted from the correction of a typesetter's error discovered in proofreading, the one in *Typee* from an error made in the process of resetting a passage after the type had been damaged. These instances are examples of the ways in which texts (already perhaps altered by publishers' editors) show traces of their passage through the printing shop. Such changes in texts come about through the actions —both inadvertent and intentional—of compositors and through the operation of the printing press itself; but they are always likely to be there, in books of all periods.

Another, more visible, residue of the printing process is also always present: the design of the pages. Every book, whether by default or by careful planning, has a design, created by the letterforms, their sizes,

---

Shakespeare (1991), pp. 12–14. For some history of the bibliographical analysis of setting by formes, see my "Analytical Bibliography and Renaissance Printing History," *Printing History*, 3.1 (1981), 24–33.

14. On "frisket bite," see Walter J. Partridge, "The Type-Setting and Printing of the Mainz Catholicon," *Book Collector*, 35 (1986), 21–52 (esp. pp. 42–44); and Paul Needham, "Slipped Lines in the Mainz Catholicon: A Second Opinion," *Gutenberg Jahrbuch*, 1993, pp. 25–29 (esp. p. 29).

15. See Peter L. Shillingsburg, "Detecting the Use of Stereotype Plates," *Editorial Quarterly*, 1.1 (1975), 2–3. Two illustrations of such damage are figures 3 and 6 appended to the condensed reprinting of my article on "The Use of Type Damage as Evidence in Bibliographical Description" in *Journal of Typographic Research*, 3 (1969), 259–276.

16. For a reproduction of the corrected state of the text, see Charlton Hinman's *The Norton Fascimile: The First Folio of Shakespeare* (1968), p. 737. (In Hinman's "through line numbering," the variant—"Looke where he haue [not] crown'd dead *Cassius*"—occurs in line 2587.) A list of substantive variants in copies of the First Folio appears on pp. xxi–xxii. The large number of press-variants of all kinds (those in punctuation and spelling as well as in substantives) are listed and discussed in Hinman's *The Printing and Proof-Reading of the First Folio of Shakespeare* (1963), pp. 226–334.

17. This variant is discussed in the Northwestern-Newberry Edition of *Typee*, ed. Harrison Hayford, Hershel Parker, and G. T. Tanselle (1968), pp. 310–311. (The point of variation—"religious attendants of the grove[s]"—occurs on p. 101, line 31, of the 1846 edition, and on p. 91, line 37, of the Northwestern-Newberry Edition.) See also my "Textual Study and Literary Judgment," *Papers of the Bibliographical Society of America*, 65 (1971), 109–122 (esp. pp. 115–116), reprinted in *Textual Criticism and Scholarly Editing* (1990), pp. 325–337 (see pp. 330–331).

and their deployment on each page; and historians of the book are becoming increasingly alert to the role these features play in readers' responses.[18] But the actual words and punctuation of the text can obviously be expected to play an even greater role; and once it is recognized that the makeup of texts, and not simply their presentation, is affected by the printing process, book historians will also see that a knowledge of what happened in the printing shop is essential to their study. The story of books in society is the story of texts and their influence; knowing how published texts came to be what they are, in their varying forms in different copies of editions and different editions, therefore underlies everything else. The fact that printing history has not automatically been swept into prominence by the rising interest in "the history of the book" shows how little understood, even now, are the connections between the printing and the content of texts.

That problem is not a simple one, however. For even if everyone granted that the details of what happened in the printing shop are a fundamental ingredient in the study of the dissemination of ideas in printed form, there would remain the question of how those details can be known. And on that issue there is no unanimity of opinion among printing historians themselves. The primary reason for this situation is uncertainty over the nature and respectability of analytical bibliography. Some printing historians have neglected it on the assumption that it is a branch of literary study, of little relevance to printing history; others have actively rejected it because they believe it to be suspect as history. The first response results from a simple misconception; the second raises the basic question of what constitutes validity in historical study.

As to the first, one need only observe that printing history clearly encompasses information on such topics as how many compositors were at work on a given book, whether they set the type pages in numerical order (or according to the sequence in which the pages would be placed on the press), and how proofreading and correcting were accomplished.[19] Generalizations about printing-shop procedures in particular periods and places can be made by combining such data from large numbers of individual books. And these data are precisely what literary scholars

18. For an excellent introduction to this subject, see David McKitterick, "Old Faces and New Acquaintances: Typography and the Association of Ideas," *PBSA*, 87 (1993), 163–186. He points out that "bibliographical analysis has much more to offer the social and enumerative historian [of reading] than, so far, seems to have been demonstrated" (pp. 164–165).

19. That analytical bibliography furnishes information for printing history was the point of my article entitled "Analytical Bibliography and Renaissance Printing History" (see note 13 above). And in 1987 I emphasized analytical bibliography in outlining an agenda for printing history—see "Thoughts on Research in Printing History," *Printing History*, 9.2 (1987), 24–25.

often amass in the process of editing texts. Their reason for analyzing books for this information is its relevance to assessing the authority of the texts, but the information itself is a contribution to printing history and could just as well have been uncovered by printing historians who had no intention of producing scholarly editions. It would be inaccurate to suggest that literary scholars in general understand analytical bibliography better than printing historians do, and the reason in both instances is the failure to see how form and content coalesce: students of literature are inclined to believe that research on printing-shop practices is not "literary," whereas printing historians assume that the activities engaged in by editors must relate strictly to texts. But at least some literary editors have seen the significance of bibliographical analysis, and the development of this field has been in their hands, with the results published by bibliographical societies or journals of literary history, almost never by journals of general history or printing history—and almost never listed in reference guides to historical scholarship.

If printing historians and other historians have frequently shared a misunderstanding of what analytical bibliography attempts to accomplish, they also have shared a skeptical view of the procedures it follows. In the first place, historians are inclined to prefer archival records—manuscript and typescript documents—over printed books when they are available. Obviously printing historians do know that to discuss typography and layout they must look at the actual printed items, just as the newer historians of reading understand why the visual appearance of printed pages is a key class of data for their work. But when historians wish to know something about how books were produced, rather than how they finally looked, the books themselves are not routinely thought of as an archival source, presumably because of the number of inferences often required in the attempt to coax their own stories out of them. If a printer's ledger records the format of a book, or the amount of paper needed for the edition, or the number of compositors who set the type, or the number of presses used for the printing, those pieces of information are conveyed as direct (or relatively direct) statements, whereas extracting the same details from the finished books would entail inferences, often a network of inferences. Archival records are frequently regarded as "primary" documents, and printed books as "secondary"; but primariness is relative to the subject of the inquiry, and when the subject is printing-shop procedures, the evidence from the objects that resulted from those procedures (objects that have survived and are available for first-hand examination) must take precedence over statements about the procedures in other contemporary documents.

Printers' and publishers' records are valuable, of course, but no one could plausibly argue that they are infallible, and the books themselves provide the final court of appeal for evaluating the claims of the records. An analogous point was well made ten years ago in an article about a related field, architectural history. Robin Lynn wrote,

The paper chase for archival documents provides only a portion of the information which the restoration architect needs. The edifice itself holds the remainder of the clues. Building alterations leave scars. Architects study them to learn how a structure has been changed. "You could have all the documents in the world," [Theo] Prudon warns, "but the building could have been built differently."[20]

The examination of a book's structure can provide the same kind of corrective to the external record. Historians of the book should heed what Robert K. Merton has called "an elementary rule of historical method": "when reconstructing the past, draw gratefully on archival documents but beware of taking them at face value."[21]

Elementary this point may be; but a tendency to assume that archival records are correct is curiously persistent. One telling example is J. D. Fleeman's investigation of William Somervile's *The Chace* (1735) in the light of the surviving ledgers of its printer, William Bowyer. He notes several discrepancies between the record of presswork in the ledgers and the press figures printed in the book—one of which is that both formes of sheet A are listed in the column for press number 3 in the ledger, whereas the figure 8 appears in printed copies on a page of the outer forme of this sheet (the verso of the second leaf), and the inner forme bears no press figure. Fleeman does not suggest the possibility that the ledger is incorrect. Instead he concludes that figure 8 here must refer to the pressmen named in the ledger as operating press number 3 (Fowle and Davis); the other two occurrences of 8 in the book, however, he attributes to a different pair of pressmen (Mazemore and Jethro, named in the ledger as operating press number 8), because the two formes involved are credited to press number 8 in the ledger. In other words, the assumption that the ledger is correct forces Fleeman to conclude that the printed figures designate pressmen and that their signification can shift—a conclusion that leaves one wondering what purpose the printed figures serve, if the ledger is the only true (and thus necessary) guide to the allocation of presswork. A simpler hypothesis that maintains the accuracy of the ledger is to regard the printed figure 8 in sheet A as an

20. "Paper Chase," *Metropolis*, 4.4 (November 1984), 24–26, 32 (quotation from p. 32). (Prudon supervised the restoration of the Woolworth Building.)
21. *A Life of Learning* (the Haskins Lecture of the American Council of Learned Societies, 1994), p. 2. Cf. Arthur Bestor's comment quoted at the end of note 11 above and John Lancaster's quoted in note 22 below.

error for 3; but it is also possible that the ledger entry is wrong, and the failure to entertain this possibility suggests how powerful is the tradition of preferring manuscript to printed evidence.[22]

A similar instance is Robert Darnton's discussion of what he calls "hidden editions" of Diderot's *Encyclopédie*.[23] He examines the wage book of the printer of the quarto *Encyclopédie* to learn "what actually happened in the printing shops" (p. 78), and he makes no attempt to verify the data from that record by reference to surviving copies. In other words, "what actually happened" in the printing process can be known, he implies, independently of analyzing the actually surviving product of that process. Indeed, he explicitly rejects such analysis: "It would be vain to draw inferences about the printing process from the examination of actual copies of the book, because the copies must vary endlessly" (p. 81) —as if complexity were grounds for refusing to examine evidence.[24] It is hard to imagine any other class of available evidence that a historian would so willingly ignore.

A more realistic attitude toward bibliographical evidence and its

22. See "William Somervile's 'The Chace,' 1735," *PBSA*, 58 (1964), 1–7 (which was the first bibliographical article to make use of the Bowyer ledgers). Fleeman's discussion of other discrepancies follows the same pattern that he uses for the one in sheet A: thus his assumption that the attribution of pressmen in the ledgers is correct forces him to state that the Long Primer figure 3, which appears in the inner forme of C and in outer E and G, signifies one pair of pressmen in the first instance and a different pair in the other two instances; similarly, he claims that the larger figure 3 designates one pair of pressmen in outer H and a different pair in M, N, and O (and, further, that this latter pair of pressmen was the same pair that used the Long Primer figure 3 in inner C). Because Fleeman does not ask what reason there could be for such a shifting use of figures, it is ironic that he concludes, "without the benefit of the printing records kept by Bowyer, a good many serious misinterpretations would have been the result of the usual kinds of analysis." For information on the ledgers themselves, see the admirable work by Keith Maslen and John Lancaster, *The Bowyer Ledgers* (1991); their entry for *The Chace* is no. 2156, p. 170. Lancaster called attention to the Somervile example in his address to the Grolier Club on 15 June 1993, during his exhibition marking the publication of the ledgers. That address, in its published form in *Gazette of the Grolier Club*, n.s., 45 (1993), 63–81, notes Fleeman's "premise that the ledgers are accurate" and provides an appropriate warning: "the ledgers —like most human documents—are not infallible, and must be used with caution like any other historical evidence" (p. 68). I am grateful to Lancaster for providing me with the materials for examining this instance of discrepancies between ledger entries and the printed item to which they refer.

23. "A Bibliographical Imbroglio: Hidden Editions of the 'Encyclopédie,'" in *Cinq Siècles d'Imprimerie Genevoise*, ed. Jean-Daniel Candaux and Bernard Lescaze (1981), pp. 71–101.

24. The variation among copies would not prevent, for example, the attempt to determine whether the pages supposedly set by different compositors do in fact display different characteristics. Darnton's comments throughout on the confounding of bibliographers by the randomness of the process by which sheets were mixed together in individual copies displays a lack of understanding of bibliography as a form of history; the goal of descriptive bibliography is not to present neat collational formulas or to seek uniformity among copies but to report as accurately as possible the true situation.

relation to external documents is found in David L. Vander Meulen's analysis of Pope's *The Dunciad in Four Books* (1743)—where again it is Bowyer ledger entries that seem not to match the surviving books.[25] Although he immediately entertains "the possibility that Bowyer erred in his recordkeeping" (p. 303), he does not automatically accept any one category of evidence as dominant; rather, he speaks of "the synergy between the artifacts and an account of those artifacts in the ledgers" (p. 309). His frustration at not being able in this instance to reach a satisfactory explanation that ties all the known evidence together is, in his view, "salutary," for it reminds one of the tentative nature of historical research, in which success is not so much a function of finding answers as of contributing to the ongoing "development of understanding" (p. 302).

The essence of any inductive process, such as the search for scientific "laws" or the pursuit of the past, is uncertainty; and what are called facts —scientific or historical—are simply conjectures that seem relatively certain (that is, relatively unlikely to be overturned by contrary evidence) to a substantial number of informed observers. (The historian's conclusions are testable in the same way that the scientist's are: by repeated reenactments of the events that led to the conclusions, whether those events took place in a laboratory or in a library.)[26] If the validity of analytical bibliographers' hypotheses is frequently questioned, those bibliographers are in no different position from other historians, or other sifters of inductive, and thus effectively infinite, evidence. Yet sometimes bibliographical analysis is criticized for involving the same inferential process that is taken for granted in other branches of history. A notable example, which goes to the heart of the issue, is D. F. McKenzie's statement that compositorial analysis has exhibited "virtuosity in discovering patterns in evidence which is entirely internal, if not wholly fictional."[27]

25. See "*The Dunciad in Four Books* and the Bibliography of Pope," *PBSA*, 83 (1989), 293–310. The points in question are Bowyer's references to cancelled and reprinted sheets and leaves (pp. 302–303).

26. The events that lead to historians' conclusions are examinations of documents and other artifacts. Some elaboration of this point, showing how scientific investigation involves historical method, can be found in Arthur Bestor's "History as Verifiable Knowledge" (see note 4 above), esp. pp. 111–113.

27. See McKenzie's Panizzi Lectures. *Bibliography and the Sociology of Texts* (1986), p. 7. I have discussed these lectures, and this passage, further in "Textual Criticism and Literary Sociology," *SB*, 44 (1991), 83–143 (esp. pp. 87–99). (McKenzie has been expressing doubts about analytical bibliography since at least 1969, when he published "Printers of the Mind" in *SB*, 22: 1–75; for responses to that essay, see Peter Davison's "Science, Method, and the Textual Critic," *SB*, 25 [1972], 1–28, and my "Bibliography and Science," *SB*, 27 [1974], 55–89 [esp. pp. 73–78].) In a later lecture, "*What's Past is Prologue": The Bibliographical Society and History of the Book* (1993), McKenzie continues to show a bias against analytical bibliography, referring to A. W. Pollard's activities as "sensitive to the primacy of trade documents as historical evidence" (p. 12) and asserting, "Enumerative

This language seems to suggest that patterns perceived in a body of evidence are, at best, true only as a characterization of the shape of the evidence, and at worst are illusory even on that level. Ingenuity, or "virtuosity," in discerning patterns is dismissed as futile, since "internal" patterns, he implies, are not connectable to the world outside the evidence. But these points can hardly be held against analytical bibliography, for the process of finding patterns in evidence is the way all historical investigation works—the way it must, of necessity, work.

What we agree to call historical knowledge is built up by the accretion of individual acts of pattern-finding, some of which invalidate previous acts and some of which confirm and extend them. It is true that each act must be interpreted in the light of whatever relevant context has already been formulated; any "internal" analysis that does not at some point recognize appropriate available sources "external" to it can of course be criticized, for we should obviously use all relevant data that we can locate. But McKenzie's belittling of analyses based on evidence internal to books, if not corroborated by evidence external to them, ultimately fails to acknowledge the limited nature of all bodies of evidence, however broadly conceived. In the first place, documents external to books hold just as many pitfalls for interpretation as do the books themselves, and any conclusions based solely on such evidence are potentially flawed for the same reasons that conclusions based on any other single body of evidence are. Beyond that, one does not in many instances have the option of checking books against printers' ledgers, for the survival of printer's archives is not common. One has to use whatever is available and interpret it in the light of what is already considered established. McKenzie overstates the authority of the latter, however, when he says that bibliographical analysis "depends absolutely upon antecedent historical knowledge" (p. 2): such knowledge (as in every other field) is itself always an hypothesis, and the new analysis may modify it. This kind of interplay, after all, is what produced the antecedent knowledge, and each new analysis plays a role in determining what is regarded as established by the next analyst. In the end, all evidence is "internal," for sooner or later one reaches a point where there is nothing outside to relate to. We are trapped in Wallace Stevens's "island solitude, unsponsored, free, / Of that wide water, inescapable." Virtuosity in making sense of what we have is thus the only procedure available to us. The degree of ingenuity

---

bibliography in Britain opened up riches . . . well beyond the reach of descriptive and analytical bibliography" (p. 17)—as if he thinks of these approaches as rivals, competing with each other. He does, however, also express a recognition of the importance of physical evidence and offers a useful statement of the "premise" underlying analytical bibliography: "that the forms [of books] themselves encode the history of their production" (p. 24).

is not the issue, but whether an ingenious explanation postulated by one inquirer is accepted by others who carefully go over the same ground. The result can indeed be called a fiction, a creation of human artifice, but the fictions that survive repeated scrutiny are the only truths we can have.[28]

Analytical bibliography seems to me a perfect paradigm of historical scholarship because it illustrates, with particular clarity, how dependent our view of the past is upon the creativity of those who engage in historical investigations. A current instance is Paul Needham's hypothesis that three works were printed by the Catholicon Press of Mainz in ca. 1459–60 (and reprinted later) from two-line slugs, cast from a setting of movable type, rather than being printed from the type itself. This startling thesis is an example of creative thinking on the part of a learned bibliographer who argues with careful deliberation and logical rigor. Whether it is accepted as "true" depends on whether it can stand up under criticism. Since its first announcement in 1982, it has in fact been criticized, and an alternative explanation has been proposed for the puzzles raised by these editions. Needham has shown, to the satisfaction of many but not all, why the direct criticisms of his position have missed their mark and why the alternative thesis does not adequately account for the observed evidence. His hypothesis is well on its way toward acceptance as a significant fact in the history of early printing. Needham fully understands the nature of this process and has on more than one occasion invited his readers to evaluate the controversy as an exercise in clear thinking (the requirements of which are themselves a human invention, of course). In 1993, for example, he said, "The issues in question do not depend in any way on a specific knowledge of incunables, but should be accessible to anyone familiar with the fundamental principles of analytical bibliography."[29] If a consensus forms in support of

28. Cf. Richard Rorty's concept of "conversation" in *Philosophy and the Mirror of Nature* (1979): e.g., the idea that "objective truth" is "the normal result of normal discourse" (p. 377). See also such statements in his *Consequences of Pragmatism* (1982) as the proposition that there is "no rigorous argumentation that is not obedience to our own conventions" (p. xlii).

29. "Slipped Lines in the Mainz Catholicon: A Second Opinion" (see note 14 above), p. 25. Cf. the following comment in his "Corrective Notes on the Date of the Catholicon Press" (*Gutenberg Jahrbuch*, 1990, pp. 46–64): "The arguments involved in these preliminary issues do not depend on bibliographical knowledge. I hope they will be accessible to every reader who is even peripherally aware of the Catholicon 'question' " (p. 61). Lotte Hellinga, in the same volume of the *Gutenberg Jahrbuch* ("Comments on Paul Needham's Notes," pp. 65–69), makes this unconsidered remark: "The more elaborate our arguments and the more they are confined to what is presented by the printed books themselves, the greater the need to recognize these inevitable limitations of our perception, and to be alert to the possibilities that lie beyond them" (p. 69). The last part of her sentence is undeniably correct: we must always be mindful of the "limitations of our perception" and the "possibilities that lie beyond them." But the "need to recognize" these points is equally present in all

his position, the result will be another historical fact produced by informed imagination and validated by repeated reexamination of the argument supporting it. We will be shown, once again, the necessity in historical research both for creativity and for intellectual rigor, as assessed by the audience at a given time.

The idea that history is revised by each generation, that what we see in the past is contingent on who we are in the present, is of course not new; most historians by this time surely subscribe to it in some form, and it is a natural element in any skeptical or antifoundational philosophy. As Charles Gullans wrote in his poem "Research," "It is ourselves we summon from the past."[30] Yet surprisingly it is still easy to arouse controversy by embracing the subjective element in historical writing, to say nothing of openly accepting the role of creativity in it. A prominent recent illustration is the celebrity achieved by Simon Schama, in both the journalistic and the academic press, from proclaiming this view in lectures and in *Dead Certainties* (1991), a book that mixes archival data and invented details in retelling the divergent accounts of the deaths of General James Wolfe (1759) and Dr. George Parkman (1849). The teasing subtitle of the book, placed in parentheses, is *Unwarranted Speculations*, a phrase that accurately conveys what some readers feel the book contains; but its parenthetical apposition to the

situations and is not "greater" when arguments are "more elaborate" or "confined" to the evidence found within printed books. The elaborateness with which one argues and the sources of evidence one employs do not in themselves make arguments questionable; what is crucial to the acceptance of an argument is the care with which one goes about collecting and evaluating the evidence (whatever it is) and then constructing inferences from it (however elaborate they may be). The controversy between Needham and Hellinga should be examined by all who are interested in the process of scholarly argumentation by which historical facts come to be established. See (in addition to the articles already mentioned) Needham, "Johan Gutenberg and the Catholicon Press," *PBSA*, 76 (1982), 395–456; Hellinga, "Analytical Bibliography and the Study of Early Printed Books with a Case-Study of the Mainz Catholicon," *Gutenberg Jahrbuch*, 1989, pp. 47–96; Needham, "Further Corrective Notes on the Date of the Catholicon Press," *Gutenberg Jahrbuch*, 1991, pp. 101–126; Hellinga, "Proof for the Date of Printing of the Mainz *Catholicon*," *Bulletin du bibliophile*, 1991, 1:143–147; Hellinga, "Slipped Lines and Fallen Type in the Mainz Catholicon," *Gutenberg Jahrbuch*, 1992, pp. 35–40; Hellinga, "Eltville and Mainz: A Tale of Two Compositors," *Book Collector*, 41 (1992), 28–54; Needham, "Mainz and Eltville: The True Tale of Three Compositors," *Bulletin du bibliophile*, 1992, 2:257–304. (See also the Partridge article cited in note 14 above and Needham's reply, "The Type-Setting of the Mainz Catholicon: A Reply to W. J. Partridge," *Book Collector*, 35 [1986], 293–304.)

30. *Letter from Los Angeles* (1990), pp. 6–7. More than half a century ago G. M. Trevelyan called it "a common opinion" (which, he said, "I myself share") that "the historian's work is partly scientific, partly artistic"; see "Bias in History," in *An Autobiography & Other Essays* (1949), p. 81. There have of course been many discussions of the subjectivity of historical scholarship. Two recent treatments (which include the history of such discussions) are Peter Novick, *That Noble Dream: The "Objectivity Question" and the American Historical Profession* (1988) and Joyce Appleby, Lynn Hunt, and Margaret Jacob, *Telling the Truth about History* (1994). (See also note 32 below.)

main title also says that whenever we regard something as a dead certainty we are engaging in unwarranted speculation. In his "Afterword," Schama states outright that "even in the most austere scholarly report from the archives, the inventive faculty—selecting, pruning, editing, commenting, interpreting, delivering judgements—is in full play" (p. 322).

Some reviewers were predictably bothered by this position and felt that it presented an overly negative outlook. But even persons sympathetic with Schama's general view may find him strangely reserved here, for in his "Afterword" he repeatedly undercuts his own relativistic remarks. He says, for example, that he does not "scorn the boundary between fact and fiction"; perhaps not, but what he does in the body of his work is to show brilliantly that such a boundary is always in flux. Similarly, he calls the narratives in his book "works of the imagination, not scholarship" (p. 320); yet presumably one of his purposes is to raise questions about how scholarship is defined, as in his assertion that scholarly reports involve "the inventive faculty." He states as an article of faith "the rather banal axiom that claims for historical knowledge must always be fatally circumscribed by the character and prejudices of its narrator" (p. 322). But why "fatally"? The banality of the observation, if it is banal, arises from its restating of a universal condition, one that can be taken for granted. In that case, the hint of a complaint underlying the word "fatally" is pointless. Historical study is not prevented by our inherent subjectivity; the limit that human perception places on verification is simply a given in everything we do, and we proceed from there.[31]

An equally fundamental point is that, even if we could be objective in reporting observed data, what has survived for us to inspect is inevitably fragmentary and requires supplementing by informed intuition. A creative account written by a learned historian may bring us closer to the past than documents alone. Whether we believe that it does so in any given instance depends on our evaluation of the process by which the account is constructed. Setting standards for responsible and irresponsible argument is not in any way incompatible with recognizing the

31. Although Schama has somewhat clouded the reasons for such a view of the bases for proceeding, his last line does seem to me to be in this positive spirit: if, he says, "our flickering glimpses of dead worlds fall far short of ghostly immersion, that perhaps is still enough to be going on with." But he could have made clearer, I think, that "enough" has no connection with quantity; whatever we have must always be "enough," if we are to do any thinking at all. He is right to speak of the "gap separating a lived event and its subsequent narration"—that is, historians' "unavoidable remoteness from their subjects" (p. 320). (And he makes eloquent use of James's *The Sense of the Past* in this regard.) But his wavering over the relation between imagination and scholarship in the effort to build a bridge to the past does not provide a satisfying preparation for a positive conclusion.

necessity for imaginative extrapolation from invariably limited evidence. Schama, speaking in a confident vein in one of his lectures, said that history's "best prospects lie in the forthright admission of subjectivity, immediacy and literary imagination."[32] The narratives that the most accomplished analytical bibliographers have produced illustrate his point, and they demonstrate why analytical bibliography is properly an inseparable part of the discipline of printing history: it deals with the great body of evidence embedded in printed artifacts, and it does so in what must be considered an historical manner, showing how stories of "what happened" can be elicited from intractable details. Printing history, if it moves forward in this spirit and encompasses all relevant evidence, may more readily be seen, by large numbers of people, to hold a basic place among the various histories that we all pursue—basic because so much of our contact with the thinking of the past, in every field, comes through printed artifacts.

In the approaching years, as we are constantly being told, electronic texts may become the dominant form of visible language.[33] Whether the study of the processes of producing these texts will be carried out under the rubric of "printing history" is less important than seeing the continuity from handwriting to letterpress to offset to electronic digitization. In his Centenary Lecture to the Bibliographical Society in London, D. F. McKenzie appropriately called for the Society to include in its domain the electronic production and dissemination of texts. Indeed, if bibliography is thought of as the field that deals with the processes resulting in the placement of texts in physical objects,[34] along with

32. Quoted from a 1991 lecture at the New-York Historical Society in Peter Stevenson, "Lights, Camera . . . Schama!", New York *Observer*, 27 September 1993, p. 15. Another historian, an economic historian, who has recently received considerable attention for stressing the importance of literary methods in historical writing is Donald N. McCloskey. In *The Rhetoric of Economics* (1985) and *If You're So Smart: The Narrative of Economic Expertise* (1990), he argues that narratives and metaphors are an indispensable part of all "factual" discourse, whether in history or in science. James Atlas, in an article occasioned by a 1991 conference in Albany on the writing of nonfiction, says that the truth of a narration is not simply a matter of "facts" (which are themselves "slippery"): "The truth is in the prose, the style, the quality of representation that compels us to believe" ("Stranger Than Fiction," *New York Times Magazine*, 23 June 1991, pp. 22–23, 41, 43 [quotation from p. 43]). The way was paved for this kind of discussion by Hayden White's pioneering and influential *Metahistory* (1973); two recent examples are his *The Content of the Form: Narrative Discourse and Historical Representation* (1987) and Lionel Gossman's *Between History and Literature* (1990).

33. The phrase "visible language" has been given some prominence by its use as the title of a journal (on matters relating to typography, handwriting, and reading) now published by the Rhode Island School of Design.

34. I use this phrase in order to encompass such texts as those of motion-picture films and sound recordings as well as of objects (like books) that display written language. My specific concern in this paragraph, as in the essay as a whole, is with the latter, but I recognize that the study of textual transmission involves other kinds of objects as well.

the influence of those processes on the reception of texts, computer technology cannot logically be excluded from it. Whether "bibliography" is the word to be used for this broad field is finally as insignificant as whether "printing history" is used for one of the field's constituent parts; the important point is to recognize that the fundamental nature of bibliography and printing history is not dependent on any single technology. One cannot deny that, as far as the technology for producing visible language is concerned, there is—to use McKenzie's term—a "new dispensation." I would prefer, however, to emphasize the essential sameness of the procedures it serves. Computerization is simply the latest chapter in the long story of facilitating the reproduction and alteration of texts; what remains constant is the inseparability of recorded language from the technology that produced it and makes it accessible.[35] In the future, the study of the current production of visible texts, both old and new, will coexist with the study of the production of such texts by earlier processes: the means by which texts were first made publicly visible, as well as the way those texts were reoffered to later audiences, will always be relevant to the act of reading. And, whatever the process, the result is an arrangement of letterforms; the design of letters and the design of layout remain central.

The history of the production, use, and influence of letterforms is fundamental to humanistic study not only because letterforms are one of the dominant vehicles for the transmission of language but also because their shapes and deployment—as with all artifactual details—con-

---

35. At the end of *"What's Past is Prologue"* (see note 27 above), McKenzie seems to think that, if the field of bibliography embraces (as he hopes it will) "the dynamics of the increasingly volatile texts of our new age," the move will "represent a radical departure" from the earlier concept of bibliography based on "the primacy of the physical artefact (and the evidence it bears of its own making)" (p. 29). But the electronic processing of texts, like the earlier methods of processing them, uses physical means to produce physical texts. (How could it be otherwise?) McKenzie refers to the capacity of computers for "modelling" as if this characteristic were new to the history of text-producing processes; but all of the technologies that have made the reproduction of texts easier—such as movable type or xerography—have also made easier the process of using old texts to generate new ones. One thinks of stop-press corrections and the alteration of standing type for a new impression, for example, or cutting and pasting followed by xerographic copying. We have lived for a long time with technology that encourages the proliferation of variant texts; and the latest instance, computerization, marks a change of degree, not of kind. It has tremendously eased the process of textual manipulation, but it has not altered the fact that visible texts are the products of physical routines, which leave their traces in the texts. McKenzie's suggestion that bibliography in the electronic age "could come to deal, less in specific manifestations of a work, than in the *formulae for their realisation*" is like saying of earlier bibliography that it could focus on printing technology rather than on printed texts. Of course the technology is always important in its own right, but it is also always important for understanding the resulting texts, whether they are on paper or computer tapes and disks. The future study of texts will have to take new technology into account, but it will be dealing with an old situation.

vey meanings in themselves. Works made of language, being intangible, do not exist on paper or on the screens of computer terminals; thus the act of reading is unavoidably the act of constructing verbal works from physical evidence. In this process, all the features of the object carrying a text are potentially useful: some for identifying what may be considered errors in the text, and others for understanding how the work was regarded by those who produced, and those who later encountered, the object. However the work is classified—as literature, biography, philosophy, science, or anything else—our reading of it, in this basic sense, depends on what printing history can offer.[36]

E. M. Forster, in his memoir of Edward Carpenter, said that Carpenter would not "figure in history," because his life did not produce the kind of "words and deeds" that attract chroniclers; but Carpenter's genius, according to Forster, was to make those who came "under his spell" realize how inadequately the human spirit has been recorded by historians.[37] Forster's observations, both on Carpenter and on historical tradition, are themselves a part of history through their embodiment in visible language printed on the pages of a book (and subject to the vicissitudes of the printing process). Our best chance of capturing the human spirit, as it has existed in different times and places, is through studying the artifacts it has produced, reading their significance in the light of how they came into being. Printing history is essential for examining a major class of those artifacts by helping us to decipher, in the fullest way possible, the physical marks that constitute verbal messages from the past.

36. It is useful to recall, in this connection, the title of a pair of lectures delivered by Alvin Eisenman at Dartmouth on 28–29 October 1992: "Printing as Memory." This wording implies not only the idea of printed texts as the memory of human thought but also the role of printing, as a technical and artistic activity, in the memorial process.

37. "Some Memories," in *Edward Carpenter: In Appreciation*, ed. Gilbert Beith (1931), pp. 74–81 (quotation from pp. 80–81).

WITH AN O (YORKS.) OR AN I (SALOP.)? THE MIDDLE
ENGLISH LYRICS OF BRITISH LIBRARY ADDITIONAL 45896

by

RALPH HANNA III

IN 1951, A. H. Smith published three Middle English poems which he found written on the back of a roll assigned the shelfmark British Library, MS. Additional 45896. All three belong to a small but well-known genre of Middle English verse: each consists of stanzaic units with a refrain which opens "with an o and an i." The first and most extensive of these works, "ʒeddyngus de Prust papelard," is unique, a fully alliterative satiric utterance put in the mouth of a non-feasant cleric (assigned Robbins-Cutler number 2614.5); the other two poems, as Smith notes (38–39), are variant versions of pieces known elsewhere.

Although "The Papelard Priest" is certainly Smith's major find in Additional 45896, he fails to investigate either of the other two poems in any great detail. But interrogating these remains will reveal some vexing problems concerning both composition and provenance. And these problems will in turn shed light upon some large-scale conundrums about Middle English literary history, perhaps an unexpected benefit from such chancy literary remnants.

Additional 45896 is a seven-foot-long roll, comprising five vellum members (for materials in this paragraph and the next, see Smith 33–37 and the plate affixed to his article). The roll itself was constructed for non-literary reasons: it was designed to hold materials concerning agricultural accounts, a common purpose for such a manuscript form during the English Middle Ages. The recto and most of the dorse contain a Latin formulary on manorial accounting, probably composed just west of Oxford around 1349. The hand which copied the formulary (and subsequently added the three poems to fill the blank fourth member of the dorse) is an anglicana of a type one can find in many documents of the 1330s and 1340s: the poems probably were copied not long after the dated formulary. Thus, these works represent, at the very latest, productions of the second quarter of the fourteenth century.

Further, the Additional roll itself and the hand which inscribed there the Middle English lyrics can be generally associated with an area removed from the composition of the formulary, the southwest Midlands. Additional 45896 was discovered in 1941 in a solicitor's safe in Rugeley, south-central Staffs. There it seemed to be associated with a second manuscript, a fifteenth-century rental for the manor of Ripple, Worcs. (just northeast of Tewkesbury). And, as Smith sees (40–42), the scribal language of the lyrics is certainly Southwest Midland (cf. such routine spellings as "mony" MANY; "heo" SHE —and "freo" FREE; "kunne" and "sunne" KIN and SIN, respectively). A recent study by the master of Middle English dialecticians, Angus McIntosh, would place the scribe's training yet more precisely, in a third western locale —southern Shropshire along that county's border with Hereford and Worcester (see Cox-Revard 44 n6).[1] Since the deposit of the roll in Rugeley appears to represent legal interests of no greater antiquity than the nineteenth century, the most likely hypothesis would be that a south Shropshire scribe copied the roll, perhaps for a Worcestershire employer; in the most attenuated account of provenance, the roll could have been acquired later for practical matters of estate management by parties in Worcestershire.

Such a placement of Additional 45896 proves immediately problematic when one begins to consider the Middle English contents. The second lyric on the dorse describes the Annunciation; as Smith is aware, this poem in some way reproduces part of another Middle English work with o-and-i refrain— in this case, the Luke portions of "The Four Evangelists" printed by W. Heuser (285–289; Brown-Robbins number 2020). Like "The Papelard Priest," "Evangelists" is composed in alliterative stanzas, and, until the discovery of Additional roll, the version Heuser presented was thought to be unique.

That poem appears at the end of Bodleian Library, MS. Rawlinson poet. 175, a manuscript produced later than the Additional roll: the hand is usually dated palaeographically in the second half of the fourteenth century. This codex, an important source for the widely dispersed *Prick of Conscience*, was certainly produced in the north of England, and equally certainly, within that general locale, Yorkshire; the Middle English dialect project places its scribe's training narrowly, in Wensleydale, North Yorkshire (see Madan et al. 3:321–322, number 14667; Lewis-McIntosh 116; Doyle 2:47–49; McIntosh et al. 3:576–577).[2] Such a provenance ought to be immediately surprising: it implies communication between two quite distant literary communities, one in the southwest, another in the north.

At least one question immediately arises from this confluence of texts: can one determine the direction of literary influence? Given that either the Additional (hereafter A) or the Rawlinson (R) copy of "Luke in his lesson" has been derived or redacted from the other, can one determine which has priority? Does the earlier fragmentary anthology on the formulary roll reflect

1. One should note similarities to McIntosh et al., LP 4218, 3:435–436, from the Kinlet area, which shares with the roll the very infrequent spelling "chal" SHALL (in the roll *sh* is usually spelled *ch*). The scribe also routinely writes the (archaic?) spelling *-st-* for /xt/, e.g. *myst* MIGHT, in this word a majority form in only three widely dispersed LPs; see McIntosh et al., 4:94–96. Of these, the most provocatively placed is LP 7650, from northwest Worcs. (and cf. the minority *myst* spellings of LP 7370, from Herefs.).

2. Yorkshire forms from the Luke portions of "The Four Evangelists" include: leres 3sg. 1, ane 5 etc., yhederly 11, yhede 11, furth 14 etc., es 15 etc., scho 17 etc., sall 23 etc. (cf. suld 31), gud 25, hegh- 26, answerd 31 (cf. harbard 48), haly 34, gast 34, ony 36, na 40, noght 41, seruand 44, als 45, has 45 and demes 46 2sg.

a West Midland poet's alliterative composition? Was this then subjected to further expansions? And if so, is the northern scribe simply the inheritor of work done elsewhere? Or did a Yorkshire poet compose the fuller account of selected moments from the gospels, transmitted in part to the west and only by accident surviving in a later copying in something like the poet's dialect?

The evidence with which to answer this question is spotty. On the whole, the two versions of the poem are so distinct that they cannot be combined into a critical text: they stand as fundamentally independent renditions. But so far as it is possible to say, the hypothesis of Yorkshire provenance for the original of "The Evangelists" appears the correct one. Several A readings appear either editorial or scribal derivatives of parallels in R. For example, in line 13, R *Comly* is confirmed by the insistent alliteration of the northern version (much of it removed from A); the latter copy here has *Semely*—which may be only an unmotivated scribalism dependent upon confusion of similar majuscules and of forms of *o* and *e*. In line 9, R *mowthed* "named (in speech)," again alliterating, corresponds to A's pallid substitution *mony clepede* (cf. also line 6, where alliterating R *was named* is reproduced as A *me clepede*). Or in line 21, where A rewrites the entire line, the alliterating R *Be noght ferd* appears to have inspired the synonymous A *Doute þe noust*. Similarly, in line 45, R *said . . . þis tale* probably suggested A *hast talked*. In contrast, no A reading looks certainly prior to its counterpart in R.[3]

One can only guess at the logic for the A redaction. But at least one possibility seems to be a sense of stanzaic proprieties rather different from that of the original. R is composed in monorhymed six-line stanzas, but the A revision deliberately sets out to differentiate the refrain from the remainder of the stanza, a process which begins in the very first line. There A extends R's line, "Luke in his lesson leres to me," into ". . . lerede me to synge;" and then converts the subsequent three verses into lines ending in -*ynge* while retaining the refrain, now rhyming separately on -*é*.

As this example suggests, the redactor behind A, in part because he rejects many traditional alliterative collocations, shows considerably less concision than his source. Perhaps the surest sign that he is the recipient, rather than originator, of "Luke" appears in the middle of the poem. In his effort to follow the account of Luke 1 closely, he rejects R's fifth stanza, which heralds Jesus's might. But he appears so bound by his textual model that he feels his version should contain an equivalent number of stanzas: this he accomplishes by splitting R's sixth stanza into two and padding out its materials (with partial retention of the rhymes of his source) to twelve lines.

Further, a meagre amount of rhyme evidence suggests that the Yorkshire scribe was copying a poem composed in his dialect. The rhymes at lines 43–48 depend upon the retention of OE long ā in the adverb WHOLE (OE hāl), customarily taken as a sign of northern Middle English. And in line 35, rhyme confirms the alliterative set-phrase "more and minne," a Scandinavianism of

---

3. In line 4, A *hayled* might be prior to R *hasted* (its line 3); in 16, A *iboren* is marginally more attractive than R *þat bene.*

restricted northerly occurrence (Olszewska 83).[4] Both these uses are eradicated in the A rendition of the poem.

But the rhymes in the A version of "Luke" raise some further difficulties. For this evidence—several forms prove to be senseless in the scribe's dialect (although he does not change them)—suggests that the scribe of A is not the source of the redaction, but only a copyist of it. The rhymes in R's sixth stanza cannot have been exact in the A scribe's Shropshire dialect: *begin, within,* and *myn* would there have short i, but *-kyn, wyn* JOY, and *syn*, the short front rounded vowel /Y/. In rendering this stanza, A converts "wyn" JOY to "w[yth]ynne" (with short i) but has an impenetrable "mynne" (probably from OE mynd-, thus with Middle English rounded vowel) and retains "syn"— which the scribe reproduces in the dialect spelling indicating rounded vowel, "sunne." Similarly, lines A 43–46 rhyme on short i, but again include a word which would have /Y/ in the scribe's dialect, FULFILL—which he again gives in a dialect spelling which implies rounding, "folfulle." Such rhymes imply that the A version of "Luke" is not a western poem at all; indeed it could have been composed in virtually any other Middle English dialect, including that of Yorkshire.

Another rhyme may provide narrower evidence of provenance. At line 46, postposited *tille* TO rhymes. This form, while not exclusively northern, certainly would limit the source of this redaction to that area or parts of the Northeast Midlands, notably Lincolnshire and Notts. (cf. McIntosh et al., 1:461–462, dot maps 618–621).

Moreover, this demonstration of the northern provenance of this A text can be extended to other items on the roll. What Smith prints as the third poem of Additional 45896, "Love him wrought," may in fact be two or three separate productions, all vaguely linked through their interest in the Passion. The first of them, again, is known elsewhere in a later copy: the lyric "Loue me brouhte" (Brown 84; Brown-Robbins number 2012) appears in John of Grimestone OFM's pulpit commonplace book, Edinburgh, National Library of Scotland, MS. Advocates 18.7.21. This manuscript is dated 1372 and written in forms one would associate with Grimestone's Norfolk origins. But he himself did have connections with areas more proximate to the Additional roll: records of the 1320s and 1330s associate him with the Franciscan convent in Dorchester (Dorset; Wilson xiii).

This portion of the third Additional text shows rather minimal differences from Grimestone's version. In the roll, the poem is not Jesus's address

---

4. The early citations at MED minne adj. are all northern (although note *Piers Plowman* C 3.399); however, by the mid-fifteenth century, the phrase had certainly entered the repertoire of more southerly dialects (e.g. Norfolk uses in Capgrave and *The Castle of Perseverance*). One should note that the original dialect of "Luke" was not identical with that of the R scribe: for example, in line 17, he writes "scho" for the rhyming "s(c)he" (A reads "heo"). For distribution of these features, see McIntosh et al., 1:308, dot map 13 ("sho" as common northern form); ibid., dot map 14 ("she" as fundamentally central and especially southeast Midland, yet sporadic in the north); 1:309, dot map 17 ("heo" as Severn estuary-Worcs. form).

from the cross but a doctrinal statement about his purpose and mission, an emphasis which recalls the redaction of "Luke in his lesson." Two pairs of lines have been transposed in one version or the other, and A ends the poem with the long-line o-and-i refrain common to all three works on the roll. But again, like "Luke in his lesson," on the basis of this second copy, the Additional roll seems to present a bobbed text—Grimestone's third tail-rhyme stanza does not occur here.

More interesting are the two lyric sections which follow. For these, both usually in trimeter arranged in a single abababab stanza with long-line o-and-i refrain, no parallel versions exist. The first depicts the horror of the Crucifixion; the second describes the loss and redemption of the world through the rearrangement of three letters, EVA becoming AVE.[5] The first of these stanzas shows non-northern rhyme forms (e.g. 18 "non" NOON rhymes with "ston" STONE and "bon" BONE, thus confirming non-retention of OE long ā). But the second is certainly northern: there the letter-name a rhymes with "fa" and "wa" (OE *fā* FOE and *wā* WOE, respectively; the ms. instructively retains the northern spellings). If the poem in fact represents a unified composition from a single source, then that probably reflects a northern border-area where rhymes of OE long ā as either a or o were equally possible, for example south Yorkshire. If it in fact joins three fragments of different sources, then at least one of these appears of pure northern origin, as is "Luke in his lesson."

Finally, "The Papelard Priest" cannot be a local Shropshire product either. Its rhymes again point toward composition in the north. Lines 22–30 show retention of OE long ā: "mare" 24 (OE māra) rhymes with a string of words with ME long a from lengthening in open syllables. The same rhyme-leash also confirms the form "ar(e)" for the present plural of BE, normal in a wide belt running from south Lancs. to the Wash (McIntosh et al., 1:334, dot map 118)—as opposed to the expected b-form in the dialect of the A scribe (cf. "betz" 5 and "biod" 44). And, a feature of similar distribution, the author's form of the third person singular indicative was -es (not -eþ), confirmed in rhyme at lines 51–57 and 62–68.[6] Again, in lines 41–47—the scribal forms are *sore, wore* WERE, *more, lore* LORE—the author of "Papelard Priest" probably, although not conclusively, shows northern forms. Whether representing *ware* or *wore*, his rhyme most likely reflects Lancashire, Yorkshire, or Lincoln (see McIntosh et al., 1:337, 338, dot maps 131 and 133).[7]

5. I can do no better than Smith (39 n2, where Carleton Brown is cited in error for E. K. Chambers) in finding parallels; see lines 19–27 of the famous "Of on þat is so fayr and briȝt" (Brown-Robbins number 2645).

6. Cf. McIntosh et al., 1:466, dot map 645: in the west, this feature occurs no further south than Cheshire and central Staffs. But the root lib(b)- recorded in 68 *libbes* LIVES, is non-northern (most frequent in Gloucs. and Herefs.).

7. This set of rhymes is distinguished from the alternate ones of the stanza, in spite of scribal spelling. For the ms. spellings totore:bore:bifore:swore, the further rhymes corne: morne imply reading totorne:borne:biforne:sworne. Participles with full -en termination appear generally through the northern half of England (McIntosh et al., 1:469, dot map 663 —and note "Luke" 22 in A with *found*, not *founden*). *bifor-* is certainly a Yorkshire form

"The Papelard Priest" thus resembles another mid-fourteenth-century rhymed alliterative satire of deficient clergymen, "The Chorister's Lament" (Brown-Robbins 3819) in something more than theme: that poem, recorded by a scribe at Norwich Cathedral Priory, on the basis of its rhymes, travelled from its northern place of composition to a very different literary community.

Thus, what initially appears a Southwest Midland manuscript in fact demonstrates persistent textual connections with the north of England. Rather than the property of a native southwestern alliterative culture, often taken to have been the sole generator of an "Alliterative Revival" in the mid-fourteenth century (see Pearsall), Additional 45896 testifies to some collison of separate local literary cultures, cultures which existed at a considerable geographical remove (see Lawton).

The first two poems of the Additional roll represent a widely dispersed movement of c. 1200–1360 or so—alliterative verse in stanzaic forms (see Bennett). Pre-eminent examples of such work are quite provocatively placed. Ten such poems occur in the Shropshire collection of c. 1340, British Library, MS. Harley 2253 (itself the product of extensive compiling from diverse locales; cf. Brook). And Lawrence Minot, probably a member of the family which gave its name to Carlton Miniott (near Thirsk, N. Yks.), composed five similar poems, transmitted in the North Yorkshire British Library, MS. Cotton Galba E.ix. These rhymed verses are clearly related to the efflorescence of unrhymed alliterative poetry coinciding with the decline of stanzaic forms and composed in the same areas—merely to cite one example from each literary community, the south Gloucestershire *William of Palerne* (pre-1361) and the Yorkshire fragments of "Will and Wit" (at the latest, s. xiv$^{2/4}$).[8]

While I choose to address issues of "Alliterative Revival" and the originary arguments which support this conception elsewhere, here I want to develop further the link between Yorkshire and the Southwest Midlands exemplified by the Additional roll. Yorkshire sources allege that the holograph of Richard Rolle's prose Psalter belonged to the nuns of Hampole (W. Yks.), and copies of the work apparently multiplied slowly. But one of the oldest survivors, Bodleian Library, MS. Bodley 953, was certainly produced for Thomas IV, Lord Berkeley, of Berkeley Castle in southern Gloucestershire, and probably, from the decoration, produced locally. Again, the alliterative stanzaic poem "Susannah," on the basis of its rhymes, is the work of a south Yorkshire poet; but the earliest copies, both drawn from the same deviant archetype, appear in manuscripts customarily localized in northern Worcestershire, Bodleian Library, MS. Eng. poet. a.1 ("The Vernon MS.") and British Library, MS. Additional 22283 ("The Simeon MS."). Certainly, literary traffic between Yorkshire and the southwest Midlands was extensive and—so far as my examples suggest—in the main one-way.

(v. more northerly *afor-*, more southerly *tofor-*); see 1:394, dot map 360. But the *-n* termination has been borrowed from another dialect, perhaps Lincoln or East Anglia; see 1:396, dot map 365.

8. For a convincing theory of the transition from rhymed stanzaic forms to long-lines, see Turville-Petre 16–17.

Although any variety of mechanisms might explain this confluence of transmission patterns, I would direct attention toward a pattern of a type generally overlooked by literary scholars. The mid-fourteenth-century "Gough Map," among other things, provides an outline of the contemporary "transportation system:" it carefully demarcates major roads. In the main, these radiated from London, and, outside the south, ran generally northwest-southeast (Stenton 10–11; R. A. Pelham, in Darby, 260, fig. 43). But Worcester was the terminus of two important routes which, unusually, traversed the Midlands. One of these roads passed through Coventry to join the Old North Road at Grantham; the second, more provocative for my purposes, ran "from Worcester, Droitwich, and Birmingham, and pass[ed] on to Derby, Chesterfield, and Doncaster" (Stenton 10), where it also joined the North Road. This second route provides a direct link between the Southwest Midlands and southern Yorkshire. Such major arteries of the transportation system would certainly have facilitated interregional contact: we should consider them likely media for literary, as well as commercial and military, interchange. Thus, early evidence of Southwest Midland verse may in fact not represent either an originary gesture or an example of coincident polygenesis in diverse literary communities; in fact, these remains may have been stimulated by importation from outside the region—and not simply from Yorkshire.[9]

Thus what began as strictly an editorial issue—which version of "Luke in his lesson" might be construed as prior to the other—ultimately comes to address large and fundamental issues of Middle English literary history. As an editorial question, the "priority" or "anteriority" of the Yorkshire version of this poem turns out to be something of a red herring: the Shropshire text of Additional 45896 cannot be consolidated into a single text with the Yorkshire version recorded in Rawlinson poet. 175. Some currently fashionable opinions in Middle English textual studies would find in such a result reason to query the entire enterprise of editing medieval texts. Although I concur that editorially the poems can only be presented in parallel, as entirely separate renditions, I would point out that only the determination of anteriority can lead beyond questions specifically textual—in this case, to broader literary and cultural problems whose importance far outweighs any possible adjudication of poetic lections.

9. For example, Brook 61 suggests that Harley 2253's rhymed alliterative complaint, "The Song of the Husbandman" (Brown-Robbins 696, Robbins-Cutler 1320.5) was composed in the southeast, not traditionally considered "an alliterative area."

WORKS CITED

Bennett, J. A. W. "Survival and Revivals of Alliterative Modes." *Leeds Studies in English* n.s. 14 (1983):26–43.

Brook, G. L. "The Original Dialects of the Harley Lyrics." *Leeds Studies in English* 2 (1933):38–61.

Brown, Carleton, ed. *Religious Lyrics of the XIVth Century.* Oxford: Clarendon, 1957.

————, and Rossell Hope Robbins. *The Index of Middle English Verse*. New York: Columbia University Press, 1943.

Cox, D. C., and Carter Revard. "A New Middle English O-and-I Lyric and its Provenance." *Medium Ævum* 54 (1985):33–46.

Darby, H. C., ed. *An Historical Geography of England before A. D. 1800*. Cambridge: Cambridge University Press, 1951.

Doyle, A. I. "A Survey of the Origins and Circulation of Theological Writings in English. . . ." 2 vols. Cambridge University Ph.D. thesis, 1953.

Hanna, Ralph III. "Alliterative Poetry." Forthcoming in David Wallace, ed. *The Cambridge History of Medieval English Literature*.

Heuser, W. "With an O and an I." *Anglia* 25 (1904):283–319.

Lawton, David A. "The Diversity of Middle English Alliterative Poetry." *Leeds Studies in English* n.s. 20 (1989):143–172.

Lewis, Robert E., and Angus McIntosh. *A Descriptive Guide to the Manuscripts of the Prick of Conscience*. Medium Ævum Monographs n.s. 12. Oxford: Society for the Study of Mediaeval Languages and Literature, 1982.

Madan, Falconer, et al. *A Summary Catalogue of Western Manuscripts in the Bodleian Library*. 7 vols. in 8. Oxford: Clarendon, 1895–1953.

McIntosh, Angus, et al. *A Linguistic Atlas of Late Mediaeval English*. 4 vols. Aberdeen: Aberdeen University Press, 1986.

Olszewska, E. S. "Illustrations of Norse Formulas in English." *Leeds Studies in English* 2 (1933):76–84.

Pearsall, Derek. "The Origins of the Alliterative Revival." In Bernard S. Levy and Paul E. Szarmach, eds. *The Alliterative Tradition in the Fourteenth Century*. Kent: Kent State University Press, 1981. Pp. 1–24.

Robbins, Rossell Hope, and John L. Cutler. *Supplement to the Index of Middle English Verse*. Lexington: University of Kentucky Press, 1965.

Smith, A. H. "The Middle English Lyrics in Additional MS 45896." *London Mediaeval Studies* 2 (1951):33–49.

Stenton, F. M. "The Road System of Medieval England." *Economic History Review* 7 (1936):1–21.

Turville-Petre, Thorlac. *The Alliterative Revival*. Cambridge: Brewer, 1977.

Wilson, Edward. *A Descriptive Index of the English Lyrics in John of Grimestone's Preaching Book*. Medium Ævum Monographs n.s. 2. N.p., 1973.

Notes on Contributors

DAVID FAIRER is Senior Lecturer in English at the University of Leeds. He is the author of *Pope's Imagination* (Manchester University Press, 1984), *The Poetry of Alexander Pope* (Penguin, 1989), and, as editor, *Pope: New Contexts* (Harvester-Wheatsheaf, 1990). His edition of *The Correspondence of Thomas Warton* was published in Fall 1994 by the University of Georgia Press, and he is author of the forthcoming volume, *English Poetry of the Eighteenth Century*, in the Longman Literature in English Series.

JAMES MCLAVERTY, Lecturer in English at the University of Keele, is currently working on a study of Pope, print, and meaning.

O M BRACK, JR., Professor of English at Arizona State University, is the editor of Samuel Johnson's translation of Jean Pierre de Crousaz's *Commentaire* forthcoming in the Yale Edition and serves as textual editor for the Works of Tobias Smollett.

KEITH MASLEN retired in 1991 from the University of Otago English Department. He is currently working on Samuel Richardson as printer. Books include *The Bowyer Ledgers*, ed. Keith Maslen and John Lancaster (London: The Bibliographical Society; New York: Bibliographical Society of America, 1991), and *An Early London Printing House at Work: Studies in the Bowyer Ledgers* (New York: Bibliographical Society of America, 1993). He is represented in *An Index of Civilisation: Studies of Printing and Publishing History in Honour of Keith Maslen*, ed. R. Harvey, W. Kirsop and B. J. McMullin (Melbourne: Centre for Bibliographical and Textual Studies, Monash University, 1993). More recently he has published a brief guide to early New Zealand directories in the Hocken Library, Dunedin, New Zealand, and contributed to proposals for a history of the book in New Zealand.

HUGH AMORY is Senior Rare Book Cataloguer at The Houghton Library. He is completing an edition of Fielding's *Miscellanies* with Bertrand A. Goldgar, is co-editor with David A. Hall of vol. 1 (Beginnings to 1790) of the *Collaborative History of the Book in America*, and is a contributor to vol. 4 of the *History of the Book in Britain* (1557–1695).

JAMES E. TIERNEY, Professor of English at the University of Missouri-St. Louis, is the editor of *The Correspondence of Robert Dodsley 1733–1764* (Cambridge University Press, 1989), has served as an editor of *The Eighteenth Century: A Current Bibliography*, and has contributed many articles and chapters to publications concerned with British Studies, 1660–1800. Currently, he is producing a CD-ROM subject index to pre-1800 British periodicals.

GWIN J. KOLB, Chester D. Tripp Professor Emeritus in Humanities at the University of Chicago, is the author of numerous publications on eighteenth-century English literature.

ROBERT DEMARIA, JR., is Henry Noble MacCracken Professor of English at Vassar College and the author most recently of *The Life of Samuel Johnson: A Critical Biography* (1993).

ANNE McDERMOTT is Director of the Johnson Project at the University of Birmingham which will see the publication of Johnson's *Dictionary* first on CD-ROM and then in a scholarly critical edition. She has published articles on Johnson and is just completing a book on Johnson's arguments.

DONALD D. EDDY is Professor of English in Cornell University. He devotes his research to eighteenth-century English books.

DONALD W. NICHOL is an Associate Professor of English at Memorial University of Newfoundland. His edition of William Warburton's correspondence with John Knapton, *Pope's Literary Legacy*, was published by the Oxford Bibliographical Society in 1992.

THOMAS F. BONNELL, a recent recipient of an NEH Fellowship, is at work on a book to be called "The Most Disreputable Trade: Publishing the Classics of British Poetry, 1765–1810." He is an Associate Professor of English at Saint Mary's College, Notre Dame, Indiana.

ANN BOWDEN and her husband William B. Todd are now engaged upon a comprehensive bibliography of Sir Walter Scott 1792–1836; a project of such complexity that it requires two computers. Now retired, she taught courses in bibliography and rare book and manuscript librarianship for more than twenty-five years at the University of Texas at Austin.

WILLIAM TODD and his wife Ann Bowden for fifteen years were co-editors of the *Papers* of the Bibliographical Society of America, in 1988 published *Tauchnitz International Editions*, and are now complicit in a Scott bibliography. He is Kerr Centennial Professor Emeritus in English History and Culture at the University of Texas at Austin.

PAMELA DALZIEL is Assistant Professor of English at the University of British Columbia. Her edition, *Thomas Hardy: The Excluded and Collaborative Stories* (Oxford: Clarendon Press, 1992), is based on her Oxford D.Phil. thesis, supervised in part by J. D. Fleeman. She has also edited (with Michael Millgate) *Thomas Hardy's 'Studies, Specimens &c.' Notebook* (Oxford: Clarendon Press, 1994).

B. J. McMULLIN is a reader in the Department of Librarianship, Archives and Records, Monash University, Melbourne, and editor of *The Bibliographical Society of Australia and New Zealand Bulletin*.

G. THOMAS TANSELLE, Vice President of the John Simon Guggenheim Memorial Foundation and Adjunct Professor of English at Columbia University, has recently published a biography of Fredson Bowers and is currently the president of the Bibliographical Society of the University of Virginia.

RALPH HANNA III teaches at the University of California-Riverside and is particularly interested in the conditions of literary production in the English later middle ages. The article represents a small part of an effort at resituating Middle English alliterative poetry in the period *c.* 1190–1550.

BIBLIOGRAPHICAL SOCIETY OF THE UNIVERSITY OF VIRGINIA

Studies in Bibliography is issued annually by the Society in addition to various bibliographical pamphlets and monographs.

Membership in the Society is solicited according to the following categories:

Subscribing Members at $30.00 a year receive *Studies in Bibliography* and other bibliographical materials issued without charge by the Society. Institutions as well as private persons are accepted in this class of membership.

Student Members at $15.00 a year receive the benefits of *Subscribing Members*.

Contributing Members at $100 a year receive all publications and by their contributions assist in furthering the work of the Society. Institutions are accepted.

Articles and notes are invited by the Editor. Preferably these should conform to the recommendations of the Modern Language Association of America. All copy, *including quotations and notes*, should be double-spaced. The Society will consider the publication of bibliographical monographs for separate issue.

All matters pertaining to business affairs, including applications for membership, should be sent to the Executive Secretary, Penelope F. Weiss, University of Virginia Library, Charlottesville, Virginia 22903.

CONTRIBUTING MEMBERS FOR 1994

RUTHE R. and MARTIN C. BATTESTIN, Charlottesville, Virginia

TERRY BELANGER, Charlottesville, Virginia

BODLEIAN LIBRARY, Oxford, England

BRITISH LIBRARY, London, England

UNIVERSITY LIBRARY, Cambridge, England

CARLETON UNIVERSITY, Ottawa, Canada

†IRBY B. CAUTHEN, JR., Charlottesville, Virginia

JACK DALTON, New York City

PETER J. D. DEDEL, Suffern, New York

ROLF E. DU RIETZ, Upsala, Sweden

GENE G. FREEMAN, Santa Ana, California

FREIE UNIVERSITAT, Berlin, Germany

GEROLD & Co., Vienna, Austria

JOHAN GERRITSEN, The Netherlands

PHILIP GOSSETT, Chicago, Illinois

UNIVERSITY OF HAWAII, Honolulu, Hawaii

INDIANA UNIVERSITY, Bloomington, Indiana

WALLACE KIRSOP, Victoria, Australia

MARK SAMUELS LASNER, Washington, D.C.

MELVIN M. McCOSH, Excelsior, Minnesota

PAUL MELLON, Upperville, Virginia

HARRISON T. MESEROLE, Bryan, Texas

CHARLES MICHAUD, Randolph, Massachusetts

DAVIS W. MOORE, Denver, Colorado

QUEENS COLLEGE LIBRARY, Flushing, New York

SOUTHERN ILLINOIS UNIVERSITY, Carbondale, Illinois

UNIVERSITY OF SUSSEX LIBRARY, Brighton, England

G. THOMAS TANSELLE, New York City

DIANA THOMAS, Encino, California

ROBERT A. TIBBETTS, Columbus, Ohio

WILLIAM M. TUCKER, Palo Alto, California

CHARLES VALLELY, Newtonville, Massachusetts

VIRGINIA MILITARY INSTITUTE, Lexington, Virginia

CALHOUN WINTON, College Park, Maryland

DAVID YERKES, Salisbury, Connecticut

---

† The Council of the Bibliographical Society notes with regret the death of Irby Cauthen, who served the Society as President from 1978 to 1992.

PUBLICATIONS IN PRINT

Distributed by the Society

The following three Occasional Publications are available from the office of the Bibliographical Society of the University of Virginia, Alderman Library, Charlottesville, VA 22903.

1. Tanselle, G. Thomas, THE LIFE AND WORK OF FREDSON BOWERS. $25.00.

2. Eddy, Donald D., and Fleeman, J. D., A PRELIMINARY HANDLIST OF BOOKS TO WHICH DR. SAMUEL JOHNSON SUBSCRIBED. $10.00.

3. Vander Meulen, David L., and Tanselle, G. Thomas, editors, SAMUEL JOHNSON'S TRANSLATION OF SALLUST: A FACSIMILE AND TRANSCRIPTION OF THE HYDE MANUSCRIPT. $25.00.

Distributed by the University Press of Virginia

Former publications of the Society not listed here are out of print. Those wishing a complete list of them should see the annual lists in successive volumes of Studies. Members will receive a 20 per cent discount on all publications. Orders should be addressed to the University Press of Virginia, Box 3608, University Station, Charlottesville, Virginia 22903, U.S.A.

Blehl, Vincent Ferrer, S.J., JOHN HENRY NEWMAN, A BIBLIOGRAPHICAL CATALOGUE OF HIS WRITINGS. $25.00.

Bloomfield, B. C., and Mendelson, Edward, W. H. AUDEN, A BIBLIOGRAPHY, 1924–1969. $35.00.

Boughn, Michael. H. D.: A BIBLIOGRAPHY, 1905–1990. $39.50.

Bristol, Roger P., INDEX TO SUPPLEMENT TO EVANS' *American Bibliography*. $20.00.

Bristol, Roger P., SUPPLEMENT TO EVANS' *American Bibliography*. $50.00.

Dameron, J. Lasley, and Cauthen, Irby B., Jr., EDGAR ALLAN POE: A BIBLIOGRAPHY OF CRITICISM 1827–1967. $40.00.

Evans, G. Blakemore, editor, SHAKESPEAREAN PROMPT-BOOKS OF THE SEVENTEENTH CENTURY. Vol. V: Text of the Smock Alley *Macbeth*. $35.00. Vol. VI: Text of the Smock Alley *Othello*. $35.00. Vol. VII: Text of the Smock Alley *A Midsummer Night's Dream*. $50.00.

Fry, Donald, *Beowulf* AND *The Fight at Finnsburh*: A BIBLIOGRAPHY. $25.00.

Gallup, Donald, EZRA POUND: A BIBLIOGRAPHY. (Published in conjunction with St. Paul's Bibliographies.) $50.00.

Grimshaw, James A., ROBERT PENN WARREN: A DESCRIPTIVE BIBLIOGRAPHY, 1922–1979. $40.00.

Herring, Phillip F., editor, JOYCE'S NOTES AND EARLY DRAFTS FOR *Ulysses*: SELECTIONS FROM THE BUFFALO COLLECTION. $42.50.

Herring, Phillip F., editor, JOYCE'S *Ulysses* NOTESHEETS IN THE BRITISH MUSEUM. $42.50.

Hodnett, Edward, AESOP IN ENGLAND. $20.00.

Johnson, Linck C., THOREAU'S COMPLEX WEAVE. The Writing of *A Week on the Concord and Merrimack Rivers* with the Text of the First Draft. $45.00.

Life, Page West, SIR THOMAS MALORY AND THE *Morte Darthur*: A SURVEY OF SCHOLARSHIP AND ANNOTATED BIBLIOGRAPHY. $28.50.

Maynard, Joe, and Miles, Barry, WILLIAM S. BURROUGHS, A BIBLIOGRAPHY, 1953–73. $27.50.

Partridge, A. C., A SUBSTANTIVE GRAMMAR OF SHAKESPEARE'S NONDRAMATIC TEXTS. $27.50.

Pound, Ezra, A QUINZAINE FOR THIS YULE. $10.00.

Ross, Charles L., THE COMPOSITION OF *The Rainbow* AND *Women in Love*. $25.00.

Roth, Barry, AN ANNOTATED BIBLIOGRAPHY OF JANE AUSTEN STUDIES, 1973–83. $35.00.

STUDIES IN BIBLIOGRAPHY, Volumes 1–47. $35.00 each. (Volume 10 out of print)

Tanselle, G. Thomas, TEXTUAL CRITICISM SINCE GREG: A CHRONICLE 1950–1985. $12.95.

Tanselle, G. Thomas, TEXTUAL CRITICISM AND SCHOLARLY EDITING. $40.00.

Tucker, Edward, THE SHAPING OF LONGFELLOW'S *John Endicott*. A Textual History, Including Two Early Versions. $26.50.

Vander Meulen, David L., POPE'S DUNCIAD OF 1728: A HISTORY AND FACSIMILE. $40.00.

Wiesenfarth, Joseph, GEORGE ELIOT: A WRITER'S NOTEBOOK, 1854–1879 AND UNCOLLECTED WRITINGS. $30.00.

West, James L. W., III, A SISTER CARRIE PORTFOLIO. $25.00.

Wright, Stuart and West, James L. W., III, REYNOLDS PRICE: A BIBLIOGRAPHY, 1949–1984. $25.00.

Wright, Stuart, PETER TAYLOR: A DESCRIPTIVE BIBLIOGRAPHY, 1934–87. $40.00.

WINNERS OF THE 1994 STUDENT AWARDS IN BOOK COLLECTING

Frank Grizzard (Bunyan's *Pilgrim's Progress*)
Matthew M. Davis (Major Authors)
Kelly Tetterton (Woolf's *Orlando*)

Honorable Mention

Gregory Ashe
Mary Fletcher Jones
Gregory A. Riley

This book was printed by letterpress from type cast on the Linotype by Heritage Printers, Inc. of Charlotte, North Carolina. The typeface is Baskerville, a design by John Baskerville (1706–1775), English printer and type-founder. Linotype Baskerville is a weight-for-weight and curve-for-curve copy of Baskerville's celebrated printing type. The pattern for the cutting was a complete font of (approximately) 14 point, cast from Baskerville's own matrices—exhumed at Paris, France, in 1929. The paper is 70-pound Glatfelter, an acid-free paper with a useful life of 300 years.